AREA

FORT McINTOSH

FORT PITT
(PITTSBURGH)

★ BRADDOCK'S
DEFEAT

JAMES HARROD'S
BIRTHPLACE

DANIEL BOONE'S BIRTHPLACE
BERKS CO. - PA. 187 MILES EAST

FORT
REDSTONE

Allegheny R.

River

Potomac

River

WADKIN'S FERRY

WINCHESTER

SIMON KENTON

SHENANDOAH MTS.

Shenandoah River

BLUE RIDGE MTS.

CLARK'S RIVER ROUTE

★ BATTLE OF POINT PLEASANT

ROUTE 1773 1774

OHIO

Kanawha River

Gauley River

GAULEY MTS.

New River

Big Sandy River

River

STAUNTON

★ GEORGE ROGERS CLARK

BENJAMIN LOGAN

TYPICAL 2 FAMILY STATION

WILDERNESS ROAD

GLADE SPRING
(JONESVILLE)

NATURAL
TUNNEL

SAPLING GROVE
(BRISTOL)

LONG ISLAND
(KINGSPORT)

TREATY
WAUTUGA

Capt. BILLY "RUSSELL'S STA.
(CASTLE WOOD)

ROGERSVILLE

Yadkin River

DANIEL BOONE'S ★
HOME 1772

DANIEL BOONE'S ★
HOME 1771

South Fc

TYPICAL 1 FAMILY STATION

LE)
LICK

BERLAND
AP

ON

OONE PARTY
BUSHED IN
CT. 1773

SALISBURY ★

The Hunters of Kentucky

"The Scout," BY DAVID WRIGHT.

The Hunters of Kentucky

A Narrative History of America's First Far West,
1750–1792

Ted Franklin Belue

STACKPOLE
BOOKS

Copyright © 2003 by Stackpole Books

Published by
STACKPOLE BOOKS
5067 Ritter Road
Mechanicsburg, PA 17055
www.stackpolebooks.com

Printed in the United States of America

10 9 8 7 6 5 4 3 2 1

FIRST EDITION

Library of Congress Cataloging-in-Publication Data

Belue, Ted Franklin.
  The hunters of Kentucky : a narrative history of America's first Far
West, 1750–1792 / by Ted Franklin Belue.—1st ed.
      p. cm.
Includes bibliographical references (p.) and index.
  ISBN 0-8117-0883-7
  1. Kentucky—History—To 1792. 2. Frontier and pioneer life—Kentucky.
  3. Pioneers—Kentucky—Biography. 4. Kentucky—Biography. I. Title.
  F454 .B45 2003
  976.9'02—dc21   2002011247

In remembrance of my old compañero of camp and trail, Warren "Hawk" Boughton (1915–2002), who taught me as much about the human spirit from his nursing home bed as he did back in the good days when we ran the woods together.

To friends Win Blevins and Richard Taylor, whose lyrical storytelling continues to inspire.

And to the memory of the late Barbara Olson and all of our brave comrades slain on American soil on September 11, 2001:

Requiescat in pace!

Also by Ted Franklin Belue
The Long Hunt: Death of the Buffalo East of the Mississippi

Edited
A Sketch in the Life and Character of Daniel Boone
The Life of Daniel Boone

CONTENTS

Many heroic exploits and chivalrous adventures are related to me which exist only in the regions of fancy. With me the world has taken great liberties, and yet I have been but a common man. It is true that I have suffered many hardships and miraculously escaped many perils, but others of my companions have experienced the same.

—Daniel Boone, Missouri years

ACKNOWLEDGMENTS

Reading Win Blevins's *Give Your Heart to the Hawks* in 1978 rekindled my love of the frontier (as did Richard Taylor's elegiac *Girty*), and meeting Win in 1982 deep in Colorado's Uncompahgre helped inspire me to write. Win's fine Mountain Man book, with its chapters and interludes, has a versatile structure I adapted for this one.

Then to Neal O. Hammon, one of Kentucky's natural wonders. Neal's grasp of history and geography, of rivers, surveys, and traces is singular, bettered only by his wit and generosity. His essays in the *Filson Club History Quarterly* and *Register of the Kentucky Historical Society* are worthy of perusal, as are his books and his yet unpublished work, "Into Western Waters, 1773–1775."

At Murray State University, in Murray, Kentucky, the good folks at the Harry Lee Waterfield Library and the Forrest C. Pogue Special Collections Library put up with my many requests, as they have always done. Dr. Jerry "Lion of the West" Herndon, who taught there for about thirty years and retired, helped proof my writing.

David Wright "colorized" the jacket's illustration, originally rendered in 1823 by F. O. C. Darly to appear in James Fenimore Cooper's *The Pioneers*. Darly was a preeminent artist of his day, and Cooper showcased his art in his "Leatherstocking Tales." Dave, a preeminent frontier and Civil War artist of our day, reproduced Darly's engraving in historically correct hues, keeping a careful eye on the original work.

This book required unusual care and attention and received it from my publisher, Stackpole Books. I would like to thank copy editor Joyce Bond for her patience, concern, and keen eyes; and Wendy A. Reynolds, Stackpole's jacket designer, whose fine work speaks for itself. Especially I wish to thank my editor, Leigh Ann Berry, whose unfailing intuition and open-mindedness inspired me to work even harder, and her assistant, Ryan Masteller, who saw the book through to its completion.

Jennifer Pfister helped mightily with the illustrations, as did David Wright; thank you both very much. Lavina Turbeville Belue kept *La Longue Carabine* fed and phone callers at bay while he ran the woods with the Shawanoes and *The Hunters of Kentucky*.

AUTHOR'S NOTE

Memory is a furtive thing, a mind's gossamer thread fixed by time and experience. Why and how memory's processes function—certain items the psyche imprints upon the brain; others the subconscious discards—remains a mystery; language thus far lacks a vocabulary rich enough to discuss memory in a meaningful way.

Lyman C. Draper and John D. Shane intuitively understood this. Such men, driven by a muse neither bothered to explain, conducted hundreds of interviews with frontier folks and wrote letters by the ream, prodding and probing—all to mine troves they hoped would be deep. Zealous to a fault, often lacking historical perspective, Draper and Shane did not stir memories idly, waiting to skim surfacing details, but plumbed the depths of their interviewees' remembrances. If they failed to unearth the gems they sought, they might, they knew, unearth gems remarkably similar as Americans bore witness to the deeds of pioneers from generations before.

With the frontier's eclipse, and in the nostalgic fullness of time, as kith and kin gathered around hearths and dinner tables to hear the old stories and family histories, yarns and lore evolved from "hearsay" and "myth" into "truth" and "fact." When visited by Draper or Shane, a rare and welcome occurrence for most rural households, these men and women retold their tales for posterity.

Draper's work as one of our nation's first oral historians resulted in his massive compendium—the Draper Manuscripts consist of 491 volumes, some longer than 300 pages—which a researcher, girded with a malleable hermeneutics, must plow with perseverance to glean the vibrant life songs contained within. It is a worthy endeavor, for the stories are surely there.

Daniel Boone's are. Boone remains the most famous hunter of Kentucky. In 1769 John Findlay led Boone, brother-in-law John Stewart, and three camp tenders through Cumberland Gap to a trace "much trammeled by the savage" that cut to the heart of the Bluegrass. Boone stayed until 1771, hunting, trapping, and exploring, exulting in the bountiful land—*Kanta-Ke!*

There were others—men like George Michael Bedinger, James Nourse, and Capt. Thomas Bullitt—who aided in Kentucky's settling but who, compared to the legendary Boone, have received scant attention. Some of these pioneers, like Spencer Records and Daniel Trabue, wrote their tales in memoirs and letters. Others, like Kentucky's first freed slave, Monk Estill, were written about.

Seeking to restore a balance lacking in popular history, mainly, that Daniel Boone—and Boone, the humblest of men, said as much—was far from being the only capable woodsman roaming the Bluegrass, *The Hunters of Kentucky* is an attempt to present a brief portion of the saga of America's first Far West via an anthology of stories, narratives, and themes that proceeds at a rather loosely imposed chronological pace, with appropriate (and overlapping) shifts in chronology, in digressions, and in narrative voice.

My focus rests upon telling that story through the eyes and the lives of common, largely unheralded men. Certainly it is regrettable that the exploits of redoubtable frontier stalwarts like Simon Kenton, George Rogers Clark, and Benjamin Logan have been largely omitted herein; all three have been the subject of sizable (and, in the case of Kenton and Clark, best-selling) biographies, which are yet available for readers wanting to know more about these famous Kentuckians. Daniel Boone, though, could hardly have been relegated to a few asides, and to be blunt, I found it a challenge keeping him out of the text. For others, like John Floyd, Michael Cassidy, William Whitley, John Redd, William Clinkenbeard, and Bland Ballard—all of whom deserve to be far better known—I simply lacked space.

To be sure, frontier Kentuckians not only killed buffalo and grained deerskins, they carved out homesteads, axed forests into oblivion, and shot at warriors who shot back. Settlers trammeled in the wake of the Long Hunters, staked claims on plats mapped by Fincastle County surveyors, recited from the journals of Dr. Thomas Walker and Christopher Gist, all of whom had passed through this mysterious Eden.

Balancing and plotting all this telling and unraveling was like orchestrating and conducting a giant, spontaneously erupting symphony. Pushing the book forward and inserting independent vignettes—called "interludes"—between chapters eased transitions and helped flesh out main and lesser characters and give background and present historical context, all the while creating a palette of moods. (Interludes may be read separately or with the chapters.) Footnotes I used sparingly, only as needed. Still, history rarely cuts cleanly or simply, nor do historical eras usually begin and end tidily. Nor did my woodsmen—by nature an independent, hard-headed lot—always fit where I wanted them to go.

There was another "imbalance" I tried to aright: *Kanta-Ke* was Indian land—hunted in, lived in. The notion persists that prior to the coming of Daniel Boone and his comrades, Kentucky was forever a vast, uninhabited big-game preserve, a "Dark and Bloody Ground" of unrelenting internecine warring, fought over by Indians but never lived in.

New archaeological evidence and recent scholarship are causing historians to rethink the Dark and Bloody Ground legend. Many scholars theorize that due to epidemics and the "Beaver Wars"—when the Iroquois imposed a hegemony from New York to the Mississippi—Middle Ground natives fled. When the wars ended and the epidemics subsided, Indians returned to their homelands, only to be confronted by a far more persistent invader—the westering American pioneer. My prologue presents this side of the story, setting the stage for the Anglo invasion.

Then, another quandary. These days, writers of historical verity often must grapple with the tedium and pretense of "political correctness." To be blunt, interloping woodsmen under fire did not line fort walls to spew epithets of kind and gentle politic to attacking "Native Americans" (a trendy phrase that debuted circa 1970 and one that many Indians, like Lakota film star, author, and American Indian Movement activist Russell Means, bristle at and reject).

No. Kentuckians bandied their foes with an onslaught of names—"reds," "savages," "Yellow Boys"—and worse. (Mostly they called them "Indians.") In a letter to Gen. George Rogers Clark, dated April 16, 1781, Col. John Floyd described Shawnees raiding the Beargrass settlements (now a Louisville suburb) as "execrable Hell hounds"; months later, the Shawanoe Hell hounds spied Floyd pounding his charger down a path and shot him.

Indians responded in kind, calling Kentuckians "White Eyes" and "Long Knives," berating them with curses learned from white traders who often plied them with rum. (Slaves were called Africans, blacks, or Negroes.) With few exceptions, as my characters spoke, so too spoke I.

Dialogue appears sparingly and was taken as is from journals, old diaries, and manuscripts. To be sure, Algonquins speaking their own tongue expressed themselves with dignity and eloquence. Many natives knew a smattering of English yet spoke the strange words as haltingly as Anglos spoke disjointed Algonquin. In reproducing pidgin dialogue from a phonetically written eighteenth-century text, a writer risks being accused of having Indians talk like Tonto parodies, an accusation I find both offensive and uninformed.

Daniel Trabue's text, for example, teems with quirky anachronisms and phonetically written dialogue keen enough to distinguish an Irish cockney from the thick brogue of a Dutchman or from pidgin English, and I have quoted heavily from it. Cryptic colloquialisms ("jumed" for zoomed, "tuckeyho" for Virginian) abound, as do depictions of customs, hunts, fights, land deals, and insights into the day's political, social, and religious fabric—all part of a common man's life. To Trabue, getting details right was more pressing than bending his rough-hewn prose to stubborn rules of grammar or syntax or spelling. "Buffalo" he spells variously as "Buffelo," "buffelo," "Buffaloos," "Buffelow," "buffelow," "Buffeloe," "buffeloe," "bufflo," and "buffeloes." (In one remarkable sentence alone he spells it three different ways.) His "Shoneys" are Shawnees.

Again, where possible I left the text intact, except in cases of profanity, where I replaced the chroniclers' censorious dashes with letters.

As in word, so too in deed. In 1778, when Flanders Callaway shot an Indian woman with smallpox and Spencer Records rebuked him, I felt that this vignette should be told. Records maintained a strong hand in defending Kentucky. Despite his religious scruples, he thought little of scalping a fallen foe, but back-shooting a defenseless old woman was a far different matter.

When Laban Records scalped a Shawnee and took his trophy home to show off and tack to his cabin garret, I wrote it as he did; likewise when Indians meted out eye-for-an-eye justice. And if folks herein tell what they are wearing or describe what they saw or felt or how they jerked meat or tanned hides or how they evaded Indians or some other nuance, to preserve their voice and spirit I did too.

A few narratives overlap. Though such happenstances were kept to a minimum, it was unavoidable. Daniel Trabue's memoir, for example, contains the only account of Daniel Boone's court-martial; as I was dealing with Boone's life in the year 1778, I logically placed Trabue's testimony of the episode in Boone's chapter. As many of these men knew each other, and hunted and fought together (and sometimes fought and sued each other), it is natural such interplay would occur; when it does, I tell such stories from a fresh perspective and in abbreviated form.

In the opening pages, *Kanta-Ke* is an unmapped, amorphous island in the wilderness—a "trackless forest" only to pale-skinned intruders and their westering sons who warily breached heavily canopied tangles of laurel and hemlock to reach the fabled canelands and savannas. By the end, *Kanta-Ke* is Kentucky, America's fifteenth state.

Ted Franklin Belue
September 2002
Murray, Kentucky

The Contested Land, 1200–1744

Kanta-Ke!

Lush without measure was the land reposing south of Speleawee-theepee, whose waters of burnished gold and henna formed the land's northernmost border. Onward, southwesterly, churned Speleawee-theepee, its length—from its headwaters at the fork linking the Monongahela and Allegheny to its spill into the Father of Waters roiling brown and muddy—a smooth flowing wash of 981 miles. Smooth flowing, that is, save for one juncture: the Falls. Six hundred miles southwest of the Beautiful River's beginning, the Falls were a two-and-a-half-mile chute of turbulence boiling through boulders caked with petrified dung of the ancient long-horned buffalo *(Bison latifrons)* where the river's level abruptly dropped twenty-six feet. Negotiating the cataracts took care: Spring rains transformed the Falls into a whirl of maelstroms able to seize elm-bark canoes and poplar dugouts and send them spiraling onto rocks and snags. Summer's drought tamed the Falls into sandbars and shallow, still pools revealing fossilized marine life that vanished as autumn's downpours shoved the river as high as one hundred feet out of its banks, transforming, again, the Falls into a tempest. Winter's icy blasts stilled the tempest into snow-dusted floes of cerulean blue that melted and refroze with shifts of wind and temperature. More rain, warming, thawing, and the Falls' cycle began anew after snowmelt.[1]

But the Falls were the only exception to the Beautiful River's calms; usually its currents lazed along at a steady three knots an hour from headwaters to mouth.

Tributaries cutting from the shores spilled into the Speleawee-theepee. Creeks emanated from springs and brackish licks. And then, the rivers—the

Muskingum, Beaver, Great Kanawha, Scioto, Great Miami, Licking, Kentucky, and Wabash—all fed by sprawling arterial webs of branches and watersheds. Their labyrinthine meanderings carved a vast linkage of portages and thoroughfares that not only watered this fertile Middle Ground the French called the *pays d'en haut,* but gave entrance to it.

Life teemed at the water's edge and at Speleawee-theepee's junction with the Scioto, 250 miles upriver from the Falls and near a rising islet of cedar and cane littered with turtle egg shards and ribboned with raccoon tracks.[2] Shellfish shoals rose from shallows as hogback ridges; jammed in side-to-side, the mussels had bred for millennia, growing into craggy, brown clumps resembling V-shaped reefs and half atolls.

Softshells, sliders, and snappers and box turtles were bounty to skunks and minks. Crawfish darting back-end first among mud turrets rimming the shore were repast for bass whose spiny dorsals cut the surface as they cached, waiting, then drove in for the kill. Warmouths and shellcrackers gobbled nymphs and minnows and red-horse chubs; shiners scattered like goldfinches before a kestrel, whirling beneath the surface in glinting, ever-changing clouds, wary of bream, the bream alert for gar, pickerel, and muskellunge, and blue and flathead catfish bearing eyes set four fingers' width apart.

The Beautiful River was home to opossums and red and gray fox, raccoon, mink, and otter. And to beaver, whose bustling colonies of kits and migrating two-year-olds swelled in the spring. Muskrats altered banks by burrowing. Beavers burrowed and denned, felled trees, and dammed pools, their lodges and logjams shifting rivers while creating wetlands. As dirt, ferns, grasses, shrubs, and forbs filled in the bogs, the wetlands created luxurious vegas that all of life—great and small—intricately hinged upon.

Deer and elk wandered shorelines, as did panthers, turkeys, wolves, and bears. By the 1500s buffalo *(Bison bison bison)* fording the Mississippi—at the Red and Yazoo Rivers, and at fork of the Ohio—altered savannas and woodlands. Old paths the wild cow herds created anew, widening and deepening lanes into trails that meandered past knobs, chiseled through tall timber, cut up and over ridges of clay and rock, forded streams and creeks, slashed through tangles of twelve-foot cane.[3] But buffalo were a late arrival, not seen by those first people living along the Beautiful River's banks and the Scioto, northward.

These men and women of Ohio land wore ear-bobs and necklaces, bracelets of stone, shell, and hammered copper, and were of slight, wiry build. Heavily tattooed like the Timucuans seen by Spanish invading the tropical peninsula, the Land of Flowers, the bronze bodies of the Fort Ancient ones revealed bold mezzotints of valor gained in war, of rituals, of nature spirit manitous; the geometric and linear blackish whorls tribal tattooists jabbed into the skin with gar teeth, then rubbed in soot mixed with bear fat.[4]

Flint maize tasseling into kernels of indigo, brick red, and greasy yellow assured the people's survival, as did pumpkins, beans, and squash. Rain, coupled with the Ohio's spring surges, and a growing season of 180 days promised years of plenty that outnumbered years of lean. Harsh winters seldom lasted long. Droughts were rarer still. Women tended gardens with care, seeding plots in grids and low-rising corn hills that little resembled the rows and fallow fields of Old World peasants. Plows—like the lumbering, ox-driven mold-board plows of medieval Europe—were unknown, as were wheels and domesticated beasts of burden, save for wolfish-looking dogs. Digging sticks with fire-hardened tips and mussel shell hoes hafted with hickory staves were tools the women, who supervised the field work, wielded with surety and efficiency.

By 1200 in the Christian Era, Indians were flourishing in central Kentucky, their towns numbering more than fifty. Village life centered around a plaza and meetinghouse in the village's midst. Around the pavilion they erected elm-bark wigwams that resembled shortened, less expansive versions of Iroquois longhouses. Town populations rarely exceeded three hundred, and often, towns were ringed by palisades. As towns grew and as game, furbearers, shellfish, wood, and fertile land dwindled, the "Big Men" gave the call to move, usually about once every generation.[5]

To their west and south were earthen complexes featuring sizable moats and platform mounds built by Mississippians and guarded by deadeye archers. Such earthworks might serve as protection from marauders during raids that were more ritual than war; or as altars to offer prayers and sacrifices to gods; or, by the Late Woodland Era, to serve as tombs. By the 1400s Fort Ancient's artisans were trading limestone-fired ceramics to Tennessee's Coosa villagers for conch shell gorgets inscribed with rattlesnakes and weeping eye motifs, and for marginella disk beads, pendants, and yaupon leaves to roast into caffeinated black drink. Yet, they remained unique among their Mississippian neighbors, never evolving the hierarchies of the southeastern chiefdoms that in 1539 so startled Hernando de Soto's six hundred conquistadores loosed in North America with two hundred horses, Canary Island mastiffs and greyhound war dogs, and an ambulatory meat locker of three hundred pigs.[6]

The Fort Ancient people fled or were dispossessed by later arrivals. Or, perhaps they died out from famine or disease, or were annihilated by enemies, leaving their dirt mounds and shell middens for White Eye investigators to theorize that the sugar-loaf mounds could not have been built by undisciplined, aboriginal "savages." Rather, the whites declared that it must have been civilized remnants from "the lost tribes of Israel," or the "Hindoos," or

perhaps even fair-haired descendants of twelfth-century Welshmen that had
built them.

Born then was the cant Kentucky had been forever unoccupied by Indians. Kentucky was, the White Eyes averred, a vast hunting reserve rendered
"Dark and Bloody" from generations of tribal wars.[7]

But no one told the Mosopeleas or the Honniasontkeronons living south
of the Beautiful River about an invading Israelite diaspora, nor of the coming
of Madoc, son of Owen Gwynnedh, prince of Wales. Nor did they tell such
fables to the Algonquins who lived there, the ones the Iroquois, who preyed
upon them, knew as "Shanwans." French traders called them Chaouanons
and the English knew them as Shawanoes or Shawnees, a wandering people
whose traditions suggest a kinship to the Fort Ancient folk.

And, to *Kanta-Ke.*

1689. Darkness was upon Huronia, and to the south and west.

Dutch and English wares arrived in New Netherlands' ports by the
bateaux full, but it was guns with thick butts and fitted with dog-lock cocks
that clasped tight the amber and black sparking stones that the Mohawks
wanted. Not the arquebuses sold to them an era before; the clumsy
matchlocks needed a long cord that watered the eyes with the stink of vinegar
when lit, and both ends smoking, and the glowing slow-match clenched in a
serpentine arm suspended over the pan to make them shoot, if the ember ignited the priming. Flintlocks—forbidden to troops in France, but *Compagnies*

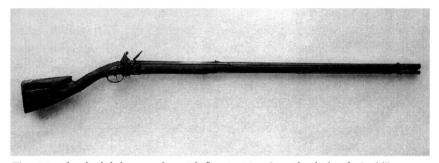

*Transitional-style club-butt musket with flint ignition (sans dog-lock safety), 44"
octagon-to-round barrel, walnut stock with persimmon wood patch-box lid, .62 caliber.*
Narragansett Armes, Indianapolis; re-creation by Chuck Edwards. Author's Collection.

The arquebus nitre-treated slow-match set in the serpentine's jaws and having been lit with flint and steel, blowing on the slow-match prior to firing to keep the glowing end free from ash ensured greater reliablility of ignition. AUTHOR'S COLLECTION.

franches de la Marines in Canada had them—cost more beaver, but the fancy guns killed with greater surety and at a good distance.

Sleek, long-barreled fowlers stocked to the muzzle in walnut, and bullet molds, black powder, and bar-lead—all bartered for heaps of plundered deer-skins; for stolen otter and beaver pelts; for booty of fisher, mink, fox, raccoon, and pine marten furs; for greasy bundles of ebony silk locks, the lank Huron scalps were very finely decorated, braided with strands of white and purple wampum, barleycorn beads, and porcupine quills, and capped with human parchment stained a dirty shade of burnt umber.

"The English have no sense," declared a warrior of the longhouse, astonished at the spill of goods, his new sense of acquisition, and the power that it gave him. "They give us twenty knives like this for one Beaver skin." But trader Robert Juet's words evinced the classic European notion of these novel business dealings. "The people of the Countrie came flocking aboord and brought us . . . Bevers skinnes, and Otters skinnes, which wee bought for Beades, Knives . . . Hatchets, and trifles."[8]

Petite iron trade hatchet, c. 1750. Jim and Carolyn Dresslar Collection.

White, star, and cobalt blue Italian beads, knives, tomahawks fitted with
pipe bowls, trade guns painted with floral designs of red, yellow, and white
with black dots, and furnished with black powder, ball, and accoutrements—
all were but a fraction of the wares the Iroquois were awash in. Linen, chintz,
calico, osnaburg, frieze, cotton, camlet, fustian, baize, and silk—fabrics had
by the bolt and at inflated prices from traders using scales rigged with lead
weights—took the place of deerskins for making garments.

Among the men, "striped neckcloaths" worn with ruffled shirts of scarlet
and indigo appeared in tandem with scant cotton breechcloths and nude
thighs, shocking missionaries who labored hard to discourage public displays
of immodest apparel. "The end of a shirt protruding from under the coat is
an indecorous thing; but not so in the Canadas," wrote Father Joseph Lafitau
to his superiors. "Sauvages" doffed deerskin leggings dyed walnut brown to
don bright-hued "worsted stockings and a cloak, but without any breeches,"
regarding pantaloons as "an encumbrance, although they sometimes wear
them as a bit of finery, or in fun."[9]

Warriors chopped copper kettles into slivers to hone into arrowheads.
Gun barrels blown at the breech from overcharging found service as hide

scrapers. Broken shards from glass bottles became arrow tips. Pewter plates were cut and polished into pendants. Buckles became headdress ornaments. Woolen sashes—gaily beaded, gaily colored—were wound into turbans and festooned with peacock feathers and ostrich plumes. Pocket watches became earrings, as did jew's harps, buttons, ribbons, tassels, hanks of stroud, and coins from the great nations of the earth.

Blankets began to take the place of the heavy elk and moose hides, which were arduous for the women to tan and smoke. Cane sugar, chocolate, honey, molasses, coffee, tea, anise, nutmeg, clove, and cinnamon tantalized palates. Sterling brooches, ball-and-cone ear-bobs, armbands, wristbands, Jesuit rings stamped with fleurs-de-lis and the Cross of Calvary, and rings having gold bezels set with colored glass—all such "trifles" eased social and religious taboos and facilitated conversion to the Church.[10]

And stashed away, always, were gable-high stacks of eight-gallon kegs, carried on foot or by horse, readily tapped and proffered, brimming with "spirituous liquors": rum, madeira, brandy, and tafia.

Strong drink—watered down and altered; adulterated sometimes to toxicity—sold even faster than the fancy new guns: "Indians," Cadwallader Colden wrote in 1727, "loved rum more than their life."[11] To "drink the water that takes away one's wits" dulled senses and impaired judgment; even better, the fiery water and sea of goods created a marrow-deep craving, a hunger and thirst that could not be quenched.

But more and more, as the Iroquois played the harlot and disrupted the Hurons' trade with Onontio (that is, New France's governors), and fattened upon the White Eye's goods, they began to forsake the old paths. The flush of wealth elevated the League's status among big men on two continents and made long its arm that began to reach farther to strike distant enemies whose storehouses of peltry the Iroquois coveted. Avarice and rum shattered totem and taboo, sacred gossamer threads that for centuries provoked fear of reprisal from malevolent Underwater Panther and Thunderbird manitous and kept intact a fragile peace broken only by ritualized mourning wars.

But the fragile peace was no more: Ritualized mourning wars became mass bloodlettings.

Deafened to the despairing cries of Onontio's Huron children, whom they hunted and kidnapped and stole from, the League, implacably and with impunity, tortured and killed the flesh of their flesh, and with iron hatchets severed arms and legs from the scalped corpses and boiled the rank flesh in copper trade kettles and quaffed the unholy broth from tin cups.[12]

Yet it was not enough.

As fur stores ran low, then ran out, tribes that supplied them dispersed in terror. Longhouse warriors scoured the land for more furs and skins to pilfer to get the precious White Eye cargo. They looked to the valley of the Ohio—a fresh, untapped lode. They lifted high maple ball-head death hammers inlaid with wampum and beads to strike anew the black-and-red-streaked war post.

West to Lake Ontario and south to the Ohio and west to the Wabash, much of the land began emptying, or nearly so, save for French-allied Ojibway and Ottawa towns along the shores of the Great Lakes and at the cultural crossroads of the Straits of Michilimackinac, which linked Lakes Huron and Michigan and a sprawl of river routes. Again, it was the Iroquois.

In their wrath, the longhouse men drove those nations loyal to Onontio out from before them, gathering peltry to sell and captives to adopt to replenish their ranks and captives to burn and eat to atone for their own dead. The most devastating epoch of the invasions was from 1649 to the 1660s. Waves of shocked refugees streamed to Algonquin towns along the Great Lakes: throngs of Wenros, Nipissings, Petuns, Hurons, Wyandots, Neutrals, and Eries. Fleeing too were the Algonquins of Ohio and Illinois country: Weas, Kickapoos, Twightwees, Tamaroas and others of the Illinois Confederacy, and the Fox, Piankashaws, Kaskaskias, and Peorias.[13]

In the Carolinas, the Iroquois fought Cherokees, Creeks, and Catawbas. Even as longhouse parties were leaving the Adirondacks to hunt the Ontario Peninsula for moose, caribou, and beaver, Shawnees ensconced in villages along the Maumee, Scioto, and Ohio trembled at the sight of more invading Iroquoian adders.

Middle Ground nations scattered, trespassing upon hunting lands not their own and kindling epic wars that remain some of the bloodiest episodes in Indian history: Mascoutens rising up against the Mesquakies (Fox), Potawatomis against Sauks, Miamias against Kickapoos and Illinois, Chickasaws against Shawnees, Shawnees against Cherokees and Catawbas.

Fueling the Fox wars was Onontio, siding with the Mascoutens. The Fox erred fatally in opposing the chief of the Canadas' fur and firearm trade with Sioux to their west. Impaled between imperial and native foes, as Onontio's children sought to exterminate them for profit, the Fox fled their Wisconsin homeland to live among Iowa's Sauks.

And, with the Beaver Wars, there came upon Huronia, and to the south and west during those dark days, a more insidious invader: malevolent destroyers that eye could not see, whose vile medicine bespoke of a strength far mightier than that of the Great Serpent, Matchemanitou. Perhaps, warned the sachems, these killers that so mysteriously came were sent to punish them: scourges of the One Manitou, the Master of Life and Death.

Influenza and measles, colds, diphtheria, viral hepatitis, typhus, mumps, meningitis, pneumonia, whooping cough—epidemics emptied villages and reaped bitter harvests among the Ohio and Lakes peoples, whose bodies lacked immunity to virulent Old World diseases. Smallpox, which appeared in its host as a "distemper" or "rash," could in less than a week reduce a healthy man to a near unrecognizable horror seated in the house of the dead and dying.

Pox victims exhibited a bewildering array of symptoms: chills, violent vomiting, debilitating bouts of dysentery, oozing lesions. A survivor was hideously pitted for life and often left eyeless, pus-filled pustules devouring cornea and iris, leaving ulcerated translucent lids shuttered over sunken, rheumy sockets. Most did not survive, and there was no knowledge of the Europeans' brutal logic of quarantine. Nativist cures—fasting and plunges into icy streams after exhaustive sweat lodge rituals—served to frustrate the shaman's efforts, exposing healthy people to the sick, weakening the ailing, and sharpening mortality.

From whence came the evil serpent's spawn of "loathsome fevers" is not known. The first strains from the Southeast arrived after 1539, brought from infected stragglers fleeing Hernando de Soto's fifty-month, four-thousand-mile death march, which took him from Tampa Bay to the Father of Waters, almost to the Ohio's mouth, and back to the Mississippi's fall into the Gulf, de Soto's Spanish knights raping, torturing, enslaving, and killing countless Indians along the way, de Soto's swelling (and escaping) swine herd infecting deer and turkeys and forests with zoonotic issues of anthrax, brucellosis, trichinosis, and tuberculosis. Then, a century later, a lethal wave of smallpox came to the Ohio via refugees fleeing the epidemics on Lake Huron's north-eastern edge that so ravaged Hurons during the 1630s and 1640s.

The Iroquois Confederation—the Mohawks, Oneidas, Onondagas, Senecas, and Cayugas—were among the earliest tribes to feel the plague's wrath. And yet, though these longhouse people perhaps gained a faint degree of immunity sooner than did their enemies of the woodlands, in 1679 they too had to lay aside their arms for a season to bewail their dead.[14]

Across the vast veldt of the Middle Ground, south and north of the Beautiful River and its tributaries, slowly, inexorably, cane and juniper thickets and hardwood saplings reclaimed abandoned hunting grounds once kept clear and open by annual firing, and ghost villages dotted with fire pits long cold and stark with dilapidated council houses; collapsing log huts, half faces, and lean-tos; and rotting elm-bark wigwams.

Hundreds of acres of desolate corn hills lay withering, many a harvest gone to seed in a gray mat of husks and leg-high weeds, stalks skewed and tangled, splayed cobs rotting into the earth. Ruination.

And always, an eerie stillness. Only wind, birds of the air, beasts of the field.

———————

To Englishmen, *Kanta-Ke* was like an isle in the Great Wilderness ripe for settlement, free for the taking.[15] Or so it seemed. While the Iroquois Wars raged.

But for New York's "Romans of the Western World," the century's dawning marked a dawn of crises.[16] Chiefs of the Five Nations had been tried and found wanting; their empire was rife with evils from within and without; the splintered League was collapsing to a rising enemy horde—one-time allies, traditional foes, and alien peoples from near and far—about them.

"Sa Ga Yeath Pieth Tow" (or Brant), one of the four Mohawk kings to visit Queen Anne in 1710. Note dramatic tattooing on face, torso, and left arm, scarlet match-coat, and club-butted Queen Anne musket. The bear designates clan kinship.

PAINTING BY JOHN VERELST, 1710.

Truly, if there was a time the Iroquois resembled Rome, it was in 1701 when the League signed treaties both in Albany and in Montreal, ending sixty years of Beaver Wars and securing a niche as fur brokers over a fiefdom they claimed "by right of conquest," reaching from New England to the Father of Waters. But by then it was Rome circa 450 A.D.—the days of the last puppet Caesars withering under the fire of the Visigoths and Attila's Hunnic assaults—that the culturally and politically addled League resembled. Not the glory of Octavian's Pax Romana.

In 1710 a delegation of Iroquois chiefs—they were Mohawks, Keepers of the Confederation's Eastern Door, arrayed in English apparel that did not detract from their shaved heads and faces tattooed with ebony dots and triangles and lines—appeared before Queen Anne, beseeching Her Majesty to protect her Indians. She, in turn, beseeched them to clasp hands with her in defending Iroquoia. Hers was a true test of diplomacy, its having been six years since the Deerfield slayings.[17]

Three years after Anne sent the troops, the Treaty of Utrecht ended the war, making the Iroquois her subjects. The links of the League's symbolic "Covenant Chain," once rusted and pulled apart, were reforged and polished, welding as one the longhouse people with the Crown.

During the pestilence and war, Shawnees had quit their towns along the Beautiful River's tributaries. Southward they went and elsewhere, to live along "Rivière de Chaouanons"—a river that in fourscore years a Virginia doctor would rename Cumberland for one of England's greatest butchers.[18] From there, as strands fraying off a hempen rope, the Algonquins moved to the red clay land to live on the Chattahoochee and Tallapoosa among the Yuchis and Creeks.

By 1680 Shawnees had built homes along the Savannah (some speculate it was from the Savannah basin that the earliest Shawnees came), where they resided until 1715; the Yamasee Wars drove them to the river's end, where they pushed out the Westos and served as slave catchers for Englishmen who swapped guns for humans. Shawnees traded at St. Augustine, bartering deerskins for cloth, yaupon leaves, egret and crane feathers, blue and white duffels, for miquelet muskets and powder and lead to war against Catawbas.

To be nearer to the commerce and safety of St. Augustine's presidio, a strand of the diaspora moved to the Land of Flowers' hummocks of live oak and moss, sable palm, palmetto, sawgrass, and brackish inlets roiling with manatees, and tarpon, snook, needlefish, mullet, bull and lemon sharks, black bass, bream, and shad, the squatters erecting lean-tos beneath towering cypresses reaching from the banks of the tannin-stained river of St. John's. By 1707 a strand had emigrated to Apalachiola to establish Ephippeck Town. Black Hoof, a famous chief, was said to have been born in 1721 during this sojourn and died 110 years later. And so it was in La Florida, among its emerald flora and exotic fauna, that these southernmost exiles lived as strangers in a strange land.

※

Northward, by 1692 Shawnees were living among the Susquehannocks and Delawares in Pennsylvania and Maryland, in towns as motley as New York's Fort Orange. Chartier's Town, "the capital of Allegenia" (named for the St. Louis Huguenot, Martin Chartier), was one such hub of expatriated accommodation in western Pennsylvania.[19] There, Shawnees renewed tribal enmities, roaming Athiamiowee—the "path of the armed ones"; white hunters called it "the Warrior's Path" that bisected Kentucky and cut through Cumberland Mountain, past Reedy Creek and Holston River—to prey upon Cherokees and Catawbas east of the Blue Ridge.

During the warmongering, some of the exiles wandered to Missouri, to Illinois, to New York, to the Tidewater. To be a "Shawnee" meant one belonged to the "Southerners" or "People of the South"—a name given in remembrance of their sojourns on the Savannah, or along the Coosa and Tallapoosa, or on the Cumberland. Or, "Shawnee" may reflect these people's Fort Ancient, Ohio, origins following an earlier emigration from the Great Lakes.

War had stirred their hearts to the English. England's victory in the first two French and Indian Wars quenched the flames of the Iroquois' wrath—flames that for threescore years had burned bright—and offered succor to La France's allies.

Provided, of course, Ohio tribes give up their ties to New France. For three decades, Algonquins and Iroquoians appeared willing to do just that. For the trade, mostly.

As trade was king, so too for Indians was this much clear: Dependency and survival became trade's pernicious counterparts. England reigned over that trade, middle-manned by Iroquois, the Crown's haphazardly loyal subjects. Reveling in their status and at peace with England and France, the Iroquois made Pennsylvania a southern wing of its protectorate.

But their relationship with the Shawnees remained tenuous. Unlike the Tuscaroras—who joined the Iroquois in 1722, making it the Six Nations—the Shawnees would not bend to the League's will.

By 1700 Shawnees numbered about twenty-five hundred, and rarely did they number more than that. About a dozen clans—with names like Turkey, Turtle, Horse, Raccoon, Rabbit, and Rounded Feet, representing wolves, panthers, and bears—and five septs, tribal divisions, distinguished Shawnees from

Algonquins and Iroquoians (like Mingoes and Wyandots) living near them. Each sept had its own duties to fulfill to keep the Shawnee as one.

"First Man" was the first division, translated from Chillicothe (or Cha-laakaatha). Keepers of the Mee-saw-mi (sacred medicine bundles that had been passed down for centuries), Chillicothes were one of the two septs from which chiefs for the entire nation were chosen. (The most obscure sept, the Thawikila or "eldest brother," was the other.) Chillicothes were involved in politics and in making decisions to relocate the villages. Their seed begat eighteenth-century leaders whose names would resonate along the frontier: Moluntha, pro-American Black Hoof and pro-British Black Fish, and Black Bob, who in the 1830s led his dispossessed "Absentee band" in a final hegira to the far western wilds of Kansas.

Piqua, the second division, implies the Manitou's creation of a wise people, a folk "formed from ashes" or "a man coming out of the ashes." Alternately rendered Pekowi, Shawnees knew the sept as the "second oldest brother." From this "talking band," as they deemed the intellectual Piquas, elders picked shamans and orators, go-betweens and fleet couriers adept at evading enemies while sprinting to distant villages via moonlit traces to bear by memory the words of chiefs.

War was the business of the Kishpokothas ("the third brother of the five"), a duty shared with the Piquas. Born into this sept in the late 1700s were two brothers: one greater, the elder; one lesser, the younger. Tecumseh, who died in a flash of musketry in 1813, built his confederation on alliances secured by the Piqua, Blue Jacket. Tenskwatawa, Tecumseh's churlish brother turned holy man, died in Kansas in 1836—shamed, morose, ignored. Yet during the War of 1812, Tenskwatawa's call to reject the White Eye path drew the masses that became Tecumseh's audience and spawned a nativist revival that withered under American fire on the banks of the Thames.

The Red Earth, or Mequache sept (alternately: Makujay or Mekoche) concerned itself with ceremonies and healing arts. Many sachems were Mequaches; the name signified "a man filled—a man . . . in whom nothing is wanting." In councils, Mequache words interpreted the traditions and aided Shawnees in keeping pure their beliefs. The Mequaches' role in spiritual matters was shared with the Piquas.

Schisms might arise between the septs, splintering the nation into two competing factions vying for tribal preeminence and led by chiefs from the Chillicothes and Thawikilas. Traditionally, Chillicothes and Mequaches stood as one against their rivals, the Piquas, Thawikilas, and Kishpokothas.[20]

After the illegal "Walking Purchase" of 1737 in Pennsylvania, in which the Penn brothers defrauded the Delaware of more than twelve hundred

A

TREATY,

Held at the Town of

Lancaster, in PENNSYLVANIA,

By the HONOURABLE the

Lieutenant-Governor of the PROVINCE,

And the HONOURABLE the

Commiſſioners for the PROVINCES

O F

VIRGINIA *and* MARYLAND,

WITH THE

I N D I A N S

OF THE

SIX NATIONS,

In *JUNE*, 1744.

PHILADELPHIA:

Printed and Sold by B. FRANKLIN, at the New-Printing-Office, near the Market. M,DCC,XLIV.

Circular concerning the details of the Lancaster Treaty, published and marketed by Benjamin Franklin, 1744.

square miles of their homeland, as White Eyes began to settle the interior and as game was killed out and woods shrank between split-rail rows into fields and pastures studded with charred stumps and cabins, Shawnees began filtering back to Ohio land, north and south of the Beautiful River, Speleaweetheepee.

The home-going was bittersweet: Their exodus had gained them disquieting knowledge of an immense pale-faced sprawl spawning east of the Dangerous Mountains (as the Cherokee knew the endless verdant of laurel and spruce and hemlock soaring misty blue northwest of Carolina land); a sprawl rife with mystery and foreboding, of impending harrowing times. And then, when that which is imperfect had come, the final dispersal.

<hr />

Pennsylvania's spring of 1744 awoke the countryside in a flush of greening verdant; no colony was more lovely than the well-watered Susquehanna basin,

Often ignored in history, mixed-blood interpreters played pivotal roles in frontier diplomacy and in native/Anglo relations. THE GASTOWEH, BY JEFF PRECHTEL.

land of the Leni-Lenape, known to Quakers as Delawares. Their towns of Paxton, Aughwick, Shamokin, Conestoga, and Tulpehocken the Munsee clan (called Loups) likened to spoke tips emanating from an immense wheel having as its hub Lancaster, due west of Philadelphia and by coach two days north of Maryland's border.

Indian towns were becoming pockets of rumor-mongering and unrest, red and white relations within them made brittle by white emigration to the Potomac's headwaters. Algonquins were defecting to the French, spates of random killings ensued, and the churning bustle of the peltry trade forced hunters west into hostile territory. Prices for French goods were being undercut by an English monopoly, exasperating New France's governor, who responded with a scheme of fort building to shore up France's hold on the Northwest.

Then, the English received extraordinary news: The Iroquois were poised to cede to them Ohio land, lacking warriors enough to drive interlopers from it or quell seditions brewing within its borders.

By June 1744 delegates from Pennsylvania, Maryland, and Virginia and traders, officials, and interpreters gathered in Lancaster to greet the 250 Iroquois accompanying their chiefs clad in full regalia. Pennsylvania agent Conrad Weiser cautioned Virginians "not to talk much of the Indians, nor laugh at their dress, or make any remarks about their behaviour." "It would," he warned onlookers, "be very much resented by them and might cause some differences betwixt the white people and them."[21]

Parleys were somber occasions and, to whites, interminably long: rituals of wampum giving, pipe smoking, and speeches performed with ceremony and pomp to mollify all factions concerned. Americans sat, at times amused, bemused, and rankled, but behind stoic visages belying nothing, enduring long-winded speeches with one mind, seeing with one eye the windfall at their fingertips, trusting in interpreters to transform the strident declarations lobbed back and forth among the Iroquois headmen into English to scribble on parchment. And then, to get their curious marks of animals and manitous inked on the paper.

One mediator attending was Andrew Montour, son of the Seneca Madame Montour (herself once a French captive), as fluent in English and French as he was in Iroquoian and Algonquin. In his heart he was Iroquois, one to whom longhouse ritual and protocol were intuitive. Eghuisera was the name the elders—the headmen and -women—had given to Montour, he, the trusted go-between to the Six Nations and English, who passed the white and purple wampum strands with care and attentiveness to detail as one might observe a religion, which, indeed, longhouse ceremonies were.

Conrad Weiser must have been grateful the enigmatic Montour had journeyed to Lancaster and now stood beside him. Moravian missionary Nicholas Zinzendorf met him in 1742; the renowned mediator may have been dressed in much the same way in the Lancaster council, where, just as with one's measured speech, one's dress was strutted and brandished in a display of plumage warfare. His facial features reflected the Gaelic countenance of his grandfather, Governor Frontenac of Canada; to perceive that, though, one would have had to peer over the fire pit at his face, shiny with vermilion blended with bear fat. Wearing shoes, eschewing breechclout for breeches, Montour's shirt lapped over his drop-fronts, which at the knees were buttoned and cinched with wool garters to hold up his stockings. The black cordovan scarf glinting with brooches and tied loosely about his neck set off the scarlet brocade of his damask weskit showing underneath his brown coat. Silver buttons shut the weskit from groin to neck; the top two buttons he left undone to let his shirt ruffles protrude, matching the ripples of his cuffs.

By day he covered his head with a wide-brimmed, low-crowned beaver, sides curled up, rolled, and flared inward. Here, though, it would have been as proper for the *métis* mediator to don a *gastoweh*, a deerskin cap beaded, quilled, and flamboyantly thatched in an amorphous, feathery array—iridescent "eyes" clipped from a peacock's train, white and black ostrich plumes, pileated woodpecker crests, spiraling tufts plucked off snowy egret and blue heron pinions, eagle tail feathers—that rose and fell in shimmering fluffs. Spiraling half crescents emanating from his temples were in fact his ear rims; as a child, his auricles were slit from apex to lobe, stuffed with beaver fur, and let heal, and here wrapped along the edges with brass wire to resemble basket handles four inches in circumference from which dangled ball-and-cone bobs.[22]

Thus stood before this harlequin assemblage of deerskin and silk, fur and velvet, tawny skin and pale, war paint and tattoos and scalplocks, queues, and talc-powdered wigs, this harlequin go-between. All knew he did not hold liquor well; that he frequented tippling houses; that he debauched to excess; that some men assembled there did not trust him. "Montour is," concluded one trader, "an unintelligible person."[23]

Maybe. But he was a skilled linguist. He remained clear-eyed and dispassionate, again and again cocking his oiled and ochered, well-decorated head to listen, relaying the Mohawk's message in Munsee to stone-faced Algonquins, relaying the words a second time in English to terse whites.

Algonquins did not like what they heard. Nor would the French: France claimed the Mississippi by right of La Salle's 1680 forays. News of the

Lancaster Treaty would give pause to the native inhabitants of the thriving, newly established Lower Shawnee Town at the Scioto's spill into the Ohio, and to those Shawnees living at Eskippakithiki in their palisaded one-acre village set on the thirty-five-hundred-acre plain between Upper Howard and Lulbegrud Creeks and twenty-five miles from the Warrior's Path.

But the tobacco-farming, landed elitists of Virginia were immensely pleased, and so, as the Lancaster Treaty of 1744 concluded, the die was cast: His Majesty George II "legally" owned the land from the Tidewater to the Mississippi—to the Crown an untrammeled, unsettled region.

CHAPTER ONE

Forbidding Gateway

DECEMBER 12, 1749

Dr. Thomas Walker jabbed the quill's clipped end into the dip well, paused, then guided its nib in a forcibly neat stroke that belied the joy in his heart. His rough-hewn "farmer's hand" was the brunt of many a jibe from his high-toned friends, so he had to work to achieve the look of control. When he wrote in haste or when his passions ran high, his script was nigh indecipherable; and just now, after receiving tantalizing news from his Loyal Land Company associates, he was both.[1]

"It is my business to write the note, theirs to read it," Dr. Walker said to his wife, who, besides having once been a widow of privilege, was Patrick Henry's niece and second cousin to George Washington. Through Mildred Meriwether, Walker acquired a home and fifteen thousand acres in Albemarle County, Virginia, near Wolf Hills,[2] and in the fullness of their years together, Mildred would bear twelve children.

Pioneering ran deep in the family's bloodlines. Eldest daughter Mary wed Nicholas Lewis, uncle of Meriwether Lewis, the secretary to President Jefferson (Dr. Walker was, in Thomas Jefferson's youth, his guardian), who, along with Capt. William Clark, co-commanded the Corps of Discovery in their epic journey to the Pacific. Mary's grandfather, Langaloo Winston, was skilled in the hunt and honest in the skin trade, which put him in good stead with his Algonquin neighbors. A "Long Hunter" thirty years before Elisha Walden's deer slayers began filtering from New River basin to exploit the Cumberland, Langaloo lived with Delawares from midsummer until the first snow (and then some, if beaver and otter were aplenty and furs prime), dressing in leggings and moccasins, bark-dyed linen and brain-tanned buck-skin, sleeping on bear hides, and eating from gut stewpots.[3]

From Winston, Walker learned Indian ways, and of the verdant wilder-ness skirting Albemarle, and of the western waters. Now, he evinced no sur-prise: The Loyal Land Company, by considerable finagling and finesse, had persuaded His Majesty George II to grant unto them eight hundred thousand acres to parcel off as quitrents.

What did startle Thomas was the fine bit of good news that the acreage need not be claimed or granted in one expansive swath; rather, Virginia's prospective barons should choose their land with care, giving diligence to lo-cate, survey, and mark the finest, most fertile tracts that were sure to yield the highest in the estate markets. Dr. Walker was to head the LLC's scouting ex-pedition beyond the Dangerous Mountains, northwestward of the Tennessee-Carolina border, to find those most excellent tracts.

Of all the Company's members—all of them bookish, rich, ambitious, and influential men who measured wealth and status in delicately manicured estates, in vast acreage, in two- and three-story stone and clapboard homes fit-ted with imported English panes, in cattle and horses, in corn and burley fields and barns, in African chattel bought and sold at slave auctions—Walker was the one man among them best suited for the heady task at hand.

And too, besides the adventure, there was the ultimate quid pro quo: land. A gentry tobacco farmer, growing "that stinking weed" that so exhausted the soil after a harvest or two, and a two-time member of the House of Burgesses who also served on the Privy Council, Dr. Walker found such prospects irresistible. So alluring, in fact, that it was said of him, "Had Vir-ginia's land companies been a spider web, Dr. Walker would have been the spider."[4]

His father had died when he was a boy. But tragedy and loss notwith-standing, Thomas Walker was intellectually keen and well tutored, energetic and disciplined. Even in his last years, his disposition, said son Francis, in-clined toward "fire and great spirit," and he remained an optimistic, merry woodsman of robust health almost until his death in 1794, a month shy of his eightieth birthday.

Neighbors swapped tales of his practical jokes, pranks bordering on the macabre and played out at the expense of Virginia's upper crust. Walker, all knew, loathed bourgeois pretentiousness.

Once, it was rumored, he had invited all the neighbors for a barbecue, laying before them plates heaped high with what his guests deemed succulent mutton, which was soon devoured and heartily complimented. Candles dim-ming, mugs full, and pipe smoke curling to the rafters, someone noticed that

Old Fowler, Walker's aging hound, had yet to show. Alas!—it was soon discovered that Old Fowler's ribs were laid bare before them. Another time Walker brewed a batch of what he touted to be exotic gourmet coffee. After his visitors supped and artfully commented on the coffee's unique aroma and delicate bouquet, he lifted the kettle lid and drew forth a decapitated timber rattler, one of his gustatory addictions.

But there was far more to this man than pranks or woodsmanship or overseeing legal matters and baronial estates. A licensed surveyor beset with wanderlust and schooled at William and Mary in the arts of physic (tutoring at Williamsburg under his brother-in-law, Dr. George Gilmer, who owned an herbal apothecary), where, perhaps, he pored over the earliest western maps as rendered by De l'Isle (1700) and Moll (1720), Dr. Thomas Walker was a unique embodiment of American possibility.

And now, missive in hand, he did not tarry. In April 1748 he had journeyed with Col. James Patton to the Holston, which flows through northeast Tennessee. Since 1743 Patton had worked hard to keep his clandestine Blue Ridge journeys a secret—"keep the noise subdued," he ordered James Wood,

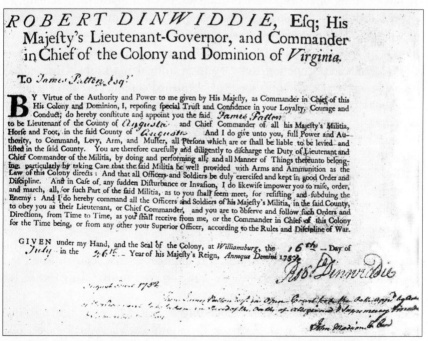

James Patton's militia commission, signed by Virginia's Royal Lieutenant-Governor, Robert Dinwiddie, July 16, 1752. DRAPER MANUSCRIPTS 1QQ:68; STATE HISTORICAL SOCIETY OF WISCONSIN.

John Buchanan, and Charles Campbell and his chain-men and hunters, while he formed the Woods River Land Company and petitioned the Privy Council for two hundred thousand acres on which to settle one hundred families, "one family for each 1,000 acres" at £3 sterling per acre.[5]

In April 1745 the Council granted the two hundred thousand acres: one hundred thousand to Patton, but, stunningly, the other one hundred thousand acres to John Robinson, the Council president. In 1748 Thomas Lee and Robert Dinwiddie, surveyor general for the southern colonies, penned into being a competing speculative venture: the Ohio Company. Two feisty rivals followed: the Loyal Land Company and Greenbrier Company.

Col. James Patton was dumbstruck. His worst fears realized, against such powerful political and financial machinations he had no hope of appeal. It hardly mattered: Shawnees killed him on July 8, 1755.

Dr. Walker had beheld what Patton had tried to keep secret: eastern Tennessee's loamy soil, spacious hardwood forests, teeming game herds. Cherokee half faces with scaffolds piled with deerskins baled and wrapped in bearskins and jerk racks smoking slabs of wild meat dotted the Holston to Reedy Creek. He saw denning otters and beavers and swarms of "English flies" (Cherokee for bees), heralding the coming of westering colonials. Buffalo were there too, the wild beef a welcome repast, their pounding hooves keeping paths clear of laurel twice head-high, which in spring burst into pink, purple, and ivory pastels. He saw elk trumpeting steam funnels from flared nostrils during autumn's frosts, their thickening coats of burnished copper, taut and shivering from ebony muzzle to tawny rump and quivering hamstrings, ending in pear-shaped patches of tan buff. He marveled at the elk's agility to nimbly clatter and skid along rock-strewn trails leading hither and thither to Athiamiowee, the Warrior's Path spiraling northward to the Great Wilderness.

By the early 1700s few Englishmen knew with surety what lay beyond the imposing sandstone chasm, Cave Gap, a massive cleft sundering the mighty Ouasioto (Shawnee for "land where deer are plentiful") north-to-south. The mountain's 120-mile ridge cresting to thirty-five hundred feet and parting the east from the west was a forbidding obstacle, its summit but a rounded splinter of its once towering magnificence that, eons before, had reached high into the foggy-blue, low-hanging cumuli that daily settled on this singular span of the Appalachian plateau.

Vestigial splinter of ancient geography or not, Ouasioto certainly impeded travel. Gaining its slopes from the southeast, via Athiamiowee, one passed northwesterly through cliffs that on sunny days cut a stark profile to travelers gazing up at its rim from Powell's Valley, Virginia. Twenty more miles took travelers to the Narrows, a water gorge carved by Clear Creek, a branch of the Shawanoe, through a rock wall jutting off Pine Mountain.[6]

Cave Gap and the Narrows were twin gates opening to a lattice work of wide, dished-out ruts and traces travelers followed across overlying escarpments, through the tall timber of dark forests, past knobs rising near salt licks, savanna and canelands, to the Great Wilderness and to the Beautiful River. Gaining the Ohio shore, the paths resumed, ribboning on to the Great Lakes. Centered as an island in the Great Wilderness[7] was its crown jewel: *Kanta-Ke.*

North and south of *Kanta-Ke* were the Indian towns. The craggy Appalachian rim veined with coal was due east. West, on past the Falls of the Ohio, lay French and Indian settlements.

By horse, or on foot (with a packhorse or two in tow), the bluegrass isle was two weeks' journey from Cave Gap—about 120 miles. Or, a riverbound traveler departing the forks of the Ohio by keelboat, bateaux, flatboat, poplar dugout, or elmbark canoe drifted to the wide maw of a famous landmark, a well-beaten lead buffalo trace fording Limestone Creek. Taking the path at a smart step, one reached the bluegrass in fine order, the entire route—from Wheeling to now Lexington—being about 370 miles one-way. The riverine route was longer, but much easier.

MARCH 6, 1750. 10:00 A.M.

Dr. Thomas Walker's company departed his home north of James River in Louisa County, Virginia, moccasined heels nudging mounts ahead. Six men astride six horses, two packhorses behind, Plott-ish looking hounds and yellow and brindled mutts panting along, dodging clomping hooves, capering and bugling in the morning's chill.

Dogs harassed bears, chased deer, locked onto buffalo ears long enough for hunters to throw down, and crawled in amongst men shivering under blankets—"three dog nights" of spring were commonplace on the Blue Ridge. Cherokees were at peace with England. Dr. Walker reckoned he knew Indian ways enough to deal with them. Still, the tranquility veneering the border remained brittle; sharp-nosed curs alert to the rustle and scent of Ouasioto's painted guardians added security. And Walker had a fondness for dogs, as did Ambrose Powell, his deputy surveyor from Culpeper County; beneath Powell's pony, plodding along, was old Tumbler. William Tomlinson, Colby Chew, Henry Lawless, and John Hughs rounded out the fellowship.

Pressing on to the James's headwaters, they spent Tuesday with Col. Joshua Fry, Albemarle's commander of the county militia. Fry—collaborating on his forthcoming "Map of Virginia" with Peter Jefferson, father of America's third president—was enthusiastic about the adventure. He and Walker talked long into the night.

Rains ensued, lasting until Sunday. They forded the swelling Rockfish and Fluvanna, buying at an outpost "Rum, Thread and other necessaries," and rode atop the Blue Ridge Wednesday, March 14, stopping at Buford's Gap on Staunton Creek (near Roanoke).

Travelers depended on Buford's Station for jerk, tallow, and bear bacon and supplies from back east, but now there was no wild meat. Walker was dismayed at the dearth of big game: "Hunters had," he lamented, shot the deer and elk for skins and "killed the Buffaloes for diversion." The half bushel of meal and hominy he bartered from Michael Campbell had to last until they found game enough to hunt.

Harsh, rainy winds that cut sharply off the Shenandoah's ashen chert and sandstone ridges swept the valley, making the men's crossing of New River on March 17 a memorably brisk one. Here, a turbid swirl of four hundred yards parted hilly banks wooded with sycamore and barely budding dogwood and redbud, wiry grapevine streamers and sparse cane; in fording the New after a downpour forced it into a high chop, one risked being swept downriver or colliding with a careering, half-submerged poplar.

Walker knew, as he had traversed this leg of the Hunter's Trail with Col. James Patton two years before, the shore was broad and pebbly, affording secure footing. Within ten years, travelers would name the ford Ingles's Ferry for the rickety, horse-driven shuttle of sawmill planks, pulled along on hempen ropes through creaking hardwood pulleys, that, for a few pence toll, one-eyed William Ingles and wife Mary steered from shore-to-shore; Ingles's descendants ran the ferry for more than a century, long after Mary—perhaps the first white woman to see *Kanta-Ke*—fled from Shawnee captivity at Big Bone Lick in August 1756 and followed the river back to Virginia, her grim seven hundred-mile Kentucky exodus taking forty days.

Guns, powderhorns, and saddlebags held arm-high, wool duffels and oil-cloth budgets bound with tumplines and hoppused Indian-style up and over shoulders, the six swam their steeds and dogs across, Walker's cur on his lap, men and dogs staring at a throng of hairy faces gazing back from the western shore: It was, Walker discovered, a commune of expatriated Brethren who had arrived in Philadelphia from Europe's Palatinate.

Their leader summoned their thin, mobcapped women, who kept their eyes cast downward, folks addressing one another as "Brother" and "Sister," lacing talk with "thee" and "thou," and "da" and "du," and kindling a fire as the men and dogs drew near to dry.

Brethren were sabbatarians, Dr. Walker learned. Brush arbor services they held on Saturdays. They rejected all creeds, save for the Bible only, holding fast to the apostle's saying as declared in I Peter 4:11: "If any man speak, let him speak as the oracles of God." Speak and practice such oracles Brethren did, as the Spirit gave them utterance: greeting one another with "holy kisses"; foot-washing to show piety; fasting; shunning icons, Papists, and Protestants; passing communion of wine and unleavened bread weekly; adding no musical instruments to their a cappella hymnody. Brethren did not vote, serve in militias, or employ a clergy, but composed hymns, suffered women to keep silent in the assembly, and held all things in common.

Oddly, Brethren men baptized adults (only) with a righteousness exceeding that of the Pharisees: immersion three times face down in the name of the Father, Son, and Holy Ghost, the triune ceremony earning them their derisive nickname: "Dunkers."

These Dunkers were from the Ephrata community, an austere sect founded in 1732 by Conrad Beissel. Brother Beissel, a mystic who dreamed strange dreams and talked with God and with angels, demanded his disciples live as cloistered as the Judaic Essenes who tented along the Dead Sea a century before Christ's birth. Beissel's followers donned togas and went about shod in Roman sandals, confusing Pennsylvanians who mocked them and reckoned the devout were a diaspora of lost Dominicans. Like Samson the Hebrew judge, Beissel permitted no razor to touch a man's head or face, thus fulfilling the Nazirite vow. Like apostle Paul, he buffeted his flesh daily, deeming celibacy the noblest of virtues but ensuring doom for his sect. To the relief of regular Dunkers, who were having a hard enough time gaining converts, the Ephrata faction died in 1768 with the death of its founder.[8]

"The Duncards are an odd set of people, who make it a matter of Religion not to Shave their Beards, ly on Beds, or eat Flesh, though at present, in the last, they transgress. I doubt the plenty and deliciousness of Venison & Turkeys has contributed not a little to this." Dr. Walker observed his "Sabbath" on Sunday, his men resting, grazing their mounts, buying hominy. Between this ford on the New and Cave Gap lay two hundred miles of escarpments and laurel thickets.

Saturday, March 24. The scouting fellowship had arrived at Capt. Samuel Stalnaker's camp on the north bank of the Holston's middle fork, which falls into the French Broad to form the Tennessee.[9] Between rains, Walker's men helped erect Stalnaker's cabin, which one year later Fry and Jefferson's "Map of Virginia" would mark as the colony's far western outpost. Stalnaker had traded with the Cherokee since 1748, the year Walker and Patton first met him; seeing him now was fortuitous, and Dr. Walker tried to hire him as a guide, but with his cabin walls up, his family at his side, Stalnaker demurred. Indians attacked his home in 1755, taking Sam prisoner, murdering his wife and son and three others.

Sunday they rested, belling their mounts to graze the plenteous grass of the low ground, departing westward of the Holston on the morrow, lightning clapping, thunder roaring, rain changing to a snowy slush blanketing ridges and precipices, six tired men leading horses whose chipped hooves, chewed tails, cocklebur-studded manes, and thinning middles stretched taut over protruding short ribs testified to the trail's vicissitudes and a diet of river reeds.

Nearing Reedy Creek after four days' journey, they ambushed two buffalo calves, killing one and notching the ears of the second. That night Walker saw nothing (nor did his men), but their yipping hounds scented Indians traveling along Reedy near some deserted wigwams seen the day before and "a large Indian Fort." "Our Dogs very uneasie."

Cherokees or Shawnees? Catawbas, maybe, from Santee land to the southeast? Colby Chew and Ambrose Powell read their sign the next morning: twenty warriors, moving fast.

"April ye 1st. The Sabbath." They rested.

Travel was tedious, seven or eight miles a day. Fallen trees, wooded crests, bare ridges, and on warmer days, umber-banded copperheads and highland rattlers slithering from dens to bask in the sun and feed and shed slowed the band's ascent. The company scaled the piney traverses of Clinch Mountain searching for Looney's Gap, a dirty white cut in this barrier bisecting Virginia and Tennessee.

Their dogs nosing along the broken land routed a slumbering he-bear, hungry and spoiling for a fight. Walker's dog waded in, but the angry bruin mauled him badly before the men shot the bear. Walker doctored his mutt, toting him in the saddle splayed across his lap until he was able to trot along on his own.

Trees blazed with hieroglyphics to scare off intruders designated passing tribes and celebrated raids and coup counts. "Indian war-marks"—sketches of forts and villages; half moons, turtles, otters, crosses, suns; and slashes for prisoners taken, an "X" equaling one scalp—warriors had gashed into beeches and smeared with vermilion and gunpowder ink. The company paused to carve in their own graffiti: "TW" and "CC." So often did Elisha Walden ten years later see "A. Powell"—distorted from a decade's growth—cut into trees bordering the path that he named the rivulet flowing nearby Powell River.

Fording the Clinch April 9 and nearing Cave Gap on the twelfth, Walker took "a large Buffaloe Road . . . and found the Ascent and Descent tollerably easie." At noon the next day they rode through Ouasioto's famous yawning cleft—Cave Gap—which Dr. Walker renamed for William Augustus, duke of Cumberland, son of George II and Queen Caroline, who spared neither the wounded Highlanders nor the Scottish prisoners at the battle of Culloden, April 16, 1746, and whom Lord Byron would immortalize as "Willy the Butcher."

Cumberland Gap, gateway to America's First Far west. Copper engraving by H. Fenn, 1872.

"April 16th. Rain." April 17. "Still Rain."

Two days later they wounded a bear that charged in and grabbed Ambrose Powell's leg, shaking him like a pup and lacerating his knee; Powell, wracked by pain barely numbed after a few stout pulls on a rum horn, was hefted into his saddle. The party picked their way over seven miles of ridges before nightfall.

Dr. Walker's blue eyes reflected the adventure of it all. At thirty-five, his frame of five foot, seven inches cut a spare silhouette fleshed out to subsistence muscularity, his step quick, his energy unflagging. Confronting them: meandering paths, canebrakes, honeycombed licks reeking of dung and saline and sulfur that drew animals from afar to perpetually lick and devour the salty dirt, transforming the landscape into a moonscape. Between cliff faces, the six forded Licking Creek and Clover Creek (named for the carpet of clover edging its banks), taking a day to girdle and debark a huge elm—"25 feet round 3 feet from the ground"—and stitch its long wedges with tugs into a canoe, bark side out, to ford the Shawanoe, seventy yards broad and running high—the last choke point into *Kanta-Ke.*

Prodigious hailstorms, symphonies of thunder and lightning, and rising waters delayed crossing in this near blossoming thatch of dogwood and crimson redbud.

Sunday morning, April 22, broke clear.

Personal rum keg, French and Indian War Era, 4" long x 3¹/₅" at base, top bung visible and mirror at one end.
JIM AND CAROLYN DRESSLAR COLLECTION.

They waited, eyes on a sandstone boulder's high shoulder poking up out of the frothy swirl; by Monday the boulder was exposed, the pellucid waters an ample ether alive with schooling sunfish, smallmouth bass, and fat, droll-eyed catfish rising sluggishly to smack the surface.

Unhitching oilcloth bundles from the packhorses to cache in the barque, along with the powder and lead, Walker's tent, extra clothes, their jerk and hominy rations, the men stripped, ferried goods to the Shawanoe's far shore, swam the horses over, kindled a fire, and shirted. Here, where Clear Creek's mouth empties into the Shawanoe and a skyward glimpse through lofty greening poplar and sycamore canopies reveals a sublime view of the Gap, Dr. Walker renamed the Shawanoe the same "good English name": Cumberland.

Dr. Walker faced a decision: Their horses were famished. One pony, lame beyond recovery—"He is white, branded on the near Buttock with a swivil Stirrup Iron, and is old"—he untethered to let roam beneath the awakening understory of hornbeam, dogwood, and black haw, the beast sure prey for gray wolf packs and solitary panthers that nightly lifted their voices in protest at the intruders' presence. This jut of tableland on the Cumberland's north bank offered water, buffalo clover for grazing, a leafy cloak from hickories, oaks, ash, and sugar maples rising majestically above lush spreads of boldly erect early saxifrage and emerald thatches of five-leaved cinquefoil. Big game was a plenty, and turkeys perched high in the lofty timber caused the men to crane their necks when shouldering firelocks to pot them.

Dr. Walker divided his party's fellowship to lead ahead a three-man van. The men left behind (after casting lots, William Tomlinson, Henry Lawless, and John Hughs) he gave directives to make "improvements": clear a plot; plant peach "stones" and corn seed; hew timber enough for a cabin twelve feet by eight; lay in a store of jerk, venison, and bear hams.

Dr. Walker, Ambrose Powell, and Colby Chew departed on their own hook, Monday, April 23, bearing northwest then west, riding twelve miles by nightfall.

Eighteen miles they reconnoitered the Tuesday following, Dr. Walker's fireside nights spent scribbling in his leather-bound journal. Land here was "poor and the woods very Thick beyond them." Stony hilltops choked with cedar, spicebush, red oak, and laurel relinquished little soil, and so the horses suffered.

Wednesday Dr. Walker pulled himself up through the limbs of a tall tree perched atop a ridge to spy out east Kentucky's landscape: Below him on the undulating hills rose hemlocks and cedars, hickories and red oaks; but few if any stands of cherry, buckeye, hackberry, slippery elm, pawpaw, coffee, or honey locust—trees that, to the eyes of an astute land speculator, denoted soil of the highest fertility.

Twenty miles below their first fording of Cumberland River four days earlier, they paced over and over an ancient Mississippian mound, marveling at it and stepping it off—"20 feet high and 60 over the Top"—and saw fresh sign (but no Indians). Walker lost a dog to a black bear.

The group reunited Saturday, April 28. Walker, Powell, and Chew beheld a singular sight: Kentucky's first cabin.[10]

"April 29th. The Sabbath." Sunday's sun warming rock lairs thick with cleft phlox in white bunches on dry outcroppings summoned all manner of snakes, heads emerging, forked tongues stabbing for a taste of field mouse or surfacing vole, keeled scales glowing purplish next to translucent tatters of dried, cast-off skins. No one saw the iridescent, sinuous blur of yellow, gray-green, and ebony crossbands strike as the horse sauntered past, parted lips and teeth tugging up tender shoots. The horse whinnied and stomped and jerked its head violently away from the taut coil at its hooves, twin blebs rising off its muzzle oozing cherry.

Copperhead, maybe? No . . .

Then: A dry, staccato buzz like #6 swan-shot spilling from an unplugged shot-snake onto dry leaves and a faint whiff like freshly sliced cucumbers: timber rattler.

Dr. Walker dispatched the reptile and calmed the horse enough to rub into the suppurating fang punctures a greasy, rank-smelling bear oil poultice

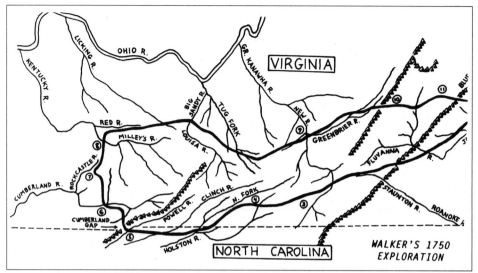

The western foray of Dr. Thomas Walker, 1750. 1) Walker's home in Louisa County; 2) Walker's Joplin home on Rockfish River; 3) trek stalled by lost horses; 4) Stalnaker cabin; 5) Cumberland Gap; 6) Walker's Kentucky cabin; 7) far western point of exploration on Rockcastle; 8) ford at Kentucky River; 9) confluence of New and Greenbrier; 10) Warm Springs Valley hamlet; 11) Augusta court house. MAP BY SAMUEL SISTLER AND ALEXANDER CANADY MACLEOD; FILSON HISTORICAL SOCIETY.

cut with "Rattle Snake root." The horse doctored, the rattler skinned, sliced, roasted, and devoured, the Loyal Land Company expedition pressed along the Warrior's Path, rousing and blazing away at a buffalo herd one hundred head strong, spying out a deserted Indian camp, slogging about in cold rains that rarely ceased.

Ambrose Powell, bear-bit in one knee, wrenched his good knee Sunday next, May 6. Three days later Powell gimped along where flinty narrows and steep, shaley walls closed in to force the party off their saddles. Rain splattering down the banks and sluicing off in the Rockcastle pushed it higher and higher, yet the greenish blue water cascading through the rock chute was far from cresting.

Three months out now. Tilting limestone landscapes and suddenly gusting wind blasts seemed to defy their horses' securing footing among surreal spires and shelving rocks; eleven days before, Colby and his pony had tumbled off a ridge and into a ravine. To balance the bodily humors of blood and phlegm, yellow and black bile, Dr. Walker lanced a vein and drained Colby of a gill, then dosed him with a shot of the powerful patent tonic "Volatile drops."

The dew's incessant dripping off the emerald canopy and the daily fording were wearing their moccasins thin, the cracking deerskin soles cut by chert, and petrified stobs and mussel shells splintering and jabbing into shriven, calloused feet. On clear days the men turned the soggy soles to the sun; at night they impaled their moccasins on sticks over fires, but not so close as to bake the soles hard as cedar shakes. Darkness found them lounging on blankets, elk hides, and musty bearskins cast beside aromatic flames fed by juniper and shagbark hickory. Dr. Walker's men munched jerk, parched corn, and roasted wild meat while tending to their nightly ritual of patching moccasins that more and more resembled tattered old wineskins.

Two days later, May 11. Wending their way up and down a tortuously strait path laced with lady fern, ivory bouquets of six-petaled hepatica, and carpeted with Virginia bluebells, prodding gaunt horses along a creek swirling viridescent past a high-lifting limestone face, the party spied a spacious "rock-castle"—"Sufficient to Shelter 200 men from Rain," recorded Dr. Walker, with his usual alacrity. They drove in their horses; as they did so, darkening skies rolling heavy and gray with cumulonimbi thundered and cracked, unleashing torrents lasting a day and a night.

Though no one realized it, the heavens' roars heralding their arrival signaled a milestone: The commodious cavern marked the farthest point westward reached by Dr. Thomas Walker's Loyal Land Company.

One huntsman—Chew or Powell, probably—a day or two earlier had shot an elk browsing the Rockcastle's banks and boned out the gamy, brick red meat, taking care to hone the blade keen to shuck the skin off free of scours. Here, now, dry and snug within the cavern, they lugged the stiffening hide down to a pool, tossing it in hair-side up and anchoring it with stones. A day or two later, after the hollow hair began to slip, they carried the hide back up to the cave, sheared off the wet swatches with a blade, then, spelling each other off—two men facing each other gripping the lank skin front and back to whip it back and forth over a rounded rock to dry it and rub free its epidermis, which would harden tough as cartilage—in an hour or two the hide was deemed "half-grained." The men cut the dirty white, fluffy skin into sheets a foot square to make "Indian shoes."[11]

Then, alas!

A quick rummaging through oilcloth budgets revealed what Dr. Walker feared—"We had lost every awl that we brought out." So he contrived a punch from a fishhook shank and cobbled awls from horseshoe nails, filing ends shiny and, waxing some linen thread and whangs, poked the holes and stitched up moccasins and saved what was left of the skin for patch leather.

The six crossed and recrossed the Rockcastle the week following, fell (again) into the Warrior's Path, veered (again) from it, winding around chimney rocks buffeted by chilly winds and enduring daily soakings of rainfall. Ambrose Powell, though, must have felt a twinge when a bull elk felled his beloved Tumbler as he gave chase, perhaps the flying clip of an ebony hoof crushing his skull. Walker dubbed the gulch Tumbler's Run.

"May 27th. The Sabbath." In a bark canoe of two days' building under soaring beeches and a wide, open-headed sycamore measuring thirty feet at its base, the party forded an oxbow of "Milley's River" (the Kentucky), and on Wednesday, May 30, walked over a burn site, horses cropping close spring's burst of grasses. Here, too, buds and leaves offered slim repast for shy elk easing from the forest's shadows to nibble lichen "mossings" growing in thick patches in the misty, riverine valleys. Hail-laden gusts yanked Dr. Walker's canvas from its poles, scattering the men beneath it and toppling trees.

Undaunted, the six departed, leaving "T. W." and four "blazes" slashed in lines of beeches bordering the traces they followed. Buffalo scratching themselves free of tattered hanks of wool crawling with vermin had rubbed tree middles gnarled and bare, alleviating the buffs' misery, but leaving their quivering flanks naked and sensitive to flies, seed ticks, and mosquitoes ravenous for a first feed.

Early June. West now of the Louisa (or Levisa) Fork of the Big Sandy— named by Dr. Walker for Louisa Augusta, daughter of His Majesty George II and sister to the duke of Cumberland—rainfall (again) stalled them. "The River is so deep we Cannot ford it and as it is falling we conclude to stay & hunt," he wrote on June 8. Powell and Walker, out hunting that afternoon, were taken aback by a distant crack of a flintlock from the river's shore to the south, toward Tug Fork. Within a day and a bit, they forded the Louisa.

Creeks. Steep valleys. Downed trees from the storm days before hindered progress as they slogged two hundred miles eastward toward the fork of the New and Greenbrier, tomahawking their way through the laurel and ivy atop steep ridges, so famished they had to kill one of their dogs and eat it. And so the trek went, with little notable about it on the homebound leg save the daily series of tiny astonishments.

On July 8 the fellowship began crossing the Alleghenies and entered Shenandoah Valley, topping the Blue Ridge at Rock Fish Gap. They got to Dr. Walker's home eight days later, ending their tramp of four months and seven days. "We killed in the Journey 13 buffaloes, 8 Elks, 53 Bears, 20 Deer, 4 Wild Geese, about 150 Turkeys, besides small Game. We might have killed three times as much meat, if we had wanted it."[12]

Dr. Walker later learned that he had just missed the island in the wilderness; he would have found the Promised Land had he pushed northwest of the Kentucky's headwaters a few days' travel. Still, he was the first Englishman to have entered Kentucky from the southeast and to pen lucid observations of a vast chunk of uncharted territory; he had renamed the Shawanoe the Cumberland, named Cave Gap Cumberland Gap, rode through the Narrows to the ford, detailing lead traces, old Indian camps, rivers and streams, licks and terrain; his path along the Rockcastle would become a leg of the Wilderness Road to the bluegrass; his "cabbin" was Kentucky's first homestead; his journal aided Fry and Jefferson in their landmark "Map of Virginia" (published in 1751 by a London firm) and served as a influential source for Lewis Evans and Thomas Pownall in their famous map (1776), though the French and Indian War stalled migration just as surely as it halted Walker's 1753 proposed expedition to go beyond the Mississippi River and across the Missouri to the Pacific Ocean, along the way making "exact reports of the country."[13]

But Dr. Thomas Walker was not the only Englishman to go west in 1750. Nor was the Loyal Land Company the sole joint-stock venture aspiring to plow the bluegrass.

George II, artist unknown.

Wars & Rumors of Wars

In the year 1749, of the reign of Louis XV, of France, We . . . have buried this plate at the mouth of the Ohio . . . as a monument of renewal of possession, which we have taken of the said river, and of all those which empty themselves into it, and of all the lands of both sides, even to the sources of said rivers . . . by force of arms and by treaties, especially by those of Ryswick, of Utrecht, and of Aix-la-Chapelle.
　　　　　　　　　　　—Capt. Pierre Joseph de Celeron de Bienville

Captain Celeron's burial of his lead plates along the Ohio's shores was tantamount to an act of war. England's response: the creation of land companies, and Lt. Col. George Washington's capitulation of Fort Necessity on the rainy July 4, 1754, a fateful day marking a flash point of grinding rivalries that had begun two hundred years earlier.

England's defeat of the Armada in 1588 and the ebbing of bullion pilfered from the Yucatán that had once poured into Spain's coffers signaled a waning of Felipe II's designs. But the Catholic monarch laid claim to Europe's first New World holdings in the Southeast, and in 1565 Pedro Menendez, His Majesty's servant, founded St. Augustine in La Florida. Menendez's accommodation by the sword renewed Spain's policies gained by battling Moors and Africans; it mattered not that he now warred against transported heretics and heathen natives.

At the mouth of Florida's river St. John's was Fort Caroline,[1] its palisades erected in the shape of a big triangle a year before by French Huguenots—disciples of John Calvin and wards of Calvinist Holland and Anglican England. Menendez's morion-crested conquistadores seized the outpost on the rainy dawn

Arquebusier, firing with matchlock on rest. Note both ends of the "slow-match" are lit. Bandolier belt for powder charges (in attached wooden flasks called "the twelve apostles"), priming flask, extra slow-match tucked into belt.

of September 20, 1565. To save on powder and ball and soggy niter-treated slow-matches that were hard to keep lit with flint and steel, causing the arquebusiers to make a botch of the executions, Menendez ordered in his lancers, who spilled open the Protestants in the same manner that they did their hogs. The groggy infidels surrendering in nightshirts numbered only about 150 and were assured mercy; upon reflection, Menendez deemed killing these mockers of the Holy Eucharist a noble way to "serve God Our Lord, as well as Your Majesty."[2]

In 1568 French corsairs razed the wood fort that Pedro Menendez had renamed San Mateo and, meting out eye-for-an-eye justice, butchered its owners.[3] Fort St. Augustine's stones were laid in 1675, and the presidio remained just that—a military town built to protect ships and priests and missions, largely bereft of families and settlers, save for Indians and Africans to serve as slaves and concubines. With little incentive to navigate the Atlantic's dangerous waters to live in immense malarial swamps inhabited by eighteen-foot alligators and to hundred-acre seas of palmetto patches infested with the world's largest rattlesnakes[4] and with harlequin cobralike coral snakes,[5] Spain's southeastern colonies hardly prospered, remaining wards of the homeland.

Soon white flags bisected with a wide white cross flew over New France's outposts: Port Royal, Arcadia (1605); Quebec (1608); Montreal (1611). These forts on their way to becoming towns boasted of pressed fur bales by the hundredfold destined for Paris, prime furs collected by a distinct class of canoe-men, the voyageurs, largely illiterate, yet wise in bartering and fur-taking.

Voyageurs[6] and their woodsrunning coureurs de bois kinsmen—maverick, unlicensed fur peddlers who skirted the borders of legality and transgressed them with a wink and who, on a whim, might side with the Dutch or English—explored the Lakes and the Mississippi and beyond, establishing in 1730 Fort Orleans three hundred miles up the Missouri. Roman Catholic holy orders—Jesuits, Dominicans, Franciscans—labored to stamp out pockets of Protestantism and vied for Indian souls, blunting the carnality of traders who, in the settlements, attended mass with utmost reverence but on the trail fornicated prodigiously, siring a progeny of *métis* and helping to establish warm relations with Algonquins. Indians held no romantic delusions about Frenchmen, nor were they ignorant of France's imperial designs, but Algonquins feared rapprochement with the English-allied Iroquois: With the bearers of the fleur-de-lis, they sought alliance and accommodation, not annihilation.

France's worry: the English. For if by land the French army was the "Terror of Europe," it was upon ships flying much canvas and heavily gunned that the Crown rested her hopes for making the world England's.[7]

France in Canada and Louisiana, Spain in the Southeast, the English filling in along the Atlantic coast, the Dutch laid hold on the Indies and cast their eyes northward, employing *boucaniers* to live on the islands to load ships with hundred-gallon hogsheads of smoked salt pork. Dutch colonists and the dogs and cats and livestock they shipped over with them brought vermin and disease and overran island wildlife; the prolific European hogs gorged to butchering size on mangoes, guavas, coconuts, avocados, papayas, and palm dates and sugar-cane mast, and devoured ground bird eggs and nestlings, and iguanas, and hawksbill, Ridley's, and loggerhead eggs, and snakes. Not even abundant spear-headed fer-de-lances[8] seven feet long could stop the feral pigs from forever altering the Caribbean's delicate ecological balance.

Slavers did a brisk business: The Dutch West Indian Company (founded 1621) took 15,430 African slaves to Brazil in 1623; by 1643 the firm was importing Africans to New Amsterdam (Manhattan Island, swapped in 1625 for sixty guilders' worth of trade goods).

In 1602 Henry Hudson's ship nosed into the river that now bears his name. By 1647 brawny, peg-legged "Hard-Headed Pete" Stuyvesant was commander general of Fort Orange (Albany) and New Amsterdam. Fort Orange was Holland's New World crossroads—a many-hued hamlet of four hundred or five hundred Dutch, Finns, and Swedes, free blacks and slaves, northern and southern Algonquins and Iroquoians, *métis* and Creoles, Catholics and Protestants, coureurs de bois and voyageurs, a few Jews and Irishmen and Scotsmen, Englishmen and Spaniards, and sundry whores of divers ethnicities, shades, and nationalities. One out of every five buildings was a tavern, and a visitor would have heard no less than eighteen languages and seen a tawny-skinned progeny that reflected the wry truth of one Iroquois's words—"we have given them our daughters to sleep with." But New Netherlands spreading south of the Delaware infringed upon cabins that were not her own. Typically fourteen by twenty feet, windowless, shingled with cedar shakes, logs left round or hewn square and chinked with moss and mud—these were the homes of Swedes and Finns.[9]

Entrenched to their north were the spiritually illumined "cities on a hill"—Pilgrims and Puritans who could abide no dealings with the ambitious Dutch and sought to rid their colonies of the competing heretical sectarians. As the Dutch in 1655 seized Swedish claims along the Delaware, so too a decade later did New England's Calvinist dissenters unleash holy war against Peter Stuyvesant's cadres. In 1674 England conquered Babel. New Amsterdam became New York. To keep open the Hudson and furs piled high and guns out of the hands of insurgents, the Crown garrisoned New York with Regulars—a first in North America.

The year 1688 saw the ascension of William of Orange and wife Mary as England's monarchs, precipitating King William's War ("War of the League of Hapsburg"), which in America left dead 650 English, 300 French, 200 Algonquins, and 1,300 Iroquois before the Treaty of Ryswick (September 30, 1697) ended it.

In July 1689 the Iroquois attacked Lachine, six miles from Montreal, killing 200 French and taking 100 prisoners—the worst massacre in Canada's history. Within a year of the Lachine debacle, a cadre of Algonquins and coureurs de bois left Montreal and ice-skated across frozen Lake Champlain, pillaging from Schenectady to Albany, in one night's carnage killing sixty English, seizing eighty captives, and torching seventy cabins. French losses: one dead Frenchman; one dead Algonquin. The fifty partisans that Rev. Cotton Mather called "half Indianized French, and half Frenchified Indians" moved on to Salmon Falls, New Hampshire, where nearly forty English died and fifty were taken hostage. For four days and nights, the partisans pounded Falmouth, Massachusetts, killing about twenty. After it was over, and as the vanquished stacked arms and signed articles, awaiting their fate, the Algonquins, deprived of scalps and booty promised them by the *Compagnies franches de la Marine,* put under the knife more than one hundred men, women, and children.

And so it went. By 1702 Pierre d'Iberville's colonies in Biloxi and Mobile threatened Spain's Panhandle forts as France cast wide her net in a bid to tie southern New France to the Great Lakes. East of the Blue Ridge, tales of land and deerskins threw Englishmen into a dither.

Then, on May 4, 1702, war.

Charles II, the childless king of Spain, named as successor his grandnephew Philip—the Sun King's grandson—allying France with Spain and upsetting

Europe's balance of power. England, Holland, and Austria sided against Germany and Italy, who sided with France and Spain. Queen Anne's War—"The War of Spanish Succession," named for Anne, successor to William—ripped into the West Indies, Florida, New England, and the Carolinas.

An uneasy peace prevailed on April 11, 1713. Terms of the Treaty of Utrecht: France ceded to England Hudson's Bay, Newfoundland, and the West Indies. Now England's empire building lay in a bold vision: to seize America's interior.

Utrecht's peace turned more brittle with each imperial feint: a fort at a river's fork; an outpost to wrest trade from one's foes; peltry bartered to one sovereign over another. As glib representatives of the global powers postured and prated in diplomatic parleys, their kings connived and conspired, jockeying troops and allies over the poorly mapped terrain of the New World.

Off Cape Breton Island rose the "Gibraltar of the New World": Louisbourg, 250 cannon muzzles jutting through apertures chiseled in the fort's thirty-foot-tall stone walls. To hold the swath from the Gulf to the St. Lawrence, the French built Fort Toulouse in Alabama, Fort Rosalie at Natchez, then Forts New Orleans (1718), de Rocher (Illinois: 1718), de Chartres (Illinois: 1721), and Assumption (Memphis: 1739). France armed Choctaws against British-allied Creeks and Chickasaws, and treated with the Osages and Sioux.

New France's population, circa 1715: twenty-five thousand.

New Hampshire, Maryland, North Carolina, South Carolina, New Jersey, New York, Michigan, Rhode Island, Massachusetts, and Maine became England's royal protectorates. In 1732 James Oglethorpe established Georgia, George I's penal colony wedged between New France, New Spain, and hostile Indians. Scotch-Irish and Germans flooded the Tidewater and Piedmont, pushing England's frontier to the Blue Ridge.

England's New World population, circa 1715: four hundred thousand.

In Parliament, 1738, Caribbean smuggler Capt. Robert Jenkins, in a flourish of drama and braggadocio, held before the assembly's eyes a mahogany sliver, hard and curled. He was England's newest hero. "I commended my soul to God, and my cause to my country," Jenkins blustered, recounting how the Spanish customs agent boarded His Majesty's ship to search for contraband; how at his defiance the saber grazed his temple and left his flesh on the deck. Spain parceled out £95,000 in reparations for Jenkins's amputated ear, which he kept in a little box. The Brits, feigning hurt pride, lashed back at Spanish and French forces.

By March 1744 the parrying escalated into "King George's War," pitting George II against Louis XV. England aimed four thousand New Englanders straight at Louisbourg. Stunningly, His Majesty conquered. On October 18, 1748, royal diplomats signed the Treaty of Aix-la-Chapelle.

Three wars. Three treaties. Thousands dead.

Yet France and Britain could not agree on the boundary between America and Canada. English settlers treading on Abenaki and Penobscot land drove Indians into the arms of the French. France's new banners of gold fleurs-de-lis on royal blue would not be easily furled as outposts began cropping up in Ohio land and as Louis XV sent Capt. Pierre de Celeron down La Belle Rivière with his lead plates. Loyal Land Company and Ohio Company emissaries Dr. Thomas Walker and Christopher Gist struck westward to counter, staking out claims said to run clear to the Pacific and spying out Indian and French presence.

Wars and rumors of wars.

CHAPTER TWO

Odysseus
of the Middle Ground

SEPTEMBER 11, 1750

Christopher Gist's graceful chirography—letters high-arced in cutting, calligraphic regularity and possessing a kind of literary cadence—and his even, phonetically rendered spelling set him apart from many of the border men, though in queued locks, in homespun and leather dress, in decorum and dark, pocked countenance, he much resembled them.

Few did not notice him. At forty-five, Colonel Gist stood six-two in moccasined feet, his frame fleshed out to two hundred pounds. His size loomed more commandingly when one met him, his genteel, courtly way an odd contrast to his half-Indian ranger dress and military bearing. Impressive, too, were his enigmatic comings and goings and willingness to suffer hardships patrolling the war zone both England and France claimed.

He reread the dispatch from Thomas Lee, Virginia's acting governor and the Ohio Company's driving force:

> You are to go out as soon as possible to the Westward of the
> great mountains, and carry with you such a number of
> Men as you think necessary, in Order to search out and dis-
> cover the Lands upon the River Ohio & other adjoining
> branches of the Mississippi down as low as the great Falls.[1]

Governor Lee had petitioned the Virginia Council for five hundred thousand acres in the West. Lee's actions did not go unchallenged: Pennsylvanians feared his scheme would divert Indians from selling deerskins and furs upriver at Logstown on the Ohio to bartering them at Williamsburg. Such a

41

deal, averred Thomas Penn, Conrad Weiser, and George Croghan—Pennsyl-vanians all, and with much at stake in this business—would incite enmity be-tween the two colonies.

Lee's answer came March 18, 1749: Two hundred thousand acres the Ohio Company would get, to "Settle 150 or more Families on the Company's Lands . . . within two years," and erect a fort at the forks. "The Ohio and Kanawha Rivers and the Allegheny Mountains" would mark the tract's borders.

To search out this land, Lee offered Gist £150, "and such further hand-some allowance as his service should deserve."[2] In all, it was not much.

Gist was dogged by a bottomless debt going back to Baltimore's 1732 in-ferno, his warehouses' cross-joists hung heavy with beaver and raccoon pelts (skinned open, tacked to boards), and with otter, mink, red and gray fox, bobcat, pine marten, and fisher pelts (cased-skinned, stretched nose to vent on grease-patinaed slats), collapsing in a pile of rubble. British Fur Company bankers pressed him for £10,000 in compensation. Gist shot wolves and lugged in heads to collect the bounty; served as coroner; surveyed; cleared roads; sold his inheritance, two estates, his slaves, his furniture and tools and horses; auctioned his forty-five-ton sloop, the *Two Brothers*. Still, it was not enough; he fled with his family to North Carolina's Yadkin Valley. Never in what was left of his fifty-three years did debt leave him. "I know Mr. Gist's credit was so bad I was obliged to pass my word at one of the Shops at Win-chester for some goods," wrote Col. John St. Clair to Gen. Jeffrey Amherst on the eve of Gist's death by smallpox in 1759.[3]

Lee's firm promised Gist £20 more to act as envoy, entreating Indians to rendezvous at Logstown in June of 1752 to renew the Lancaster Treaty to shore up the king's grip on the western waters. Being Lee's "liaison" would give him cover to spy out French presence clear to the Falls and Louis XV's Middle Ground trade.

Gist penned his reply and blew the ink whorls to tan and set the leaf aside. Lee's request would delay his homegoing to his wife, Sarah, and their five children: A Cherokee uprising, Catawba scouts had warned him, threat-ened settlements as far east as Salisbury.

His Catawbas could patrol three hundred miles of Allegheny wilds with-out him. His family would go north if threatened.

OCTOBER 31, 1750
Woodsrunning while beset by fever slowed him, but Gist arrived at Col. Thomas Cresap's at Old Town to make ready for his twelve-hundred-mile odyssey, wrapping oilcloth about the compass and jerk hanks and corn pone,

Appalachian pack-frame for horse-back transporting of furs and wares, c. 1760.
MUSEUM OF THE FUR TRADE, CHADRON, NE: PHOTO BY DAVID WRIGHT.

packing budgets, his seventeen-year-old African hefting bundles onto the packhorse. Gist had visited here as a teen mustering out for Ranger's Mobile, Maryland's militia. Opessa, a Piqua Shawanoe shaman who had fled Ohio during the Beaver Wars and had scribbled his mark on William Penn's Philadelphia Treaty of 1701, had founded Old Town in 1722, where he and his Delaware wife lived under the rule of wise Sassoonan. Cresap—called "Big Spoon" for his generosity—had settled in Old Town in 1741 to trade with Iroquois and Algonquin fur takers.[4]

Gist departed Cresap's home on the Potomac that Wednesday for three days hiking a leg of the Warriors' Path over Warrior Mountain and northward to the "Juniatta." His chills remained unabated. His brow burned. Rains worsened to snow, then freezing rain, hiding deadfalls, icing rocky paths, swelling high-banked meanders off the Susquehanna. Gist for three days waited it out under a lean-to, he and the boy feeding off a bear he killed, the boy chopping wood, keeping the fire stoked and their hut in repair, fetching water, keeping watch on the belled packhorse, and attending to Gist.

Forty-six miles Gist tramped the week next, west along the Juniata Path. Friday and Saturday they slept in an old cabin; the rain and snow ended at dawn Sunday, causing Gist to strike for the Kiskiminitas, the Susquehanna's forks, the broken land, shoals, and his wracked body slowing him. By night-fall, when he encamped to skin a gobbler, he had gone six miles.

Seven miles northwest, midway, thereabouts, between the Juniata and Ohio, and near a Loup village, flowed Loyalhanning Creek.[5] "Lawel" (meaning "middle"), "hanna" ("a stream"), and "ing" ("at the place of"), combined into "Loyalhanna" or "Laurel hanne" or "Loyalhannan," the Delaware town Gist got to on Thursday, fifteenth of November.

He turned northwest, enduring cold, wading icy streams. En route to Shannopin's Town (twenty Delaware lodges clumped a few miles above Monongahela's fork at Two Mile Run), the path forked and he came to Cock-Eye's camp.

The next day he axed down some saplings, slashing the ends sharp to jab in the dirt in a circle, and bent them waist-high and tied them off to make a low, one-man wigwam. He dug a pit at the center. Outside the frame, he struck flint and steel and blew the spark in the spunk into a flame, fed in tow and shavings, then kindling, let it catch up, then fed in sticks finger-thick and let that go and heaped on the logs until fire and smoke billowed forth. Only then did he add the fist-size rocks to redden; with sticks he finagled the rocks to the hole. Working quickly, he tossed skins over the frame and pegged the edges, making the hut's insides black save for its glowing center. Tugging off his hunting shirt, he crawled in, dragging a full gourd. He sat by the hole spilling water, the hissing forcing him to the hut's edge, gasping. "I was very sick, and sweated myself according to the Indian Custom . . . which gave Me Ease, and my Fever abated."[6]

He suffered a relapse in his trek to Shannopin's and laid by from Monday until Saturday (November 24), setting his compass far from his Leni-Lenape hosts. Opposite Shannopin's was Queen Alliquippa's estate. She, a Seneca go-between who in 1748 treated with fur broker Conrad Weiser (who greeted

Screw-barreled Queen Anne Pistol, c. 1740, showing open lock frizzen and round-faced cock at rest. Grotesque head chiseled in sterling barely visible on walnut butt. PHOTO BY DAVID WRIGHT.

her with a four-brace pistol salute), Joshua Fry the mapmaker, and trader James Patten. In 1749 New France's emissary, Capt. Pierre Joseph de Celeron de Bienville, on his lead-plate mission, courted Alliquippa's favor, but his audience with the queen did not go well: "She is entirely devoted to the English."[7]

Gist and his boy passed Alliquippa's home, walking the Ohio's west bank en route to Logstown, eighteen miles below the forks, on the north shore. There, in the 1740s, Kakowatcheky's Piquas settled to hunt and tend their corn hills and raise pumpkins, squash, potatoes, beans, cucumbers, and melons. In 1748, when Conrad Weiser visited Logstown, Shawanoes, Mingoes, Delawares, and Iroquois honored him with a hundred-gun salute. Weiser presented Kakowatcheky with "a Stroud, a Blanket, a Match Coat, a Shirt, a Pair of Stockings, & a large twist of Tobacco," hoisted the king's colors, and declared to the chief that the Council of Philadelphia loved him.[8]

The next summer, when Celeron's flotilla of 250 Indians, *Compagnies franches de la Marine,* and coureurs de bois spied the Union Jack fluttering over Logstown and pulled ashore to protest and hammer Louis's coat-of-arms into a tree, jeering warriors loosed his way "a mighty discharge of balls" and "gave the French to understand that the land was theirs." Put off by this— "often accidents happen from it . . . I told them to cease firing"—Celeron left Logstown sure its citizens "had evil designs . . . seduced by the bait of a cheap market given to them by the English."[9]

This winter, "Loggs Town" was astir with rumors of a raid on Lower Shawnee Town: No one saw the Ottawas or Canadians who crept in unawares, tomahawking a Shawanoe man and kidnapping a woman and two children. Thirty Iroquois had just left to attack Catawbas woodsrunning the Alleghenies to Carolina, and George Croghan had warned them of a rival Long Knife firm, the Ohio, invading the Youghiogheny. Delawares were outraged: Had not Tishcohan with the chin hair and Lapowinsa with the serpent and bird tracks tattooed upon his forehead negotiated the Walking Treaty with Penn's sons in 1737, and then wound up defrauded? Treating with Long Knives would be as bad.

On Sunday, November 25, Christopher Gist stepped into Logstown's maelstrom. Indians ringed him about. "A Parcel of reprobate Traders" from the Monongahela gathered, enjoying his plight immensely.

Why are you here?, the warriors demanded; the Long Knife covets the land, they accused; the Long Knives wish to settle here, they taunted; you are not safe here Gist, they warned.

At first, Gist hung fire: "They began to suspect me . . . I found this Discourse was like to be of ill Consequence." Then, overhearing that Croghan— "who is a meer Idol among his Countrymen the Irish traders"—had left here a week before, he spoke with bravado: He was on royal business, he said. He carried a message from the Great Father to be delivered, by orders of Virginia's royal governor, to Croghan himself.

"Tho I was unwell, I preferred the Woods to such Company." He and the boy set off north by northwest to Beaver Creek, after six miles rendezvousing with fellow Ohioan Barney Curant, whose men rounded out Gist's fellowship to eleven—a tolerable number in these parts.

Bottomlands butted between the river and knobs looked to be some of the richest land any of them could remember seeing. The tableland was nearly its equal. It was all very fine. Beaver Creek was running high, so they did not see the sacred petroglyphs carved in the Beaver's channel, the malevolent underwater panthers and big-winged thunderbirds, opposing gods of the lower and upper spheres whose perennially warring spirits guarded the way.

The company left the Ohio.

> Friday 30.—Set out 45 W 12 M. Crossed the last Branch of Beaver
> Creek . . . killed 12 Turkeys. Tuesday 4.—Set out late S 45 W about
> 4 M here I killed three fine deer.

Traveling cross-country, the Conchake Path taking them into Tuscarawas Valley, Gist steered northwest, making ten to twelve miles a day, jotting notes on soil, land, game, timber, runs fit for mills. Elk's Eye Creek (a branch of the Tuscarawas) opened to an encampment of seven Ottawa families headed by Mark Coonce, a métis who lived with his Iroquois wife. Coonce (Ojibways bastardized his name into "Maconce," for "bear cub") was a friend to the French and guided war parties against Susquehanna settlers.

Coonce was friendly enough—until he learned Gist was tending to the king's affairs, then he turned sullen. December 9 the company left, keeping along the Elk's Eye southwest twenty miles to Muskingum (near Coshocton), a town "of about one hundred Families," mostly Wyandots, blood remnant of the Hurons.

George Croghan was here with the half-Seneca interpreter Andrew Montour. Gist bought horses and corn. Croghan was a storehouse of news.

Croghan knew Gist's presence boded ill for his interests. Six months before, at Old Town, Barney Curant had invited Seneca George, Broken Kettle, and The Stone to barter their peltry to Long Knife traders, promising higher exchange rates than Croghan gave them—"a match-coat for a buck; a strowd for a buck and a doe; a pair of stockings for two raccoons; twelve bars of lead for a buck."[10] If Curant's offer startled Seneca George, Broken Kettle, and The Stone, it surely startled red-nosed Croghan standing at Curant's elbow.

And now, Gist's mission depended upon Croghan's favor and discretion.

On Christmas morning Gist roused himself, pulled on a knee-length shirt, coat, and moccasins, swept aside the skin flap hanging stiff, and stepped into the snow. Behind him, raised atop Croghan's cabin (built at a cost of £150), hung the red, blue, and white folds of his sovereign's colors. In the muffled din of the awakening village—snores, grunts, and voices from wigwams; long, breathy whooshes upon ash-dusted embers; axes splintering kindling; the hollow stomping of hooves; and always, dogs barking—he returned to the warmth, fetched out his prayer book, and leafed through to read about Mary and how the babe leaped in her womb with joy before she knew Joseph and about the innkeeper.

He hesitated. Monday a week before, forty troops of the *Campagnies franches de la Marine* and twenty Ottawas, painted, hair roached, brandishing graceful *fusils de chasses*, fell upon Croghan's men—Luke Irwin, Thomas Burk, and Joseph Faulkner—packing seven horseloads of deerskins and furs, and whisked the entire lot to Fort Sandoske (near Lake Erie), garrisoned by twenty of the French troops. Irishman Croghan, with that drunk Montour—Montour: he who whooped with laughter one second, tore the air with curses the next—had comrades here hostile to any disruption of trade.

The sun fully risen, Gist walked between cabins and wigwams, prayer book in hand, toward trader Thomas Burney's blacksmith's shop. Burney shied away, but a Wyandot throng compassed him about to hear the Gospel first proclaimed west of the Blue Ridge at Muskingum. As Montour interpreted, Gist preached with an utterly sincere heart Anglican notions of salvation by "Faith and good Works . . . which the King and His Church recommended to his Children."

"Annosanah" ("the go-between") he would be to his listeners from this day on, the crowd honoring Gist with a bestowal of this title of a holy man who had once lived among them. After his sermon, the women and men asked Annosanah to baptize their children so that when they died, they might see Paradise. Annosanah demurred, snared between duty, theology, and his scalp. He was no minister, he said, and though the One God loved all children, the Wyandot children were yet unlearned in His faith.

Annosanah retired to his lodge, and the next day recorded in his secret journal:

Wednesday Dec 26.—This day a Woman, who had been a long Time a Prisoner, and had deserted, & been retaken, and brought into the Town on Christmass Eve, was put to Death in the following manner:

They carried her without the Town & let her loose, and when she attempted to run away, the Persons appointed for that Purpose pursued her, & struck Her on the Ear, on the right side of her Head, which beat her flat on her Face on the Ground; they then struck her several Times, thro the Back with a Dart, to the Heart, scalped Her, & threw the Scalp in the Air, and another Cut off her Head.[11]

Some of Barney Curant's boys buried her.

Gist tarried at Muskingum two weeks past New Year's. In Croghan the Pennsylvanian, he had found a comrade-in-arms and a fellow Anglican (which put the Irishman in fine stead with the entrepreneurial Quaker Penns). Truly, it was hard not to like Croghan, whose bawdy wit and Irish brogue (he pronouncing his name "Croane" or "Grahoon" in one unending, guttural syllable, the "r" spoken with a hard, curling roll pulled from his glottis) so enlivened companions sharing his campfires. Croghan lifted many a glass of madeira to the king's health, even in polite society ending his tippling with ribald toasts—"To days of sport and nights of transport!"

Traveling with the Dubliner ensured a level of legitimacy hitherto beyond Gist's grasp. Croghan played along with his masquerade, for upon the one real issue Virginians and Pennsylvanians stood united: George II, with all haste, must fully extend his power to the Mississippi to drive out the *Compagnies franches de la Marine.*

In their advance, the two men sent their retinues southward, on to Lower Shawnee Town. Ohio's weather seemed as double-minded as its Indians. Blustery winds, plummeting temperatures, and sleet-crusted ankle-deep snow marked most days; then it warmed, winds blowing from the south.

On January 9 Mike Taffe, a Pennsylvanian from upper Ohio land, entered Croghan's lodge with some very bad news: Two months before, Lakes Indians had seized trader James Patten and his wares. Croghan's loss: £9,000. Patten, sent shackled to Fort Niagara, was sentenced at Montreal, jailed at a prison hulk in Quebec, and was bound across the Atlantic to rot in a Rochelle gaol.[12]

On the thirteenth Croghan, with Montour interpreting, met with Muskingum's headmen. His council went as expected, Croghan promising them the king's protection, declaring that the Long Knife in their midst, Gist, was their friend sent by his royal governor to invite all Indians to a grand parley the summer next at Logstown.

He concluded: Go to Logstown; treat with the English; see with your own eyes the English Father's benevolence; partake of his plenteous gifts and rum.

Croghan sealed the verity of his words with four wampum strands.

On Tuesday, January 15, Gist and his African left Muskingum with Croghan and Montour. Ohio was lovely—bountifully watered and mostly unbroken; timbered and fertile. Elk and whitetails were daily sights. Buffalo capering in the black mud of wide-open licks and stamping grounds reeking of dung wallowed down cane stalks to devour the tender shoots. Gist shot a cow for her tongue.

They turned southwest, en route to White Woman's Creek, whose name hearkened of tragedy, and of redemption. It was during Queen Anne's War, in February 1704, that the raiders had descended upon Deerfield, Massachusetts—three hundred miles from Montreal. Its townspeople had feared nothing: New England's winters always halted warring, insisted Deerfield's fathers. No one knew the 350 Canadians and Abenakis were near until they had struck, killing fifty-six. With prisoner ties of braided nettle, Abenakis had

Typical buffalo drove east of the Mississippi, numbering about twenty-five head.
LAND BETWEEN THE LAKES, KENTUCKY; PHOTO BY DENISE SCHMITTOU. AUTHOR'S COLLECTION.

bound one hundred captives and fled, cluttering their wake with twenty head-bashed corpses splayed grotesquely in gore-splattered drifts. Ransoming had been the fate of survivors, save two: Eunice Williams, daughter of Puritan minister John Williams, who grew to adulthood among her captors, married a Mohawk, embraced Catholicism, and lived as a white Indian[13]; and Mary Harris, who married a Loup and bore him many sons.

Now, white-haired and past fifty, Mary Harris lived at her town four miles from Coshocton. "She still remembers they used to be very religious in New England, and wonders how the White Men can be so wicked as she has seen them in these Woods." Gist tarried a day.

One hundred twenty-six miles and eleven days past White Woman's Creek, past the Hockhocking and potholes gurgling blue and salty that hunters boiled meat in, past Meguck Town's snowy, rye-covered plain forested with walnut and hickory, and poplar, maple, and cherry, the riders neared the Scioto River to hail a "Delaware Town of about Twenty Families," ruled by Wawundochwalend, whose "Negro Man" he sent busking about tending to these visitors, who lodged two days and a night.[14]

January 29 was blustery, snow calf-deep. Wawundochwalend's town was ten miles—"SW 5 M, S 5 M"—from the Scioto's fall into the Ohio. North of "Shannoah Town," corn hills of flint maize cultivated two seasons before lay fallow; no women were tending them to see their approach. Nor did sentries watching from Lower Shawnee Town's rock lockout on the south shore see the riders top the sharp slope of the Scioto's east bank and wend down it to the ferry, moored opposite them.

Gist and Croghan touched off firelocks to "hello" the camp. It was not a difficult ford. Barney Curant's men ferried them over the narrow river.

———⋙◆⋘———

Count de Jouy had deemed Lower Shawnee Town "a kind of a republic" a year before Pierre de Celeron had stopped there. Celeron's was quite a visit: Fearing ambush, he sent Thomas de Joncaire ahead in a canoe with Abenaki warriors, white flag high. As the van steered to the Scioto's mouth with shouts of *Vive le Roi!, Vive le Roi!* a wall of Shawnees rose over the north bank and opened fire. Joncaire's delegation hastily reversed paddles.

The republic astir, within hours the Shawnees had built a rock "fort" to do battle with the White Eye intruders. Were it not for the intercession of an Iroquois and a bout of calumet smoking, Celeron's float trip might have ended in a wash of blood. Though the races got along peaceably enough after that, still, Celeron's brand of diplomacy soured the palaver and relations were hardly amicable. Five English traders doing business there he ordered away; only the fear of losing his own life kept him from killing them. When Celeron nailed Louis's royal placard to a tree, the Shawnees tore it off and trampled it, mocking the captain's high-mindedness. Celeron upbraided the multitude—"You had a French heart, and . . . let it be corrupted by the English"—and, for safety, bivouacked his men "opposite the village" until departing August 26, 1749.[15]

Pierre de Celeron did accomplish one deed: He drove Lower Shawnee Town's citizens into the arms of the English.

This Shawnee capital had its origins in 1729, the year Chillicothes and Thawikilas—weary of William Penn's lying sons and the rum trade, vanishing game, diminishing land, a buzzel of towns, and haughty Iroquois chiefs who castrated the Leni-Lenapis' manhood, deeming them "Petticoat Indians"—began a Algonquin hajj to their homeland. Septs from Maryland and southern septs joined them. Filtering back were westering Shawnees who had never left *Kanta-Ke,* but who, in the 1600s had migrated to the Father of Waters' confluence with Speleawee-theepee, where they had battled the Chickasaws in 1715, the year their eastern kinsmen fought the Cherokees.

And so began their homegoing to the Scioto's mouth, an extraordinary site.

Speleawee-theepee permitted river travel east and west. Overland trails from Virginia, Pennsylvania, and Maryland linked Lower Shawnee Town to Logstown, Muskingum Town, Pickiwillany, and Sandoske; a portage away was Lake Erie. The republic sat at the apex of Athiamiowee's eastern prong, the great buffalo avenue bisecting Kentucky and Tennessee and skirting Georgia to the Spanish trail.

As Fort Detroit was to the French at the Lakes, Lower Shawnee Town was to the freedom-loving Shawanoes driven by Mohawk adders from the land where the navel strings of their grandfathers had been cut and their blood had soaked into the earth. Miamis, Piankashaws, Delawares, and Mingoes gathered at their town. Lakes Indians—Ojibways and Ottawas—bearing gifts of tobacco, wampum, and rum, and warm salutations from Louis XV, often visited, mindful of swaying Shawanoes' hearts to raise the fleur-de-lis atop their ninety-foot-long council longhouse and plant before it the Cross of the Savior.

Three hundred warriors defended Lower Shawnee Town, its population of more than twelve hundred inhabitants forcing its hunters to range far. More than one hundred lodges dotted the north shore's plain abutting Scioto's west bank. Across Speleawee-theepee, here three-quarters of a mile wide, and nestled below the bluffs, were forty more lodges as diverse as the ones on the far shore: Log cabins with deerskin doors and windows, and chimneys; cabins of squared poplar, clapboarded, cedar-shingled; elm-bark sugarloaf wigwams, longhouses, and half faces—three-sided huts with open fronts, "no more than three or four feet tall in the rear," tall enough for a man to stand, spacious enough to cache staples and peltry, moss stuffed in the cracks to make the sides airtight, and "the whole slope of the roof from the front to the back of slab, skins, or . . . the bark of hickory or ash trees"; and "skin-houses"—buffalo hides stretched across poles.[16]

Strains of Algonquin and Iroquoian, smatterings of French and English, Dutch, Swiss, and African emanated from wigwams. Countenances reflected the world's empires—faces hued light and dark shades of white and brown, black and red, adorned in flashy ensembles of trade silver. Men dressed in greatcoats and leggings, in blue and scarlet trade shirts of linen and silk lapping over wool sashes cinched to clouts. Chemises and leggings, shirts and English coats served as women's attire, dried eel skins binding their clubbed ebony hair, a vermilion streak down the part, vermilion half-penny dot on each check.

Here, along Speleawee-theepee's southern, high-rising bluffs, Shawnees had erected a rock tower to keep watch along the river and to the southwest, Athiamiowee's ruts shearing off to the older Shawnee town of Eskippakithiki, some twenty-five or thirty miles north of the Kentucky River.

Christopher Gist and George Croghan arrived on Tuesday, January 29, 1751.

Croghan's outpost here, built in a square, each wall three hundred paces long and with four gates and two sally ports, cost £200 to build. At Croghan's Lower Shawnee Town fortress, rising a quarter mile from the Ohio, his men did a brisk trade, ever alert for *French* partisans.

On Wednesday, January 30, Algonquin Big Men ushered Gist into the council house.

Croghan spoke first, Montour interpreting:

> That his Prisoners who had been taken by the French, and had made their Escape from the French Officer at Lake Erie as he was carrying them towards Canada brought News that the French offered a large Sum of Money to any Person who would bring to them the said Croghan and Andrew Montour the Interpreter alive, or if dead their Scalps; and that the French also threatened those Indians and Wyendotts with War in the Spring.

His traders "had seen ten French Canoes loaded with Stores for a new Fort they designed on the S Side Lake Erie," Croghan ended.

Then: Montour:

> That the King of Britain had sent Them a large Present of Goods, in Company with the six Nations, who had sent Me out to invite them to come see Him, & partake of their Father's Present next summer.

Then, finally, Big Hominy the chieftain, his words delivered with two four-strand wampum hanks:

> That from the Beginning of our Friendship, all that our Brothers the English have told Us has been made good and true. . . . We are but a small People, & it is not to Us only that You speak, but to all Nations—We shall be glad to hear what our Brothers will say to Us at the Logg Town in the Spring, & We hope that the Friendship now subsisting between us & our Brothers, will last as long as the Sun shines, or the Moon gives Light.

The council ended.

Croghan's news of the invasion of Lake Erie, of arms and provisions shipped to the Lakes, left the town's inhabitants alarmed and Croghan with need to make haste to Pickiwillany, the Twightwee town some 150 miles northwest on the Great Miami.

Old Brit ruled the Twightwees (their tribal name being an onomatopoetic rendering of the call of the Miami Confederation's totem, the sandhill crane, whose winged manitou stood sentry over Pickiwillany's lodges scattered along the Great Miami's headwaters). Pickiwillany was Pennsylvania's far western fist, and Croghan's traders wintered there, caravaning the king's wares to the Maumee and Auglaize to sell to Ottawa, Potawatomi, and Ojibway hide hunters in lands trammeled by *Compagnies franches de la Marine* garrisoning Forts Miami, St. Philippe, and Sandoske.

Pickiwillany was an incubator of rebellion. Until 1747 Old Brit was La Demoiselle, a name he had taken to show his love for Louis XV. But, his heart seduced by madder red raiment bordered with gold lace, Long Land muskets, blue beads, and Caribbean rum and flattery, La Demoiselle became Old Brit, abandoning the Maumee for the Great Miami just as he abandoned his

French name. In 1749 his Twightwee rebels numbered fifty men; by 1751, about four hundred families—"& daily encreasing"—lived at Pickiwillany.[17]

Croghan feared for his men's safety housed there. Big Hominy and The Pride (who had departed Peter Chartier's Shawnees when Chartier's band visited in 1745) felt no different, but the delegation would not depart until February 12. While at Lower Shawnee Town, Gist, not neglecting his spy duties, observed a curious dance ritual one of his nights there, as two rows of Shawnees circumambulated the town's perimeter in lock-step twin figure 8's that spiraled ever inward to lap at the town's center to thread the council longhouse, and out again. Young men and young women sang and cantered apart in a sort of low-kneed jog-trot on the balls of their feet, toes in, shifting to heels in time to shell shakers, dew-claw rattles about the ankles, drums resonating up and down La Belle Rivière, the women's bold refrain sung separately and repetitiously—

> I am not afraid of my Husband
> I will choose what Man I please

> I am not afraid of my Husband
> I will choose what Man I please

The woodland revel was three days and three nights of feasting and singing and dancing and raucous merriment. Now on this, the third night, inside the longhouse the women pressed against the bark walls in a sweaty, greasy row of tallow-smeared bodies, keening away, knees humping, elbows lifting and falling, doeskin-clad feet shuffling dirt, heads cocking side-to-side as eyes cast about the capering line of lean, muscular warriors whooping and foot-stomping past, eying the narrow-hipped, sloe-eyed sirens. As they shambled by, the women reached out to grab the clouts of their chosen suitors and fall in behind them, the cacophony droning on and on until the women made their choices. When the shell shakers and rattles ceased, and at the final "thrum"—the drum's last booming, hard-hit note of punctuation to signal the end—the couples slipped away for a night of lovemaking.

On February 12, 1751, Croghan and Montour departed Lower Shawnee Town for Pickiwillany. Gist, eager to spy out "the Strength & Numbers of some Indian Nations . . . lately revolted from the French," left his boy to care for his horses and struck out with them.

He did not yet know it, but on this day his financier, Gov. Thomas Lee, died, forever crippling the Ohio Company's expansionist dreams.

Croghan in the van, they rode to Pickiwillany, encountering some Shawnees and Delawares, Montour gleaning any intelligence he could.

Averaging thirty miles a day and bearing northwest, the troupe forded the Little Miami, and on Sunday, February 17, rafted saddles, weapons, and clothes across the Great Miami and swam the horses over to a rousing gunfire salute.

Old Brit was humored by it all: Croghan the famous Yankee trader from the Monongahela's forks—here, and in his honor. And with him, a tall, silent Long Knife holding on to his saddlebags. Twice they met with Old Brit, smoking the pipe, exchanging wampum, Croghan raising the Union Jack atop Old Brit's longhouse and presenting the Twightwee chief with £100 in tobacco, trade shirts, and vermilion.

It was a fortnight in territory under the arm of Louis XV. Four Ottawas sauntering into Pickiwillany's longhouse, holding aloft the French standard, shattered the calm as all grabbed for tomahawks and dirks, fusils and pistols. Old Brit dismissed them—but only after accepting two brandy kegs, matchcoats, strouds, and a ten-pound carrot of tobacco leaf linen-wrapped and bound with twine.

Gist made his pitch for Logstown's parley, forthcoming in 1752.

The Twightwees might come, Old Brit responded ambiguously, if the women had gotten the corn in. A half answer.

Gist returned alone to Lower Shawnee Town at the Scioto's mouth, Sunday, March 3. As news of the goodwill between Croghan and Old Brit passed from ear to ear, 150 flintlocks loosed skyward a ragged volley, the Indians joyful at prospects of allying with Old Brit, the stolid Miami who cast down before the Ottawa Louis XV's standard.

Gist must have been elated that his mission was nearing the tramp home with his African boy, his horses, and his most recent acquisition, a Carolina parakeet[18] fletched in yellow and green that whistled and smacked and perched on his shoulder to nibble cracked corn and tallow flecks. One task yet remained: to view La Belle Rivière's cataracts—the only riverine obstruction from Monongahela's forks to New Orleans—and spy out the French presence.

A Mingo guide warned him: Hide hunters were hunting the Falls. They would kill the Long Knife or take him hostage. "As I had a great Inclination to see the Falls, and the Land on the E Side the Ohio, I resolved to venture as far as possible." Gist was undeterred.

Warriors to the westward ferrying Speleawee-theepee at Limestone Creek crossed in a twenty-man woolly skin barque sewn of four bull buffalo hides. Perhaps the Shawnees living at Scioto's mouth had such a bull boat too, moored upon the Ohio's bank, skin hull upended sunward and caulked with suet and ashes.

Gist touched *Kanta-Ke* soil on Tuesday, March 12. For five days he debated a trip to the Falls. Every day he saw traps and tracks—sixty French, he reckoned—and Indian sign. High-ended cracks of flintlocks lightly loaded jarred his solitude. "I was now much troubled that I could not comply with my instructions."

On Monday, March 18, 1751, he turned southward.

He marveled: *Kanta-Ke* was even more beautiful than Ohio land. He pressed on, from Powell's River, detouring northeast to Tall Rock, then to Salt Pond and to Ingles Ferry, through Flower Gap and toward the Yadkin Valley. He kept up his diary, writing of passes, land, trees, and rivers, and of his pet parakeet, whose death left him sad—"tho it was but a Trifle I was much concerned about losing Him, as he was perfectly tame, and had been very brisk all the Way." He did not write any more about his African boy.

It was May 18, 1751, when Gist reached the Yadkin's torched cabins and heard the cries of deep lamentation. The Cherokees done it, an old man said: They scalped five here months before; his family had fled to Roanoke, thirty-five miles north. Gist left his cabin to reunite with Sarah and their sons and daughters.

Afterward, Christopher Gist felt he had "erred"—if erring is to esteem one's life of loftier value than a glimpse of real estate—by not pushing on to the Falls. Alone, he might have risked it; but he feared that the African boy, left to fend for himself, would give them both away. And too, if, while on his return leg, he had spared a few days to stitch a canoe to pole up the Kentucky, he might have mapped its extent and marveled at its dolomite and limestone "chimneys." But any Indians or French watching the river might have seen him.

Yet he sensed his epic reconnoiter was far from a failure. He had observed French spies, George Croghan's traders, and Ohio Indians—and he knew the way to some of their towns. Verdant valleys teeming with deer and buffalo seemed to him as endless, sublime parks hemming the Ohio. Southward, cherry, buckeye, elm, pawpaw, coffee, honey locust, and maple stands shaded "the finest Meadows." Undulating rises spoked with traces and gouged with licks and pungent stamping grounds flourished with rye and bluegrass.

Surely Nathaniel Gist shared his father's saga with his Yadkin woods-running companion Daniel Boone—eking out a livelihood as a Long Hunter, already with three children and a wife to provide for—when the two roamed the Holston in 1760; Boone, who had been living in the Yadkin since 1751, may even have learned of *Kanta-Ke* from Gist himself or read from his detailed, well-written journal.

Gist returned to the Ohio Valley the winter of 1751, again clandestinely mapping Ohio Company land while promoting Logstown's parley. While at the forks, one Delaware bluntly put it to him: "Where does the Indian's Land lay, for the French claimed all the Land on one Side the River Ohio and the English on the Other?"

"My Friend," Gist answered, "we are all the King's People and the different Colour of our Skins makes no difference in the King's Subjects: You are his People. . . . You will have the same Privileges as the White People have."

William Penn had heralded the same glad tidings two generations before, but with one difference: He meant it.[19]

American scalp on bone hoop. JIM AND CAROLYN DRESSLAR COLLECTION.

Crucible of Fire

*A finer sight could not have been beheld, the shining barrels of the mus-
kets, the excellent order of the men, the cleanliness of their appearance,
the joy depicted on every face at being near Fort Duquesne, the highest
object of their wishes—the music re-echoes through the mountains.*
                                   —Col. George Washington, July 1755

*En route to Fort Duquesne with Maj. Gen. Edward Braddock, Captain
Jack . . . offered his services for the expedition. His merits as a guide and
"Indian-killer" were not unknown to Braddock, but the proffered services
were coupled with stipulations for freedom from the discipline of the army
and rejected. This singular man . . . was at the head of a party of bold
woodsmen, clad, like himself, in Indian attire, and following very much the
Indian mode of warfare. . . . It was a misfortune for Braddock that he
neglected to secure the services of such an auxiliary.*
                                   —Winthrop Sargent, 1856
              The History of an Expedition against Fort Duquesne in 1755

After the suicide (by hanging) of his sister Fanny on September 8, 1731, Edward Braddock's spirit hardened as he drank to dissipation, rarely leaving pubs
until bottles outnumbered him five to one. He scrapped and dueled, joining the
army and rising in rank to major general, and with his hardening, his ruddy countenance locked into a sneer accentuated by thick lips, heavy eyebrows, crowned
with a powder white wig, queued and tied off with ribbon. Torrents of profanity

Edward Braddock

punctuated his haughty, foul-mouthed diatribes—"I never knew him do anything but swear," averred Col. Joe Yorke—but his demons granted him clairvoyance: His last night in London he confided to actress Anne Bellamy that he "was going with a handful of men to conquer whole nations . . . to cut their way through unknown woods as sacrifices sent to the slaughter." He handed Miss Bellamy his will, naming her executor of his estate of £7000.[1]

He was a burly fellow and stout, his build lending him an air of leadership. Save for that, his personal attributes should have thoroughly disqualified him from field leadership in America: His age (sixty); his imperious bearing; his tongue that cut like a lash; his gout, which often kept him confined to a litter; his unwillingness to adapt to the task, heavy with global import, now before him.

Pennsylvania assemblyman Ben Franklin warned him about wilderness war. Braddock, he said, "smil'd at my Ignorance, and reply'd 'These Savages may indeed be a formidable Enemy to your raw American militia; but upon the King's regular and disciplin'd Troops, Sir, it is impossible they should make any impression.'" Justice William Allen bade him godspeed, but his journal reveals his sum of Braddock—"an improper man, of mean Capacity, obstinate and self-sufficient, above taking advice, and laughed to scorn all such as represented to him that in our Wood Country, war was to be carried on in a different manner from that in Europe."

Braddock, though, had his virtues. He was politically astute, obedient to William Augustus, duke of Cumberland, who appointed him, and he was a martinet and administrator with forty-five years' experience. Under fire he was infinitely brave, sure that in a properly conducted battle irregulars would always crumble under the king's men.

The *Norwich,* Sir Edward's transport, entered Virginia's Hampton Roads Harbor in February 1755. His boot soles had barely touched the New World before the major general stepped into a coach that whisked him away for a council of war in Williamsburg. Braddock's mind churned, the wheels spinning off the miles underneath him, and pursing his lips to pun "mount Seir" into "monsieur," he engaged in a bit of self-banter, as was his way, reciting from Ezekiel's thirty-fifth chapter:

> Thus saith the Lord God; Behold, O mount Seir, I am against thee, and I will stretch out my hand against thee, and I will make thee most desolate. . . . Because thou hast said, These two nations and these two countries shall be mine, and we will possess it.

These few verses seemed a Divine prediction of success. He did not doubt his plan's efficacy, hammered out months ago in London's Whitehall war room: To hack a war road 110 miles long along an old Indian path—leveling rises, building bridges, blasting out stumps, clearing brush, filling holes—to deliver men and artillery to the Ohio's dogleg with the Monongahela to oust the French from Fort Duquesne, built on the site of Fort Prince George, begun by Virginia's Capt. William Trent, captured by La Frances a year before.[2]

Irish Regulars—the 44th and 48th Foot—landed three weeks after Braddock's arrival. A bustle of gaunt soldiers ordered about by mounted officers, the Irishmen marched to the Potomac's Maryland shore, their gait relaxing into a shamble as Hampton Roads slipped into the distance. They bivouacked at Will's Creek to rendezvous with their commander at Fort Cumberland.

With the proud Brits lay many advantages. Artillery and trained Regulars, colonials mustering from Virginia and Maryland and farther north and south. Christopher Gist (accompanied by his subordinate, Andrew Montour) was head scout and twice saved the life of his protégé, the twenty-two-year-old Virginian George Washington, now Braddock's advisor serving without pay to obtain a royal commission. Ben Franklin patched up provincial squabbles enough to deliver 259 horses, 150 wagons, and provisions to Virginia's "Commissary of Provisions and Stores," Dr. Thomas Walker. George Croghan and Sir William Johnson, blood brother to the Mohawk, promised to deliver hundreds of natives to the English. Stashed in Braddock's portmanteau was a detailed sketch of Fort Duquesne's polygonal interior, showing pickets, palisades, and battery, paced out to scale by Capt. Robert Strobo, a captive at the outpost, and delivered at great risk by Indian couriers.

On May 29, the mighty twenty-two hundred lumbered from Fort Cumberland, an unendingly unfolding phalanx twelve feet wide and stretching more than a mile along Nemacolin's Path, blazed three years earlier by Colonel Gist and Col. Thomas Cresap. Braddock's army was a polyglot of English, Dutch, Africans, Catholics, Protestants, Jews, Irishmen, and Scotsmen, followed by wagons, artillery, cattle, and swarms of venereal camp followers. Visitors passing nights visiting fire pits were taken aback at the myriad dialects and languages. But one race was conspicuously absent: Indians.

Braddock deemed the "exotics" troublesome. His three-day meeting with Algonquins and Iroquoians ended with a broadside—"No Savage Shall Inherit the Land." Enraged, the Indians left to join the French. Forty warriors lingered, lured by promises of booty and captives, but as their women commenced whoring, enticing the soldiery with salacious glances and lifted chemises, Braddock dismissed them all, save for seven Mingo scouts led by famed chief Scaroudy.

The pageant's glory fizzled under the groans of each mile as axmen cut and cleared, and pale, thin men fed on sowbelly and hardtack stepped to "The

Henry Bouquet's negotiation at Tuscarawas in 1764 shows features typical of parleys, including Indians with severed ear rims, wampum belt, pipe smoking, and mediator. Central figure in breeches and leggings thought to be translator Alexander McKee.

Grenadier's March." Teams strained under the lash to yank through Maryland's wilds siege guns, eight-inch howitzers, and twelve-pounders.

Thirty-five miles this clogged river of humanity flowed the first seven days. From afar, such a harlequin of colors, drums and fifes, brass and steel, swaying hurdles of bayonets, tromping bootsteps and creaking wagons, and man and beast engulfed in a whirl of dust and noise appeared as a sort of inchoate comedic procession spontaneously reacting to a serendipitously shifting script, with "the Knight [Sir John St. Clair] swearing in the van, the Genl cursing & bullying in the center & the whores bringing up the rear."[3]

And so it went, from May 29 until July 9, 1755, the day a detached force of England's finest—fifteen hundred Regulars and militia with eight Mingoes—forded a loop of the Monongahela, wagons clanking behind them, en route to Fort Duquesne, ten miles distant, where Capt. Claude-Pierre Contrecoeur's fretting had turned to despair. His outpost could hold but two hundred of the sixteen hundred men camped about his perimeter. No answer to his dispatch had arrived. Indians and partisans bickered, anxious to flee this slip of western Pennsylvania as spies spilled news of Braddock's approach.

But Captain Contrecoeur had in his ranks a bold officer with a desperate plan: Capt. Daniel de Beaujeau, with his cadre of thirty-six officers, seventy-two troops of *Compagnies franches de la Marine,* 146 coureurs de bois, and 637 Lakes and Middle Ground Indians—Mingoes, Ottawas, Wyandots, Mississaugas, Ojibways, and Potawatomis—would hit them in a mad dash of a sortie, buying Contrecoeur time to evacuate Fort Duquesne.

At 1:00 P.M., July 9, de Beaujeau's partisans collided with Braddock's thin red line, the French spotted at two hundred yards by George Croghan and Scaroudy. Croghan's Light Horse and Lt. Col. Thomas Gage's advance work party wheeled into formation and opened fire. Three volleys to shouts of "God Save the King!" and, unbelievably, a hollow smack and the macabre sight of de Beaujeau's bursting skull halted the French-Canadians for a moment, but the coureur de bois contingent and the Indians hallooed like enraged devils and treed, scattering along ravines, and commenced a nibbling fire that became a maddening death roar.

Braddock was everywhere, cursing, cajoling his men, stubbornly waiting for the enemy to fall back. Whistling bullets zinging past his own head sounded "charming," Lieutenant Colonel Washington later wrote. "The French and Indians crept about in small Parties so that the Fire was quite round us, and in all the Time I never saw one, nor could I on Enquiry find any one who saw ten together."[4]

Braddock's Regulars did as they were trained to do: They stood, pale, aghast, and trembling, shooting and reloading, shooting and reloading and shooting again, in their fright and horror and in the confusion and din firing up into the air or at each another. Around them, bodies pitched and crumbled into groaning heaps of scarlet, blue, and white as garishly painted apparitions, leering and yelping through choking sulfurous clouds, poured salvo after salvo into the Brits' wavering ranks.

Capt. Adam Stephens's Virginians treed, firing from cover, and most militiamen did likewise, pinning themselves in crossfires between Regulars, grapeshot blasts, and fusil fire. Teamsters, like the broad-shouldered twenty-one-year-old North Carolinian, Sgt. Daniel Boone, already a renowned Long Hunter but here a wagoner serving with Maj. Edward Dobbs's militia, were behind the van when the carnage began, watching the spectacle unfolding before them. Boone waited until he saw there was no hope, then he grabbed a horse and fled. As did Gist, as did Montour, as did Croghan, as did Croghan's *Kanta-Ke* packhorse man John Findley, an artful yarn spinner and Sergeant Boone's new friend of camp and trail. As did all who could.

Four horses were shot from beneath Braddock, and Washington ditched bloodied mounts one after another. His Virginia regimental pierced and tattered by four balls, the dashing lieutenant colonel in this three-hour debacle so distinguished himself that his name would resonate on two continents. The massacre might have gone on had not a musket ball plowed up through the major general's arm and churned deep into his lungs. Their commander down, the army gave way, men dropping guns, stripping off gear, fleeing in a trampling rush, calling upon the Savior, running until exhaustion or a bullet or a scalping knife felled them.

More than four hundred British lay dead, and more than five hundred were wounded. Twenty-three French were killed. No one knows how many Indians died. Not many, probably.

Had the Indians pursued them across the Monongahela, it would have been worse. But plenteous booty, twenty captives to stake and burn, and a two hundred-gallon rum cask ended the glut as warriors ceased killing to scalp and loot and drink themselves into oblivion. The British limped 110 miles back to Fort Cumberland.

"Who would have thought it," uttered Maj. Gen. Edward Braddock, his last words on the thirteenth as he expired on his road that became his tomb, creaking wagons and bloodied men and horses passing over his grave to conceal it.

Pittsburgh: summer 1776

Dr. Thomas Walker's visit to the Monongahela's forks on the eve of the Revolution was for "official business"—mostly to shore up Loyal Land Company dealings. Walker was relieved: The Six Nations, Wyandots, Shawnees, Delawares, and Cherokees seemed sufficiently duped by his resolute, deadpan prevarications: "We have before told you all that we had no intention of incroaching on your Land, which are the real Sentiments of our hearts."

All things in order, his fortune and baronial estate secure, indefatigable Dr. Walker transformed a Tuesday picnic for fourteen into a history lesson. Borrowing a canoe, Walker and crew poled up the Monongahela and beached near Braddock's killing field.

After dining, Walker led them on a tour of the desolate landscape, taking care not to step on broken skulls scattered about by wolves and foxes, stooping to finger cracked harness leather and tack and bridle and rusty pipe tomahawks and shards of artillery shells, piles of bones, splintered muskets. Twenty-one years of growth had deformed the scars musket volleys and cannon fire cut into the maples, oaks, and hickories, pushing their deeply gashed trunks twenty feet above the earth; the scars no longer looked fresh, but the bark wounds were vivid enough.

Dr. Walker narrated, treating his listeners to a "warm and glowing" rendering of what had taken place here—"the hellish yells of the Indians, and the groans and shrieks of the dying and the wounded falling upon their ears."

He had barely survived killing. As the French and Indians turned against the English, he had tried to flee but made a botch of it—his riding boots had so cramped his feet he could barely walk. He had flashed a private a gold coin to help him yank his boots off. Nothing doing, had hollered the private, ducking fire, scampering for cover. Walker cached, hid out in the woods, he did—he showed them where—until he cut his boots free and fled in the night. At Fort Cumberland he had found his slave (who himself had feigned dead during the ambush by laying betwixt a heap of dead horses) waiting for him.

Dr. Walker's ramble continued. He pointed out the shallow ford where the army had crossed. How noble the boys had looked, muskets and bayonets agleam, flags unfurled, stepping smartly to fife and drum, the neatness of it, cocksure officers snapping off commands.

"How brilliant the morning—how melancholy the evening," he concluded.[5]

Indeed. "Braddock's Defeat" was an American crucible, blending ideas, dynamics, and players as gold purified in fire, a catalyst sparking the exploration and settlement of the West and, ultimately, a new nation.

CHAPTER THREE

Deer Slayers &
Fincastle Surveyors

SUMMER 1763

Wawundochwalend gazed at his puffy eyes in the palm-size looking glass; the trade mirror was inletted within a square basswood frame, its little handle bored through with a hole for its thong. The indigo blue welt ending above his tanned chin had risen to a bas-relief tinged in tiny red beads welling from a swirl of pinpricks; in a day or two, the dots would vanish and the ache from the scabrous ridge, shiny and lathered in bear fat, would ease, its swelling ebb, and the fine rusty scale slough free. His Lenape tattooist, with the needles bound tightly together in the stylus's end and crushed poplar charcoal and tallow pigment, had inscribed into his skin this manitou to commemorate his valor against the beaten French. In the final French and Indian War, his Delawares had esteemed themselves stalwart allies to George II. Wawundochwalend had earned the right to be tattooed, and to celebrate the event, he took his totem's name: Twakachshawsu, the Water Lizard.[1]

England was in her ascendancy. Logstown's Treaty had been concluded on June 13, 1752. Christopher Gist, Twakachshawsu's guest north of Lower Shawnee Town for two days and a night, had fulfilled his duties well as the Ohio Company's liaison. The Six Nations, and Shawnees, Wyandots, and Delawares, had reaffirmed the Lancaster Treaty of 1744, giving Pennsylvanians George Croghan, Conrad Weiser, and William Trent rights of trade in the western waters and granting them "leave to build two forts."[2]

Old Brit's Twightwees did not attend the parley at Logstown. Old Brit— by forging his own covenant chain with the Iroquois and Pennsylvanians to control English trade and grow fat on the land and rebuff the stern face of

*Teedyuscung (1700–63),
Delaware leader who sought
accommodation with whites
and was murdered by land-
hungry settlers, depicted here
in colonial dress, was typical
of Middle Ground
Algonquins trying to deal
with the arrival of white ways
and culture.*

Onontio, New France's governors—had put in motion his own death, which came when he had it least in mind.

That June, Charles Michael de Langlade, an illustrious, slightly built *métis* lieutenant allied to the Ottawa, and 250 Lakes warriors torched Picki-willany and looted the king's stores. Langlade's tawny cadre slew Old Brit and hacked apart his corpse and boiled it in a big iron kettle and devoured the chief's heart and feet and hands before the horrified eyes of his family. Andrew McBryer and Thomas Burney were the only traders to escape the orgy of death and pillaging. McBryer's luck did not hold: In late 1752 French-Canadians and Lakes Indians seized him. At the least, Lieutenant Langlade's sacking of Pickiwillany had cost Croghan £1,000 in wares.[3]

By 1760 the Shawanoes—Canada's governor swaying their young men's hearts with gifts and rum and, wary of English invaders firing rifle-guns to protect the men with spyglasses and poles, long-linked chains and glass-fronted spinning devices that divined from whence came the four winds—had begun migrating northward.

Eskippakithiki was no more. Lower Shawnee Town had vanished into a sprawl of abandoned corn hills, huts, tattered wigwams, and a long, parallel row of post holes where once had stood the council longhouse on Speleawee-theepee's north shore, before a flood swept it down river. Braddock's defeat, Fort De Chartres's surrender to the redcoats, and fear of reprisal for defections to *les françaises* had led Big Hominy, The Pride, and Newcommer to move the Shawanoes up the Scioto to a well-watered site in the heart of Ohio land, Chillicothe.

As *Kanta-Ke* emptied, there arose from the East a man-made flood pushing down the Blue Ridge's western slopes, coming in violation of Great Britain's Proclamation of 1763, which promised Indians, after the Seven Years' War, that England's colonists would forever live to the lee of the Appalachian ridge.

American hide hunters spilled from the New River basin, from the Carolinas, from eastern Tennessee, coming as solitaries, in twos or threes, in thirty-man brigades. The Long Hunters.

The Water Lizard knew all of this.

SUMMER 1766

When he was not reading Psalms or meditating upon Isaac Watts's *Upon Prayer,* the devout James Smith found time to compose these verses, which he sang to Jamie, Joshua Horton's eighteen-year-old African on loan to him:

> Six weeks I've in this desert been,
> With one mulatto lad,
> Excepting this one stupid slave,
> No company I've had.
>
> In solitude I here remain,
> A cripple very sore,
> No friend or neighbor to be found,
> My case for to deplore.
>
> I'm far from home, far from the wife,
> Which in my bosom lay,

Far from the children dear,
Which used around me for to play.

Perhaps the signs compelled his destiny, he being born between Venus rising and Mars in 1737, in Carlisle County, Pennsylvania. James Smith believed
in the mysterious forces of the stars and planets, and that their rotation and
placement in the heavens at the time of a person's birth affected one's fate, so
he reckoned he must have had it coming.

After Smith had stomped on the cane stob, at Smith's behest, Jamie whittled him a crutch and took Smith's knife and awl and scalloped out the torn
flesh festering around the stob, then, gripping the stob's head between the
jaws of a two-handled ball mold, he yanked the jagged sliver from Smith's
foot. Jamie made a gel from bark off the root of a linden to bath Smith's foot
in, wrapping the ooze in green moss around his ankle to keep swelling down.
He built a cane and stick lean-to, and took Smith's rifle-gun and hunted buffalo while tending to the man and watching for Creeks, Cherokees, and
Shawnees who might smell their fire and spy their jerk rack. Jamie "had nothing on him that was ever spun," wearing a clout, buckskin leggings and moccasins, a bearskin "dressed with the hair on which he belted around him," and
a coonskin cap.

Well, at least this time, Smith reflected, he was here of his own doing.

It was not so in 1755, after he hired on as a road cutter and found himself to the west of Maj. Gen. Edward Braddock's van, hewing timber under a
boiling sun. Days before the ill-fated July 9, four or five Mohawks and
Delawares attacked him and Arnold Vigoras, killing Vigoras, but sparing him.
At Fort Duquesne he heard the scalp halloos and saw the French and Indians
return in glory, driving before them packhorses heaped with booty and then,
after the horses, a score of Braddock's finest lurching along tethered with
woven nettle prisoner ties. Behind them and to the side came the bloodied,
sooty, wild-eyed fighters, hallooing for acknowledgment from the jubilant soldiery, partisans, and natives, and clutching a great many dripping scalps, brandishing bayoneted officers' fusils and muskets, wearing grenadiers' caps, belly
boxes, canteens, and scarlet, blue-faced regimentals. The women painted the
English black and beat them, and the men staked them. James did not watch
as they put the captives under the firebrands and hot irons, but he could not
shut out their wailing and "the Indians . . . yelling like infernal spirits."

Burning was not to be Smith's fate. To ease the spirits of the dead and
atone for the slain Yankees and take fire from the hearts of the English, he was
adopted. So too, later, was a boy near his age, Arthur Campbell.

A warrior had roached Smith's hair, wetting and dipping his fingertips in a bowl of ashes to yank it out to leave three hanks. Around the first two was wrapped a "narrow beaded garter"; the third was braided and "stuck full of silver brooches." Fitted with ear- and noserings, armbands, and wampum strands around his neck, and scrubbed free of his white blood, he donned "a new ruffled shirt . . . a pair of leggings with ribbons and beads, porcupine quills and red hair—also a tinsel laced cappo." The Indians streaked his face and head in vermilion and tied a shock of red-headed woodpecker feathers to his scarlet, mostly bald crown.

As "Scoouwa," Smith had lived with his Mohawk brothers for five years, learning and mastering dialects and skills. As Captain Smith to his guerrilla-fighting rangers in 1763, he had dressed his crack forces in "breechclouts, leggings, moccasins, and green shrouds." As he described it, "In place of hats we wore red handkerchiefs and painted our faces red and black like Indian warriors and I taught them the Indian discipline as I knew no other."

And so it was now in his half face near the Cumberland's banks this summer of 1766 that he sat, contemplating Providence, clad in his "old beaver hat, buck-skin leggings, mockasons, and a new shirt," hoppusing high upon his shoulders Indian-style when he traveled a filthy thin blanket bound with a cordage tumpline. Capt. James Smith, a Presbyterian white Indian turned Long Hunter and destined to be a missionary to the Indian people, was having plaguey hard luck at the deer-slaying trade.

Weeks before, Joshua Horton, Uriah Stone, the older James Smith (no relation), and William Baker had beseeched Smith to go on to Illinois land with them; Smith had refused and had given them a rather novel excuse: He missed his wife and children.

When Smith returned Horton's slave to his North Carolina household that October, Horton told Smith what misery had befallen them. He and Stone and the rest, he said, had ridden to the Illinois and had had a good hunt, heaping up deerskins and loading the bales on a New Orleans-bound bateau—only to have their hide-laden vessel commandeered by French trappers.

The deer season was a bust. Stone was going to try it again, with a bigger party.

James Smith was not interested. He went home and got himself arrested and put under armed guard, the townsfolk and high sheriff figuring anyone dressed that shabbily was no better than a horse thief and probably was one.[4]

SUMMER 1769

By June Uriah Stone and his Long Hunters—Abraham and Isaac Bledsoe, Casper Mansker, Obadiah Terrill, John Baker, Joseph Drake, Ned Cowan, Henry Smith, and John Rains; maybe twenty fur takers in all—were en route to their destination: *Kanta-Ke.*

Grubstaking themselves, their supply horses loaded as heavily as their pockets allowed, their oilcloth budgets secured with ropes and smelly, bone-hard tugs that reeked after a rain and turned slimy and were hard to untie, the Long Hunters rode through Cumberland Gap to Cumberland River and on, striking the Hunter's Trace, alert to sudden rustles of cane different sounding than the shimmering rustles zephyrs and wind devils wrought. The hunters cached their packs in a spacious half face and divided into teams of threes and fours, agreeing to rendezvous at the skin depot about once a month.

Mansker's band headed west, struck the Big Barren, then struck a lead trace and rode south, into Tennessee. Ten of Stone's hunters returned to the New the next April, horses loaded with furs, deerskins, bear bacon, and bearskins bulging with rendered fat. Mansker, Stone, and Bledsoe bartered their wares at Natchez and boarded a clipper bound away to North Carolina.

By fall, Casper Mansker had returned to the Cumberland with Col. James Knox, Joseph Drake, Henry Skaggs, and the rest—the largest brigade yet, forty strong—to reach *Kanta-Ke's* Dix (Dick's) River to harvest deerskins in the red before the frosts plumped the skins and blued them. They passed the Knobs' swath of salt licks, where James Dysart saw a buffalo herd of nearly one thousand head; buffalo had so devoured the salty earth "that they could in places go entirely underground."

Knox's brigade pushed on to the Green's lush veldt, then on to the Skin House branch and Caney Fork nearing Russell's Creek. Mansker heard an eerie sound quite unlike any other he had heard before and shushed the men as he slipped forward to investigate, only to spy another Long Hunter, Daniel Boone, sprawled on a deerskin singing. The Boones, Daniel and Squire, lingered with the Long Hunters a week or two. The brigade camped, fleshing and beaming and laying up skins, rendering tallow, jerking wild meat, and smoking bear hams.

Twenty-five out of the forty returned east in late 1770. Mansker, Knox, the Skaggses, Dysart, William Miller, and one or two others hunted on, splitting into two parties, hoarding powder and ball, living off wild meat, leaving behind seven men to guard the station camp and prepare skins for market. They would rendezvous in March. One band turned north, the other west.

That March, the Long Hunters returned to a dismal sight: Indians had driven off their comrades and ransacked the station camp. The deserted half face was wrecked, the peltry rotting and exposed to the rain and sun and wolves, a grim message carved in a beech: "2,300 deer-skins Lost, Ruination By God."

Col. James Knox blamed Capt. Will Emery's roving party of Shawnees and Cherokees. But Knox had no thought of heeding Emery's unwritten message.[5]

SPRING 1773

His men knew it and admired him for it: At thirty-three, Thomas Bullitt was a survivor.

Captain Tom had distinguished himself on Brig. Gen. John Forbes's campaign in September 1758; and what a debacle that had been—the English driving the French from the Ohio's forks. Royal Governor General Vaudreuil's Canadian colonials, reinforced by a contingent of Louisiana's *Compagnies franches de la Marine*, did not go willingly. Swiss mercenary Col. Henry Bouquet ordered Maj. James Grant forward with eight hundred men to reconnoiter Fort Duquesne. Grant's van stumbled about in the night beating drums to keep spirits high, alerting French and Indians who whooped the death cry and poured forth, colliding with Capt. Thomas Bullitt's fifty men guarding the baggage train. Bullitt rallied, fighting his way back to Forbes, who readied for a second feint. On November 24 the mustached, white-and-blue-coated *Compagnies franches de la Marine* torched their fort's palisades and touched off Duquesne's powder magazine, some fleeing through the smoke and fire down the Ohio to the Illinois country, others scattering southward laden with rum kegs and sleek, twenty-bore *fusils de chasses* and Tulle hunting muskets into Overhill Cherokee land to incite Willaniwaw's red men against Fort Loudon's Yankees.

General Forbes commended Bullitt's valor. Even Col. George Washington, Bullitt's commander, managed to speak words of praise at the grand ceremony, but it was a struggle. "Bullitt," he confided to a friend, was "no favorite" of his. "His opinion of himself always kept pace with what others are pleased to think of him—if anything, rather ahead of it."[6]

Captain Bullitt's tour of duty put him on a path straight as a leather thong to the bluegrass island beyond the wilderness. A son of Fauquier County and trained at William and Mary as a surveyor, Bullitt worked hard to ingratiate himself to Virginia's newly appointed royal governor, John Murray, fourth earl of Dunmore, viscount of Fincastle, who arrived at Williamsburg on December 2, 1771, and appointed Bullitt Virginia's chief surveyor.

About land acquisition, Bullitt and Dunmore saw with one eye; already his lord owned fifty thousand acres of land bordering Lake Champlain. As the New Year eclipsed the old, Dunmore severed Virginia's western county of Fincastle from Botetourt in hopes of a better chance of pushing open Fincastle's amorphous edges, which included all the lands south and west of the Great Kanawha, North Carolina's uncharted border, and to the west, *Kanta-Ke*.

Undoubtedly, Fincastle's officials—Col. William Preston, Capt. John Floyd, Col. William Christian, Maj. Arthur Campbell, Col. William Russell, and Col. Evan Shelby—were very pleased.

Either Bullitt or Dunmore's nephew, Dr. John Connolly (or perhaps one of Fincastle's leaders, expansionists all), hinted an intriguing idea to Dunmore, and one based upon a well-known truth: For each militia stint in the French and Indian War, Virginians had earned warrants redeemable in public land: An ensign got one thousand acres; two hundred acres went to a sergeant; and privates received fifty.[7] As the lure of land had so swelled county levies with hungry-eyed fighters willing to die for a farm in the West, Dunmore was advised it was time Virginia made good.

Kanta-Ke was beckoning, and not just to Virginians, but to North Carolinians, Pennsylvanians, and Sir William Johnson's real estate moguls of New York. Already new rival firms—the Indiana Company, Vandalia Company, and Westsylvania Company were but three—were marking lines upon plats of the Promised Land that in 1607 Virginia had claimed as hers alone. Joseph Martin, aided by Dr. Thomas Walker, had founded his station in 1769 in Powell's Valley—more than a hundred miles past the thinly settled Holston and William Bean's Station.

To protect Virginia's stake in the Far West, the time to act was now.

Col. William Preston, Fincastle County's official surveyor and nephew of the late Col. James Patton, promoted Captain Bullitt's vision with vigor. But behind all the plotting was Lord Dunmore, though even he was not the first to broach such an ambitious idea. In 1767 George Washington had told his agent, William Crawford, a rising star in his army, "Any person who neglects the present opportunity of hunting out good lands and in some measure marking them . . . (in order to keep others from settling them) will never regain it."[8]

Lord Dunmore solicited George Croghan's help in his scheme. Old Croghan, the hard-drinking Irish trader—always a stalwart ally in one's quest for empire in Ohio land; in return, of course, for a substantial quid pro quo of the same thrown his way—had shifted Pennsylvania's base of peltry commerce to Fort Pitt (erected on Fort Duquesne's rubble). In a rare gesture of colonial goodwill, Dunmore rendezvoused there the summer of 1773 to appoint John Connolly his ambassador at this triune forking of the Allegheny, Mononga-hela, and Ohio, the West's riverine gateway.

Dr. Connolly did his lord's bidding, reeling off a spate of exaggerated war circulars. He had it "by good authority," declared one, that "the Shawanese were ill disposed towards white men"; all colonists should take up arms and make ready "to repel any insults offered."[9] Dr. Connolly's firebrand missives transformed Fort Pitt from a military fur depot into a heavily garrisoned stronghold set on high alert. Settlers forted up, bracing for a fresh wave of ver-milion-streaked terror.

Capt. Thomas Bullitt's proposed foray into the western waters to mark off land grants for veterans—the *Virginia Gazette* published news of it on Oc-tober 30, 1772—all knew, violated England's Proclamation of 1763, which forbade emigration west of the Blue Ridge, and the Treaty of Hard Labor (1768), which outlawed speculating and settlement beyond the Great Kanawha—Virginia's tenuous fault line barely restraining a rising tide of ex-soldiery, squatters, market hunters, and farmers.

Lord Dunmore could not have escaped the clamor Bullitt's circular pro-voked. Word was, Dunmore had secretly promised two thousand acres near the Falls of the Ohio to Dr. John Connolly and another two thousand to his friend, Charles Warranstaff. Dunmore himself, as befitting George III's royal governor, sought his ten thousand acres surveyed below the Falls so as "to get richer and wider bottoms . . . upon the banks of the Ohio." George Washing-ton, upon hearing all of this, sent a second letter by courier to William Craw-ford: Make haste to issue a claim for the West.[10]

So it was, seven months later, that Capt. Thomas Bullitt's flotilla em-barked at the Kanawha's mouth to float the Beautiful River to the Shawnee land Virginians deemed Fincastle County, pulling ashore en route to the Ohio's Falls to lay out boundaries and streets for five towns, one of which George Rogers Clark would in five years name Louisville for King Louis XVI, King George III's great antagonist and America's first ally.

SUMMER 1773

Nearing Lower Shawnee Town's ruins, and peering past pines and cedars to watch the four warriors, James McAfee and his brother Robert lay by with brothers James and George, their eyes on the red men swimming seventeen horses—some saddled; others with pack frames—to the Scioto's mouth from the Kentucky shore. They must have cached the plunder from their raid, James thought, as he discerned none.

Tradition places this American long rifle as belonging to the McAfee family, who migrated from Botetourt County, Virginia, to Kentucky in 1779. One unique feature of this piece is the period replacement Fredericksburg rifle lock engraved FREDG 1777, which may have been acquired by the McAfees during their militia service. Barrel length: 42", .52 caliber. A leather "calves knee" lock cover has remained with the rifle.
GILES AND CAROLYN CROMWELL COLLECTION.

It was just a few days now before they were to rendezvous (again) with Capt. Thomas Bullitt, who was on a dangerous mission. Waiting, the McAfees and forty men hid out in a rocky bottom to spy out what was left of the old Shawnee citadel—"19 or 20 houses in it, compactly built together in the compass of about 2 acres of ground in it & a good deal of cleared land & fruit trees which had been about the time of the first wars."[11]

Captain Bullitt and his Delaware scouts and white hunters returned to the McAfees' camp on June 15. His was an epic tale.

A week or two before, Bullitt told them, they had walked into Chillicothe unseen and unheralded—save for the village dogs, which always barked and so no one heeded them. Only when they entered Chillicothe did the Indians see them. Shawanoe sentries—incensed that the four English and three Loups had appeared so suddenly in their midst—steered Bullitt's entourage into a wigwam. As the Shawanoe Big Men debated the seven's fate, heavily armed guards kept them hostage, only to free them at ten the next morning to what they were sure was to be their death party.

As the Big Men hustled the Long Knife intruders toward Chillicothe's center, more than one hundred screaming warriors charged in, arrows notched in taut strings stretched on yellowish *bois d'arc* bows. Others brandishing tomahawks and spears with conical tips cut from iron kettles slashed at Bullitt's coat. Volleys of fusil fire singed their feet and legs. Live rounds blasted overhead. And all the while, the angry faces; the yelling; the women's tongue trilling; naked, chittering berry brown children darting in and out of squatty longhouses and wigwams, cabins, and lodges hedging this, Chillicothe's promenade.

Neither Bullitt nor his comrades dared flinch, but walked on to meet their end, if indeed, this was what was to be.

Then, as suddenly as the din had begun, it stopped. The Shawanoes began to erupt in laughter. Captain Tom shook hands all around, honored, he told them, that his Shawanoe brothers would pull such a fine jest in his behalf.

Bullitt's Chillicothe stay lasted five days. Through his Delaware go-be-tweens, he explained his presence in their land: In 1768 at Fort Stanwix, the Six Nations had relinquished stewardship of *Kanta-Ke* clear to the mouth of the Tennessee River; in 1771 John Donelson replotted the region's southern boundary of white territory to be the Kentucky, instead of the Levisa. Donelson's "mistake" nearly doubled white territorial claims, but the Chero-kees, duly compensated for the slight oversight, had let it stand.

His bowdlerized history recitation falling upon a stoic audience, Bullitt went on: The Shawanoes had not been compensated for their *Kanta-Ke* hunting grounds; but within two years all would be righted, a just sum paid

John Murray, fourth Earl of Dunmore, viscount of Fincastle.

in full and in person by Lord Dunmore, the Long Knife governor who longed to visit their homeland and butcher a fatted ox and sing with his red children the war song; White Eyes might settle *Kanta-Ke* but would welcome their Shawanoe brothers and sisters to hunt and trade and dwell on Speleawee-theepee's shores. Lord Dunmore was too ill to deliver these glad tidings himself, Bullitt said, concluding, and had sent him to speak in his stead.

Such was the message his Delawares had related to the Shawanoes. Bullitt's men listened, disbelieving.

In a way, it was downright laughable: The likelihood of pudgy, ruddy-faced Lord Dunmore in kilts and balmoral bonnet, brandishing his dirk and Scottish steel pistols and strutting Chillicothe's dirt avenues to pay off a passel of half-naked Shawanoes was as likely as His Majesty George III touring the Illinois country to pay off *la française* for blowing up Fort Duquesne twenty years before.

Captain Bullitt wound down his tale. After his parley, he said, some of the very Shawanoes he had feared meant to brain him actually furnished canoes and an armed escort to see them safely down the Scioto to the Ohio.

And now, here he was. Back among his own.

And with him here, besides the McAfees, were deputy surveyors Hancock and Richard Taylor, and Abraham Haptonstall, Willis Lee, a Scotsman named James Douglas, and Kennedy the Irishman. And with them, Matthew Bracken, Jacob Drennon, John Mann, John Smith, Michael Tygert, John David Wolper, and twenty-year-old Isaac Hite with his band of seven. Black-bearded James Harrod stood out among this young, mostly clean-shaven crew of bachelors. Like the Taylors and Haptonstall, this was not Harrod's first bluegrass jaunt, and he and the Taylors guided Bullitt to the canelands.

Captain Bullitt's duplicity bought his Virginians time enough to float from the Scioto's mouth to the Falls by canoes, dugouts, and bateaux, erecting sails to cruise faster, frequently landing and going ashore to sight along theodolites and compasses atop Jacob's staffs that measured horizontal and vertical, pulling Gunter's hundred-link chains (or, in a pinch, well-stretched buffalo tugs) equaling twenty-two yards, and red-flagging, drafting, and pacing off more than one hundred thousand acres of rectangularish plots bordered on one end by the Ohio or Kentucky or a creek or spring, and trees or rocks or lead traces on the others.

For four months, Captain Bullitt's surveyors tramped the bluegrass. Once Shawanoes and Kickapoos visited them at the Falls; after a parley, Bullitt swapping them a "rifle-gun" for directions to a lick, they departed. The men worked on, unharried save for a desire to quit this land and register their claims to legalize them and collect their fees.

Back in Virginia by October 1773, Bullitt faced Col. William Preston, Fincastle's official surveyor, who refused to enter his claims, and for two very good reasons: Bullitt had neglected to employ Fincastle deputy surveyors, as required by Virginia law; and Bullitt's party had staked his surveys in Shawanoe land under treaty to the Crown.

Bullitt, too, most likely neglected to tip Preston a little gratuity for all his troubles in overseeing Fincastle's disputable claims. No matter: Lord Dunmore could negotiate these waters.

Sir William Johnson, New York's mediator to the Six Nations and the Crown's Indian agent who also had his sights set on *Kanta-Ke,* dispatched a stern letter of inquiry to Lord Dartmouth, George III's secretary: "I find that a certain Captain Bullitt with a large number of people from Virginia are gone down the Ohio beyond the limits of the proposed government with the authority . . . to survey and lay out land there."[12] England was not pleased.

The fourth earl of Dunmore, viscount of Fincastle, enjoying remarkably fine health back in his governor's palace as the Loyalist toast of Williamsburg, was as deeply troubled by England's accusations as he was by the illegality of Bullitt's grants and his rapidly vanishing Ohio Valley fiefdom at the Falls. To the inquiring king's men who investigated, Lord Dunmore denied any and all complicity in the land grab, shifting blame upon rebellious, bull-headed Americans who, he said, did "not conceive that Government has any right to forbid their taking possession of a Vast tract of Country."[13]

His own defense he laced with prevarications and lies; yet, of a truth, Dunmore was facing a rather novel besetting worry: wealthy, influential American rebels.

George Washington, Patrick Henry, Thomas Jefferson, and other Virginia Dynasty men were casting aspersions upon the notions of a "royal governor," and accusing the Crown of absolutism, and declaring that they—as freeborn Americans—would rather die than live under the yoke of tyranny. Such was seditious talk in these dark days rife with hints of secession that led to Boston's "Tea Party" on December 16, 1773.

What transpired among Fincastle County's land barons, Captain Bullitt, and "His Excellency," no one knows with perfect certainty, but on that same December 16, Dunmore ordered Preston to register Bullitt's surveys for Dr. John Connolly and Charles Warranstaff. Preston did so. Bullitt was able to assure Col. William Fleming on March 12 that all was well—no need for Fleming to fret over his new claims.

Sir—

His Excellency having come to a Resolution to Receive such of my Surveys as may be Certified by the County Surveyor (untill a meeting of the Council Can be had in April to Finally Settle the matter) take this opportunity to acquaint you that you need not be at the Trouble and expense to order any Further Survey as I will at any Time make out your plot, and Certificate and until the Meeting afores'd the county Surveyors possessing them will be Sufficient.

> I am with Esteem yours,
> Thos Bullitt
> Williamsburg

SUMMER 1774

War drums resounded from council fires on the upper Ohio and to the south as the Shawanoes unearthed the hatchet to color with blood, garnering their allies and dispatching fleet Piqua couriers to chieftains in neighboring villages. Chillicothes were especially outraged: Capt. Thomas Bullitt and his intrepid Long Knives had played them for utter fools, fearlessly attempting to steal *Kanta-Ke* from beneath them, and they had very nearly succeeded.

But back in the East, Col. William Preston was preparing to tidy up Captain Bullitt's unfinished business by launching a second surveying expedition into the western waters, to be led by his friend and deputized Fincastle County surveyor Capt. John Floyd. Floyd sensed something was awry on April 20, when he landed his flotilla at the Great Kanawha's mouth to hire an interpreter he knew lived there. "Take care of your scalp," the woodsman replied, refusing Floyd's generous offer of western land and English pounds.[14]

The mood was brittle, tense. A month before, a band of white hunters had murdered an unarmed Loup canoeing the Ohio. On May 15 some drunk bordermen lured the family of Talgayeeta, the respected Mingo chief whites called John Logan, to Yellow Creek (flowing into the Ohio from the Indian shore, fifty miles below Fort Pitt), plied them with rum, shot them, cut up their corpses, and scalped them. The barbarous act sent shock waves up and down the frontier.

Fort Pitt hunter Spencer Records believed that Capt. Michael Cresap— the Pennsylvanian trader who, it was accused, shot and scalped some unarmed

Excerpt from Col. James Robertson's dispatch to Col. William Preston, August 11, 1774:
"I have Offered £5 for the first Indians hand that will be brought in to the fort. . . .
they Left a war Club at one of the wasted Plantations well made and mark'd with two
Letters IG (well made) so that I think there is a White man with them." DRAPER
MANUSCRIPTS 3QQ:73-73[1]; STATE HISTORICAL SOCIETY OF WISCONSIN.

Indians near Wheeling on April 25—instigated the murders. Others named
Dr. John Connolly's ruffians, who, weeks before, had fired on Shawanoe hide
hunters en route to trade at Fort Pitt. More than a few blamed a scurrilous
gang of woodsmen led by the hunter Jacob Greathouse.

It hardly mattered. Logan's Mingo alliance of ex-patriot Shawnees and
Cherokees rose up against settlers living on the ridge spanning Virginia and
Tennessee in a seven-month killing spree settlers and frontiersmen remembered as Lord Dunmore's War, whose nefarious dealings with Thomas Bullitt
and William Preston and the rest had helped ignite it.[15]

Logan's savagery left a wake of scalped corpses littered with vermilion-
streaked death hammers as calling cards. On September 23, at Fort Blackmore
on the Clinch, commanded by militia captain Daniel Boone, the raiders
slaughtered livestock and ran two slaves to their deaths in a gauntlet held beyond rifle range as forted-up inhabitants looked on helplessly. By fall most of
the whites along that leg of the Alleghenies who had not forted up were heading east, images of terror that had seared their mind's eye looming up before

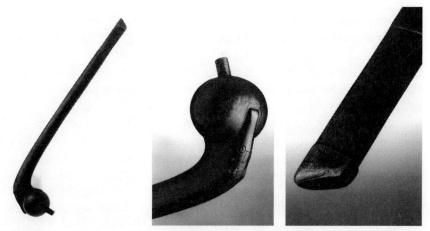

The "IG" ball-head war-club collected during Lord Dunmore's War. Club is feather-light but rock-hard, 22" in length and made of maple, featuring incised otter face gripping ball in mouth and wood spike. JIM AND CAROLYN DRESSLAR COLLECTION; PHOTOS BY DAVID DAMER.

them, driving them along the dark, narrow paths winding to safety as if so many tawny, fiercely painted hellhounds were on their trail.

Near Cumberland Gap, Logan's clout-clad wraiths slew John Roberts and his wife and family; it was Maj. Arthur Campbell, once a white Indian himself, who came upon Roberts's little boy wandering in the woods and was dismayed at his sad condition—"one blow with a tomahawk . . . cut through his skull, but it is generally believed his brains is safe, as he continues to talk sensibly"—and doctored him as best he could, but so grievous were his wounds that the Roberts boy died.[16]

Incensed, James Robertson in Tennessee informed Colonel Preston at Fort Wheeling in Fincastle County that "the men Seems Resolute for a Sculp or two," and put up as bounty "£5 for the first Indians hand brought to the fort."[17] Captain Boone collected a ball-head war club left beside John Duncan's body near Moore's Fort and sent it to Major Campbell, who on October 1 wrote Preston, "Mr. Boone preparing to go in search of the enemy . . . thinks it is the Cherokees that is now annoying us."[18]

Already Captain Boone, the blue-eyed, wide-mouthed Yadkin Long Hunter who knew Christopher Gist and had survived Braddock's Defeat and, en route to the disaster, had sat spellbound by the fire pits listening to John Findlay's tales of *Kanta-Ke,* was a much admired scout. At thirty-nine, he took to Indians far better than most whites, dressing half-Indian himself in moccasins, clout, and beaded deerskin leggings dyed black, clubbing back his hair in a beige plait, hunting with Cherokees, visiting their towns and camps, and able to speak a smattering of Cherokee and Delaware. Pony-built he was: five-eight, wide-shouldered, 175 pounds, his robust frame firmly seated on stout, muscular thighs. Rebecca, his dark-eyed, black-haired wife of eighteen years whose height was equal to his, had by now borne eight children; Jesse had just turned a year old.

Boone knew *Kanta-Ke* better than any Long Knife alive, first hunting there in 1765 with brother Squire, but skirting only its eastern rim and, like Dr. Thomas Walker, missing the island in the wilderness. Then again in May 1769 he sojourned there with Squire and brother-in-law John Stewart (who never returned, shot by Indians), three camp tenders, and old Findlay, in his last years an itinerant tinker still seeking a tug at the brass ring and who led Boone through the Gap and to the bluegrass.

Shawnees, led by the mixed-blood Capt. Will Emery, captured Daniel twice, stripping him and his men (who fled) of deerskins, weapons, powder and ball, traps, and horses. Squire went home, reoutfitted, and rendezvoused with Dan, who had stayed behind to explore. Again they hunted and trapped and laid by, graining deerskins for eastern markets and enjoying a good hunt on the Green with Casper Mansker's Long Hunters, who left the Boones and moved farther southward to scour the Cumberland watershed of deerskins. In May 1771 a band of Cherokees accosted the homeward-bound Boones, pack-horses heavy, and robbed them clean.

After two years of toil, Daniel Boone returned unto his own, badly bent but far from broken: He had found the island.

Far better, he knew the way. From Col. Isaac Shelby's to Moccasin Gap: twenty-five miles; from Moccasin Gap to Martin's Station: fifty-five miles; from Martin's Station to Cumberland Gap: twenty miles; the Gap to Flat Lick: eighteen miles; Flat Lick to Laurel River: twenty-seven miles; Laurel River to Hazel Patch: thirteen miles. At Hazel Patch, the Warrior's Path forked. If traveling to Otter Creek, then from Hazel Patch to Boone's Gap: twenty-seven miles; then Boone's Gap to Otter Creek: twenty-eight miles. Or if traveling from Hazel Patch to Boiling Springs: sixty-five miles.

In September 1773 Boone had tried again, five Yadkin families departing with him, others joining as his cavalcade threaded the misty mountains thick with rhododendron and hemlock, sky hanging foggy and blue. Shawnees and Cherokees hit them in Powell's Valley on October 9, killing Boone's firstborn, James, and Henry Russell, the two Mendinall boys, a youth named Drake, and a slave. "The Murder of Russell, Boons; & Drakes Sons is in every ones mouth," wrote Maj. Arthur Campbell to Col. William Preston on June 20, 1774. Virginians counted them as Lord Dunmore's War's first white victims.[19]

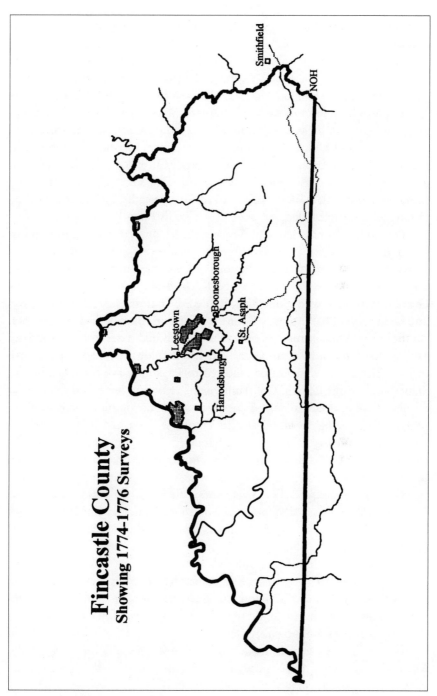

Fincastle County
Showing 1774-1776 Surveys

Smithfield

NOH

Boonesborough

Leestown

St. Asaph

Harrodsburg

MAP BY NEAL O. HAMMON.

Boone had cached near Clinch River, winter's chill cooling hostilities for a season.

And now, by this summer of 1774, Colonel Preston's greatest concern: the safety of Capt. John Floyd's retinue of Fincastle County surveyors—Hancock Taylor, James Douglas, and Isaac Hite and the rest—and Floyd's hunters and chain pullers, land jobbers and outliers. Sixteen had begun the expedition; more threw in as the flotilla drifted down the Ohio. Floyd's party reached the Falls on May 29, only to learn that James Harrod's thirty men had been there and were camped near Salt River.[20] On July 24 Floyd discovered ominous signs upon returning to one camp. Two fires burned, wares were scattered about, this stark message carved into a nearby beech: "Alarmed by finding some people killed. We are gone down this way."[21]

Preston fired a missive to Col. William Russell on the Clinch: Dispatch two scouts to *Kanta-Ke* posthaste; warn the surveyors; return with intelligence.

Stepping forward to accept Preston's task was the quiet North Carolinian, Capt. Daniel Boone. With him came Michael Stoner—a stout, humorous German marksman who himself had hunted the bluegrass in 1767. There was one hitch: Stoner had no gun. Boone handed him his rifle and got another.

Boone and Stoner rode more than eight hundred miles in sixty-two days, finding that most of Fincastle's surveyors had fled for their lives—"well drove in by Indians," Captain Boone reported to Preston—save for a handful he guided back to the Clinch. Col. James Knox, who had left Floyd to hunt on his own hook near James Harrod's newly established clump of hog-pen cabins near Boiling Springs surveyors called Harrod's Town, led in a few others. James Douglas's party took a far more hazardous route, canoeing past the Falls to the Mississippi and on down to New Orleans to secure passage on a vessel bound for Virginia.

But not all escaped. The Shawanoes killed hunters James Cowan and James Hamilton. Two of Captain Floyd's men, Hancock Taylor and James Strother, were shot crossing the Kentucky in a pine dugout. Still, John Floyd had managed to survey and claim, in all, 206,250 acres, more than 40,000 of them, sixty-five square miles, at the Falls alone.[22]

On October 10, at the battle of Point Pleasant, Virginia, an estimated force of one thousand Ohio Indians killed seventy-five Long Knives and wounded about one hundred out of Col. Andrew Lewis's force of fifteen hundred. Native losses: unknown.

Fearing retaliation, Cornstalk, the renowned principal Chillicothe Mequache chieftain for the entire Shawnee nation, reluctantly signed articles with the Virginians: Shawanoes would live north of Speleawee-theepee, the bloody river now to be the boundary between Indians and Long Knives.

Cornstalk warned the White Eyes: His words held little sway among younger warriors whose hearts Long Knife duplicity had hardened for war.

Thus, Lord Dunmore's War ended.

Chief John Logan, his seed exterminated—"There runs not a drop of my blood in the veins of any living creature. . . . Who is there to mourn for Logan? Not one!"—sought solace in strong liquor.[23]

Unbelievably, it seemed, the Shawanoes had ceded their claims to *Kanta-Ke*.

"Opening in the Forest," by David Wright.

The Long Hunters

Every tree cut, every deer slain . . . directly affected the livelihood of the Indian.

—Arthur K. Moore, *The Frontier Mind,* 1957

A century before cowboys, the Earps versus the Clantons, and Buffalo Bill Cody's Wild West (which helped create and perpetuate mythic notions about the Great American West) was a distinct breed of woodsmen, the Long Hunters. Popular histories and academia have rendered little unto these stalwarts whose brief era and scant numbers composed the van of westering Anglo-American settlement. Lore and legend swirl about them like so much karmic dust blowing off the Blue Ridge's rounded peaks, which they traversed from the 1760s to the 1770s, wending their packhorses down the Warriors' Path and up through the yawning, white-faced chasm dividing Cumberland Mountain.

Long Hunters were uniquely American, a pioneering fraternity of poor men from the "lower classes" whose veins pulsed with the blood of their English, Scotch-Irish, French, and German forebears. Parched corn and jerked meat, buffalo tongue, marrow bones, and beaver tail kept them fit, hardened for the trail, and inured to hardships they encountered as they left their wives, passels of lean, barefooted children, and dirt-floored, one-room cabins dotting Virginia's New River, the Carolinas, and eastern Tennessee to hunt the Middle Ground.

Some names of these hardy, freeborn men: Capt. James Smith, who hunted the Cumberland in 1766; Benjamin Cutbirth, who saw the rolling Mississippi before his cousin Daniel Boone did; Hancock Taylor, whom Shawnees shot mortal on the Kentucky in 1774, so as blood leaked out of him for four days and Abraham Haptonstall held him up to sip water, he signed his surveys to make them legal;

87

the Skaggs boys, who named a trace that became a Kentucky road; Isaac Bledsoe, who survived a buffalo stampede only to be killed by Cherokee; Anthony Bledsoe, who like brother Isaac was also killed by Cherokee; the McAfees, who surveyed along Salt River with Capt. Thomas Bullitt; Casper Mansker, who heard Daniel Boone singing on the banks of the Green back in 1771; Uriah Stone, who had a Middle Tennessee rivulet named for him; club-footed Obadiah Terrill, who died lonely and without issue, but whose first name metamorphosed into Tennessee's Obey River; James Dysart, who rarely left camp to hunt without a book to read; James Knox, whose station on Green River was raided by Indians—he "Lost 2300 deerskins" and suffered "Ruination by God"; Huguenot Timothy De Monbruen from Illinois, who hunted French Lick and wore a foxskin cap and blue frock; Isaac Crabtree, who survived Indian attack and got revenge; Michael Stoner, the stout German friend of Boone and one of the best shots on the frontier; and the Boones, Daniel and brother Squire and brother-in-law John Stewart.

In Tennessee, North Carolina, West Virginia, and Kentucky, many a river, county, city, town, and road are named for them, and romance and enigma shroud their appearance and livelihood: Long Hunters were not voices crying in the wilderness proclaiming the coming of civilization; Long Hunters did not wear buckskin dripping with fringes and rarely donned coonskin caps.

Footwear could be straight-last shoes buckled or tied, or pucker-sole moccasins or harder-soled Fort Ligonier-style "shoe-packs" cut from half-dressed hides, whipped closed with a whang. Side-seam deerskin leggings reached midthigh; hunters wore them "Indian-stile," with clouts of leather or cloth, or Anglo-style, yanking the leggings up over their knee-breeches cuffs. Tucking the leggings' ends into moccasin tops, flaps turned up and tied off about the ankles with a three-ply buffalo wool cord, protected from thorns and snakes and kept out rocks and twigs. To keep leggings taut and high on the leg, hunters wrapped above their calves but below the knees a thong of some sort, from Indian-made quilled rawhide strips to intricately beaded fingerwoven wool garters a foot and a half long and two inches wide or, more simply, a slender slip of whang leather.

Hunters swapped skins for worsted stockings at outposts in Tennessee's Holston Valley; perhaps in winter they (and Indians, as they wore stockings too) wore stockings under their leggings for warmth. To insulate from frostbite and ice-covered creeks and thinly iced pockets of snowmelt they stepped in and crashed through, hunters stuffed moccasins with beech leaves, wads of buffalo wool from spring's shed, or deerhair. Far greater risks than snow and ice were floods and rains. A prolonged soaking left feet swollen and sore, soles ragged and flayed, the wrinkled skin peeling off in puffy layers and tearing free, ripping deep into the pink inner flesh. Woodsmen knew the malady as "scalded feet." To cure it, they laid up for a few days to apply a balm made by pulverizing slippery elm bark with the poll end of a belt ax and boiling it in water to render it into viscous gel cool to the touch.

Shirts were plain, reaching to midthigh or knee, billowy at the chest and shoulder, and tied at the wrists and collar or buttoned with buttons of horn, bone, wood, or antler. Over the shirt, hunters might wear a linen or flannel weskit—fashionably worn past midthigh before the Revolution, a few inches below the hips after that. In the settlements, weskits were mandatory for gentlemen; folks of the better classes deemed a man not wearing one a boor. On the trail, such distinctions among men of equal estate held no concern; still, a weskit buttoned from neck to crotch added warmth with little bulk during April's cool evenings and had the handy advantage of pockets, which breeches, shirts, and frocks lacked.

Headgear was typically a hat but could be (and was) anything from a head rag that doubled as a handkerchief, to a wide-brimmed, low-crowned beaver, to a tricorn, to a Quaker hat with upturned edges. Coon, skunk, and red fox skins, with faces and tails attached, were stitched into caps (fur caps hinted of Indian wear), as were blankets, scarves, goose skins, and crudely woven flats of matted buffalo wool—anything to keep heads dry and warm.

One garment became a badge of this fraternity: the hunting shirt. More frock than a pullover "wagoner's shirt," hunting shirts were sewn ten to twelve stitches to the inch of plain or single-block prints of calico, osnaburg, linen, cotton or blend, or of buckskin. Buckskin hunting shirts, good for warding off morning chills and

Brain-tanned buckskin coat worn by John Peter LeMayeur, George Washington's dentist, c. 1785, and patterned similar to Revolutionary War rifle-man's frock, with fringed belt with tab (right end of belt purposely behind to show coat's double row of fringe and silk thread floral embroidery in colors red, blue, light green, pink, and brown), black velvet collar and cuff binding, and cape. VALENTINE MUSEUM, RICHMOND, VA; PHOTO BY DAVID WRIGHT.

breaking the stiff winds of winter, were the least desirable: In summer a buckskin shirt was hot and clammy, lacking cloth's breathability; downpours transformed it into soggy chamois that never fit the same after being stretched out to dry and resmoked to waterproof it.

Steeping broths of butternuts, black walnut hulls, chestnuts, oak bark, and salt (if it could be spared) to act as a mordant colored garments tea beige to coffee brown; iron scrapings added to dye vats (or a thirty-gallon kettle) turned clothes black. Indigo grown in the Carolinas and Tidewater yielded sky blues. Imported European dyes turned hunting shirts into brilliant scarlets, royal blues, and myriad yellows and greens. Many a wearer—including Revolutionary War militiamen fighting the Brits in the colonies—left his hunting smock undyed, a tawny zinc gray.

Cuffs, hems, and borders of capes (if the garment was caped; some hunting shirts were not; others were embroidered) were frayed off along the ends into a feather fringe that served no function other than being the day's style. (Frayed edges might break up a hunter's silhouette and shed rain more freely.)

Open-fronted and belted shut with a strop buckled in front or a beaded sash tied in back to keep the ends out of the way, a hunting shirt marked a man as a woodsman—even if he were not. At Boonesborough, wrote Col. Richard Henderson in May 1775, hunters hired out to provender folks who lacked skill enough to keep themselves fed. Some of the more inept settlers, though, "from conceit, from having a hunting shirt, tomahawk, and gun, thought it was an insult to offer another man to hunt for them"[1] and took to the woods and blasted away, crippling buffalo and driving off herds.

This garment, which signaled "woodsman" to settlers, signaled "poacher" to Indians. Nicholas Cresswell, a young Tory visiting Kentucky seeking adventure and land, was warned by a Fort Pitt trader, a Mr. Anderson, prior to his foray into the Middle Ground, "that the Indians [were] not well pleased at anyone going into their Country dressed in a Hunting shirt." Cresswell, adaptable, eminently curious, and willing to "go native," switched dress and alter-ego, outwardly leaving behind his Anglo trappings and persona to blend with Munsee customs—"Got a Calico shirt made in the Indian fashion, trimmed up with Silver Brooches and Armplates so that I scarcely know myself"[2]—and so fit in better than he thought, bedding the handsome Delaware women and taking a Mohawk mistress.

As in their diversity of dress and look, Long Hunters embodied an amalgam of skills, bloodlines, and habits—traits typical of westering Americans with a thirst for adventure in pursuit of cash. One trait they shared: They were commercial hunters and typically riflemen, market hunters who scoured the Cumberland basin for white-tailed deer.

Long hunting commenced by April and ended in late fall, after second or third frost, when deerskins thickened as veins swelled to grow the heavy bluish coats needed to survive snow and ice and dearth of browse; winter-killed hides,

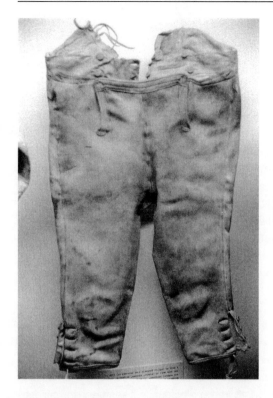

Buckskin English breeches, c. 1780, showing button closures, garter ties, narrow "drop-front" fly, and rear tie enclosure. MUSEUM OF THE FUR TRADE, CHADRON, NE; PHOTO BY DAVID WRIGHT.

half-dressed and dried, cracked along vein lines. After skinning the carcass, the skin yanked free and hair and epidermis scraped off with a fleshing tool, the men whipped skins over a staking board to dry and render them pliant ("half-dressed") to store on scaffolds away from wolves and covered over with buffalo, elk, or bear hides.

Pack teams took deerskins back east, where they were either shipped to Europe or bark or salt-alum tanned into breeches and leggings, weskits and shirts, frocks and coats, shoes and boots, dance slippers and moccasins, book bindings and saddles, gloves and harnesses. One "Breeches-Maker, and Glover" open for business in 1739 in Williamsburg, Virginia, advertised that he made only

> the best Buck Skin Breeches, either of the common Tann'd Colour, or dy'd Black, or of Cloth Colours, after the *English* Manner: Also Buck Skin Gloves, with high Tops. . . . He also dresses leather after the *Philadelphia* Manner, not inferior to Oil'd Leather Dress, for Goodness and Fineness, upon the Flesh or Grain.[3]

Such leather workers drove a bustling cottage industry that made one half-dressed male deerskin weighing two and a half pounds (a "buck") the equivalent of

40 cents, or one Spanish dollar, a pound. At Fort Pitt in 1767, commissary Alexan-der McKee received 178,613 "Fall Skins" and 104,016 "Summer Skins"—figures typical of the region's exchange from the 1740s to the 1780s and comparable to the southern trade out of Charleston and New Orleans, proof that Indian and Anglo hide hunters were slaughtering millions of deer in the Mississippi watershed.[4]

But in summer's heat, mosquitoes, flies, and gnats filling the air, and larval seed ticks clustered on low-hanging sumac, with timber rattlers and copperheads basking on ledges and cottonmouths poised along riverbanks and in malarial swamps, long hunting was a grueling job, fraught with accidents and possible death from snakebite, frostbite, starvation, falls, disease, gangrene, infections, shootings, buffalo gorings, and bites from rabid wolves.

Besides such calamities, rains, floods, humidity, grease burn, hide rot, and ex-posure were constant worries; wolves, bears, and panthers ransacked caches; di-minishing herds meant fewer hides to flatten in presses to pack in bearskins in lots of fifty and bind with tugs (buffalo hide ropes) to load on packhorses, two bundles per horse.

Preparations for long hunts began in winter; departure dates were set for spring. Daniel Boone's first foray into Kentucky commenced in May 1769 and lasted until May 1771. Such a two-year jaunt (Boone was scouting land while evad-ing Shawnees and Cherokees, who twice robbed him, as much as he was downing deer) presented problems, notably, keeping oneself in powder and ball; keeping one's rifle oiled, cleaned, and "in order"; keeping hidden lest keen-eyed Shawnees read one's sign in their territory.

Even for teams of twenty to thirty hunters, such was the deadliest challenge of all: dealing with Iroquoians or Algonquins who might befriend in the first encounter, steal or kill in the second. In these risky ventures, safety was in numbers, but num-bers spooked deer. So after establishing a base—a "station camp"—hunters split into twos and threes to hunt salt licks in the cool of morning or hide to evade roving red men crossing the Ohio. In 1748 Ohio and Great Lakes Indians stole forty-eight horseloads of deerskins from George Croghan—a staggering loss to the Irish-born Pennsylvania trader.

Antipathy was mutual and inevitable. Unlike Fenimore Cooper's fictional pro-tagonist, Natty Bumppo, Long Hunters saw little admirable about Indians, though they adopted Indian dress and skills, and sought to supplant Indians in the deer-skin trade. Platitudes about "Natural Men" were reserved for Europe's bourgeoisie in parlors sipping tea cut with latte, imbibing Enlightenment ideals of Rousseau and Montesquieu, mulling over the mores and eternal destinies of the New World's indigenous inhabitants.

Long Hunters did not much countenance such thoughts; in a tight spot the Nimrods might shoot Natural Men on sight and slice off a scalp with the steady coolness of cutting free a tom-turkey beard. A sixty-pound beaver back-stabbed with a single-tine trade gig was one less blanket beaver to trip the dog of a hand-forged double-longspring trap. A whitetail felled by a .50-caliber long rifle meant another bloated carcass left naked by the trail and marked by spiraling buzzards. Yet, had an arrow or Shawnee bullet felled the deer, its fate would have been the same.[5] In 1773 a Delaware hide hunter slaughtered thirty deer in seventeen days; another took forty-seven bucks in a month. Missionary David Zeisberger estimated a native might shoot 150 deer a year, observing that "Delawares use no other than rifle-barrelled guns."

Interloping Long Hunters poaching from the Cumberland watershed to the Ohio and west to the Green and Mississippi, land understood by all to be Indian territory, forced contacts and confrontations between the races.[6] How, through Indian eyes, to deal with this persistent intruder? Accommodation was one tack; annihilation another. Both roads led to Indian removal. Long Hunters did not go west to dispossess, but were dispossession's harbingers. In their wakes came settlers, surveyors, land jobbers, speculators, publicists, clergymen, and lawyers who turned paths into macadamized roads and salt licks into real estate ventures to spawn towns and cities and county seats.

Today's inheritors of their birthright can read their names on rusting signs along blacktops that once were traces, as on marker 217 in Scott County, Kentucky, on State Highway 227, near the town of Stamping Ground:

> This area first explored April 1775 by William McConnell, Charles Lecompte and party from Penn. Buffalo herds had stamped down undergrowth and ground around the spring— origin of town's name. McConnell and Lecompte in Blue Licks, 1782.[7]

Virginia's U.S. Route 58 threads down Boone's trail through Powell's Valley. If travelers do not park their cars and get off the pavement and walk, though, they will sense less than a glimmer of what Boone saw and felt there in 1773 when Indians knifed his firstborn son, James. Amid the day's rush at the old hub of French Lick, a contemporary reconstruction of "Fort Nashboro" is eclipsed by shadows cast by Nashville's gigantic Coliseum. Sport fans might be startled to learn that Indian and Anglo blood mingled upon their arena's soil, buffalo and elk and panthers and wolves crisscrossed it into earthen mazes, man and beast sipped freely from the Cumberland River without suffering the ills of heavy metal contamination.

Perhaps, on an atavistic level, industrial man, holding fast to his "independence" that is seated upon shrinking resources, upon silicon chips and blips of flashing light, upon science, industry, and technology, upon vain gospels of gross national product and eternal economic growth, is a little wary of his preindustrial pioneering forebear. If so, it's understandable. For the spirit of the Long Hunters symbolizes something vastly deep and precious in the human psyche: Long Hunters were rugged, self-reliant individualists who truly were free.

CHAPTER FOUR

Into Western Waters

SPRING 1775

The battle of Point Pleasant, beginning at dawn October 10, 1774, ended Lord Dunmore's War, stalling Shawnee raids for almost a year and opening the disputed lands south of the dark and bloody river, the Ohio. Already James Harrod's men were back establishing themselves at Harrod's Town, and the Transylvania Company—financed by Col. Richard Henderson and his partners and led by Daniel Boone—would be arriving to settle on the Kentucky.

It was the following spring that Nicholas Cresswell,[1] twenty-four, left England for America. In the employ of William Murray (founder of the Illinois Company), and en route to Alexandria, Virginia, on April 3, 1775, he "hired a horse" for £4 and dined with the son-in-law of a Mr. Snickers. As the night wore on and rum loosened the talk, Cresswell told him his plight: He was traveling west and was seeking a guide. The man suggested he stop in Winchester—it was right on the way, anyway—and look up George Rice, a good woodsman who himself was bound for the western waters.

Arriving the following afternoon, Cresswell went to Rice's home to explain his intentions: He was from England; he was not a hunter; and he knew nothing of Indians. After his claims were filed, and assuming he could locate suitable land, he would pay a guide five hundred acres for his services. Was Rice interested?

Come morning, Rice replied, he was riding to Fort Pitt; Cresswell was welcome to go along. "Bought some Blankets, Gunpowder, lead, flints, camp kettle, frying-pan and tomahawk," Cresswell recorded in his diary April 4. Fearing rattlesnakes the warming days were sure to draw from their dens, he purchased a pair of wool leggings.[2]

After lunch the next day, the two men left and rode ten miles, stopping at Rinker's Tavern. On April 6 they made thirty miles, Cresswell recorded—"over barren hills and bad ways." Hogback ridges became foothills, and after a shower that spring night, water froze in a skillet lying ten feet from the fire that Cresswell kept ablaze.

On Friday, April 7, they ascended the Appalachians, riding thirty miles before camping west of Patterson's Creek. That night, as they kicked up a bed of dry leaves to spread their blankets on, Cresswell complained that he had barely slept the night before. That was because, Rice said, he had gone to bed with his clothes on. Cresswell stripped and slept well.

On the morrow, big rocks and fallen trees—one pine measured 130 feet—forced them to dismount to pick their way over ledges and around trees that blocked the sun, casting a pall upon tangles of laurel that they had to push through before trudging into a narrow chute: the Shades of Death. "This is one of the most dismal places I ever saw," Cresswell wrote. Still, they had gone twenty-eight miles.

Sunday, April 9. Before them rose Little Meadow Mountain, a pinnacle that they wended their way over; probably near Will's Creek, they crossed western Maryland to ford the Youghiogheny. It was a fine day, made finer that night by a brace of grouse spitted over low blue flames that hissed when fat dripped off and hit the coals.

Cold, heavy rains fell Monday as Cresswell and Rice rode through a mile-wide swath of severed treetops lying many yards from the trunks they were torn from. Root clumps heavy with clods reared out of the ground, and oaks two feet thick lay snapped like kindling. The men were passing through "Fallen Timbers," ravaged years before by a tornado that left a wake of destruction for more than one hundred miles due west. At Great Meadows, they passed what was left of Fort Necessity[3]; in overgrown fields a mile or two beyond the ruins, they began seeing signs of Gen. Edward Braddock's army slaughtered near Fort Duquesne. That night they slept in the cabin of Zachariah Connel, Rice's brother-in-law.

Cresswell spent two weeks exploring and taking notes. At the site of Braddock's Defeat, he "found great numbers of bones. . . . We could not find one whole skull, all of them broke to pieces in the upper part, some of them had holes broken in them about an inch in diameter, suppose it to be done with a Pipe Tomahawk." Mortar shards and rusty ordnance lay among leather scraps, scabbards, shoes, tatters of dingy, madder red regimentals. Trees were barked from artillery fire.

A score of miles below the fort, Rice felled two walnuts, and after he burned a trough and gouged out the char with an adz, twin dugouts began to take shape on the Youghiogheny's banks. "One of them we called the

Right view of skull of soldier killed by Indians in raid led by Tory partisan Simon Girty against Americans garrisoning Ohio's Fort Laurens, winter 1778–79. Note punctures from ball-head war-club.

DR. RICHARD M. GRAMLY; PHOTO BY PAMELA SCHUYLER-COWENS.

Charming Sally, the other *Charming Polly.* They are about thirty feet long and twenty inches wide . . . dug out something like a manger." By April 28, Friday, the men launched the vessels to try them, the river's mouth widening to a gauntlet of shoals and choppy rapids.

On Saturday, April 29, they met James Nourse, who was going west to secure claims on Kentucky River for his brother serving in the navy of George III. With Nourse were his indentured servants, Tom Ruby and George Noland, and Edmund and Reuben Taylor and Ben Johnston, en route to Harrod's Town to live with John Gabriel Jones.[4]

The parties agreed to travel together. As Nourse and his men were sharing the dugouts, Nourse would share his tent with Cresswell. The travelers floated *Charming Sally* and *Charming Polly* to the forks of the Allegheny and Monongahela. Destination: Fort Pitt.

Loaded with gunpowder, lead, salt, corn, pork, rye for the horses, their dogs, and their budgets, the dugouts sat so low in the river that often the men waded the craft over shoals that sloshed water over the gunwales. One turbid stretch churned for two miles; Edmund Taylor's dugout smacked a rock and at the loud *thunk!* bucked and spun about, and the men feared she would capsize, so they lashed the vessels together, and all hands waded and shoved until they passed the shoals.

Supper was boiled chicken, fatback, and bread. Clouds blew in, then rain.

Breakfast was bacon broth thickened with crumbs. Nourse shaved and spent Sunday in his tent reading. By noon the rain turned to a drizzle, and dirty-faced squatters emerging from hovels on the bank came down to talk; Nicholas had no truck with the "rascals," but the land, he said, was "rich beyond conception. . . . The soil in general is Black and of a Fat Loamy nature." Walnut and cherry trunks three feet thick rose nearly forty feet to their first limbs.

Noon the next, still raining, Rice shot a turkey, and they pulled to the bank to retrieve it. Tom Ruby baited a hook with its liver, tied the hook to a linen thread, and cast into the river, but he tied to a stump instead of a limb and his line snapped when he got a bite and lost fish, line, and hook. Where the Youghiogheny joins the Monongahela, the channel widened, creating eddies that float nymphs to big fish lurking in such places; townsfolk had raised a weir from each bank to the stream's middle, and at the juncture was a fish trap big as a cart.[5]

That night they ate the last of their turkey, endured rains, and slept little, reaching Fort Pitt the noon following, Tuesday, May 2. Nourse stripped off a linen shirt over his flannel weskit and shirt, picked off a few lice, and shaved. Cresswell bought "lead, flints, and some silver trinkets" to trade with Indians and ate with Mr. John Campbell.[6] Reboarding at 2:00 P.M. at the Ohio's headwaters, the *Charming Sally* and *Charming Polly* slipped into calmer currents, gunwales clearing by three inches.

Floating past McKee's Island—a mile-wide islet where the Shawnee-Scotsman Alexander McKee, the British Indian agent, lived with his family—Cresswell and Nourse logged entries about the land. McKee's was the first of a three-island chain ending with Montour's Island (named for John Montour, the half-Seneca uncle to Andrew Montour[7]). At Montour's, they camped. Chores done, Tom Ruby baited and cast and struck fire to keep down mosquitoes. He gazed into the dusk, then sat upright, staring at a canoe veering out of the haze to his fire, and sprinted off to warn the others, but laughter greeted Nourse's company as a band of woodsmen splashed ashore to stay the night.

A leak discovered in one of the dugouts delayed their voyage. Hours later, they passed the men they had camped with and four Kentucky-bound vessels, glided past Beaver Creek, emptying into the Ohio,[8] and nearing dusk landed to bake bread. Pushing on, they lashed *Charming Polly* and *Charming Sally* together and steered into the channel, keeping watch in two-hour shifts, veering from snags and sandbars. By dawn, Thursday, May 4, they had arrived at Fort Fincastle at Wheeling.

Erected on a promontory jutting into the Ohio, Fort Fincastle was "a quadrangular picketed Fort . . . built last summer by Lord Dunmore," and well garrisoned. Here Capt. George Rogers Clark joined the fellowship and they shoved off; within hours clouds thickened the sky, and as the wind picked up, Clark pointed them into a cove of Grave Creek.[9]

Friday morning they hove to a trio of mounds; the largest resembled "a round hill something like a sugar loaf, about 300 feet in circumference at the bottom, 100 feet high and about 60 feet in diameter at top where it forms a sort of irregular basin."[10] "Tom and I cooked, G. Rice helping me," Nourse recorded, "a small fish the two the liquor being made into soup, dined 9 of us on the most delicate meal I had made, sauce melted butter with walnut pickle."

Trolling behind the dugouts on Saturday yielded two catfish in spite of rainy gusts kicking the Ohio into a chop and forcing the voyagers to strip and stow their clothes in their budgets. Near Muddy Creek, Clark said, was Capt. Michael Cresap's cabin[11]; when sighted, they rowed to it, pulling the dugouts from the surge.

As the rains slacked, some men left to hunt, others to fish. The hunters returned empty-handed, but Ruby had a string of catfish; in minutes three big cats were gutted and browning in sizzling sowbelly, and the men sat before a fire and under a roof, laughing at their fortune. Barking dogs and strange voices made them rush the door as three dugouts of whites pulled ashore for a night's rest.

On Sunday, May 7, Cresswell shaved and shirted. Morning broke clear. They skimmed down the Ohio, shooting past two islets, pulling ashore on Big Tree Island.[12] One sycamore stretched their surveying tape fifty-one feet, four inches; where the tree branched some twenty feet higher, "its forks were larger than most trees." Captain Clark dug up a reddish root—"puccoon," he called it—that Shawnees claimed cured snakebite.[13] They floated past the Muskingum and dined on fish and bacon. Ben Johnston tossed out a line and hauled in a twelve-pound cat.

The sun set. They stopped at the mouth of Hocking Creek to view the ruins of Fort Gower, abandoned during Dunmore's War.[14] They ate dinner among its timbers, then lashed the dugouts for the night's ride; by dawn they had made another sixteen miles, and as the sun rose they untied (as was their custom) the vessels from each other to row. Morning brought rain, and they rigged blankets and tents into canopies, but gusts whipped their tarps into a bellows and made the dugouts shudder, and so they pulled ashore twelve miles above the Great Kanawha, spreading wet blankets to sit, pipes lit, to talk over news heard from travelers who had pulled in: Shawnees had killed some hunters on the Kentucky.

"My courageous companions' spirits began to droop," wrote Cresswell Monday night, May 8. Tuesday they landed at the mouth of the Great

Kanawha near Fort Blair, at Point Pleasant. Capt. William Russell commanded Fort Blair's hundred-man garrison, and Nourse and Cresswell breakfasted with Captain Russell, Lt. Isaac Shelby, and Ensigns Roberts and Sharp. Russell had just returned with a bateau load of flour and corn from the Big Sandy and, at the Clinch, had heard about the murders.

"Two of them killed were Boone's men," Russell said, and word was the same warriors had attacked Sam Tate's party, killing two more. The Chillicothes accused the Mingoes; a few blamed Dragging Canoe's Cherokees; there were rumors the Piquas to the north had dug up the hatchet. No one, he said, was sure who had done the killings.[15]

"My companions," wrote Cresswell, "exceedingly fearful and I am far from being easy," but he was set to go on "as far as anyone will keep me company." Said Nourse, "The company all resolved to continue there rout, myself undetermined, but having come so far, loath to return without my errand." They passed the Guyandotte.[16]

On Wednesday, May 10, near the Big Sandy, they landed at an encampment of twenty-two men led by Capt. Charles Smith, a deputy surveyor. Breakfast was venison. As the men ate and talked, Tom Ruby landed two catfish, which he gutted and chopped into chowder as James Nourse took a few minutes to write to his wife.

My dearest Love—

We arrived here this morning. . . . Capt. Smith, who promises to send you this as soon as ever he gets home, but I flatter myself I may possibly be at home near as soon as he, for he talks of calling at some places to make improvements, but whether I shall go down to Kentucky is at present uncertain, we having a report that some Indians have done mischief. . . . I long most ardently to hear of you all. I hope to God the small-pox keeps clear of you. . . .

Your most affectionate and faithful Husband,
James Nourse[17]

Thursday's breakfast was coffee and buttered bread. The men washed and mended clothes. Ruby fished. The hunters returned with turkey eggs. Nourse swapped Smith a hunk of bacon for two catfish and, Smith directing, got "an iron pot with half a pint of water and between each layer, butter, pepper and salt putting sticks to keep the fish from the bottom and then put the fire over and under the pot."[18] Friday's breakfast was bacon and eggs. Nourse kept

Ruby busy washing linens and dying his hunting shirt as the company debated any dangers that might lie ahead.

One problem was the dugouts; they were too narrow to move freely in and awkward to handle. "I believe they are a set of Damned cowards," wrote Cresswell, who persuaded them to lash the dugouts together once and for all, fixing the "canoes together by two beams,"

> one athwart the heads, the other at the stern, setting the Canoes about one foot apart. In the middle . . . a strong pin, on that hung the rudder, made something like an oar, but bent down towards the water and projected about two feet astern of the Vessel, rigged her out with four oars.[19]

The task took all Saturday. *Charming Sally* and *Charming Polly,* now redubbed the *Union,* heeded the helm well.

On Sunday, May 14, storms moved in early; as night became day, moods turned brittle. Edmund Taylor—"a red-hot liberty man"—locked horns with "torified" Cresswell over American rights under Crown law, the dispute ending "in high words." Said Cresswell, "Taylor threatened to tar and feather me."

Shoreline colors were a variegated matte of tan and brown blended with listing green slashes as gusts off the river bent the tall, leafy grass. Droves of buffalo stomped down the cane and capered along the Ohio and lounged in shade cast by tulip poplars and fat sycamores and wallowed in mud flats and swam the channel. Deer gazed from the water's edge, ears up, tails flitting, watching, waiting, fleeing at a bound. Wapiti walked the bank; by fall their racks would be pushing through the cane, long-leaf sumac, and grapevines.

That Monday afternoon, the crew shipped oars to dine on day-old bacon. Off the *Union's* twin bow, they spotted a big blotched-brown pancake basking, poking a fleshy snorkle above water.

Rice shot; as it bobbed and tilted and began sinking in a swirl, the men scooped the soft-shell in. Though dead, for hours the turtle lay oozing blood, twitching and turning, its claws raking the dugout's bottom, serpentine neck writhing about. Rice sliced through the shell's halves and yanked free its plastron.

Huzzah! The turtle was a she, bulging with eggs. The company feasted on turtle fried in hog fat, fried turtle eggs, and turtle soup, "which," wrote Cresswell, "made us an excellent supper." They boarded to drift the night and with a full moon they made good time and a cool breeze kept those on watch awake.

Clark reckoned they were below the Scioto.[20] As the early-morning sun burned off the haze, they landed on an island marked on their charts as being fourteen miles past the river's mouth[21] and walked to an array of sand circles to dig the turtle eggs from the halos. Slitting the leathery shells to mash out the yolks and embryos, they whipped up a batch of pancakes "equal in goodness to those made with hen's eggs," Cresswell declared.

The crew chopped a sapling into a mast, rigged it with a sail, and fixed it to the *Union*. Gusts shifted northwest, then west; the men could not fight such a headwind and stripped the mast and tossed it overboard. Cresswell and Rice shot turkeys—"an excellent supper."

Wednesday, May 17, those on watch had slept; luckily they had not run aground, but high water had so altered the shore that Clark was not sure how much farther they had to go. They floated past a rivulet Ben Johnston guessed was Bracken Creek, ten miles above the Little Miami.[22] Nourse saw turkeys strutting the banks and shot and steered the *Union* ashore. Tom Ruby's limb lines baited with fresh liver reaped a cat. Edmund Taylor and Cresswell, along with George Rice, Ben Johnston, and Captain Clark, took the dogs hunting; by dusk Clark had hoppused a buck to camp. Then, barks and two shots. Cresswell and Johnston ran and saw Rice and Taylor ducking behind a tree, Rice charging his piece. One hundred yards away hunkered a wounded buffalo. Rice fired.

The bull bolted a quarter mile, dogs nipping hooves. Then he stopped and just stood, a mighty, shaggy-headed, black-eyed foe, pawing and wheezing blood, as the hunters jogged up to end him. He weighed a half a ton, "from his breast to the top of his shoulders measuring 3 feet, from his nose to his tail 9 feet 6 inches." "We eat all day long," wrote Nourse, "from turkey to beef, from Beef to Venison, fish, &c." Cresswell spent two days making jerk.

> The meat is first cut from the bones in thin slices like beef steaks, then four forked sticks are stuck in the ground in a square form and small sticks laid on these forks in the form of a gridiron about three feet from the ground. The meat is laid on this and a slow fire put under it, and turned until it is done.[23]

On Friday the nineteenth, they neared the Great Miami. Supper was catfish and jerk. They spied an elk and bear—both out of range. "Were rather imprudent in having a fire so late on shore, it being quite dark before we quitted it," wrote Nourse as the men reboarded.

They had not seen the Kentucky: Had they drifted too far?

The heat drove the men's tempers skyward, and moods soured when lighting and rumbling thunderheads brought rain. Cresswell squeezed off a shot at the tawny blur of a panther; the big cat bounded along the shore to leap into the scrub. They moored to a stump, passing a sultry night bobbing with the chop.

Sunday they arrived at the Kentucky, rain falling, men grumbling; they rowed to a point thick with beech, where Cresswell helped set up Nourse's tent as he shaved and shirted, and the two passed the day and night dry. Outside, the men slept without fire, their dogs baying at howling wolves drawing near. "Had Indians been near," Nourse said, "they might have found us by the Dogs."

Anxious to go, the men boarded. Miles later they got to Drennon's Lick. Named for Jacob Drennon, who, with Matthew Bracken, explored there in 1773, Drennon's was a fifty-acre blue-black stamping ground pocked by wallows and ribboned by traces.[24] Buffalo rubbing against the few trees there had girdled them about their middles. No grass grew around the lick; the ground was so scalloped out from the herds devouring the salty dirt that Drennon's resembled a colossal beehive of cavernous, half-covered, thin-walled pits.[25]

The *Union* scraped along, men rowing and poling. They patrolled the banks at shallow stretches, one on each side, pushing through cattails and reeds head-high, stumbling in bottoms made mucky by rain. Buffalo sign was abundant. Parakeets and passenger pigeons whooshed and scattered by the score. Cresswell put in his stint; by noon the waters deepened.

Hours later, they shot a deer. Twilight slipped into night.

Nourse's men promised to put out the fire when they finished cooking and he retired, awakening to an orange-yellow illumination. He stormed out, the crew scrambling to douse the flames, wolves smelling meat, the dogs skulking about and howling as the wolves yawped back. "All hands well tired and Damned cross," wrote Cresswell Monday, May 22.

By Tuesday afternoon, they had gone thirty miles up Kentucky and dragged the *Union* over shoals into calmer waters. At a ford merging with a trace two wagons wide and four feet deep and edged with sloping borders, the men shot two yearlings and cut out the best meat.

Wednesday morning, May 24. Cresswell's journal:

> Surrounded 30 Buffaloes as they were crossing the River, shot two young Heifers and caught two calves alive whose ears we marked and turned them out again. About noon Captn. Michael Cresop met us . . . it is about 100 miles to Harwood's Landing the place our company intends to take up land. No danger of Indians. Captn. Clark left us.[26]

Buffalo are "fierce if wounded," Cresswell observed. "If you get to leeward of them you may go up to them, or at least within shot, but if you are windward, they run long before they see you."[27]

Wednesday they camped at a trace crossroads. Dragging the twin-bows clear and supping on wild beef, they pricked and primed and spread blankets. Ben Johnston bedded down in a dugout, awaking hours later, his screams alerting the men to a buffalo drove trotting through camp and splashing into the river, hurdling Johnston's dugout and smashing through the second. Splintered and cracked, with fourteen-foot splits along the hull and the stern underwater, the men spent Thursday, May 25, caulking the *Union* "with the bark of the white elm pounded to a paste, which is tough and glutinous."

Sweat rolled off them as they toiled on Thursday, cursing the heat and their broken vessel. In the melee, buffalo had kicked their flour keg overboard; someone rescued it and pried it open to dump the soggy flour on a tent cloth to dry, but they threw the filthy mush away, forcing them to reduce rations to one pint per day per man.

Friday morning, May 26, the *Union* crept up the Kentucky and they shot an old bull—someone had notched its ears years before, Cresswell saw—while skirting over shoals, steering past rocks, tying ropes to the bow to slog along the shore. The cool water provided relief, but cordelling under the sun was made worse by brushing against tick-infested sumac.[28]

Saturday: The morning's currents swept them past a gravelly islet of cedars, and they beached at Elkhorn Creek when winds kicked up. Cresswell retired to Nourse's tent: "Rice does everything in his power to quarrel with me, am determined not to give the first affront." The men, tired, grumbling, and hungry, did not build a shelter, hoping for the clouds to pass. The thunder came about midnight, with lightning candelabraed against the black sky, then a pummel of steps as the crew scrambled for trees and blankets, Nourse's tent flaps parting as Ben Johnston and Edmund Taylor crept in. Hours later, the claps diminished to faraway booms, and the rain moved off as the forces retired.

Sunday morning broke clear. Nourse stropped his razor and walked to the creek's edge and wet a soap bar to sop and shave off a week's beard. Returning to his tent, he dressed in the cleanest clothes he had. At 2:30 P.M. both men and dogs clambered aboard.

Two and a half hours later came a rumble they heard and briefly felt, as buffalo bounded up and over the Kentucky and across a ford. "A great quantity," Nourse wrote. "All sizes."

All hands grabbed guns, powderhorns, and shot bags and bailed out of the *Union* nudging to shore. Taylor came running back with word of three downed buffalo; behind him were the hunters clutching hearts, tongues, and shank bones. "Our stupid company will not stay to jerk any meat, tho' we are in want of provisions," said Cresswell, who shot a yearling. They camped on an islet and feasted.

6:00 A.M. Monday, May 29. They poled up the Kentucky, eyes alert for the great trace that Reuben Taylor said would lead to a tract his cousin Hancock had surveyed for him a year before. Four hours passed. As the men steered to shore to eat breakfast and disembarked, suddenly Rice swung on Cresswell, cursing. Cresswell turned, startled, as Rice vented his wrath, punctuating his profanity with a tomahawk, threatening to kill him. Cresswell shouted back, and both grabbed for guns as Nourse stepped between them. "I have expected this for sometime," Cresswell wrote, reckoning Rice, fearing Indians, had choreographed this to get out of his contract. It worked: He fired him.[29]

Beaching the next day at the trace bisecting the Kentucky, Nourse, Taylor, and Rice hiked overland along this path "as well trodden as a market-town path for about twelve miles" eastward to Elkhorn Creek,[30] stampeding five buffalo herds. Rice shot a calf, and the men cut forks to roast the "heart, liver, kidneys, sweetbread and about ten pounds of the best meat."

Here, bottomland was

> timbered with oak . . . sugar trees, Walnut, Ash, and Buckeye . . . the growth of grass under amazing—blue grass, white clover, buffalo grass and seed knee & waist high: what would be called a fine swath of Grass in cultivated Meadows.[31]

On Wednesday, May 31, the three returned to camp. Ruby landed a forty-pound catfish measuring six inches from eye to eye. Nourse cleaned his gun. Cresswell reflected: The trip had been an adventure, but all the good land, he feared, had already been surveyed. And then there was Rice.

Thursday, June 1. Nourse rousted them at 5:00 A.M; undertows forced them to pole the *Union* against rapids three times in as many hours before beaching her at a trace arcing down the bank. Buffalo had trodden the trace bare, its rounded walls and belly a dusty, stratified bric-a-brac of rock, earth, and pebbles appearing "to be paved." The men walked to a spring, stepping through their dogs scampering past a spiderwort, its green leaves like sprouting spears,[32] bees buzzing about its pastels of blue and purple to gather pollen on bags on their hind legs. Barking shattered their humming as the dogs rushed an old bull buffalo so weak it could not fend them off. The men shot the beast, leaving it without even hacking out the tongue.

Friday, June 2, 6:00 A.M. Eight canoes passed them—"bound for Redstone and Fort Pitt," a man hollered, floating by[33]; one crew stopped to give them half a doe. Cresswell fitted Nourse's tent with an elm bark floor and a slab outside for a mat. "Land good. Pleasant weather. Our company continually quarreling, but I have the good luck to please them all but Rice, whom I treat with contempt."

Saturday the company was poling up the Kentucky. Morning's cumuli grayed, and the crew heaved to shore. Nourse and Cresswell had the tent up in five minutes; the rest slashed elms to patch together a lean-to. By afternoon the deluge ceased, but thunder persuaded them to go no farther. In a day or two they would reach the landing—a day's walk from Harrod's Town.[34]

Sunday, June 4, 1775:

> Cloudy set off about 6 oclock, rowed about 3 hours, rained again, went under a cave in the rocks stayed about 2 hours (having passed six bad ripples this day) about 2 oclock arrived at Harwood's Landing.
> —James Nourse[35]

> Arrived at Harwood's Landing in the evening. Saw a Rattle Snake about 4 feet long. A bark Canoe at the landing. We have been Fourteen days in coming about 120 miles. My right foot much swelled, owing to a hurt I got.
> —Nicholas Cresswell[36]

On Monday morning Nourse, Rice, Taylor, and Johnston packed their budgets; Harrod's Town was a fifteen-mile hike, Johnston told them; his friend John Gabriel Jones lived there. Cresswell's ankle kept him standing off-kilter; he mashed a wad of damp herbs into a poultice to bind with a linen rag around the swell, watching Nourse whittle a sapling into a staff. Ruby, Noland, and Taylor would stay at the landing with Cresswell.

The trace was cluttered with branches and rutted with gullies brimming full after the rains. Sitting five weeks in a boat had not helped their leg muscles; walking with his staff, greatcoat hoppused high upon his back, twice Nourse fell. Johnston hobbled along cramped and sore.

Harrod's Town was "8 or 10 log Cabins without doors nor stopped . . . about 70 acres in Corn."[37] Men feared hunting because of attacks—one had occurred on a trace nine miles from Harrod's—so there was little meat.[38] Mr. Jones fed them "bear fat and hot bread for dinner . . . and hominy for supper, hominy for breakfast."[39] Thom, Jones's servant, filled noggins and trenchers as talk swirled around two topics: land and Indians.

Between the Virginians and the Transylvania Company, much of the land had been claimed. Men from Boiling Springs were throwing up pigsty cabins and claiming every spring within eight hundred miles.[40] But for now they had ceased surveying: Alarmed at the death of four men days before, Harrod's Town and Boonesborough had dispatched spies to reconnoiter.[41]

Nourse's party returned to Harrod's Landing the next day. Half lame, Johnston rode a horse belonging to Mr. Jones, who had sent along Thom to help him get his possessions to Harrod's Town. Talk was sparse and the men kept a sharp eye. By evening they heard the hounds and spotted a fire.

All was well. Ruby's limb lines lay slack. Cresswell's ankle was stronger; more than ever, he was ready to turn back east, but news of the killings, he said, "struck such a panic that I cannot get anyone to go down the Ohio with me on any account." On Wednesday Johnston drew his ration, leaving "about 20 pounds of flour a hand and about 1 gallon of corn," Thom promising to get his baggage to Harrod's on Thursday.

On Thursday, June 8, came a canoe paddled by four men. Greetings hailed the outcasts poling into the shallows. Dressed in breechcloths, leggings, and tattered hunting shirts that barely hid their nakedness, the haggard woodsmen tanned dark as mulberries more resembled river pirates. John Clifton and Joseph Brashears were Americans; Thomas O'Brien from Ireland; the fellow in breeches, Henry Tilling, English, and it was he who declared his crew were "bound up the Ohio to Fort Pitt."

"Determined to go with them," says Cresswell, "but don't much like their looks. A confounded ragged crew." Cresswell, with "three ragged shirts, two pair linen breeches in the same condition, a hunting shirt and jacket, one pair of stockings," was the best dressed among them. He drew his ration: a gallon of salt, two pounds of bacon, two quarts of flour, and a half peck of corn. He cut the *Union*'s lashes to reclaim *Charming Sally.*

They turned in, only to be awakened at 3:00 A.M. Tilling, Clifton, Brashears, and O'Brien were peering through the fog, aiming at apparitions bobbing at the far shore: Thom and George Noland had commandeered *Charming Sally* and stolen two pounds of powder (though they had no gun). The runaways stroked hard, leaped to the bank, and bolted into the darkness.

Friday morning, June 9, Nicholas Cresswell paddled off with Tilling.

JUNE 1775

James Nourse, his leg badly inflamed, rested two weeks at Harrod's Town, applying "British Oil" to slow the swelling, and Tom Ruby thatched him an arbor. Days were muggy and hot; at night he rolled up in his greatcoat. Food was bacon, cornbread, hominy, "boiled beef and buffalo, cabbage plants, Fritters and wheat bread."[42] One day he feasted on a buffalo, endive, and lettuce stew, "as good as ever I would wish . . . but no bread."

Quiet, bearded, and spare, James Harrod shared meals and secured Nourse a horse for £16. Harrod's cabin at Boiling Springs had "a log floor and a chimney, but not stopped." On June 17 Nourse witnessed the flogging of the two runaways, George and Thom.

Knob Lick, Nourse noted Monday, June 19, en route to Boonesborough, was "100 acres without a Stick or Grass." Traces leading to Knob Lick appeared "to be trod as much as any Public road." On Wednesday Nourse, Johnston, and Harrod arrived at Boonesborough, ate buffalo and deer stew, mush mixed with flour and fat, and visited Richard Henderson; eight days earlier Daniel Boone had left for the Yadkin to bring his wife and family to Kentucky.[43]

Nourse recorded his first of two claims on Licking River:

> Where the buffalo path fails continue course till you meet
> with paths that run that way, follow them and they will
> lead you to a very plain buffalo path . . . you come to a
> broad run blazed a tree upon the path to be taken marked
> J. N.[44]

Tuesday morning Boonesborough's gates swung open as Nourse and Tom Ruby departed, joined by David Wilson, North Alexander, Jonathan Jennings and his two sons, Henry and Levi, and a slave.[45] They made thirteen miles, "fell into a buffalo path, passed through some fine land, and some water to a lick called the Blue Lick" (Boone's Blue Lick); Boone's Trace took them past Twitty's Fort, where three months earlier Indians shot two woodcutters and a slave.

> Wednesday, June 28, 1775: missed our way, got up a steep mountain
> beat all about the ridge,—found another steep place, where we got
> down off the Mountain.

> Thursday, June 29: Kept down the buffalo path—crossed a large
> meadow at least a hundred acres—about nine o'clock got into the
> right path.[46]

Near the Rockcastle, they killed a buffalo cow, slit her udders, and drank her milk before barbecuing her. Enduring heat and mosquitoes, bad food (or no food), Monday, July 3, the men forded the Cumberland and rode through the Gap and Powell's Valley. By Friday they neared the Holston to dine with Isaac Bledsoe. On Saturday Nourse crossed the New at Ingles' Ferry and

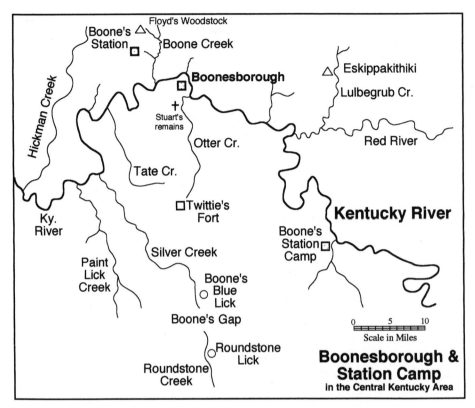

MAP BY NEAL O. HAMMON

jotted the mileage in his last entry at Bristol—"To the town of Fincastle, 46."
Two days later he arrived at the Potomac.

On the first day of Nicholas Cresswell's trip, he and his comrades floated
thirty miles below Harrod's Landing, stopping at a camp to stay the night and
buy jerk. Especially worrisome was *Charming Sally:* The leaking dugout was
mended past repair. Another worry: the flour stores—fifteen pounds to feed
five men. Two days later, on June 11 Cresswell's company got to Drennon's
Lick: "An immense number of Buffaloes." Traces were "as large as most public roads." Buffalo ate the "reddish Clay found near brackish springs," wrote
Cresswell. "I have seen amazing large holes dug or rather cut by them."[47]
Brine formed crusty suds along gurgling pools, and the men boiled sixteen
gallons of water to render a pint of salt.[48]

    The men blasted at 200 buffaloes from a range of twenty yards, "but
killed none." "I suppose here is 50 acres of land trodden by Buffaloes. . . ."

Incredible numbers come here."[49] They fetched a pine canoe from a drift-wood heap, her stern broken, bullet holes punched through her hull[50]; but the holes could be pitched and *Charming Sally*'s stern could be reshaped to fit the canoe, and by the next day the repairs were done.

That day they fell in with more hunters heading to Fort Pitt, a "motley, rascally, and ragged crew": two Irishmen, two Englishmen, two Dutch, a Swede, two Virginians, a mulatto and a slave, a Welshman, and two men from Maryland. The party's three canoes gained the Ohio, watching for the trace leading to Big Bone Lick—a three-mile hike southeast of the river.

Thursday, June 15: Proceeded up the Ohio, where we killed a Buffalo and camped.

Friday, June 16: Killed another Buffalo.[51]

They landed, spending Saturday poking along Big Bone Lick[52]; Indians believed the bones were those of "White Buffaloes" that had died drinking the brine.[53] Huge bones—"of enormous size but decayed and rotten. Ribs 9 inches broad, Thigh bones 10 inches diameter"—littered the banks. The men stripped to dive for souvenirs; Cresswell grabbed an eighteen-inch mastodon tusk, "of good ivory," but "a damned Irish rascal" broke his "Elephant tooth," which so angered him that he could "write no more" that day.

On June 19, eight miles from the mouth of the Miami, they "saw two buffalo bulls crossing the river." Paddling to a bull, the front man grabbed its tail; for half an hour the beast towed them up and down the Ohio. They blasted the bull point-blank eight times; still it swam to shore and lurched off.[54]

They passed the Scioto June 26,[55] Cresswell in the stern steering as Tilling, Clifton, Brashears, and O'Brien prodded the craft on with twelve-foot poles. "All hands very weary and very crabbed." A day later they nearly ran aground, but as they poled to the far shore to float the deeper waters there, Indians two hundred yards above them made haste to cut them off. Four canoes—twenty-one warriors—swept downriver toward the whites.

Terror reigned. Wood and food sailed over the gunwales. Cresswell stoked his musket with "an ounce bullet and seven swan shot," then rammed a pistol ball on top of that: "I was determined to give some of them their quietus." At Tilling's nod, Cresswell leaned on his oar; the other vessels veered sharply, the men digging poles into the bottom as twenty-three more Indians burst from a brake and manned six canoes.

Jacob Nalen's, he a Swede, led the van and bore three rifles. Ten yards behind Nalen was Cresswell's dugout. Of the five aboard her, only two had their smoothbores in order, and O'Brien, nearly dropping his musket in the river, lay flat, crossing himself, thumbing a rosary. Brashears prayed, muttering "Ave Mary's," hugging his wooden crucifix. Bringing up the rear was Williams's craft (he a Welshman) with two muskets.

Clifton and Cresswell took up oars. Tilling was steadfast. Brashears and O'Brien wept, beseeching the Virgin Mary Full of Grace. Cresswell cursed, aimed at O'Brien's head, and threatened "to blow his brains out if he did not take his paddle." O'Brien sat up, howled a prayer to St. Patrick, and stroked—"Desperate as we imagined our situation to be, I could not forbear laughing to see the condition of this poor fellow." Brashears screamed, rocking and nearly capsizing the dugout.

Thirty yards now. Nalen's crew raised up.

"Howdy do, brothers!"

Indian woman in Middle Ground dress and adornment: trade silver, beads, scarlet matchcoat, wool strap dress, neck knife sheath, turkey feather fan with quilled handle. "AHNAWAKE," BY DAVID WRIGHT.

It was Catfish and his Delawares, wanting tobacco and salt. Cresswell, humored by it all, found the Indians pleasant and their women attractive. The gifts given, Catfish thanked them and whisked down the Ohio.[56]

Wednesday afternoon a pounding rain forced the men to land "five miles above Sandy Creek." Cresswell spread his blanket on a log as water swirled through the camp; by morning the Ohio was up four feet.

The crew got to Fort Blair on June 30, to news of April's Boston massacre and the skirmishes at Lexington and Concord. "Yankee men," Cresswell observed, were "the nastiest devils in creation. . . . The army here is ragged, dirty, sickly and ill-disciplined. If my countrymen are beaten by these ragamuffins I shall be much surprised."

Their corn ration had sprouted, but they boiled it and ate it with elk fat. Their jerk cache was a smelly brown mush sloshing in rainwater and swarming with maggots. Brashears hurled the keg into the river. Cresswell scavenged a bloated carp from an eagle.

Near the Great Kanawha, Tilling and Brashears headed overland to Redstone, and Clifton had left a few days before that. Cresswell got to Wheeling on July 9 and lived with some Delawares on the Muskingum. "Employed an Indian Woman to make me a pair of Mockeysons and Leggings. . . . painted by my Squaw in the most elegant manner. Divested of all my clothes, except my Calico short breechclout, leggings, and moccasins."[57]

Months later, worn from bad food and "Bacchanalian excesses," nights spent "feloniously drunk," wenching with so many tavern girls and Indian women that he was "alarmed with symptoms of the itch," Cresswell showed up at James Nourse's on November 6, and the two spent a week together regaling each other with their adventurous tales.

Anticipating America's war with England, already Nourse had enlisted in Virginia's militia. A defender of Crown law, Cresswell could not abide "redhot liberty men," and in June 1777 he sailed from New York back to his father's Suffolk estate, taking with him a tomahawk, a *gastoweh,* snowshoes, and a buffalo powderhorn.[58]

That year, the war spilled violently into the West, pitting nations against nations, red men against white, sparking on both sides a glut of atrocities and terrorism.

"The Warrior," by David Wright.

Warfare & Tactics

Most officers, including Greene, Lincoln, Muhlenberg, Wayne, and Washington himself lamented the large number of rifle-equipped troops who could not be made into useful line infantry until muskets could be found for them.

—De Witt Bailey,
The American Revolution, 1775–1783: An Encyclopedia

With few exceptions the conflict in the back country was largely a defensive struggle waged mainly between the frontier militia and the Indians and Loyalists partisans; it was a war of sporadic, destructive raids on native villages, isolated settlements, and remote garrisons.
—Jack M. Sosin, *The Revolutionary Frontier, 1763–1783*

Lost upon Nicholas Cresswell was America's great irony: Its rabble of citizen-soldiers and fledgling nationhood and blurred social distinctions resulted in a revolutionary social order portending of revolutionary war. Yet "the shot heard 'round the world" on Lexington's green in April 1775, which birthed a nation "dedicated to the proposition that all men are created equal," owed its origin to simple friction—to a sharp, delicately knapped sliver of flint slamming into a frizzen, an L-shaped piece of steel. The "clatch" kicked the frizzen back to expose a tiny pan brimming with black powder and sent sparks sizzling in the pan, which jetted a flame through a hole to detonate a charge that blasted a lead ball down an iron tube and toward its mark.

It was a flash of global irony frozen in space and time: There was a lot of world history and the telling of man's civilization in that shot that ignited fifty or sixty grains of sooty black powder, and with it, U.S. history.

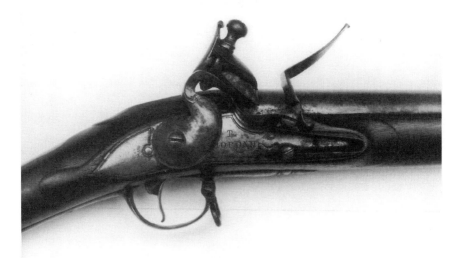

Flintlock mechanism of English Long Land Pattern (or "First Model") Brown Bess musket, c. 1730, showing round-faced cock in uncocked position, flint secured in leather and clenched in cock's jaws, with open frizzen showing the touchhole, barely visible above lip of frizzen pan. Sling swivel on trigger guard. HISTORIC MANSKER'S STATION, GOODLETTSVILLE, TN; PHOTO BY DAVID WRIGHT.

Global irony because this novel form of gun ignition—the flintlock firing mechanism—which the French invented about 1610, was founded upon ancient technology and ancient alchemy.

Striking flint (or chert or amber, which is petrified resin) against tempered iron to create a cascade of sparks to fan into a flame, and from there, fire, hearkens of early man and his first cradles of civilization. Steel and the mystic art of forging peaked in Japan (c. 1600) under Tokugawa Shoguns. In Persia (Iran) that century, Muslim metallurgists of Shia Islam's mystic Sufi sect learned to lap and relap the orange-hot ore upon itself, culminating in the terminal form of hand-forged edged weaponry, damascus. Black powder—an explosive blend of ten parts sulfur to fifteen parts charcoal to seventy-five parts saltpeter—originated in 1000 A.D, mostly to bedazzle Sung emperors with fireworks displays and smoke bombs. Within two centuries, Mongols adapted black powder's use to war, as did Arabs. After the Renaissance, Europeans refined Asian hand cannons to invent sophisticated firearms: the arquebus (matchlock), the wheel lock, and last, the flintlock, the ultimate in eighteenth-century firepower.

Flint, steel, and black powder: Taken together, global irony that on a spring day in 1775 left 250 British dead or wounded, and 146 American colonials, sparking an epic war, the American Revolution.

East of the Blue Ridge, steel was the primary tool of death on the killing fields of the War of Independence fought European style. And, the practical, all-purpose, big-bore musket. Regardless of allegiance—French or British, German or American—and aside from variations, eighteenth-century manual-of-arms tactics were rote and simple: Opposing armies in phalanx formations faced off at one hundred yards or more and waited, sunlight glinting diamonds off polished bayonets aloft and menacing and affixed to musket muzzles on square lugs that served as front sights.

Then—staccato drumming shattered the stillness. Cord side-bands, cinched taut to tighten goatskin heads and gut snares still damp from dew, shifted the drum's timbre from a dull, hollow thud to a sharp, high-end tap that could be heard for a distance.

Alerted, hearts echoed the stark cadence as pulses quickened and nostrils sucked in deep draughts to exhale as gasps from mouths uttering prayers and last wills and testaments to stolid comrades on either shoulder. Eyes cut hard and squinted and widened to stare at the formidable wall before them: men and beasts, muskets and ordnance, a bristling hedge of bayonets, hangers, swords, sabers, spontoons, and halberds.

On command (and every move made was made on command of voice or drum), the vanguard and lines of men behind the front line slow-marched forward, stepping to the beat. Knees low, feet straight, eyes forward. Within forty to sixty yards of each other, the lines pulled up and stopped. Came the orders above the din: "Prepare your firelock!" "Make ready!" "Fire!"

A long *whoosh* of synchronized flash, flame, and smoke belched from muzzles and pans. Smoke shrouded the field and the soldiers. Gunfire merged with cannon blasts—salvos of bullets and grape, canister and round-ball—wreaking havoc upon man and beast, trees and land.

Aiming for pinpoint accuracy had no bearing in the training of rank and file: To "pick off your man" was not a goal. Rather, it was to launch as much lead in the air as possible—bloody walls of it, hurtling along at the speed of sound—and to deliver it in sequential waves obliterating the foe before you. Men yanked from their oiled leather belly boxes prerolled paper cartridges tied and folded that held powder and ball; they bit off the paper's top and sprinkled a few grains under the frizzen to prime the pan, then upended the musket to charge it and ram a .75-caliber one-and-a-half-ounce lead ball with wadding down the barrel; they loaded rapidly, ideally as one body, to achieve four shots per minute. (Often the rate was less than that.)

On order, what was left of the van snapped long arms downward, a brilliant arc of shiny muzzles turning in a single spiraling wave of wood and steel and of white, blue, and red uniforms, rippling the distance of the van's length and ending with gun barrels hovering waist-high above the ground and parallel to it.

Long Land Pattern Brown Bess musket, c. 1730, stocked in walnut, .78 caliber, 46" barrel, wooden rammer and fitted with sling swivels. Front sight is bayonet lug. Note bulbous swell at forestock, a characteristic feature. HISTORIC MANSKER'S STATION, GOODLETTSVILLE, TN; PHOTO BY DAVID WRIGHT.

Bayonets became pole spears as Regulars rushed the lines forward, disemboweling the dying and wounded that they trampled as the horde closed upon itself. Clashing steel and clubbing muskets, the brutality turned hand-to-hand. Victors stood their ground and seized the ground of their foes. Losers panicked and fled. "Draws" were rare.

Such was eighteenth-century warfare as properly conducted on a gentleman's field of honor.

In the Middle Ground—the Revolutionary War's western theater—British-allied Indians were the foes, not redcoats. Americans warred in forests; there was little campaigning choreographed to European standards and scant maneuvering upon pitched battlefields.

Death on the border came by bullets and long knives, tomahawks and war clubs—rarely by fusillades of sustained rounds of musketry and artillery shell. Though smoothbores—fowlers, smooth-rifles, fuzils, and muskets of various sorts—probably outnumbered rifles west of the Blue Ridge, it was the "rifle-gun," able to drop a man at two hundred yards, that gave the much-feared sniping riflemen on both sides a tactical (and psychological) edge. Ordering "Every Man to his Tree"—to fight "Indian-stile" on one's own hook—was standard fare in ambuscades where skirmishes were smaller, yet, when taken in proportion, were as bloody as skirmishes in the East.

Frontiersmen who specialized in brush fighting (called scouts or "spys"), honed such skills to a high art, an art developed by Capt. Robert Rogers during the French and Indian War; Brits adopted Rogers's tactics against Francophile Indians and their Indianesque coureurs de bois and métis allies. During the War for Independence, Butler's Rangers acted as the Crown's guerrillas.

Frontiersmen served as "guerrilla riflemen." In August 1778 Daniel Boone and five stalwarts rafted the Ohio, smeared bear oil and pigment on their faces, and donning head rags and turbans, attacked Paint Creek Town on the Scioto.[1] They killed one Shawnee—Simon Kenton lifted the scalp—and wounded two others, stole horses and peltry, then recrossed the Ohio hell-bent for Boonesborough.

Such was classic border warfare: undisciplined, catch-as-catch-can, brutally raw and bloody. Americans fighting Brits and Indians as Indians. And Brits and Indians reciprocating in kind.

Daniel Boone was not a typical guerrilla fighter. (But his image as the "rippin'est, roarin'est, fightin'est man the frontier ever knew!" stubbornly persists.) Boone—an unchurched Quaker by upbringing, possessing a reflective, philosophical bent and an even disposition that caused him to avoid a fight until forced on him (he admitted to killing three Indians in his adventuresome life)—had, as one relative put it, "little of the war spirit."

But Lewis "Death Wind" Wetzel and Andrew Poe reveled in their abilities to "out-Indian" Indians and in the chase and coup, shooting and reloading on the run. Wetzel, ears bored and silk tassels dangling from each lobe, taunted his prey by growing his hair down to his calves and keeping it clubbed in two tight plaits tied with ribbon—a pair of greasy, raven-hued trophies that went uncollected. Many a time Wetzel returned from the trail silent and taciturn, his dark linen hunting shirt stained with gore, dripping scalps hitched to his sash.

It was blood sport. Bluff and bravado rewarded with scalp bounties and cash from auctioning off booty, rife with glory and exhilaration from hunting the ultimate prey. Capt. Sam Brady and his boys—and Lew Wetzel was one of them—were the best at the lethal game.

Old John Cuppy, the last of Brady's men to die, remembered his captain as a tireless six-footer of lean, rawboned frame, blue eyes, and shoulder-length black hair. "Brady was . . . tall, large—with muscles of steel, when he ran he appeared to fly over obstacles, and never appeared fatigued. He could throw a tomahawk straighter and further than anyone I knew."[2] After surviving Valley Forge, Princeton, and the Paoli massacre, Sam Brady put Fort Pitt under his protectorate and made the region his personal war zone, and keeping open the fork of the Ohio, Monongahela, and Allegheny became his quest.

Brady trained his men as he trained himself, building camaraderie and keeping his troops pert and fit for the trail—a tough cadre of threescore crack-shot spies able to suffer privation without grumbling. "Spies," recalled Cuppy, "often practiced before going on a scout, shooting at a mark, throwing their tomahawks and sticking them in a tree at two or three rods and jumping over fences."

A spy's pay was six shillings and three pence per diem, but it beat army pay and conditions were better, though spies scouted in cold and heat, enduring snakes and mosquitoes. "In cold weather, we would kindle a fire to lie down by, taking off the moccasins and drying them off, and in warm weather, sometimes a small fire to raise smoke for the night to drive off gnats." Wild meat was tolerably finer than hog-and-hominy army rations and hard biscuit, salt pork, and tainted beef from Fort Pitt's commissary. "Sometimes we took along wheat bread, and bacon and flour to make ash cakes, and sometimes chocolate;

and could always get venison, turkies, and sometimes bear meat, but never any parched corn meal."[3]

Eschewing regimental coats, weskits, and breeches worn by enlisted men, Brady, observed Cuppy, insisted that his charge dress in part-Indian, part-white, a versatile blend of woodland wear.

> Spy dress—a handkerchief tied around the spy's head of any color, sometimes a capeau (shorter than a hunting shirt) of cloth or a hunting shirt and moccasins; and thick, loose woolen leggings reaching above the knee, so thick that a rattlesnake could not penetrate through with their fangs.[4]

One ranger wore war paint and a coonskin cap topped with a hawk feather. Leggings of wool or deerskin deflected pit viper fangs, but a timber rattler struck Thomas Edginton during a sortie on the Tuscarawas River—"his woolen leggings having parted, and down on that leg, left it exposed."[5] Brady called off the chase. With two ponies, some hickory saplings, and a blanket, he rigged up a horse litter to get Edginton—"much suffering from the bite"—to Fort Pitt for treatment. Three months later, Edginton resumed his place with Brady; on his next mission, Indians seized the ill-fated man, and he spent two years a Shawnee captive.

Gen. "Mad" Anthony Wayne in April 1793 employed Sam Brady, John Cuppy, and six scouts, who descended the Ohio in a keelboat with one hundred Regulars. On a dare, Captain Brady challenged Wayne's army to a shooting match. Wayne, much amused at the audacity of this frontiersman, offered a keg of whiskey to the winning side. The mark was "a piece of white paper the size of a silver dollar placed on a tree sixty paces away." Shots were to be fired offhand.

Wayne's Regulars blazed away. Out of one hundred musket rounds, one nicked the mark.

Brady and his riflemen checked their pieces and fired. Each man hit the mark "save one and his ball hit right beside it." Hezekiah Bukey, a master trick shooter, stuck "a knife with the point in on the under limb of a tree, so the edge of the blade was facing him, and fired at thirty paces off hand and split the ball on the edge of the knife."[6] After Bukey's exhibition, Wayne's men gave it up. The keg staved in, Brady's men commenced to "dipping in their cups, becoming quite merry on their grog."

Such was guerrilla warfare in America's first Far West.

CHAPTER FIVE

The Pathfinder

WINTER 1777

Along the American Revolutionary War's western front, Kentuckians marked 1777's grim harvest as the bloody "Year of the Three Sevens." Torched cabins; bloated, mutilated corpses of men, women, and children; cadres of walking wounded; burned crops; and slaughtered cattle, hogs, and goats left nerves frayed and ragged, bringing cries of lamentation to settlers south of the Beautiful River.

Settlers did not grieve alone: Death songs filled longhouses and wigwams throughout Ohio land. On October 10 the renowned Shawanoe chieftain and warlord at Point Pleasant, Cornstalk, his son Elinipsico, and two other warriors, Red Hawk and Petalla, were bayoneted under a flag of truce during a parley at Fort Randolph, Virginia. Fort Randolph's commander knew he had little time, but sharpening a turkey quill was a task for Col. William Fleming, seated at his desk set wobbly on the puncheon floor. Pared down, the translucent nib had become a sliver as he scooped a shallow crescent from its rear, shaved fuzz off its underside, and slit, imperceptibly, its tiny square tip. He laid the quill by his inkwell sitting near a strand of wampum.

Odd. This tiniest of movements caused Colonel Fleming, age forty-eight, to wince. Not so much from actual pain, but from the memory of the searing buck-and-ball blast that parted his arm and shoulder during Col. Andrew Lewis's Point Pleasant campaign. Col. John Todd had visited him daily as he lay convalescing to help him with his journal, Fleming dictating his words to Todd. From the looks of the twisted, pale blue sheathing of proud flesh hardening over the reddish scar, and from his own medical knowledge, which he prided himself in, Fleming knew he would never fully mend.

Shawnee warrior wearing scalplock, slit auricles with sterling ear wheels. Shirt, beads about neck, and breechclout are blue, scarlet stroud leggings with deer hair in metal cones, and fingerwoven garters. "SAUVAGE DE LA NATION DES SHAWANOES," BY JOSEPH WABUN, 1796. BIBLIOTHEQUE NATIONALE, PARIS.

So be it. Now, to the writing. These last few days, the bitter cold that made his arm ache had so frozen the ink that he had had to set it near the hearth to thaw it.

Colonel Fleming dipped his carefully hewn nib and withdrew it, pushing the quill steadily, pausing to gather his words and redip. No less than the fate of Kentucky County, hewn from Fincastle the December before by Gov. Patrick Henry, was at stake. Educated at Edinburgh, his high-toned script lent an authoritative flourish to his missive:

To the Chief and Warriors of the Shawnee Nation—

We are commanded by the Governor of Virginia and his Council of great Men to write you a letter. . . . We are concerned, that the path between your Country and ours should be sprinkled with Blood, and made so Dark, that neither our People nor yours can walk therein; and that our great Council Fire, before which your Fathers and ours, and yourselves and us, have sat and smoked the Pipe of Peace, should now be put out . . . by an Accident.

We are grieved, that this Accident, we mean the Murder of the Cornstalk, his Son and two more of your people should have been committed by Virginians; as it was an Action unworthy of the Character of Warriors and brave Men. . . . We expect you will the more readily overlook it, and not attempt to revenge it on the Innocent & Helpless.

You may, by the Governor's proclamation, know that the Crime is to us an Abhorrence; that a great Reward is offered, and every method fallen upon to bring those People to Justice and if they can be taken, you may be assured they will be tried and punished by our Laws in the same Manner as if they had killed 10 white People.

To avoid for the future, We would invite some of your old wise Men and Warriors to come to the Mouth of the Kanawha, where you will be met by Commissioners, whom our Governor will send there to talk with you, and to hold a Treaty of Peace for the good of both Countries.

But as your People and ours live on this same Land, breathe the same Air, and drink the same Water, we ought to live in Peace like Friends, and take no Notice of the advice of our Enemies, who came over the great Waters to kill us both, or make us kill one another. . . . In the meantime, lay down the War hatchet.

We send you this string of white Wampum, and esteem ourselves Your Friends and Brothers.

> I Remain, Yours Most Truly,
> Col. William Fleming
> Botetourt Militia
> Fort Randolph, Virginia[1]

The courier carrying the important missive to Black Fish was a six-and-a-half-foot-tall woman of great dignity, the Grenadier Squaw, Nonhelema. The Grenadier Squaw was in deep mourning. She was Cornstalk's sister.

Colonel Fleming dared not guess how Black Fish, war chief of the Chillicothes and Cornstalk's successor, would react to his dispatch, which stretched even his credulity. All at the fort knew Patrick McCowan, one of the killers, had gotten off with a mere reprimand, and that McCowan reveled in the glory of his shameful deed.

The voice of Cornstalk's blood, Fleming knew, now cried aloud from his grave, demanding no less than eye-for-an-eye vengeance.

WINTER 1778

For Daniel Boone, the new year began auspiciously.

On February 7, while he was hunting buffalo to feed his men camped on the snowy banks of the Lower Blue Licks, rendering the Lick's brackish water into bushels of coarse, dirty salt so desperately needed by the forted-up Kentuckians, four Shawnees ran him down and tied his hands with tugs and led him to a glen concealing a war party 120 strong. Blue matchcoats edged with gold silk ribbon, and red, gray, green, and brown wool blankets, wool cappo coats, and scarlet regimentals were draped over the warriors warming by a long trough of campfire. Snow near the fire had melted; in the dirt and damp, stroud blanket rolls upon cane piles lay kicked out to the ashes.

In place of blankets, some men used deerskins tanned with the hair left on, hoppusing the hides high on their backs when traveling, shilling-size holes poked along the hides' edges so that, when fording a creek, they could thread branches through the holes to fashion coracles to put their clothing and budgets and accouterments in as they swam or waded, pushing their hide saucers before them.

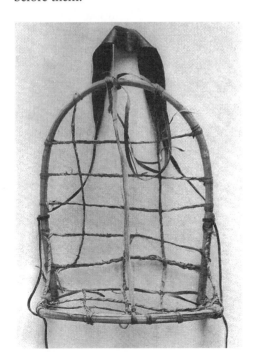

Ojibway packframe of ash or maple and bound with basswood bark, showing tumpline, which was worn across forehead or chest. Bureau of American Ethnology, Smithsonian Institute.

Maple and basswood bark pack frames sat on some blankets. On others, bearhide budgets tied with fifteen-foot tumplines—"Sapper's strings"—woven from nettle and buffalo wool, four fingers wide in the middle tapering to two fingers wide at the ends. Otter turbans adorned with white beads and silver brooches, knives, powderhorns, pipe tomahawks, ball-head war clubs, and roaches of deer tails, turkey beards, and quills were abundant. Propped against trees were *fusils fins*—slim, smoothbore guns, lightweight, stamped with fleur-de-lis proof marks on octagon barrel flats at the breech. As plentiful were English Brown Bess muskets in Long- and Short-Land patterns; the thick-wristed Besses lacked the fusil's grace but were rugged arms, made for service, and much desired. Some Shawanoes carried rifle-guns and trade guns fitted with grotesque serpent side plates cast in brass; where side plates used to be opposite some lock mortises, there were only squared-off iron lugs.

Slung over the shoulders of warriors were leather bags dark from black walnut hull dye, embroidered with red, yellow, white, and black porcupine quills woven into animistic motifs, dripping with deerhair tufts dyed red and crimped in brass cones. Moccasins hung on sticks, drying soles up in smoke rising from the fire. Men chewed jerk or parched cornmeal mixed with sugar and pounded beans or hickory nuts, washing the gruel down with a broth of jerk boiled in water. Some of the red men had slit ears adorned with copper wire, wampum, and sterling ball-and-cones.[2]

So it was then that at this war camp all eyes gazed upon the stocky, brown-haired, blue-eyed, fair-skinned Big Knife captive with the wide mouth. Among them, Boone saw, were a few woods-running Britons; the notorious Capt. Will Emery, the bandit who had twice captured him in 1769 and had despoiled Col. James Knox's Long Hunters; and Louis Lorimier, a much respected French trader who spoke fluent Shawnee.

Lorimier stood barely five foot and was spider thin, his hair a pungent pomade of bear fat and castoreum yanked back in a tight queue, heightening the hawkish jut of his nose, and tied off with a dirty ribbon that dangled to his hips. His knee-length justaucorps was worn and tattered, long devoid of

French fusil fin, c. 1730, with octagon-to-round 57" barrel, walnut stock, 24 gauge (.58 caliber), and an overall length of 73¹/₂". PHOTO BY DAVID WRIGHT.

epaulets or gold braid, and he wore leggings with a breechclout and elaborately quilled moccasins.[3] He was a veteran of the Seven Years' War, and his honesty had gained him respect at Piqua Town, where he and his Shawnee wife, Charolotte Pemanpieh Bougainville, operated his famous trading post, which was a bustling hub of exchange. Now allied with the British, Louis Lorimier—a sagacious diplomat and go-between, a gentleman of Old World polish and manners—enjoyed tremendous influence in Ohio land among Indians and whites alike.

Pompey, a young African, was with them too. During a raid years before, the Shawnees had kidnapped Black Dick.[4] Pompey interpreted for Boone and Black Fish, the imposing, sturdily built war chieftain, who informed Boone that he and his men were en route to burn Boonesborough and kill all of the people there to avenge Cornstalk's murder.

First, though, he was going to kill Boone's men at the Lower Blue Licks who were boiling water into salt. His scouts, Black Fish said, had spotted smoke billowing from the near-continuous fires stoking the white men's big iron kettles and heard their axes and had spied them out as Boone's men worked on, unaware.

At dawn the next day, in a wild bet to head off a mass execution, and then the slaughter of the defenseless Kentuckians at the yet unfinished fort, Boone, bound and under guard, led Black Fish's delegation to the Licks as the war party fanned out into the surrounding thickets. As the salt boilers realized the Shawnees were upon them and frantically kicked out of their blankets to grope for guns, powderhorns, and shot bags, Boone shouted: "Don't fire!—if you do, all will be massacred!" and so he gave them up, his men staking arms.

Black Fish's magnificent coup—nearly thirty Long Knives taken and not a shot fired!—atoned for Cornstalk's death, protected his men, and restored Shawnee honor. But Louis Lorimier argued with Black Fish to press on to Boonesborough. It could be easily taken, he said. The younger Shawanoes, hot for a blood reckoning and desirous of loot and scalps, sided with the French trader as Black Fish wavered, reconsidering his deal struck with Boone the day before. Boone's salt boilers never knew how close they were to being slaughtered until they heard their captain's impassioned plea when he addressed Black Fish's council of war:

> Brothers . . . You have got all my young men; to kill
> them, as has been suggested, would displease the Great
> Spirit, and you could not then expect future success in
> hunting nor war. If you spare them, they will make you
> fine warriors, and excellent hunters to kill game for your

squaws and children. These young men have done you
no harm, they were engaged in a peaceful occupation,
and unresistingly surrendered upon my assurance that
such a course was the only safe one for them; and I con-
sented to their capitulation, on the express condition that
they should be made prisoners of war and treated well. I
now appeal both to your honor and your humanity; spare
them, and the Great Spirit will smile upon you.

Black Fish spared them, but at first it seemed the Great Spirit did not
smile upon Captain Boone.

Quickly stomped out in the ankle-deep snow, the gauntlet's path
stretched maybe one hundred yards, gloating warriors capering along its edges
in bold display. A shivering aisle of lashing switches, hickory wiping sticks,
and war clubs rising and falling to the fell whoops of war as the Shawanoes ca-
joled and stamped before the captured White Eyes.

Black Fish steered him through their midst to the row's open end and
told Captain Boone, speaking through black Pompey, to try to run to the pole
at the row's far end, to not fall down. Else he would be beaten to death.

But Boone, stripping to his clout and leggings, unexpectedly charged.
Veering, he feinted left then right, cutting back side-to-side, clipping thighs
and knees as he hurtled like a stone from a sling down the narrowing lane of
strident voices and thrashing limbs that tightened into a shoulder-wide alley
of waving canes and clubs. He staggered on, ignoring his torn neck and bleeding back, only to spy a broad, squatty fellow, greasy and menacing, blocking
the path's end. Boone braced himself and rushed head-down, head-butting
him in the gut like a he-goat. He hurdled the prostrate warrior and seized the
post. Only then did he hear their gales of laughter.

Hi-yah!

Black Fish was very pleased. Captain Boone, he acknowledged, was a
great warrior.

With the whites in tow and heaped high with kettles and their own property that was now Shawanoe booty, for ten days the reds trudged along snowy
traces to the Ohio, living on meager rations of jerk and parched corn, and
after that ran out, slippery elm broth. One warrior shot a deer; the men devoured it entrails and all. Captives and captors crossed the icy Ohio twenty at
a time in their buffalo-hide ferry boat. Days later the Shawnees entered Old
Chillicothe in glory, driving their prisoners before them in the leg-deep snow,
forcing them all, save Boone, to run a long gauntlet in which all the villagers
participated. All the salt boilers survived, though Ansel Goodman, stripped

naked and his hands tied with buffalo tugs, was so severely beaten and bruised that he was barely able to stagger to the gauntlet's end.

Indian families adopted many of the whites. But the pig-headed ones—James Callaway, Nathaniel Bullock, Jesse Copher, Ben Kelly, Bartlett Searcy, and eight or nine others—they marched to Detroit to exchange for each American hostage £100 bounties in sterling ear-bobs, ear-wheels, brooches, noserings, and arm- and wristbands, as well as powder and lead. The redcoats clapped irons about the captives to ship most of them to Canadian gaols; some Americans they kept at Detroit; a few were shackled and sent to rot in the hated prison hulks moored in Montreal.[5]

Black Fish adopted Boone. He and his wife loved Sheltowee—"Big Turtle," a name befitting his robust stature and tenacity for life—as if he were flesh of their flesh, bone of their bone. But Sheltowee the ingrate fooled his parents into thinking he was content.

That May Andrew Johnson, the first of Boone's salt boilers to escape, fled from Old Chillicothe straight to Harrod's Town, bringing with him the first real news of his comrades' fates and what had really happened at the Lower Blue Licks on February 8. Johnson brought with him something else: He knew the way to the Shawanoe towns, something previously unknown. Johnson stayed at Harrod's Town for two weeks—recuperating and planning—then, with William Whitely, Nehemiah Pore, and a few others, he rafted across the Ohio to attack a Indian hunting camp, killing one or two Shawnees and stealing back seven horses.

On Saturday afternoon, June 20, a stout man in Indian garb and having roached hair and clutching in one hand a crudely stocked rifle with its lock tied on with a whang, and in the other a roasted buffalo tongue, stepped from the sycamore grove lining the Kentucky's west bank, crossed the stump-filled ground to Boonesborough's gates, and hailed the fort.

It was Daniel Boone.

All were stunned. Many were glad to see him. Others were not so sure.

Save for Boone and Johnson, all the salt boilers, the flower of Kentucky's youth, were still missing. Many were adopted white Indians, and others were feared dead or rotting in French-Canadian prison barges. Andrew Johnson's talk that Boone surrendered his men rankled Kentuckians. Hints that Boone was a traitor already were circulating.

William Hancock, the third to escape, arrived July 17 with ominous news of a big war party forming to be led in part by Brits and coureurs de bois and Black Fish.[6] Poor Hancock: He had fled from his Indian father, Captain Will, and Old Chillicothe naked; in crossing the flooded Ohio, his log and grapevine raft hung on some flotsam and swept him twenty miles downriver. Exhausted and starving, more than once he had all but given up during his week of wandering, when at last he saw a tree with his brother's name carved on it, got his bearings, and made for Boonesborough.[7]

Col. Richard Callaway took Hancock's deposition after the men carried him inside the fort: "The Indians informed that they should come four hundred strong and offer the English flag to the inhabitants, and if the terms were rejected, they intended to batter down our fort with their swivels, as they are said to have four sent them from Detroit."[8]

William Hancock did not stop there. While Daniel Boone was at Detroit, dining with the much despised Lt. Gov. Henry "Hair Buyer" Hamilton and accepting his gifts and supping his fine wine and filling himself upon the king's dainties, he deposed, Captain Boone "agreed with the british officers that . . . the fort should be give up, and that the people should be taken to Detroyt and live under the Juresection of this graceous Manjesty King George III."[9]

To Colonel Callaway, and to others, such as Col. Benjamin Logan, this was sedition. Boone should be court-martialed, they said.

Yes, Boone said to his inquisitors, Hancock spoke the truth, but there were reasons behind his duplicity—"he was a Deceiving the Britesh officers and Indians," he explained. Besides, his actions spoke for themselves. A fight to the death was nearing; he had returned "home to help his own people fight and they must make what preperration they could but the indeans would certainly be their in a few days."

Boone wrote his own dispatch to Col. Arthur Campbell of Virginia a day later.

Boonesborough, 18th July, 1778

Dear Colonel:

Enclosed is my deposition with that of Mr. Hancock, who arrived here yesterday. He informed us of both French and Indians coming against us to the number of near four hundred, whom I expect here in twelve days from this. If men can be sent to us in five or six weeks, it would be of infinite service, as we shall lay up provisions for a siege. We are all in fine spirits, and have good crops growing, and intend to fight hard in order to secure them. I shall refer you to the bearer for particulars of this country.

I am, &. etc.
Daniel Boone[10]

Men from Logan's Station—perhaps fifteen—rushed to Boonesborough's aid. Harrod's Town sent what men could be spared.

Boone, stung by Callaway's accusations and anxious to restore his reputation, hit upon a plan to learn the enemy's strength: a preemptive strike on a Shawnee camp on Paint Creek. Colonel Callaway, one of the two ranking officers at Boonesborough (Maj. William Bailey Smith being the other), opposed it. Undaunted, on August 30 Boone and eighteen handpicked woodsmen smeared their faces with vermilion, wrapped turbans about their heads, and shedding breeches and stockings for leggings and breechcloths, crossed the Ohio and attacked.

They got back on September 6 with some plunder, one scalp lifted by Simon Kenton, and some very bad news: Black Fish's forces were hours away.

As the next day's dawn lifted, Black Fish and nearly 450 warriors, some British officers, and a few French-Canadians appeared on Hackberry Ridge overlooking Boonesborough. After two days of parleys, the masquerade imploded, precipitating a nine-day siege. Thirty-seven Indians and Pompey, the black Shawnee, died in the attack.[11] Two defenders—one black and one white—were killed.

And yet, though Boonesborough was spared, it was a time of casting about blame and suspicion, a time of recrimination. Behind the fort were two fresh graves; twenty-five young men were missing and feared dead—among them, Col. Richard Callaway's two nephews. James Callaway had been shipped to Canada; Micajah was living life as a Shawnee. Boone, Colonel Callaway said, was to blame for all of it, and he demanded Boone be tried for treason.

That October, Boone's court-martial trial was held at Logan's Station, established in 1775 by Col. Ben Logan and Col. John Floyd.

Colonel Callaway spoke first. His charges: When the Shawnees caught Boone, he was alone, ten miles from camp. To save his own life, he had surrendered his own men; at Detroit he had struck an unholy bargain with the "Hair Buyer," Henry Hamilton. Boone's reckless raid on Paint Creek had dangerously weakened Boonesborough's defenses and had actually incited Black Fish to attack. Finally, Boone's offhanded willingness before the siege to parley beyond range of the fort's marksmen perched on the palisades put all of Boonesborough's officers at risk.

Concluded Callaway, the prosecutor: "Boon was in favour of the britesh . . . all his conduct proved it." Callaway took his seat.

The defendant rose and, after being sworn in, stoically faced his accusers.

Daniel Trabue, a young Virginian who had arrived at Logan's that spring, recounted the tense moment as Boone gave account of his actions:

> Capt. Daniel Boon sayed the reason he give up these men
> at the blue licks was that the Indeans told him they was
> going to Boonesbourough to take the fort. Boon said he

Excerpt of Boone's court-martial from Daniel Trabue's narrative. DRAPER MANUSCRIPTS 57J:33; STATE HISTORICAL SOCIETY OF WISCONSIN.

thought he would use some stratigem. He thought the fort was in bad order and that the Indeans would take it easy. He (Boon) said he told the Indians the fort was very strong and too many men for them, that he was friendly to them (and the officers at Detroyt) and he would go and shew them some men—to wit, 26—and he would go with them to Detroyt and these men also, and when they come to take Boonesbourough they must have more warriers than they now had. Boon said he told them all these tails to fool them.[12]

Callaway protested. Boone, he retorted, "ought to be broak of his commission."

But "Boon," said Trabue, "insested other wise."

The jurors were not long in rendering their verdict: not guilty. To underscore their vindication they promoted Boone to major of the militia.

Kentuckians debated the issue for years, but Daniel Boone, always sensitive to criticism and deeply wounded by the episode, rarely spoke of the matter.[13]

Earlier that summer, as Boonesborough swirled with gossip, Rebecca Boone had returned east with her brood: Levina, twelve; Rebecca, ten; Israel, nineteen; Daniel Morgan, nine; and five-year-old Jesse Bryan. After his acquittal, Daniel rode back to the Yadkin, sixteen-year-old Jemima Boone Callaway and her husband, Flanders, riding alongside with Boone's son-in-law, William Hays.

By mid-November Boone had found his "little girl" at the farm of her Uncle Billy Bryan and moved his family into a cabin belonging to his in-laws, Joseph and Aylee Bryan. For Boone and his in-laws, it was not a happy reunion. "The history of my going home forms a series of difficulties, an account of which would swell a volume."[14]

He hunted the Blue Ridge that winter; Rebecca loathed returning to Boonesborough's rumor-mongering and through the land soiled with her firstborn's blood, but Virginia's House of Delegates had declared the holdings of North Carolina's Transylvania Company—Col. Richard Henderson's estate of some twenty million acres—"null and void" and planned to reallocate all land sales, granting four hundred acres with an optional thousand-acre preemption to any man erecting a cabin and planting a corn crop.[15]

By September 1779 Daniel had little choice: He had to return due to the insolvency of his Transylvania claims. As always, many were ready to follow him.

The emigrants—friends, relatives, adventurers—numbered fivescore, the biggest wave of Kentucky-bound whites since James Harrod had tried to settle there in 1774. Spirits ran high, but emotions filled those leaving homes and kith and kin behind. British guerrilla raids along the Tidewater and the southern colonies had raised war fevers white hot, sundering families and friends into rebel or Tory camps. Arsonists torched Tory crops and cabins. Patriots seized king's men, stripped and tarred and feathered them and, if they survived that, ran them out of town straddling a beam. Willing to risk all, many Tories believed they would fare better in the West, where life's struggle blurred allegiances.

And there was a more sure voice beckoning westering whites: land!

By late September 1779 the North Carolinians had fitted bulging packs, portmanteaus, haversacks stuffed with jerk, and knapsacks to horses, to livestock, to men's backs, and loaded churns and kettles into ox-driven carts. They packed, giving away what they could not take.

One hundred strong. Boone and his family. Mr. and Mrs. Levy Dickey. Families like John Dobson's and William Bryan's, Boone's brother-in-law. And John Longnecker, Andrew Ireland, and a host of others.

Robert, James, and Peter—Samuel Houston's teenage boys hailing from the Shenandoah Valley—drove a dozen cows and six horses burdened with axes, cane hoes, a sifter and churn, and two thirty-gallon malt kettles fixed over a packsaddle atop a bullock. For Daniel, transporting his two big-bore wall guns (a gift from Col. James Carter of Rowan County's militia to defend Boone's proposed new settlement) would prove taxing.[16]

"We began our journey all afoot," recalled one of the pioneers who made the epic trek. Weeping, the departing hugged those remaining. A curt HEP!; a commemorative volley to salute those left behind; and Boone's cavalcade lurched forward in the direction of the Clinch. Rain had pushed the river out of its banks. After a day and a night's wait, still the surge ran strong and many feared crossing.

"Follow me," called out a voice. It was Jemima Boone, kneeing her pony to the front of the van. Behind her sat little Jane Dobson, John Dobson's eight-year-old girl. Jemima plunged in. Behind her, the throng snaked along. Horses and cattle staggered as mud grabbed hooves and wheel rims.

Suddenly, in the river's midst, Jemima's horse reared, catapulting the two girls into the cold water, and John Dobson and some boys dove in to fish them out and get them to shore and strike fire. Jane sat gasping, but Jemima swam to the bank, laughing. "A ducking is very disagreeable this chilly day, but much less so than capture by the Indians," she said, and from that day on, her family would call her by her nickname, "Duck."

Remembering well the Powell Valley tragedy in 1773, Major Boone faithfully made his rounds, offering encouragement to his guards standing two-hour shifts. By October 9 Boone had his own problems. His lead mare, laboring under the weight of the heavy swivel guns, suddenly dropped dead, forcing Boone to cache his pair of heavy barreled, big caliber amusettes.[17] To transport his churn and the sifter and free up a horse for the women, Boone axed down a sapling, trimmed its fork into two five-foot-long sled runners, notched three branches to sit crosswise over them, tied them on with bark strips, and fitted a bark mat in the wood sled's center.[18]

On clear nights, families slept out under blankets, buffalo robes, deerhides. On rainy nights, the travelers erected half faces topped with bark and newly fallen leaves. "We thought we were living in luxury," said one, "until we exhausted our salt." October 17 they struck Boone's Trace. Five days later the emigrants "were received with rapturous delight" at Boonesborough.[19] Dick Callaway, though, continued to direct his venom at Boone, who spent the last weeks of 1779 waiting for his claims to be approved so he could leave Boonesborough and establish his new fort, Boone's Station.

Even upon returning and securing his land, for Boone it was hardly a season of rejoicing. Col. John Bowman had raided Old Chillicothe the spring before, and Shawnees heeding Black Fish's cries had pushed the fighting Kentuckians back to the Ohio. Bowman's militia claimed few casualties but stole plenty of corn and horses and heaped up valuable loot—clothing, trade silver, and Simon Girty's scarlet vest and double-barreled gun. Black Fish—"dressed in a beautiful white shirt richly trimmed with brooches and other silver ornaments"—was shot in the thigh.[20] It took Boone's Indian father six weeks to die of gangrene poisoning.

In December 26, 1779, Dan and Rebecca, again heavy with child, along with their kin—William Scholl, Ned and Samuel Boone and their families, and William and Susannah Hays among them—left Boonesborough and rode six miles northwest to Boone's four-hundred-acre tract on Boofman's Fork, erecting open-faced huts during the Hard Winter, eating "buffalo, bear, deer, and turkeys—all very lean and poor."[21]

In February 1780 Boone and his cohorts rode to Virginia to register Kentucky land claims. In his saddlebags he carried $20,000 in depreciated Continental currency, cash friends entrusted to him to secure their surveys. On the way, the men stopped at an inn. After supper, Boone arranged a buffalo robe on the floor before the fireplace and bedded down. When he awoke well past dawn, his first groggy thought was of his money bag. He searched, but it was gone—stolen.

It was a hard blow for a man who struggled to provide for his family, especially so since Virginia had voided the claims of Henderson's Transylvania Company. Boone was never compensated for his land, nor for blazing the Wilderness Road. With the theft came the inevitable accusations that he had squandered the cash. Many, like Thomas and Nathaniel Hart, rallied to his defense, but Boone sold what was left of his land to pay off the debt to clear his name.[22]

In March 1780 settlers at Boone's Station dismantled their lean-tos to salvage what timber they could for cabins and stockades. The men augered loops in the palisades, pegged walls, chinked cracks with mud and buffalo wool or mud and deerhair, dug fire pits, put up mud and wattle and rock chimneys. So it was then during the spring thaw and with the rise of Daniel's fort that the Boone's rejoiced at the birth of their last child, Nathan, born on the third.

The Kentuckians busied themselves shooting buffalo for meat, shearing the hides free of black and brown wool. Tough, easy to card and spin once washed and combed free of cockleburs and mud, they wove the two-ply wool into stockings so durable, one declared, that such hose "would have served an Israelite during his forty year march through the wilderness."[23] Women made an equally durable cloth with warp threads, those that ran lengthwise in the loom, of nettle fiber, and woven with woof threads, those that crossed the warp, spun from the buffalo's wool.

Peter Houston warmed water in his thirty-gallon malt kettles, stirred in alum, salt, ashes, and deerskins, and a day or two later, after the hair slipped free, he scraped the flesh sides free of clots, flesh, sinew, and gristle, and pulled and stretched them dry. Of these, Houston said, "leather trousers and jackets were made; principally for the men, but some of the women were under the necessity of wearing them." Houston smeared his tanning decoction on buffalo hides to slip the wool, covering "the flesh side with the solution made the consistency of paste."[24]

Then, in April 1780, came more attacks as redcoats at Detroit made ready to assault Americans south of the Ohio. Gen. George Rogers Clark— the Long Knife's fame had peaked after his British conquests in the Northwest the year before—marched his men to the forks of the Ohio and Mississippi near Mayfield Creek to build Fort Jefferson to try to hold the West against Chickasaws led by white and mixed-blood partisans. Fort Jefferson—garrisoned by 225 militia and 275 civilians—was occupied for thirteen months, twenty days.

The Chickasaws harassing Fort Jefferson, the Lakes Indians invested Vincennes while another detachment struck the settlements near the Falls to create cover for Capt. Henry Bird's army of Ohio Indians, Rangers, and Regulars en route with two fieldpieces. Bird reached Cincinnati on June 9. After a parley with the Shawnee, his party crossed the Ohio and struck a trace ribboning the Licking to Kentucky's interior. With the artillery, it was no contest: Ruddell's Station surrendered June 25; Martin's Station on Stoner's Creek succumbed June 26. Bird impressed more than three hundred German Loyalists hostages into duty, but the Indians brained twenty of the captives with war clubs and scalped them.

George Rogers Clark, buttressed with his one thousand-man army and armed with a six-pounder, crossed the Ohio August 1 as Shawnee scouts watched them snake along the Little Miami. In six days Clark reached the first Indian town—it was deserted. His men looted, torched wigwams and tasseling corn plots. Clark's army burned Old Chillicothe and two days later fired Piqua on the Big Miami. Twenty Kentuckians died in the foray; twice that were wounded; Indian losses were high. Col. Ben Logan and Clark returned as heroes, but little is said of Boone during this strike, which left Ohio Indians reeling and starving, ready to strike back.

On an October day that year, Daniel and Ned Boone, who much resembled older brother Dan, were working their way back to Boone's Station after hunting the Lower Blue Licks, each leading a packhorse loaded with meat. The riders halted to graze their horses at a brook flowing past a stand of hickories.

Their horses unloaded and belled, the men drank and rested in the grass. Ned gathered black walnuts.

"I have an uncommon dread on my mind," Daniel said. "This is a likely place for Indians."

Ned replied that there were no Indians for miles. He slammed rocks on the hulls to pick out the nut meats.

Daniel admonished Neddy to "keep a good lookout" and walked the bank to hunt.

Shawnees had picked up their trail near Lee's Town and tracked them. Half the warriors crouched, watching Ned. The rest followed Daniel.

Daniel roused a bear and fired, sending the bawling beast crashing into the cane. When he heard the gunfire behind him, Boone dove into the cane, reloading, sure Ned was dead or dying. He shot the Shawnees' baying mutt trailing him and pushed on.

The Indians joined their kinsmen, who had cut off Ned's head to take back to prove that they had, at last, killed old Boone. With four horses, Ned's rifle-gun and accouterments, and their grisly trophy, they fled to the Ohio.

Boone loped the twenty miles back to his fort. By dawn he and a score of militiamen returned, interring Ned's headless corpse by a hickory, cutting "N. Boone" into its bark, on the way home stopping to lay in a load of wild meat for Ned's widow, Martha Bryan Boone, and her five fatherless children.[25]

Fall, then winter. Indians ceased raiding. Whites stayed south of the Ohio.

Daniel Boone shored up his family and put the year and Ned's murder behind him, but the Revolution still ravaged the East. On January 17 at Cowpens, South Carolina, Gen. Daniel Morgan and his men routed Lord Charles Cornwallis's second wing—led by the infamous Col. Banastre "Bloody Ban" Tarleton, slayer of American men, debaucher of American women. By February Cornwallis was marching to Richmond, leaving Tarleton's dragoons to plunder Carolinian homes as far as Wilmington.

In April Kentuckians sent Boone to Richmond to represent newly formed Fayette County, but fears of British rangers caused the assembly to be moved to Charlottesville. Boone, "dressed in real backwoods stile" in "a common jeans suit, with buckskin leggings beaded very neatly . . . manufactured by the Indians," wore under his buckskin hunting shirt his red wool waistcoat fitted with sterling buttons engraved with his name.[26]

By the first days of June, Banastre Tarleton's legions loomed near, scattering Virginia's assemblymen. Thomas Jefferson had just fled to Monticello when Colonel Tarleton's Light Horse arrested Boone and a few militiamen. Tarleton detained him for a few weeks. Boone swore loyalty to George III and was freed.

In September he rode to Berks County, Pennsylvania, to visit the land of his youth. Cousin James Boone, the family scribe, marked the event in the family Bible: "October 20. Then Daniel Boone came to see us for the first time."[27]

Brutal fighting above the Falls at Squire Boone's Painted Stone Station marked September. On the fourteenth, some Shawnees raiding cabins along Beargrass Creek, led by mixed-blood Tory defector Capt. Alexander McKee, ran down a horde of settlers fleeing to Lynn's Station (near Long Run Creek), killing, some said, more than sixty whites in this, the Long Run massacre.

November found Daniel Boone back at Richmond. A few protested as he tried to be seated, insisting Boone had sworn an oath to George III. But the fray cooled and Boone took his seat. By January he was back on Kentucky's cutting edge of the western frontier.

For Daniel Boone and pioneer families living south of the Ohio, it mattered little whether *Kanta-Ke* was an Algonquin or Iroquoian word, or whether it meant "Land of Great Meadows" or "Dark and Bloody ground." His Shawnee captors had warned him: Stay out of Kentucky. Kentucky would exact the ultimate toll, and to his biographer, John Filson, Boone the pathfinder would say: "My footsteps have often been marked with blood. I can truly subscribe to its original name."[28]

"Daniel Boone," line-and-stipple engraving by James B. Longacre, from National Portrait Gallery of Distinguished Americans, *1835, based upon Chester Harding's portraits of Boone rendered from life fifteen years before.*

From Boone to Bumppo to Poe

The Last of the Mohicans is probably the first film I saw as a child. It was a black-and-white 16 millimeter print, and I must have been three or four—it's the first sense memory I have of a motion picture.
—Michael Mann, producer, writer, and director,
1992 adaptation of *The Last of the Mohicans*

In 1783 Daniel Boone met John Filson, a rather queer duck even by frontier standards. Reed thin, spectral-eyed, medium tall, and tetchy as a schoolmaster (which was his trade in Chester County, Pennsylvania), Filson and Boone warmed to each other well. As Filson queried the woodsman, Boone told of his first explorations of *Kanta-Ke.* Filson took notes, preparing for what would be its first history.

The following October a Wilmington, Delaware, publisher released *The Discovery, Settlement, and Present State of Kentucke . . . To Which Is Added, an Appendix, Containing, The Adventures of Col. Daniel Boon.,* which described the West's new "Garden of Eden" in florid prose. Filson's map pointed the way to the new land and to its forts, rivers, and paths, sparking westward migration.

Kentucke secured Daniel Boone's place in history, depicting the conflict between civilization and the wilderness: Boone the trailblazer—"an instrument ordained to settle the wilderness"—versus Boone the nature lover, living in nature in a state of grace, retreating from civilization yet by his livelihood destroying that which nurtures him. When Boone died in 1820, he was a legend and Filson's book continued to sell, influencing writers from Lord Byron to James Fenimore Cooper.

It is the latter who is most cherished in America's heart: Fenimore Cooper's hero, Natty Bumppo—a pure and undefiled Rousseauian "natural man" and redoubtable Leatherstocking—is vintage Americana. Drawing from Byron's roman-tic verse, Sir Walter Scott's heady plots, and Filson's purplish renderings, Cooper purveyed his child of the untrammeled forests into a trove richer and deeper than John Swift's legendary silver mines. ("Untrammeled" only to Bumppo; "savages," to use Cooper's sensitive rhetoric, had trammeled the woods for ten thousand years.)

Cooper worked nature's son hard, wringing life enough out of Natty's incarna-tions for his moccasin-clad feet to unrelentingly tread the gore-soaked pages of *The Pioneers* (1823), *The Last of the Mohicans* (1826), and *The Prairie* (1827). Cooper's canonical "Leatherstocking" trilogy became holy writ: the first eastern Westerns.

In short order, Cooper became one of America's first authors to garner worldwide acclaim. Appetites whetted, his audiences—spanning more than thirty

"The Pathfinder Did Not Stir," by F. O. C. Darley. AUTHOR'S COLLECTION.

"THE PATHFINDER DID NOT STIR"
The guide, holding his trusted rifle, Killdeer, stands guard over his party as they hide in ambush during their first encounter with the Iroquois.

countries—clamored for more adventures of cavalier Bumppo. But the author faced a minor complication: He had killed Natty off in *The Prairie.* Cooper's dip-pen undeterred, thirteen years later Natty arose to gallivant again in *The Pathfinder* (1840) and in the last Leatherstocking epic, *The Deerslayer* (1841).[1]

Even allowing for his resurrection, Natty Bumppo was a curiosity. At shooting matches few tested him, knowing what a terror he was with a rifle and that red men had nicknamed him *La Longue Carabine.* Chatting away, "Be all ready to clench it, boys!" and such big talk as Cooper deemed proper for huntsman Bumppo to utter, Natty would sight down the flat of a borrowed rifle and, possessing a prodigious dose of marksman's intuition, splatter a fly on a nail hammered in a stump one hundred yards off, then for good measure blast two more balls through the hole and atop the nail's head without creasing the hole's sides. Folks justifiably called him "Hawkeye."

La Longue Carabine was good in a tight spot, and Cooper made sure his hero wound up in lots of tight spots: Damsels in distress Natty rescued handily and in majestic fashion; "blood-thirsty" Hurons he potted far and near, dropping them clean; "pesky redskin varmints" trying to fool him by stepping in their own moccasin prints he tracked over granite faces, through rushing streams, across leaf-cluttered paths; black-hearted renegades he showed no mercy; in flatboat attacks he sprang out of the blue off overhanging limbs to land on decks to seize listing rudders; when bookish ignoramuses lost their way in the howling wilderness, unlettered Natty stepped unannounced from behind trees to lead them to the right fork, the whole time lecturing on the sublimity of nature's bosom and the grass under his feet; if a twig was stepped on and snapped, Natty Bumppo heard it and reacted to it. Always.

Most peculiarly, though the helpless "females" Hawkeye rescued became smitten by him and got the vapors and fell to swooning from the mere aura of his woodsy presence and his romantic, high-flown talk, courtly Pathfinder rarely swooned back. He was too pure. Besides, as he once pensively reflected aloud when probed on the delicate topic of his secretive love life, he already had a sweetheart:

> She's in the forest—hanging from the boughs of the trees, in
> a soft rain—in the dew on the open grass—the clouds that
> float about in the blue heavens—the birds that sing in the
> woods—the sweet springs where I slake my thirst—and in all
> the glorious gifts that come from God's Providence![2]

Of a truth, no mundane earthly love could vie for the untainted affections of this stouthearted mortal, "'unless, indeed,'" declared Pathfinder, as he "continued, dropping his head for an instant in a thoughtful manner, 'it be the open mouth of a sartain hound, when I'm on the track of a fat buck. As for unsartain dogs, I care little for their cries.'"[3]

Fenimore Cooper's "Leatherstocking Tales" resonated with Americans flush with Manifest Destiny beliefs in Anglo invincibility. "Cooper Indians," as Mark Twain called them (Twain loathed Cooper's grandiloquent prose and more than once mocked it in print[4]), fit well into white stereotypes of Indians as either "noble anachronisms" or "savage reactionaries." Chingachgook and Uncas, Hawkeye's adopted Mohican kinsmen and Cooper's "noble red men" (and he does not feature too many noble ones), are symbols—in the end a vanishing race going the way of the great auk before a superior one.

But bad Cooper Indians are not just bad—they are subhuman vermin: Cooper Indians always skulk; Cooper Indians always drink to riotous excess; Cooper Indians at best are suspicious characters prone to violence; Cooper Indians at worse are implacable killers. Worse, on a subliminal level, Cooper Indians, if given a chance, might rape. Thus a lingering, underlying current of the greatest threat of all: miscegenation.

Soon, Cooper's "correct" images of Indians and frontiersmen birthed an industry of pulp novels and melodramatic stage shows that unleashed a uniquely American literary genre: the Western. But Natty Bumppo refused to be hemmed in by pages and lo!, the word became flesh and blood and arose to conquer a bold new frontier: celluloid.

In 1909 Biograph released D. W. Griffith's silent two-reeler, *Leatherstocking,* followed by Republic's *In the Days of the Six Nations,* Powers's *Last of the Mohicans,* and Thanhouser's *The Last of the Mohicans.* (Hot on celluloid Bumppo's trail was celluloid Boone: The Edison Company produced *Daniel Boone* in 1907; in the 1920s four more "silent" Boones took to the screen.)

In *The Last of the Mohicans* (Associated Producers, 1920), Bumppo outshined all upstarts in his first feature-length role. Cooper Indians became Hollywood Indians and set back accurate depictions of native material culture by nearly a century or so: Magua (on the trail in a bearskin loincloth, rolled-down black socks, and Algonquin-esque fringed loafers) is a childlike psychopath, as are his comrades who can barely stay sober long enough to kill and maim and stomp around the war-post. Magua's pals slink about, powderhorns worn backward and low to the ground, rubber knives wobbling between clenched teeth, and arrayed as Neanderthals with skulls painted on their chests, terrifying white folks (and a lot of "good" Indians) who dare cross them. Save one: Hawkeye, who takes them on and rids the New World of a lot of Hurons, including Magua.

In 1936, in United Artist's *Last of the Mohicans,* Hawkeye uttered his first audible words. (So does Chingachgook, who had grave reservations about any budding romance between son Uncas and Cora Munro and said so, speaking his mind in this paragon of native elocution: "Pale face squaw no good Mohican. Fair hair make heart of Uncas weak like water."[5]) Pathfinder's clarion voice and cherubic countenance belonged to Randolph Scott. Clad in fringed buckskin and coonskin cap, toting an original flintlock Belgian trade musket, Scott is a dashing nimrod who faces down Hurons armed with .50/70 trapdoor Springfield rifles.[6] (Besides breechloaders and robotic "sign language," this edition of *Mohicans* features smoke signals, tepees, and chubby Anglo "braves" in bad wigs ill fitted to pale-skinned pates.)

As the screenplay ladled out stereotypes to the incessant tom-tom beat of the "Injun" soundtrack, there appeared a new twist: England's George II becomes "German George," a nod, perhaps, to George II's Hanoverian lineage, but one that resonated in a far different way to viewers cognizant of Chancellor Hitler's Third Reich arising from Berlin's rubble.

That same year Bumppo faced his chief rival: Boone. But director David Howard so assaulted history with his maudlin, low-budget *Daniel Boone* that beefy Dan'l (George O'Brien) came and went and stayed off Hawkeye's stage. Howard's shift of metaphor and iconography, however, is praiseworthy: His winsome hero capers about wearing a coonskin cap, while archnemesis Simon Girty (John Carradine at his swarthiest) scowls and wears his own cap fashioned from skunkskin.

The year 1992 was America's—and Kentucky's—year of celebration. For America: the quincentary, which summoned forth legions of pro- and anti-Christopher Columbus factions. For Kentucky: the bicentennial, a time of new Boone and Kentucky books and one Boone painting. Appearing in movie theaters during this wave of nostalgia and patriotism was Twentieth Century Fox's version of "Hawkeye," in *The Last of the Mohicans.*

Lean and lithe, sensitive to all sentient beings, educated, long-haired, and handsome but a crack-shot rifleman, "Nathaniel Poe" (Daniel Day-Lewis) more resembles a New Age pianist in walnut-dyed homespun than a trans-Allegheny Indian fighter. (Director Michael Mann, whose earlier work includes the television series "Miami Vice," feared audiences would erupt in laughter should a moniker like "Natty Bumppo" be forced down the incredulous craws of savvy moviegoers.) Nathaniel roams his woods, which are magnificently green and located in Asheville, North Carolina's Pisgah National Park; Fort Edward, a three-hundred-by-four-hundred-foot replica built on the shores of Lake James, is the doomed outpost where much of the action takes place.

Michael Mann's Chingachgook (Russell Means) is stolid and capable, as is younger and livelier Uncas (Eric Schweig). Cora Munro (Madeline Stowe) is steadfast and sure, a more willful heroine than Fenimore Cooper ever penned, and Poe discreetly couples with her atop the fort's blockhouse. Magua (Wes Studie) is defiant, tormented, twisted; for the first time, viewers understand what fuels the genocidal flames burning within him and sense in his seething rage a justified reckoning when he vows: "When the 'Greyhair' is dead, Magua will eat his heart. Before he dies, Magua will put his children under the knife, so the 'Greyhair' will know his seed is wiped out forever." Indian "extras" are more than a thousand American Indians bused in from Oklahoma and elsewhere, "Kentucky" rifles and (French) Charleville and (English) Brown Bess muskets are period reproductions that actually shoot, and Mann spent in the range of $50 million to produce a genuine epic.[7]

Here, Poe is far more human than his Leatherstocking predecessors of film and page: He loves and loves truly. Yet like Cooper's Bumppo, Mann's Poe evinces inner conflict: He is torn by race and upbringing. Like Filson's *Boon.,* so too is Poe nature's child and a homespun harbinger of the coming Anglo civilization; like Boone, he is "Heading West. To *Kanta-Ke*." Chingachgook—"last of the Mohicans"—faces the end with stoic, Spartanlike resignation. But much unlike Natty Bumppo, Nathaniel Poe must leave Chingachgook to cleave unto Cora and unto his own, just as Daniel Boone fled Black Fish and Shawnee life in 1778 to cleave unto Rebecca and to be reconciled unto his kith and kin.

Thus, long after Filson and Cooper, long after American independence and Kentucky statehood, and just on the cusp of the millennium's eve, America's fictional Leatherstocking had come full circle to metamorphose with America's archetypal Leatherstocking. And rightly so.

CHAPTER SIX

Huguenot Long Knife

WINTER 1778

Came the cry from the West: Stores of powder and ball were dangerously low in the dark land beyond the Clinch. Heeding the plea of the Kentuckians was the famed Long Knife, George Rogers Clark. Tall, strongly built, ruddy along the cheeks, his wavy, auburn hair receding though he was in his midtwenties, Clark, an imposing, charismatic man of fierce disposition, was ready to take the fight to the West.

George Rogers Clark now owned hundreds of Kentucky acres; in 1777 he had returned to Virginia with an ambitious plan to push the British out of the region. Gov. Patrick Henry had approved the scheme and had commissioned him a lieutenant colonel, authorizing him to raise seven militia companies of fifty men each. Lt. James Trabue from Charlotte County heeded Clark's call and signed on—illegally, it seems; Governor Henry had insisted Clark muster troops west of the Blue Ridge. With James came his younger brother, seventeen-year-old Daniel, who, at five-eight, 160 pounds, much resembled his older brother. And with Daniel came his stout bulldog, able to fell man or bear or buffalo.

In late January or early February 1778, James and Daniel left their home in Charlotte County, Virginia, passing through Chesterfield, Powhatan, Cumberland, and Bedford Counties, then crossing Blue Ridge Gap into Botetourt County. From the Philadelphia Wagon Road, they boarded Ingles' Ferry to cross New River, and rendezvoused with other Virginia volunteers at Fort Chiswell.[1]

Fewer men than expected joined Clark, and by the time the Trabues got to Fort Chiswell, most volunteers had already left for Kentucky. The Trabues' band—seven riflemen well provisioned and a slave boy—rode south to the Holston, the thriving outpost begun in 1746 in Washington County, Virginia, visited in 1750 by Dr. Thomas Walker; by 1778 the frontier community spilled into western North Carolina and northeastern Tennessee, making it a vast commercial hub for white and native hunters exploiting the game and furbearers abounding in the Appalachian watershed. Elisha Walden—the lean, raven-eyed Virginian who helped start the commerce of long hunting— was seen there in 1761, his packhorses laden with peltry and deerskins.[2] Jerk, corn, flour, powder and ball, wares, and cloth might be had, depending on the season and flow of traders and artisans—tinkers, blacksmiths, and coopers—living there. The Trabue party outfitted themselves for their journey and left that March.

Daniel, dark-eyed, black-haired, and tanned berry brown, was rapturous as they departed this last slip of settlement and exulted at the sights on the trace unwinding before him. Budding laurel tops were a warm green, their bushy crowns held aright by gnarled, spindly limbs rubbed bare from horse traffic. Massive conifers—pines, spruce, and hemlock—soared heavenward, towering about cold streams cascading over granite boulders and into deep, swirling pools glinting metallic red, silver, and gold from schools of trout and shad. Azure sky reached down, deepening into a drape of silky blue-gray touching the browns and greens of the dark forest, as the path threaded past oaks, sycamores, and hickories whose first limbs jutted so high above the earth that travelers had trouble potting turkeys roosting on the heavy branches.

As Daniel rode westward, sensing he was about to enter the Promised Land, he reflected upon the lives of his forebears driven from France after Louis XIV rescinded the Edict of Nantes in 1685, ending toleration between Catholics and Calvinists. Daniel's maternal great-grandfather, an affluent French officer who, fearing arrest, abandoned his estate and vineyards, dressed his wife as a man, armed her with a sword, and fled to England. Daniel saw in their lives a saga akin to that of the Israelites fleeing Egypt during the despotic reign of Ramses II. Perhaps in his musings he thought of other Huguenots like Francis "Swamp Fox" Marion, or the Tennessean John Sevier, or roguish Bennett Belue, the Carolinian Tory who fraternized with Cherokees and Chickasaws, deserted his French wife for an Indian woman, and piloted John Donelson's flotilla up the Cumberland a few years after Donelson had replotted the south's boundary of white territory to be the Kentucky instead of the Levisa.[3]

As they rode into the gorge that in 1751 Dr. Thomas Walker had named for Ambrose Powell, their jubilation dissipated: Charred, lonely cabins marked the valley as a defile of death. Three miles south of Cumberland Gap, they camped in an old shack; that night high winds beat a steady rain on the cedar shakes, but by dawn the storm had passed, and it was a crisp day the men faced as they packed budgets and ate and saddled their horses. When they passed by a thatch of rhododendron growing on the banks of a rivulet flowing below the mouth of Cudjo's Cave on the north side of the Gap, the sun had fully risen.

Nine miles past the Cumberland River, the Warriors' Path merged into the Wilderness Road, blazed by Capt. Daniel Boone's woodcutters three years before. Here red men and white often collided; shallow graves piled over with logs and half-rotted corpses picked clean by talon and claw and well chewed by wolves were macabre sights along the way. At the junction of these two great roads, the men spotted fresh tracks that were not tracks of white hunters.

They slid off their horses, giving the slave boy the reins. James ordered all to prime and to put two bullets in their mouths, then he and another Virginian took the van.[4] Beside Daniel and to the rear stood Locust, full of brass, fury, and bravado. His unerring aim, Locust bragged as loud as he dared, had slain more than one Indian, and many a savage's blood had darkened his tomahawk and knife. Now he chaffed at the wait, ranting, his profane tirades making Daniel feel "chikinhearted"—"I wish I could have courrage like Lucust. I would be glad."

The militiamen walked fast, staring at the tracks, Locust spewing death and destruction. Crossing a creek roiled by tracks that had splashed up the bank and rounded a bend, they saw two Shawnees crouched in the trace,

Great Lakes quilled underwater panther bag (6" x 5½"), black walnut dyed brain-tanned deerskin, blood-root dyed deer hair in metal cones. Artisan: Michael J. Taylor. Author's Collection.

eating. Daniel fired, his shot spooking them into flight and abandoning a pile of loot from a raid upon the Cherokee. James Trabue's Virginians pursued them two hundred yards but saw the Indians no more and returned to a horde of wares and weapons: five bows with quivers full, three shot bags and powderhorns, blankets, shirts, stroud leggings and breechclouts shiny with silver brooches, a brass kettle, and seven budgets stuffed with more surprises.[5]

The slave boy grabbed a fetish fletched with blue-black raven feathers. "Lord. Lord. What is this?" he asked.

"This is their thing they pow wouw with or congure with," said James, "but I thought I told you to mind the horses."

"Lucust is their," the boy replied. But as he said it, Locust darted up; he was, he said, too afraid "to stay by his silf." James, rarely given to profanity, cursed Locust "for a Dam Coward."

After finishing off the Indians' venison, the men rode on. Miles later, near Flat Lick, where the path forked—the Warriors' Path arced to the Ohio then to the Scioto; the Wilderness Road wound northwest to the Bluegrass—the men nosed their horses left and onward, their trade goods in budgets and blankets strapped to their mounts. At daylight on April 16, the men devoured their last ration of bacon and did not eat again until Sunday, when they prodded their worn mounts through Boonesborough's gates. It was Easter and "the people all ran out over Joyed to see strangers," Daniel recalled. They were "hospetable to us with what they had. But I thought it was hard times—no bred, no salt, no vegetables, no fruit of any kind, no Ardent sperrets, indeed nothing but meet."

Black Fish's Shawnees, Daniel learned, had seized Daniel Boone and twenty-six salt boilers on the Lower Blue Licks the February before. As word of the hostage taking spread, Boone's Trace, Skaggs' Trace, Harrod's Trace, and the Wilderness Road swelled with fleeing travelers. When the Trabue party got to Boone's fort, only eight families and a few militiamen were there.

On Monday morning, the party auctioned off its Shawnee booty, each man earning 50 shillings. Even "the negro boy," Daniel reported, "got his shear," but the craven Locust got nothing. Daniel bought a few wampum strings, a shot bag and powder horn, and some trade silver.

Within two weeks, Daniel Trabue left for Logan's Station. Built in 1775 by Capt. Benjamin Logan, Logan's covered an acre, its walls measuring 180 by 240 feet, bolstered with roofed blockhouses on two corners.[6] A defensive cog in the thinly populated Bluegrass, Logan's was better provisioned than Boonesborough; besides meat, there was "plenty of Milk and Butter and some Bread." To his joy, Daniel met some fellow Virginians en route to join George Rogers Clark and decided to make Logan's his Kentucky home.

On Daniel's first bear hunt, his feisty bulldog clamped down on the bear's head and got knocked sprawling. After holing up for a few days to heal, he became a renowned catch dog, and huntsmen taking to the woods often borrowed the tenacious canine. John Sappington's dog was a good hunter, as were Simon Kenton's, whose curs once dashed across a frozen river to a trotting buffalo and clamped down until dogs and buffalo crashed through the ice and drowned.[7]

Every morning nearing first light, Capt. Ben Logan rode out with a handful of men to reconnoiter, and Daniel joined in many of these scouts, but he saw few Indians.[8] Traces snaking in and out of the cane and through hardwoods were dangerous places to travel, and more than once while he lived at the fort his horse was stolen.

On May 27 Lieutenant Colonel Clark arrived at the Falls of the Ohio. Above the Falls on Corn Island, his men began planting corn and felling trees to erect cabins and blockhouses. Joseph Lindsey, who had come to Harrod's Town in 1775, was appointed commissary and sent to New Orleans for supplies. Months later Lindsey returned with a keelboat laden with goods.

Corn Island would be Clark's base until he built Fort Nelson on the Ohio's southern shore. Troops rendezvoused with Clark for his push into Illinois; on June 24, 1778, Clark and his homespun troops 175 strong shot the Falls, the auspicious day heightened by a solar eclipse.[9] They landed at the Tennessee's mouth; from there the Long Knives trudged overland across barrens and waded neck-deep swamps into the Illinois wilds. None of the Loyalists suspected the Americans were near until the night of July 4, when Clark's ragtag Kentuckians seized Kaskaskia. It was a stunning victory.

Lt. James Trabue signed on with Capt. Richard May and served as purchasing commissary, provisioning Kentucky's four forts: Boonesborough, Logan's Station, Harrod's Town, and Louisville.[10] One of his most vexing tasks was keeping afresh gunpowder stores in dank powder magazines; when kegs got damp, the mix of saltpeter, ash, and sulfur separated, the saltpeter settling at the bottom, ash and sulfur lumped on top. Kegs had to be upended and rotated or opened and the powder dried and sifted, forcing James to work hard to ensure that forts never lacked for gunpowder.

On July 13 brother Daniel Trabue had succeeded Azariah Davis as quartermaster sergeant of Logan's Station. During the next twelve weeks, Daniel bought "84 bushels of corn, 724 pounds of pork, 2,779 pounds of 'tame beef,' and 2,820 pounds of buffalo meat." Clark's men frequented Logan's, and often in times of grave danger, Daniel had to travel to other stations to purchase meat and corn.[11]

May's quartermaster was paid the same as a private: 1 shilling, $4 per day. When he had time, Daniel slipped out of the fort with one or two others to hunt to keep the garrison in meat. Fort life was boring and filthy, punctuated with lean times, and though Daniel stayed on guard, still, horses continued to vanish mysteriously and men and cattle continued to die—killed by Indians.

The previous February widow Ann McDonald had wed James Harrod. Her parents, the Coburns, lived at Logan's. That summer, when Samuel Coburn and his wife moved to Harrod's Town to live with their daughter and her new husband, the men of Logan's helped them cart their belongings. When Coburn, accompanied by a Mr. Walker and a Mr. McCoy, returned to Logan's for the last time, he spent the evening packing and by morning was making his rounds saying good-bye.

Captain Logan warned him he was taking a risk in going to Harrod's with only two men, but Coburn shrugged it off. Logan asked him to wait a day, then he could get more men to help him fetch the last of his things.

Coburn protested. There was no sign of Indians, he insisted. The three rode out of the fort.

Two hours later one of them ran back: It was McCoy. Indians had fired on them at the mouth of Knob Lick Creek; Coburn and Walker were dead; the warriors had chased McCoy toward Harrod's, but he eluded them and doubled back.

Two miles down the trace, Logan's men found Walker and Coburn, their bodies scalped. Tracks led to a canebrake, and beyond that, to the horses and Coburn's belongings. From the sign, it looked as if there were about ten of them, and Logan, fearing the attackers were en route to his settlement, sent his brother-in-law Alexander Montgomery with orders to Captain May to ride to Flat Lick (two miles southeast of Logan's) to reconnoiter. Logan and his men piled logs over the bodies to keep the wolves and vultures from gnawing them.

When May got Logan's orders, he gave the word for all to ride, but McCoy wanted no part of it. As Daniel Trabue made ready, brother James called out, "O Dan, Stay! We must not all leave the fort." Thirteen-year-old Ben Briggs, who rode with May, told what happened next: The whites came to a salt lick, dismounted, and hid in a gully, waiting. Soon the Indians appeared; May whispered orders to hold fire until he gave the word. They drew beads.

"Boys look! Don't you see that Indean their with a Naked belly? Don't none of you shoot at him. I want to kill him my self," James said.

The Indians moved closer. Then May's gun snapped—a misfire! "They all emedeately thought that Capt. May wanted to cheet and have the first fire to kill one Inden and they emedeately all fired." James Trabue's Indian fell to the earth along with two or three others.

"Dam son a bitch, come hear!" yelled an Indian treed near a brake. But the first fire ended the skirmish. The warriors vanished, leaving behind blood-splattered leaves.

SUMMER 1778

Indians had attacked two of Col. Benjamin Logan's men: William Poage was shot and killed, and Hugh Leeper was shot twice in the upper part of his left breast, bullets blasting clean through him. He bled badly, and for a few days no one thought he would live, but he did.

After Andrew Johnson's wild foray—Johnson, the first of Daniel Boone's salt boilers to escape back to Kentucky—Lt. John Bowman asked Simon Kenton to spy out the Shawnee towns, and Kenton, along with Sgt. George Clarke and Alexander Montgomery, made ready. Daniel Trabue agreed to go, and the four dressed in leggings and clouts and packed extra deerskin moccasins, and each had horse halters of half-dressed buffalo hide and to eat, parched cornmeal and jerk.[12]

But James, just back from Boonesborough and hearing of the scheme, rushed to the side of younger brother Dan. "If anything would happin to you how could I Ever see our Mother? She would say, 'James, how come you to lit Daniel to go on such an errand?'"

Daniel reluctantly left the horse stealing to the trio, and it was just as well: Montgomery was killed, Clarke barely escaped, and Kenton was captured, his captivity leading to months of torture, nine gauntlet runs, a broken arm and collarbone, a blow from a pipe tomahawk that left a dent in his skull deep enough to cup a hickory nut, and more than once, near death at the stake.[13]

Simon Kenton, illiterate save for being able to sign his name, remains one of the most illustrious hunters of Kentucky. LINE-AND-STIPPLE ENGRAVING BY JAMES B. LONGACRE, NATIONAL PORTRAIT GALLERY OF DISTINGUISHED AMERICANS, 1835.

That September Trabue heard his first news of Boonesborough's desperate siege from William Patton, who lived at the fort but was out hunting when the fight began; ensconced in a makeshift hideaway and scarcely daring to draw breath, he had watched the saga play out. On September 17, in the battle's dramatic climax, native archers dazzled the sky with waves of fire arrows, iron tips wrapped with shagbark hickory, stuffed with tow, and doused with gunpowder, then ignited and sent arcing through the air, smoking and sizzling yellow and red, to strike in the cedar shakes roofing the fort as defenders scrambled aloft to dislodge the blazing shingles and snuff them out. Overcome with fright and in a near swoon, Patton staggered to Logan's Station with grim tales of horror: "They run up to the fort—a large number of them—with large fire brands . . . and made the Dreadfullest screams and hollowing that could be imagind." He swore that he "actuly Did hear the Indians killing the people in the fort."

Ben Logan issued orders: Cattle were to be driven in; a ditch that led from the fort to the spring was covered over with log puncheons; roasting ears and pumpkins were put in stores; and "Every pail, tub, Churn, kittle, and pot" was soon brimming.

Logan set about to round up the cattle; an hour later he was back, his white horse smeared from blood streaming down his left arm which flopped from side to side as he galloped along, forcing him to clench his thumb in his teeth to keep the arm from snagging in the wall of cane. Benjamin Pettit, who had once lived with the Cherokee and knew something of their ways, set and splinted Logan's arm and rubbed his wounds with a viscous gel he boiled from the pounded inner bark of the elm. Logan bore his wounds manfully and offered encouragement, but even by the following April his arm was not fully mended.

A few cows wandered up to the stockade gates, mooing balefully, arrows sticking out of their rumps. Hours later sentries spotted a line of men walking Indian file three hundred yards in the distance. Kentuckians lined the palisades, straining to see past spires of cedar and cane.

"Dam you! Come on!" someone muttered, and children ran about peeping out of the chinks in the walls. "Lord, have mercy on us," a woman cried aloud.

Then, "Yonder they come!," followed by glad shouts of relief as the men stepped into view.

"It is our boys. Open the gates!"

It was the fifteen dispatched two weeks before to serve as reinforcements. Boonesborough had not fallen, bringing the folks at Logan's Station their first real intelligence of the West's most prolonged siege. After hugs and thumps

Dam you come on I heard the same thing repeated along on this side of the fort, (next to wards boons burough) who they could see them I actually felt better at this time than I had felt for these two Days I told these men I thought I could soon make a good shoot and they all said they woud try to make shore shoots when they advanced nigh the fort some of the woman was the first that spoke out and said it is our boys and as they come nigher we found out it was our boys shore enough, the fort gate was flung open come in howdey John Dick sam harry Tom Jarret Manufe & C some a crying for Joy some a laughing for Joy, as they had thinking thur

Excerpt from Daniel Trabue's narrative. DRAPER MANUSCRIPTS 57J:33; STATE HISTORICAL SOCIETY OF WISCONSIN.

on the back, the men reported to Logan, in bed in his cabin. Daniel Trabue was there when the cadre greeted their maimed commander. "Capt. Logan smiled for the first time sence he was wounded. If I ever seen people glad, it was at that time."

Daniel Trabue resumed hunting, searching out the big black bears that averaged more than four hundred pounds each, their dark, fatty meat making a superior cooking oil lacking the strong bite of hog lard and less prone to turn rancid. He rendered about twenty-five pounds of tallow from each bear and discovered that it took less salt to cure bear bacon than it did wild or tame beef, venison, or pork. Bear heart and kidney were nutrient-rich delicacies, and Kentuckians used bearhides as bed covers and as wrappings to protect deerskins strapped on packhorses bound for market.

By fall, as Indian raids ebbed, Daniel yearned to go east to see his family; on Christmas Eve 1778 he and two friends began their return trip to Virginia. Christmas dinner was roasted bear cub—"as good a christmas Diner as I had ever eaton." By nightfall a crust of snow lay on the ground, and that first night they slept in two-hour shifts and did so every night.

In a week's time they passed Powell's Valley; at the Clinch settlements they bought food and whiskey, and Daniel, after resting a few days, struck out on his own. Surviving floods, blizzards, and bowls of rancid mush and soured milk, he crossed Ingles' Ferry in Montgomery County, arriving by mid-January at his home in Chesterfield. In the evenings, as news of his return began to circulate, friends and relatives would come to greet "Kentucky Daniel" and ask about the West, sitting in astonishment as he told of his run-in the year before on the Wilderness Road. He ended his tale in a flourish, reaching inside his saddlebags to withdraw his wampum strands and sterling brooches and other booty gained from the exploit.

SPRING 1779

In the spring Daniel Trabue received word from brother James of a staggering coup: That February George Rogers Clark's half-starved army had forced Lt. Gov. Henry Hamilton into surrendering Fort Sackville at Vincennes, and Clark had authorized Col. Richard Callaway to escort the British hostages—including the infamous, much-hated "Hair Buyer" himself—to Virginia. Callaway was now in Williamsburg; come July, James's missive read, Daniel was to rendezvous with him in Chesterfield to assist him in securing horses, gunpowder, lead, and other supplies.

Daniel was delighted! Unlike some who found the old Virginian churlish, he idolized the man and made ready to receive him. Callaway arrived on the chosen day to a feast and to a crowd eager to hear him tell of the rescue of his daughters Fanny and Betsy and Jemima Boone in 1776 and about the siege. But mostly, they wanted to know about the land: A year before, Virginia passed "An act for establishing a Land office, and ascertaining the terms and manner of granting waste and unappropriated lands." "The Land Act of 1779" had passed that same season to settle the conflicting claims in western lands.[14]

Was the soil as rich as it was rumored? Was good land abundant and priced right? Yes, yes, he replied. Yes to all of it. Kentucky's soil was dark and rich, loose as a bank of willow ashes. Why, one could claim land and plow it on the same day!

Some men, just in hearing Callaway's stories, immediately bought Kentucky land warrants; a few days later, as Callaway and Daniel Trabue and a slave were busy loading forty packhorses with goods, forty Virginians signed on to defend the party at the rate of 2 shillings a day. They arrived at Boonesborough in July, and Trabue rode to Logan's Station—"I was truly glad to be at Logan's Fort again. Their was many more people at this fort this year then the year before."

More joyous tidings came on August 20 with the return of Lt. Col. George Rogers Clark and his army to Fort Nelson at the Falls: Kaskaskia, Vincennes, and Cahokia were now American outposts. Clark now dreamed of Detroit, heavily fortified, well garrisoned, and deep in Indian country; but what he had achieved in the Old Northwest was amazing enough, and many of his men were clad in British regimentals and shirts appropriated at Vincennes, where they had commandeered seven keel boats loaded with six tons of supplies worth $50,000. Kegs of rum, wine, taffia, and sugar made up a large part of the loot, and all of it, plus a sizable arsenal of confiscated Brown Bess muskets and hundreds of pounds of powder and ball, was stored in Fort Nelson's magazine.[15]

On the fort's south side, Clark ordered a spacious "ball-room" to be built, with hewn log sides and a puncheon floor, to host a shivaree. "A number of Jentleman and Ladies Attended," wrote Daniel, who was also there, "and when these Fort Ladys come to be Dressed up they did not look like the same. Every thing looked anew."

Rum toddies and horns of madeira flowed freely, and there was plenty to eat and much to toast. A black fiddler named Cato rosined up his horsehair bow and tore into a lilting jig as James and Ann Harrod kicked off the first dance. Clark dramatically recounted his tales, punctuated by spontaneous bursts of "Hip, Hip, Huzzah!" from the crowd, and as fancy shirts and dresses of linen and chintz danced and whirled into the night, at least for a brief span, thoughts of hard times slipped into the past.

Autumn boded ill. By October 1779 Col. Richard Callaway had secured official rights to operate a toll ferry on the Kentucky a few score yards beyond Boonesborough's pickets. On March 10 settlers hearing lightly charged pops rushed to the water's edge to find Callaway and Pemberton Rawlings dead, their bodies gashed, their two slaves gone. Days later a white captive at a Shawnee town saw Callaway's black-and-silver scalp stretched and drying near a campfire.

WINTER 1779

Beaver nosed along creeks, pushing before them cut willow and tulip poplar saplings to wedge in dams and lodges and green sprigs for food. Mink worked the banks and otters the shallows to ready dens for the coming winter; the otters' mud slides and bold, widely splayed, webbed, weasel-like tracks and pellet-shaped scat of delicate trout and frogs' bones, translucent crayfish hulls and pressed muskrat hair, were easily discerned. Squirrels' nests high in trees began to show themselves as leaves bursting yellow, red, madder brown, and faded green twirled and twisted in cascading half arcs to the earth, driven by gusts of wind and rain. Deer coats grew thick, fading from a hue of reddish brown to gray-blue. Brown, woolly curls sprouted on buffalo; buffalo turned poor early and turkeys froze to death roosting in trees, their nose slits freezing over. Overhead, a primal cacophony rent the air as geese from Canada flew over cabins and forts in long Vs. Hunters read the signs and would go out, sniff the air, and say that it was sure to be a harsh winter. It was. The freezing weather that began the first of November did not let up until March.[16]

The "severity of this winter caused great difficulty in Kentucky . . . and the inhabitants lived chiefly on the flesh of buffaloes," Daniel Boone said. At the Dutch Station near Beargrass Creek, "several . . . perished for want of provision" and some roasted buffalo skins to eat.[17] A wagonload of wild meat, hides, and tallow sold for $100 of inflated Continental cash. Livestock died, and Kentuckians sickened miserably from devouring the putrid, lank blue meat cut from carcasses dotting brown pastures. Cane—a forage crop—was often sleeted over; as months wore on, none thought it odd to see "cattle laying with their heads to their side as if they were asleep; just literally froze to death." Even buffalo starved.[18]

When the settlers boiled off maple sap, bony, half-starved buffalo would trot up to lick the runoff and suffer being shot from cabin doors. Simon Kenton believed that after the Hard Winter, game herds never recovered.[19] Corn sold for $165 a bushel, and many people died for want of it.

During the Hard Winter, Daniel Trabue hunted buffalo with his fellow Virginian "tuckeyho boys," and one day, with an arrogant Irishman who could not abide such rough-hewn company.

> One of the men we had with us was a young Irishman who was constant contending and Disputeing with the other young men that was from old Virginia about words and customs, etc. So some time that morning I shot a Buffelo bull and he fell down. We all went up to him. Some of the men had never seen one before this one. I soon Discovered I had shot this buffelo too high and I told some of the boys to shoot him again. This young Irishman said, "No"; he would kill him and Jumed at him with his tomerhock and strikeing him in the forehead. I told him it would not Do, he could not hurt him, the wool and mud and skin and skull was all so thick it would not Do. But he kept up his licks, a nocking away. The buffelo jumped up. The man run, the buffelo after him. It was opin woods, no bushes, and the way this young Irishman run was rather Desending ground and every Jumped he cried out, "O lard! O lard! O lard! O lard!" The buffelo was close to his heels. The man Jumed behind a beech tree. The bufflo fell down, his head against the tree, the tuckeyho boys laughing, "Ha! Ha!

Ha!" One of them went up and shot the buffelo again and killed him. The Irishmain exclaimed againt them, saying this was no laughing Matter but that these boys or young [men] (he said) was such fools they would laugh if the buffelo had killed him. These young men would Mimmick him, "O lard! O lard!" etc. and breack out in big laughter. The Irish men said he would go no further with such fools.[20]

SPRING 1780

The Hard Winter had been a severe test; the settlers were relieved to have it behind them, but spring brought new worries. Raids at the Falls, along Beargrass Creek, at Limestone, and south to the Bluegrass erupted like the brush fires of summer, as warriors struck "in small Companies, Done much Mischief in steeling horses and killing people." In June, when Capt. Henry Bird's army of 150 British partisans and 700 Indians invaded Kentucky, James Trabue was captured at Ruddell's, marched to Detroit, and shipped to Canada.

And then, more bad news: brother William Trabue had been one of the 400 Virginians taken captive by the British when the Crown's army seized Charleston on May 12, 1780. With two brothers in English jails, and a third, Edward, campaigning in the southern theater, brother John Trabue urged Daniel to return that summer to Virginia to secure their grants and comfort their widowed mother. So, in the summer of 1780, after two and a half adventurous years on the frontier, Daniel returned to the war's eastern front.

James and William escaped within a year, and Daniel fought at Yorktown in 1781, and on July 4, 1782, wed Mary Haskins and prepared to return to Kentucky.[21]

America's Revolution was ending in the East. But it was, Daniel Trabue feared, far from over in the West.

Hanging a bead. PHOTO BY MARCUS COPE, LAND BETWEEN THE LAKES, KENTUCKY. AUTHOR'S COLLECTION.

Buffalo for the Killing

June 30: About noon we landed to go after a herd of more than a hundred buffaloes, both bulls and cows, of which we killed five and wounded more than twenty. We cut out only the tongues.

July 1: About noon we landed on a sand bar to amuse ourselves with hunting. We brought down eight animals. We contented ourselves with cutting out their tongues.

July 2: About noon we . . . went after a herd of nine buffaloes, all of which we killed.

July 5: The most worthless Frenchman can kill a buffalo in this region.
—Diron D'Artaguiette, inspector general, Louisiana;
Mississippi voyage, 1723 journal entries

To be sure, America's wild cattle, which sustained Kentuckians before domestic cattle did and which Daniel Trabue helped shoot out of existence west of the Blue Ridge, were New World transplants. Myth and lore aside, no "vast herds" of buffalo—as influential storytellers like Thomas Ashe and Henry W. Shoemakers once wrote to gullible readers, confusing the issue—ever roamed east of the Mississippi River.

Bison, taxonomically speaking, is the proper name for the beasts. *Buffalo* is rightly applied only to Old World kine, like the Cape buffalo of the East African savanna and the water buffalo of Southeast Asia and the Ganges delta, not to the bison of Poland's forests that so remarkably resemble New World buffs. Yet it was the European bison (or "wisent") that sired the historic *Bison bison bison,* that same bearded ungulate whose image the U.S. Mint struck on the "buffalo nickel" on the flip side of the "Indian head," a humble, homespun coin, a collectible bit of Americana and one that no numismatist ever refers to as a "bison nickel."

Like other mammals (most notably, horses and men), the ruminants crossed the land bridge spanning the Bering Sea between Siberia and Alaska during the ice age. Wild bovines throve in the more temperate climes of North America, devouring luxurious sweeps of grama and needle grass and filling in the Far West with truly huge herds that totaled no less than thirty million head. The coming of buffalo, and horses (an export from Spain) on which to hunt them, ushered in a sort of golden age for tribes of the Northern and Southern Plains that lasted two centuries.

For American explorers, like Meriwether Lewis and William Clark and their Corps of Discovery, stampedes must have been an exhilarating sight, as the men sidestepped and flanked the swirling throngs of brown wool, black hooves, and taut muscle, whose galloping shook the earth and pocked it like a moonscape and kicked up billowing yellow dust clouds that veiled the sun. Traditional peoples of the Plains marveled at such sights too; and often they gave thanks to the Master of Life for this one-ton gift capering on cloven hooves that could sprint faster than a mustang and dotted the Great Plains in the millions.

Heady scenes of so much charging flesh and brawn were not seen east of the Mississippi, though the redoubtable Long Knives, Casper Mansker and Isaac Bledsoe, had a dangerous brush with a herd in 1766 and feared being crushed on horseback. And at French Lick (now Nashville) in 1777, William Bowen, who had dismounted to track a wounded buff into a brake, was charged by the brute, gored clean through, and stomped into the dirt and cane stobs. Poor Bowen lay there, broken and dying, for seven days before death from gangrene mercifully fetched him on the eighth.

Nor was the buffalo's impact upon the lives and material culture of Woodland Indians as profound as it was upon western tribesmen. Yet, just as packs of gray and red wolves, panthers and elk, and flocks of passenger pigeons and Carolina parakeets inhabited the East, so too did buffalo.

This new niche opened near the headwaters of the Arkansas, Red, and Yazoo in the 1500s: A few stragglers swam the Father of Waters—ebony horns, grizzled heads, and flaring snouts cutting gently undulating wakes that parted in a broad V—and gaining a hold, splashed ashore.

In this manner buffalo penetrated the Southeast, crossing the wide river, their numbers growing as their range extended to the Tidewater, Tampa Bay, and near the southern hem of the Great Lakes.

By the 1700s buffalo droves of twenty to one hundred head and more, up to six hundred, teemed in the Cumberland Valley near French Lick, in Kentucky's

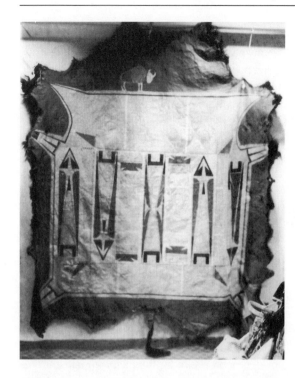

Great Lakes brain-tanned buffalo robe, magnificently painted in geometric and linear designs. ARTISAN: TOM CONIN. PHOTO BY DAVID WRIGHT.

bluegrass and Green River country, on Illinois's prairies near Fort De Chartres, and north and south along the Mississippi's shores and those of its tributaries.

For about three hundred years, buffalo roamed east of the Great River. Buffs grazed their way through airy meadows dotted with canebrakes, munching pastel carpets of resplendent wildflowers and wild strawberries growing in thick mats beneath soaring big timber of high canopy. Indians created these parklike meadowlands, firing lands in rhythm with the coming of spring's deluges, rejuvenating and broadening the greening borders of hunting grounds to entice whitetails and elk. Buffalo were a novel bonus.

Here, too, buffalo flourished and exerted their strong presence upon the landscape. Their wide lead paths—called traces—became the eastern frontier's first roadway system, leading to salt licks and waterways, canebrakes and forests, and laying open the land near the headwaters of the Mississippi and southward. As generations swept by, railroad ties were laid on the old traces, and in time, asphalt covered them, as the traces became secondary roads and highways. Proof, one old-timer observed, that Kentucky had three road builders: "the buffler, the Ingin, and the Ingineer."[1]

Throwing down with a .50-caliber long rifle on such a fleet mound of muscle and bone and sinew—one that could wheel on a shilling to charge, bluff, or pound away, head low and arched out parallel to the earth, mouth leering open flashing the squared-off teeth of the bottom jaw as the lip pulled down and nostrils flared and pinched back to the round, empty eyes of ebony hue—could be a risky proposition: A galloping buffalo, adrenaline pumping, could absorb a lot of lead.

A head shot might kill or stun, but only if the ball hit behind the ear where the skull was thinnest and plowed into the brain. Aiming dead-on was no good: Bullets smacking the horny boss and thick skull could have done as well going up against an anvil.

Peter Harper, William Clinkenbeard, and Enos Terry were hunting the bluegrass in 1779 when Harper blasted a buff at ten steps, hitting the beast just above the eyes and between the horns. The buff shuddered its withers and blinked. The ball glanced off and landed at Harper's feet, flat as a halfpenny. The intrepid Long Knife retrieved it—lead was a hard-to-get but eminently vital frontier commodity—and chewed it round, recharged, patched the deformed ball, and rammed it down and let fly. Direct hit, frontal. The buff trotted off to a dry creek bed, where the three Kentuckians hemmed it in and began stoning the beast, which finally had enough of the aggravation and, with a few headlong rushes, ran the men off and beat a retreat.

These amateurs could hardly be labeled *bona fide* "meat getters"—market hunters who profited from the sales of wild meat (elk, deer, buffalo, and small game) to forts and stations. Spencer Records and John Finch slew six buffs with six shots—fine shooting that provided good return for the paltry investment of a patched ball and charge. Long Knives, if possible, retrieved bullets during field dressing, recasting the spent balls and galena shards in two-handled molds, pinching off the sprues with a hunting knife (and saving them to remelt), and storing the shiny, newly run balls in a stitched-up deer scrotum pouch inside the shot bag.

Hunters roasted the best cuts of wild beef. George Morgan's teams of meat getters working the Cumberland and in the Illinois country packed tons of salted buffalo in hogsheads to ship to New Orleans, Mobile, Biloxi, and Pittsburgh. Woodsmen jerked buffalo meat to eat or sell and devoured hot, steamy marrow with gusto. Frontiersmen sliced hides into tugs; tanned robes into quilts and saddlebags; sewed green (untanned) hides into bags and heavy-duty winter shoepacs (called "buffalo socks"), made with the hair side turned inward; and stuffed buffalo wool into shoes and moccasins to keep their feet warm. Women washed the wool free of mud and cockleburs, then spun it into yarn to knit or blend with nettle to weave into cloth.

For good eating, the succulent tongue was the ultimate prize. Like marrow, its freshly cooked texture had a unique, buttery flavor, and fat dripped off the tongue's tip as it slow-roasted. Tongue could be split, sliced, and smoked on a grid placed over a bed of hickory coals. Smoking took two or three hours. Smoked tongue—like most wild meat—was best medium-rare and moist and was good by itself or chopped up and boiled with parched cornmeal or mush or in a stew. In his 1843

Buffalo-related items, from left to right: 1) hide for moccasin liners; 2) powderhorn; 3) winter shoe-pacs; 4) wool from spring shed to stuff moccasins; 5) dried 12' tug; 6) sheath. AUTHOR'S COLLECTION.

reminiscences, Hugh Bell, a Kentucky hunter renowned for his smoothbore shooting, yarning, and pranks on fellow huntsmen (for fun, Bell liked to entice snakes to crawl down his Brown Bess musket barrel so he could blast them against trees), explained the art of tongue cooking: "First scorch the tongue a little, then peel off the outside coating, then stick it upon a spit made of spice bush with the lower end in the ground."[2] If no spicebush was at hand, a sassafras branch worked just as well.

Bone marrow was also a delicacy. Hunters preferred shank bones. They laid the bones on coals one end at a time, split them with the poll end of their hatchets, and gouged out the hot marrow. Femurs took five or six minutes of cooking on each end to steam marrow in its own juice.

Good straight from the bone or spread on bread like butter, either way, marrow must have been addictive. James Knox, a brigade leader during the classic Long Hunter era, treated himself to thirty-six marrow bones one Christmas morning. In another such gastronomic glut, August Ross gorged on as much shank marrow as he could choke down, then topped it off with six hard-boiled goose eggs. Ross, bloated and miserable, spent that night hanging over the stern of his canoe, "feeding the fishes."[3]

Buffalo jerk was a staple for Indians and Kentuckians; Daniel Boone, typical of most hunters, toted a haversack heavy with buffalo jerk and johnnycake.

French-Canadian voyageurs called the hunks of half-inch-thick, smoked and sun-dried (or boucanned) meat *plats côtes* and learned from the Indians how to cut the beef from the bones and spread it on a sapling grid suspended over a smoky, slow-burning fire. Wild meat "dried in this manner," Father Julien Binneteau reported in his relation (letter) dated 1699, "keeps for a long time without being tainted."[4]

By the early 1800s buffalo east of the Mississippi were gone—killed out. And with them, the canelands, grasslands, and barrens that sustained the droves were slashed and burned into split-rail fences, farms, pastures, tobacco fields, planta-tions, and river-driven gristmills. Like Esau of the Old Covenant, man the hunter had risen up and subdued, selling his stolen birthright for mammon's sake.

The eastern buffalo's fate was not repeated in the Far West, albeit narrowly, though the brutal lessons of the East went unheeded. Foolishness, ignorance, and greed pushed western buffs to the lip of the final abyss, stopping short of extinction barely in time to save the breed.

As in hunting buffs during the Far West's heady frontier days of iron rails and steam-driven boxcars, slaughtering buffalo east of the Mississippi needed no justi-fication, as Daniel Trabue's remembrance of a winter hunt shows:

> Mr. Smith and I . . . found 11 buffeloes in one Gang. Shot down one. Set on the dogs after the others and going about one Mile they stopt them. We boath shot at once and killed 2 more. They broak and run off. The Dogs run after them, stopt them again. We concluded to shoot the leaders—to wit, the Old cows—and then the younger ones would not leave them. . . .
>
> We killed 2 more and the rest stayed their fighting the dogs. And we kept shooting them down as fast as we could until we got them all killed but one and that was a calf.
>
> He run away. . . . We guted them first ones that was killed and went to where the main body was a lying. When we got their, their was the buffeloe calf. The dogs took after him. The snow was Deep. He ran off round about and returned. And as he run over the dead buffaloes he fell down and the dogs ketched him and we tyed him. Made a good worm fire and guted all our buffeloes before we went to sleep.
>
> We had fun with that buffeloe Calf the next day. Their was a long rope cut of buffaloe hide and put around the horns and one of the boys would git on his back. The buffaloe was let go. He would run the length of his rope which was held by 2 of the other boys. He would kick and Jump until the man

would fall off but as their was snow their was no Damage Done. We thought at first we would tame him but after several such frolicks, thinking he would be too troublesome we killed him and slaughtered him. So we killed the whole Gang which was 11.[5]

Aside from Daniel Boone's law passed at Boonesborough in 1775 for preserving the wild cattle and their grassy range, little thought was given to stopping the wanton carnage or careless destruction of the buffs' habitat. Men who fancied themselves woodsmen strove mightily to kill buffalo and did. Yet, like the Indians upon whose land they were trespassing, the Kentuckians depended on big game for food. In twoscore years free-roaming buffalo, like panthers and wolves, would vanish forever from the Ohio Valley and east of the Mississippi.[6]

CHAPTER SEVEN

To Earn One's Freedom

1779

James Estill and his brother Samuel, along with James's slaves, Monk and his wife, had moved from Greenbrier County, Virginia, to Boonesborough, where they lived for a year. At twenty-eight, James Estill—the Delaware called him the "Great Man" for his valor—was a veteran of Indian wars. Kentuckians elected James a Boonesborough trustee, and Col. John Holder promoted him to captain in his militia. Brother Samuel was a fighter too, and Indians knew Sam better as the "Big Man," as he stood more than six feet and weighed over four hundred pounds.[1]

That year, Thomas Warren and his wife came to Kentucky via the Cumberland Gap. When Warren and his wife got to the Bluegrass, he was walking, she was riding, and their horse was footsore and weak from lack of graze. The two were famished when they spied Capt. James Estill galloping down a trace a few miles from Boone's fort.

They hailed the woodsman. Estill reined to a halt, greeted them, told them how to get to Boonesborough, and rode off.

Warren and his wife rode on. Miles later the two found the cane piled high next to a freshly killed buffalo—a gift from Estill. Warren cut out its tongue and skewered it over a fire, ate, and they pushed on.[2]

"We found a poor distressed, $^1/_2$ naked, $^1/_2$ starved, people; daily surrounded by the savage," wrote Josiah Collins at Boonesborough.[3] Indians hovered nearby to steal a horse, shoot a cow, or pick off settlers. At Hoy's, Irvine's, Strode's, Logan's Station, Harrod's Town, and Boonesborough, whites lived under constant threat.

Monk Estill

Monk Estill, like John Nutt at McConnell's Station and Daniel Boone, made black powder for the fort and nearby stations, digging cave dirt rich in guano or shoveling up dank earth from beneath outhouses to mix with water and drain through V-shaped log vats stuffed with straw. "Run your durt Like Ly after Lating it stand 24 hours then Boyle it one hour," wrote Boone in his journal. Boiling off the liquor left spindly, needle-shaped niter crystals to crush into saltpeter dust and mix with willow charcoal and sulfur. Then "Boyle your Brimstone till all the gaus is oute then Way your proportions, put them in a pott, stur thim togather till the Sulphur Melts and all unites With the Niter." That done, a maker doused the mix with urine, rendering it a black, smelly goop to be mashed flat to sun-dry; urine better oxygenated the mixture and caused the powder to "flash" with surety. Gunpowder was usually packed over the Blue Ridge or flat-boated from Fort Pitt; few seem to have known how to make it, and brimstone was hard to come by.[4]

Monk received from George Michael Bedinger a gourd of apple seeds, which he planted his first Kentucky spring and nurtured; settlers deemed Monk's orchard "a great benefit to the country."[5] He tanned garment-weight deerskins taken in their summer red coats; heavy elk and buffalo winter hides he made into quilts, saddle rugs, and shoepac leather, steeping them in rain-water-filled vats of shredded chestnut, hemlock, sumac, or oak bark oozing dark, acidic tannins that penetrated the raw skins, breaking them down for currying and softening. Rev. John Evans Finlay visited the Bluegrass and watched Kentuckians tan cowhides:

1) Take off the horns from the hides, then soak the blood out of them in ye water pool.
2) Then put ye hides into ye lime pit . . . carefully observe when the hair comes off, will be in a week or less—during this time draw them out twice a day letting them stay out 20 or 30 minutes to air.
3) Then unhair them, and put them into bast—bast them twice a week in cold weather and three times in warm . . . twice a day. Ye bast is a mixture of water and hen dung—You will know by the water when the lime is quite out of the hides then they are sufficiently basted, out of the bast rub hides with a rounding edge iron over a hollow tree out of ye bast.
4) Then handle them in a strong mixture of bast in box or pit of bark—and 4 calf skins in a handler. . . . leather is laid down in a clean pit—a layer of clean dry bark and a hide and so on and then pour on water and in four or five weeks raise and lay down as before.[6]

Deerskins might need four to six months to absorb the tanning solution before being removed from the vats to beam and oil with renderings from boiled hooves; a buffalo bull hide needed up to a year. Softening—a two-man job of whipping the damp hide back and forth over a tombstone-looking beam set upright in the ground until the skin dried—was hard work. Monk, a stout chunk of a man standing five-five and weighing two hundred pounds, muscles hardened from slave life, excelled at it. In the settlements, two tanners could do five hundred skins a year. Not in the West: By day Indians might lie in the shadows waiting for a clear shot; by night they raided the hide vats.

One day soon after Monk's Kentucky arrival, the cry of a woman in labor and a slap and shrill squall came from Monk's cabin. It was the first of many black children born in Boonesborough. Monk's wife was faint from exhaustion when the women attending her eased from her her son, cut and tied his umbilical cord, and swabbed the baby clean. Monk named their boy Jerry.[7]

In March 1780 Monk and his family moved to Estill's Station, established by Capt. James Estill about four miles southeast of Richmond, on Little Muddy Creek. Strode's Station, to the north, was as critical to the safety of the Bluegrass as its sister forts to the northwest, Bryan's and Ruddell's Station.

Strode's Station had begun as a lean-to. Col. John Strode had left Virginia for Kentucky in 1776, heading ten miles north of Boonesborough to his thousand-acre preemption, where he wintered in a half-faced shelter, blazed trees to mark his property, slashed and burned timber, torched the cane, and planted corn the next spring. A year later he was in Virginia, many of his Berkeley neighbors (Strode's "Torified ways" notwithstanding) willing to cross the Blue Ridge with him. By 1780 his fort had a blockhouse, gates, and palisades and housed thirty families, many of them Loyalists. William Clinkenbeard planted hemp there in 1779. "'Old Man' Strode," he would say, was "pretty much a coward."[8]

By February 1781 only seven men guarded Strode's Station. Spies spotting sign near Boone's Station ten miles away had put out the call for help, and eight of Strode's defenders—John Douglass, John McIntyre, John Hart, Frederick Couchman, Samuel Taylor, John Kirk, William and Isaac Clinkenbeard—rode to Boone's to wait for a raid that did not come.

Meanwhile, back at Strode's, some Wyandots hid in the scrub bordering the fort's split-rail garden fence, thatching it with leaves for cover. Jacob Spahr heard the rustling and went to see; he walked within ten steps of the red men, who shot him down. Patrick Donaldson ran to his aid, but as he slowed to vault the fence, a bullet slammed into his head. The Wyandots shot another man before fleeing beyond range, driving the cattle before them.

As the people watched, the Indians slaughtered the livestock, laying aside fusils for bows and arrows to save on gunpowder. For thirty-six hours, between bouts of feasting, the warriors terrorized the settlers with impunity—shooting, shouting profane threats, showering the outpost with fire arrows. The white men fired at the phantoms; women ran balls, wiped brows, dipped gourds of water, and braced cabin doors with billets, fearing a breach and death by tomahawk. But the last action did not come. The Wyandots vanished.

Miami
River

Little Miami
River

Big
Bone
Lick

Ohio River

Limestone

Ohio River

Eagle Cr

Licking River

Drennons
Lick

Kentucky
River

Lower Blue Lick

Painted
Stone

Ruddles
Martins

Upper Blue Lick

Falls

Elkhorn Cr.

McClellans

Bushy Cr. Farm

Louisville

Leestown

Beargrass
Stations

Bryans

Strodes

Lexington

Salt River

Cox

Woodstock

Bullitts
Lick

Town Fk

Boone's
Station

Boonesborough

McAfees

Kentucky River

Beech Fk

Harrodsburg

Dicks River

Twittie's Fort

Boiling Springs

St. Asaph
(Logans)

Whitley's

Rolling Fk

Crab Orchard

Green River

Skagg's Trace

South Fk
of Ky.

Hazel Patch

Rockcastle
River

Cumberland River

Mountain

Cumberland
River

Mountain

Pine

Virginia-North Carolina boundary

Cumberland

Cumberland
Gap

Kentucky Frontier c.1780

0   20   40   60

Scale in Miles

NOH 98

MAP BY NEAL O. HAMMON.

Savage mischief or not, still, crops had to be planted and chores tended to. William Clinkenbeard worked his soil to plant hemp seed. Monk Estill felled trees to erect into palisades, hauled wood and water and food, hunted, fished, planted an orchard, put out his own garden, and tended the garden of James Estill. In Peyton's Cave, he mined saltpeter and guano for gunpowder.

Early in 1781 the men of Harrod's Town appointed Capt. James Estill judge for a quarter session. During an ambuscade on Muddy Creek that spring, a Wyandot bullet shattered Captain Estill's right arm, leaving it a splintered mess of bone and flesh nigh impossible to properly set.[9] For three months he sat, listening, pouring over disputed claims and conducting Harrod's Town's court, bearing his aching arm in a linen sling, picking out bone bits that pushed up under his skin.

SUMMER 1781

Indians by the score gathered at Wapatomica, a Shawnee town on Darby Creek south of the Scioto, which flowed through Ohio land and to the Beautiful River. Warriors wandering about fire pits and clusters of smoke-filled lodges, cabins, and wigwams must have been taken aback upon hearing divers tongues of ancient stock, like the Huron-Petun dialects, which hearkened to the days before the White Eye invasion. In the weeks that followed, disparate strands of Algonquins and Iroquoians—Shawnees, Wyandots, Wolf clan of the Delawares, Mingoes, Potawatomis, and Cherokees, whose blood mingled with that of the Shawanoes and Catawbas to darken the soil of the Warriors' Path—forged an alliance in the crucible of a common flame.

One stoking the coals was Simon Girty. In the 1760s Girty had esteemed himself as a market hunter in Illinois for Philadelphia's fur-trading firm of Baynton, Wharton, and Morgan; in the Revolution he had esteemed himself as a scout at Fort Pitt, albeit a rather surly one due to his fondness for rum and brawling; after turning Tory the night of March 28, 1778, with deserters Matthew Elliot and the half-Shawnee Alexander McKee, Girty esteemed himself as a loyal "go-between" for the British Indian Department.[10]

Girty's look of pure malevolence was not so much his own doing. Months before, his brother James had aided the mixed-blood Mohawk from New York, Thayendanegea (whites knew him as Joseph Brant), when he traveled to Shawnee land and, on August 25, devastated Col. Archibald Lochry's Pennsylvania battalion, killing Lochry, thirty-six of his men, and capturing all seventy survivors.

Image purporting to be that of Simon Girty and on display at Fort Malden Historical Park. Used with the consent of Dwight Girty of Windsor, Ontario, the great-great-great-grandson of Simon Girty.

Days later, as Brant rejoiced in his cups, he and Simon Girty, deep in his cups too, tangled in a fit of drunken egos. Brant drew steel and slashed Girty a dreadful gash across his temple, cutting past skin and bone and nearly killing him. For the rest of his days, Girty, his eyesight fading, would don a black silk scarf pulled to his brow to hide the ghastly scar.

But now, after a feast of boiled puppy and smoked buffalo tongue and stew, and after passing of the pipe-tomahawk, aromatic gray wisps from its steel bowl filling the air with scents of tobacco, willow, and sumac, Girty the thick-necked white *sauvage* cut a stocky figure as he stood at Wapatomica's council fire, a brace of silver-mounted pistols in his belt. A master in the art of woodland elocution and adroit in native diplomacy, he spoke in Algonquin, punctuating his sonorous brogue with graceful gesticulation, declaring in a baritone voice that soared to a crescendo as he ended:

> Brothers:
> The Long Knives have overrun your country, and usurped your hunting grounds. They have destroyed the cane, trodden down the clover, killed the deer and the buffaloes. . . . Unless you rise in the majesty of your might, and exterminate the whole race, you may bid adieu to the hunting grounds of your fathers—to the

delicious flesh of the animals with which it once abounded.[11]

Girty sat down. The elders passed the war club. Each struck it to the earth.

Hi-yah!

Scalp halloos cut the night as excerpts from Girty's words and news of the war vote rippled across Wapatomica.

Girty and the rest slipped out of the council house to walk through the rows of wigwams to the village's center. Twin lines of warriors with faces painted black with red about the eyes, others with red faces and eyes of black, sang and danced to drums that pounded until the sun rose. The undulating roil of lean men slick with bear fat and stripped to breechcloths and moccasins circled the war post counterclockwise in a wide oval, pausing in step, rhythmically rising and falling toe-to-heel to a cacophony of wavering, strident cries, their bobbing heads having scalp locks plaited with red and blue silk ribbons and ringed with sterling brooches, or arrayed with eagle feathers, or magnificent *gastowehs* fitted with plumes of peafowl and ostrich.

The sachem had painted the post black and streaked it with vermilion and crowned it with a war diadem—dried scalps with locks of brown, auburn, and black, bunches of split feathers that fluttered with the wind, and the ancient medicine bundle that many feared to look upon. A host of boys joined the throng, as the oval closed and ranks of the painted men of many nations struck the post with hatchets, pipe-tomahawks, and ball-head death hammers of maple fixed with polls of wood, flint, and iron.

Thus spake the oracle: Come spring, the furies of Wapatomica vowed, they would vent their wrath south of Speleawee-theepee.

SPRING 1782

Lord Cornwallis's surrender to George Washington at Yorktown, Virginia, October 1781 had little impact on the war in the West. The British held Canada and were secure in their fortress at Detroit, keeping Ohio Indians armed, fed, and clothed. It was not hard to maintain their Loyalist sympathies. Nor was it hard to persuade warriors who saw their way of life vanishing to harass Kentuckians.

On a February night in 1782, twenty-five Wyandots and two coureurs de bois crossed the Ohio to attack Strode's Station. They traveled by night and hid in the cane during the crisp days, rarely striking fire or firing their arms.

Scouts spied their derelict raft drifting on the Kentucky churning past Boonesborough. Runners relayed the news to Col. Benjamin Logan at St. Asaph's. Logan dispatched fifteen men to Capt. James Estill with stern orders: muster reinforcements and reconnoiter.

Logan's couriers reached Estill's Station. Runners hastened to nearby forts. Twenty-five men heeded the call.

On Saturday, March 19, Captain Estill's forty horsemen rode from his outpost, leaving behind women and children, Monk Estill and other slaves, and Alexander Robertson, shot by Indians weeks before. James Estill had set aside his sling, but his mending arm still ached from the Muddy Creek ambuscade.

Estill gambled, heading his militia to a ford on the Kentucky. As they rode away, and as the sky darkened and it began to snow, the Wyandots skirting the trees ringing Estill's Station moved in behind smoldering log piles of newly cleared land that the settlers had heaped about.

For the settlers, the cold night passed as any other. But not for one thirteen-year-old girl.

She dreamed of a ladder reaching down from Heaven to her earthly home, bidding her come. And as her dream clouded as she began to slip into consciousness, she saw a little girl appear and grasp the ladder's bottom rung and pull herself to the second rung, and then to the third, and then ascending, until she disappeared.

March's chill brought her to. Jenny Gass lay there, then arose and dressed and went to warm by the crude hearth in the Gass cabin. She told her dream to her mother, Sarah, and to James and John, her brothers, and to her sisters, Mary and Sarah; her father, David, was not there to hear it; he had ridden off with Estill. But the dream was so real she felt that she must go and tell the other nine families at the station about it.

And so she went, as the people listened to her, pleased to find this maiden knocking at their door to tell of a dream that had so moved her. From cabin to cabin she went, until she had told all, and some hugged her, sharing in the joy that a strange dream had so wrought upon this fair one.

But most soon forgot about Jenny's dream. It was sugarmaking time and there was much to do.[12]

Monk Estill left the outpost to haul in a load of firewood on his wood sledge. As he bent to tie a thong near the sled's bottom, the warriors rushed in, seized him, bound him with tugs, and interrogated him.

Forty men now defended the station, Monk lied. They knew Indians were about, he told them.

Yet his audacious lie worked. Convinced Estill's was heavily garrisoned, the Indians argued among themselves.

The fort's gates opened. The slave Dick and Jenny Gass walked out, heading toward the woods to tap sugar maples, walking a quarter mile to the grove. Dick freshed out the old bore holes. Jenny hung troughs beneath the holes to catch the sap.

"Run, Jenny. Indians are coming!" called Jenny's mother from the ramparts.

All able-bodied hands manned the loops. Those that could not shoot stood at hand to cut patches, run balls, make bandages, and yank tow to plug wounds. Jenny's brother John, a year younger than she, drew a bead.

"Run, Jenny, run!" Sarah Gass screamed again.

Dick dashed behind the fort, sprinting to safety. Jenny ran for three hundred yards, her apron fluttering, her image one of cotton and linen and hair streaming from a mobcap. She had sixty yards to go when they shot her down and dragged her behind a tree.

Little brother John fired, in his anguish pulling his shot wide. Musket fire burst from behind the walls as the Yellow Boys fled to the brush piles. As the staccato ended and the defenders huddled below the palisades to load and prime and peer through the loops, a warrior jumped up on a log, waving.

"Lun, Henny, lun!" he mocked, grinning his eerie grin and dancing his death dance, wringing gore from his lank hair trophy.

Then, coolly and with resolution, the red men eased beyond range and went about loading and priming and firing, and then doing it again, shooting the cattle and sheep, chiding the whites as they did so. Two or three unhitched the team from Monk's sled and led them away. With Monk—a tie binding his wrists—in tow and hustled along, the Wyandots and the Frenchmen disappeared, leaving much sign in the bloodied snow.

Warily, the men emerged from Estill's Station to gather the fair one who had fallen to take back to her weeping mother; the women would ready Jenny's body for burial upon return of her father. Peter Hackett and Samuel South armed themselves and rode out the gates into the bitterly cold night swirling with snow and ice. Twenty miles and later, at dawn, the youths found Estill's party camped at Sweet Lick at the fork of Red River and Drowning Creek.[13]

At their report, five of Estill's men rode to the fort, but Hackett and South stayed as the scouts picked up the trail. The men crossed the river in two elm bark canoes, swimming the horses alongside.

They tracked them all Monday. "They made as much trail as possible, desiring pursuit," recalled James Wade. Estill's men slept on their arms that night, resting near a rise called Little Mountain.[14]

The Wyandots left before first light Tuesday morning, March 22, their fire smoldering as Estill and his band spied it. After reconnoitering, they reined up. Then, lo!, a distant shot; then another.

"Boys, we are going to fight them," Estill said. "Those too tired should stay. They mean to fight, so decide now."

Ten men, their mounts worn from the chase, would bivouac and act as reinforcements. Estill split his ranks and gained the van, horses galloping forward in four single-file lines.

As the sun fully rose, they saw the Wyandots fording at a wide trace buffalo had gouged into the slopes banking Little Mountain Creek. On the far shore across the creek were a few warriors hunkered over, dressing out a buffalo.

And then the Wyandots saw them.

Hi-yah!

Captain Estill slowed his horse. As his rifle cracked, so too did that of Ensign David Cook. Two Indians on the ridge, sitting side by side near the buffalo carcass, tumbled away from each other and rolled to the side—both hit by Cook's bullet. The rest forded and took flight in a sparse bramble of cane.

"Every man to his man and every man to his tree!" cried Estill. Several men took the horses to the rear and out of range.

Here the cane rose head-high. As the ridge rose, so too rose the cane, to twice head-high. David Lynch, who had hunted the Green with Casper Mansker's Long Hunters in 1771, stood by Estill as he hailed his men in the fire. Lynch reckoned the battlefield to be "not more than 125 yards wide and 200 yards long." Between the antagonists flowed Little Mountain Creek, a hindrance to both sides in that it kept them from routing their foes, a blessing to both sides in that it kept their foes at bay.[15]

The Wyandots' headman, Sourehoowah, hit mortal in the first volley, hid in a thicket to exhort his men to give them heart. At his beckoning, each warrior singled out his prey, turning Estill's offense into a series of one-on-one sorties that left men dead and dying.

As Estill's line began to waver, a voice boomed over the din. "Don't give up, Captain Jim! There are twenty-five of them! You can whip them!" Monk Estill, still a hostage, cheered them on.

Gray puffs of gunpowder soot clouds whooshed amorphous smoke rings head-high through cane and sumac. Gun barrels waxed hot, unbearably hot,

Edge-beaded scarlet wool side-seam legging (left leg), c. 1780, edge flaps bordered with silk ribbon (purple on front flap and along bottom edge; green on rear; blue along thigh enclosure), hand-stitched with black linen thread, 12-15 stitches to the inch. ARTISANS: MICHAEL J. TAYLOR AND LAVINA BELUE. AUTHOR'S COLLECTION.

blistering the grimy hands loading them, as both sides fought with no thought of quarter. For whites, it was for Jenny Gass and the killing of their sheep and cattle, a portent of starving times ahead; for the reds, it was for the intrusion upon their homeland and Big Sam Estill's murder of their two kinsmen the year before.

Sourehoowah, his life oozing away, stood and made ready to lead his men across the creek to outflank his foes. A young man in scarlet leggings joined him; it was Split Log, a man at seventeen. At Sourehoowah's word, Split Log seemed to be everywhere, hallooing, cajoling, breathing fire into Sourehoowah's warriors edging down the trace. Split Log's recklessness drew the admiration of his kinsmen as his red wool leggings drew the fire of William Irving. But as Irving felled Split Log on the Indian shore, and as he grasped his shot bag and horn to reload, a blast of buck and ball tore into his center, dropping him a wheezing mass of bleeding flesh.

The Kentuckians rendezvoused in the tall cane, watching Sourehoowah maneuver his painted cadre toward Little Mountain Creek. Estill countered: His band would flank right, Lt. William Miller would defend the left flank, and militia ensigns David Cook and John South would hold center. The Indians bearing down, the militia lines streamed forth pell-mell.[16]

Estill hollered for his men to shore up, to tighten ranks. But they were spread thin and could not pull themselves back in good order. Smelling blood, the Indians began crossing the creek.

Monk escaped during the fray; Estill dispatched him to the battle line's rear to hold the horses. The Wyandots gaining Estill's left flank, the commander ordered Lieutenant Miller to ford and counterflank. Miller and six or seven men began wading when a bullet slammed into Miller's gun cock, shattering the flint from its jaws. Two of Miller's men pitched forward, roiling the water red. His firelock useless, his men dying, Miller's unit clambered to shore and over the bank without firing a shot.

Joseph and Reuben Proctor grabbed him as he bolted past to give him a flint and get him to turn and fight. But Miller shook free and ran on, racing past the horses, shouting to Monk, who urged him to fight, that "it was foolhardy to stay and be shot down."[17]

Ensign Cook's division rushed in to hold the ground Miller had fled, but the fighting grew so hot that Cook gave way. Cook fired, ran to hide in the brushy top of a fallen tree, weaving in among the branches and tangling his shot bag's straps. As he hung there, an Indian shot him point-blank, the ball exiting at the collarbone. John McMillan swore, "By God, I will have an Indian," and made a one-man charge against a volley that slammed him to his knees, dead.

When Joseph Proctor reported to Estill—himself bleeding from three wounds—that half of his men were dead or wounded, Estill ordered retreat. As the whites dropped back, a bullet smacked into Adam Caperton's head. Spitting blood, his lower jaw dangling like an unhinged shutter loosed from the top plate, Caperton clamped his jaws shut with his hands and dashed through the cane after Estill, trying to tell him something no one could make out.

As Estill tried to aid his dying friend, a warrior yanked his scalping knife and ran Estill down, and the two locked. Proctor snapped his gun to his shoulder, thumbed it to full cock, but dared not fire for fear of hitting his commander.

The Indian bore down, stabbing wildly, as he leaned hard into the groping, upright arms that rose up from beneath him, trying to hold him fast. Pushing hard against the man beneath him, he jabbed again and again. Estill's right arm quivered, bowed like a green hickory bent out of kilter, and gave way as the blade plunged down. As the Indian arose, victorious, Proctor's shot prostrated him across Estill's corpse.

Capt. James Estill dead, his men retreated, leaving eight dead, and the wounded to hobble away to get mounts.[18] William Irvine, breeches red from his own blood, now faced a hatchet-wielding Wyandot. Four times he leaped from behind a tree to brain Irvine; four times Joseph Proctor backed him down with his unloaded gun. Irvine staggered to Estill's horse, swung himself up, and kicked the animal into a trot, but three miles later he swooned and slipped off. James Proctor, riding alongside, pressed his wound shut and hoisted him back in the saddle. James Berry, shot through his thigh, would have died were it not for Monk, who threw Berry over his shoulder and lugged him twenty-five miles to safety. The others, carrying and dragging the survivors behind them, fled to Estill's Station, Boonesborough, Hoy's Station, Tanner's Station, and Irvine's Fort.

Three days later half-Indian Peter Harper led fifty men from Boonesborough, Paint Lick, and Estill's, McGee's, Holder's, and Strode's Stations to the killing field. Trees barked bare bore testimony of the ferocity of the battle. Buzzards swooped heavily and spiraled away. None of the dead were mutilated; the Wyandots had fled, crossing the Ohio to push on to Wapatomica and Upper Sandusky.

Harper's party placed the dead next to fallen trees to cover with logs and clutter. Joseph Proctor rummaged through Estill's weskit for his line and plumb to take to his wife, Mary, and found in Adam Caperton's pockets two silver knee buckles. They buried John McMillan with Forbes, but buried John Colefoot and McNeely separately.

News of Estill's Defeat shocked Kentuckians, proving Indians could strike in the heart of the Bluegrass with masterful strategy, lay waste a fortified station, and brutally trounce its defenders on the field of battle. But the grim revelation was only a prelude of a more horrible carnage.

On what would prove a portentous Thursday, August 15, Capts. William Caldwell and Alexander McKee, the Girtys, fifty Rangers, and more than four hundred Great Lakes Indians passed unseen to Bryan's Station, five miles northeast of Lexington. They killed four whites and wounded three, stole horses, beat down corn rows, fired hemp fields, killed more than 300 hogs, 150 cattle, and all the sheep. Caldwell's raiders retreated Saturday, August 17.

That night a force of Kentuckians rendezvoused at Bryan's, and by Sunday morning 182 mounted militiamen were on the trail of Caldwell's warriors and partisans. Daniel Boone calculated their numbers at 500 and warned of treachery.

On Monday, August 19, 7:30 A.M., at the Lower Blue Licks, the militia's spies fording the Licking River saw nothing. Boone, though, captured by

Remnant of lead buffalo trace followed by Kentuckians before the Battle of Blue Licks, August 19, 1782. PHOTO C. 1900; THE FILSON CLUB, LOUISVILLE, KY.

Black Fish's warriors at this place in 1778 and vastly familiar with its deep, sheltered ravines and hollows, warned of an ambush. Maj. Hugh McGary, maddened by the delay, swore he came for a fight and splashed across the river, calling all who would not follow him "damn cowards."

On the far bank, they regrouped into three lines: Boone was on the left with seventy men, including his twenty-one-year-old son, Israel; Stephen Trigg took the right flank; Levi Todd commanded the center. They "advanced . . . in good order," Caldwell reported, within sixty yards of the warriors.[20] Stillness—then scalp halloos shook the woods, from which came gunfire as the wraiths poured from ravines, war clubs and tomahawks held high.

The Kentuckians fell back and ran for their lives. Only Boone's flank held, barely. It was over in ten minutes.

Indians captured seven of them to take across the Ohio to burn. Jesse Yocum, who escaped, "did not know how many they burned, but the smell of a human was the awfullest smell he ever smelled in his life."[21] On August 24 Col. Ben Logan and 470 men returned to bury the slain. Boone reported the horror to be "almost unparalleled."

> We . . . found their bodies strewed every where, cut and
> mangled in a dreadful manner. . . . Some torn and eaten
> by wild beasts; those in the river eaten by fishes; all in
> such a putrefied condition that none could be distin-
> guished from another.[22]

They found Col. Stephen Trigg's body—quartered. Out of 182 Kentuckians, at least 70 were dead or missing, and Logan's men interred more than 40
corpses in a common grave. Boone took Israel's body back to bury at his station, his boy's last words—"Father, I won't leave you!"—before the ball tore
out his throat, to forever haunt him.

The ambush devastated one-thirteenth of Kentucky's militia. As bad,
many settlers fled back east, leaving the West open to more attacks and causing 1782 to be remembered as the Year of Blood.

In Paris on November 30, 1782, the warlords signed articles. American
borders leaped west of the Blue Ridge to the Mississippi and south of the
Great Lakes to Spanish Florida.

But in Kentucky, there was no lasting peace: Gen. George Rogers Clark,
Cols. John Floyd and Ben Logan, and 1,050 men attacked Indian towns
north of the Ohio—"sparing neither towns nor wigwams nor a vestige of anything upon which the savages could subsist." Daniel Boone commanded
one flank. Whites vented their wrath on the Shawnee—a tribe marginally
represented at the attacks on Bryan's Station and Blue Licks. Stunned, the
Shawnee fled to face a winter of disease and starvation as the army piled up
plunder.

Thus ended the Year of Blood, but even with peace declared, the Brits,
stung by the loss of their colonies, armed the Great Lakes and Ohio Indians
against the United States' far western citizens. "Whole families are destroyed,
without regard to age or sex," Col. John Floyd wrote to Gov. Thomas Jefferson on April 16, 1781, with word to inform General Clark: "Infants are torn
from their mothers arms and their brains bashed out against trees . . . scarcely
a day without our distressed inhabitants feeling the fatal effects of the infernal
rage and fury of these execrable Hell hounds."

He dispatched a note to Virginia for guns and supplies. "We are all oblig-
ated to live in forts in this country . . . forty seven have been killed and taken
by savages . . . since January last."[23] Indians spied Floyd riding along the western fork of the Wilderness Road and shot him.

Yet, there was at least one bright moment that grim year, and thereby
hangs a tale: Monk Estill, for his courage and valor at the battle of Little
Mountain, was granted his freedom and became Kentucky's first freed slave.

"Pompey, the Black Shawnee," armed with modified Short Land Pattern *(Second Model) Brown Bess, fully accourtered, and wearing a magnificent* gastoweh. Photo by David Wright taken at Mansker's Station, Goodlettsville, Tennessee, during producer Gary L. Foreman's filming of the critically acclaimed episode "Boone and Crockett: The Hunter-Heroes."

Killing Pompey

Though they have never appeared in a school text, Hollywood movie, or a TV show of the Old West, Black Indians were there as sure as Sitting Bull, Davy Crockett and Geronimo.
—William Loren Katz, *Black Indians: Hidden Heritage*

Monk Estill, like all frontier Africans living with their masters, existed in a shadowy realm governed by hazy laws of slavery brought from east of the mountains. Africans were property. Few owners cared about their chattel's history, and often anonymity blurred identity: Cato, Moses, London, Pompey, Caesar, Jack—common names given to slaves whose place in Kentucky history is barely a footnote.

Two Africans fought in Boonesborough's siege in 1778. London, Nathaniel Henderson's slave, crawled from the fort in a trench dug under the walls to fire at Shawnees torching the palisades. Pompey, a fugitive interpreter, hunkered below the Kentucky's banks and perched in treetops to snipe at Kentuckians. Bullets felled them both, yet only Pompey is remembered. His death left a void in Shawnee society: Pompey knew white ways and was bilingual. For Kentuckians, the "black renegade" carved a niche as the audacious African sniper who took on death with a sneer and gave no quarter until the Noseless One abruptly greeted him head-on. But mostly, Pompey is famous because lore credits Daniel Boone with the legendary shot that slew him.

Of course. Boone.

In typical accounts, Pompey hid out in a tall sycamore, blackguarding incendiary diatribes laced with bawdy references to white women. His high-amplitude utterances of things not said in polite society were sure to rankle and incense, and did, provoking from Boonesborough's defenders not a little hot lead and sputtered tirades of racial invective against this saucy black who dared to spout so recklessly. For three days this sort of ribald bandying went on, until, as the story goes, Captain Boone stoked up trusty Tick-Licker with a stout charge and, hanging a bead high in the broad-leafed canopy, leveled down on "the Negro" and let go a one-ounce round.

Down came Pompey from off his perch, forehead pulsing red. Up rose a mighty shout from behind the fort's walls—"Pompey's dead!" Shawnees echoed the cry—"Pompey Ne-Poo!"

If Daniel Boone told John Filson about Pompey when Filson met him in 1783, Filson did not retell it in 1784 in *The Discovery, Settlement, and Present State of Kentucky*. Nor did Filson's plagiarist, John Trumbull; two years after the release of *Boon.*, Trumbull republished it, launching it at home and abroad by embellishing Boone's exploits but omitting Filson's philosophical musings about ancient Greece and "the loin of a buck" and such, which readers did not care about. Had Trumbull known Pompey's fate at the hand of his famed slayer, most likely he would have printed it: Such fodder in proslavery/anti-Indian Manifest Destiny America—how a noble Anglo-Saxon defending hearth and home from the red menace rose up and slew a sassy African-turned-Indian—was literary gold.

Nor did Rev. Timothy Flint—who knew Boone—tell the Pompey tale in 1833 in his *Biographical Memoir of Daniel Boone, the First Settler of Kentucky*. It was not until 1847, in his fulsome biography, *The Life of Daniel Boone, the Pioneer of Kentucky*, that Rev. John M. Peck—a Baptist minister who visited Boone in 1818—first presented the story of Pompey's dramatic death:

> While the parley was in progress, an unprincipled Negro man deserted, and went over to the Indians, carrying with him a large, far shooting rifle . . . [and] ascended a tree . . . when Captain Boone . . . fired and the Negro was seen to fall. After the Indians had retreated, his body was found, and his forehead was pierced with the ball, fired at the distance of one hundred and seventy-five yards. The Indians . . . would not touch his body.[1]

Reverend Peck was so awed by the venerable woodsman, he later admitted, that when he met the elder Boone and his family, he could scarcely speak and found it impossible to take notes.

Did Daniel Boone shoot Pompey as he sniped away perched high in a tree nearly two hundred yards from Boonesborough?

Nathan Boone, Daniel and Rebecca's last-born son, did not think so. Nor did his wife, Olive. In 1851 Boone historian and antiquarian collector Lyman C. Draper met the couple at their Missouri home to ask them their recollections about the Boones and frontier life. Their talk shifted to the siege of Boonesborough and the slaying of Pompey. Said Nathan, "I do not recall any particulars of Pompey's being killed, but an Indian peering his head in the fork of a stump was shot from the fort, but I don't know how or by whom."

The query was put to Mrs. Boone, who replied, "I don't recall any details of Pompey's death either, but neither Nathan nor I ever believed Peck's story that Daniel Boone killed him."[2]

Perplexed, Draper judged Peck's pronouncement about Pompey's death to be "a singularly confused statement." To his profound regret, Draper had allowed Reverend Peck to peruse his carefully guarded, meticulously annotated notes (a rare privilege that became far rarer after Peck published his Boone book as Draper struggled to write his own) and surmised Peck had skewed several accounts—like the one below told by Joseph Jackson—and in doing so had inadvertently produced a hybrid tale that Draper typically referred to as Peck's "Negro story."

Said Jackson to Draper in 1844:

> Another adventurous Indian frequently placed himself in the fork of a tree . . . pulling up his breech-clout and exhibiting his person in a bantering, derisive manner. Several shots had been ineffectively fired at him, when Captain Boone's famous "Tick-Licker," as he termed it, a gun of more than the common caliber, carrying an ounce ball [fired] . . . and the bold, saucy fellow was seen to tumble lifeless from the tree.[3]

Never one to let a historical sliver wane into insignificance, Draper became obsessed with unraveling the considerably snarled line of the Boone-and-Pompey backlash and wound up interviewing more than forty people about the matter.

One correspondent, E. J. Roark, wrote to Draper:

> While the siege of Boonesborough was going on, there was a Negro with the Indians called Black Dick. Dick climbs up a sycamore tree so he could poke his cap on a stick just below the top of the forks—and meanwhile Boone's men, misled by Dick's trickery, would make the fur fly from his old cap. Finally, Simon Kenton said, "I see now," discovering Dick's white eye shining through the forks of the tree below like a star in a

dark cloud—"Now," says Kenton, "I will take another shot.
Watch me fetch Dick." Down came Dick, sure enough.[4]

In this rendering, "Black Dick" must be Pompey, though this is the only account
where he is called by that name. But Draper knew Roark's folksy yarn lacked cred-
ibility. Simon Kenton was away stealing horses before the siege, and upon returning, he hid behind enemy lines while the siege was in progress. Kenton did not
shoot Pompey.

In a conflicting account, again the voice of Joseph Jackson, age eighty-eight
when Draper interviewed him about the event that transpired some sixty-six years
before, said, "Pompey was killed . . . by John Martin." But there is no record of Joe
Jackson's being at the siege; Jackson, captured by Shawnees in February 1778
with Boone's salt boilers, was a prisoner at Old Chillicothe.[5]

Then, according to Ephraim McClean, William Hancock, a fort defender and,
like Jackson, one of the salt boilers, claimed it was his bullet that felled the infamous Pompey:

> Billy Hancock was on the stairs firing on the Indians and his
> old lady had been running bullets for three days and nights,
> and was so overcome, that she fell asleep . . . and exclaimed,
> though asleep "Pour it to them, Billy; the day is a rolling!" A
> big Negro by the name of Pompey came running up, carrying
> a flag, and demanded the surrender of the place. As Pompey
> approached, Hancock leveled his long fowling-piece on him,
> and dropped him.[6]

Was Hancock telling the truth? Was McClean? As Draper copied his "poorly
written letter," noting the inaccuracies, he wrote "erroneous" and "probably erroneous" in the margin. Draper did not believe McClean. Nor, for that matter, did
William Hancock's son, Robert.

The strongest evidence for identifying Pompey's killer, Draper finally averred,
lay in the words of John Gass, a Boonesborough siege survivor and redoubtable
hunter of Kentucky whose sister, Jenny, was brutally killed in a Wyandot attack on
Estill's Station in 1782. In 1844 Gass told Rev. John D. Shane:

> Pompey came to the place where they had dug into the bank
> and put his head up two or three times. Some of the men
> shot, while others . . . [set] to watch, could see the bullet[s]
> strike the water. William Collins, a first-rate marksman, held

"Pompey," by James Daugherty, 1939.

> his gun cocked and waiting: and when Pompey put his head
> up again, he fired. That time no splashing in the water was
> seen. Pompey was not heard of again.[7]

Still, Gass's memory was far from perfect: He claimed Simon Kenton fought inside the fort during Black Fish's prolonged attack, which he did not. And there were other inconsistencies.

And so Lyman Draper in his last years was still penning notes to anyone who could help him figure out who had killed Pompey. Reuben Gold Thwaites (heir to Draper's position as secretary of the State Historical Society of Wisconsin) did not use "the Negro story" in his trustworthy *Daniel Boone,* published in 1902.

But in 1939 author John Bakeless revamped Reverend Peck's prose to recapture the heady moments of Pompey's death (complete with dialogue and fresh insights on race relations) in this startling revelation:

> "You black scoundrel," muttered Captain Boone as he raised
> old "Tick-Licker," . . . "I'll fix your flint for you!"
>
> At the crack of the rifle, Pompey came tumbling out of the
> tree, dead. When the siege was ended, his was the only body
> found. . . . No Shawnee cared in the least what happened to
> the black body or the woolly scalp of a Negro slave.[8]

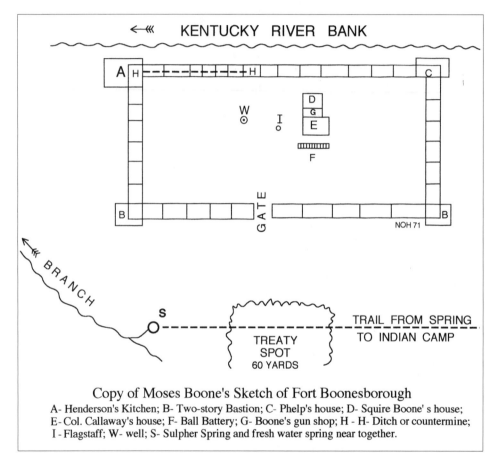

KENTUCKY RIVER BANK

A — Henderson's Kitchen; B- Two-story Bastion; C- Phelp's house; D- Squire Boone's house; E- Col. Callaway's house; F- Ball Battery; G- Boone's gun shop; H - H- Ditch or countermine; I - Flagstaff; W- well; S- Sulpher Spring and fresh water spring near together.

NOH 71

TREATY SPOT 60 YARDS

TRAIL FROM SPRING TO INDIAN CAMP

BRANCH

Copy of Moses Boone's Sketch of Fort Boonesborough
A- Henderson's Kitchen; B- Two-story Bastion; C- Phelp's house; D- Squire Boone' s house;
E- Col. Callaway's house; F- Ball Battery; G- Boone's gun shop; H - H- Ditch or countermine;
I - Flagstaff; W- well; S- Sulpher Spring and fresh water spring near together.

Besides using Peck's rendering, Bakeless also based his account on the contradictory letters of Elijah Bryan, a distant relative of Boone. In 1883 Bryan had written Draper that Boone told him that during Boonesborough's siege:

> He saw the smoke of the gun away up a big forked hickory tree. The Negro pushed up his head in the fork of a hickory to see what his shot had done to the fort and [Boone] drawing a bead on his forehead raised [his rifle] a little . . . bang went "old Tick-Licker"—down came the Negro . . . he supposed it at 200 and 50 yards. . . . This ended the siege.[9]

In a second letter, Bryan alters the range to 180 yards—a bit less spectacular, but still fine shooting for any Leatherstocking in the heat of battle.

Bryan's narrative is suspect: Pompey's death did not end the siege, which lasted nine days (not counting the two additional days of perfunctory negotiations that failed, precipitating the siege); he was not shot out of a tree; he was shot on the riverbank and not at the extreme ranges Bryan's letters suggest. Bryan's letters lack the ring of verity, but it does not matter: The specter of Pompey being blasted out of his tree was resurrected anew and arose to live again in numerous Boone and Kentucky books and melodramatic stage presentations.

Yet, the details of Pompey's death, like his life, remain elusive. Sifting the lore surrounding him demonstrates the difficulty in divining yarns, tall tales, and stories to glean truth from myth. But therein is revealed at least one truth: That five men claimed credit (or had credit thrust upon them) for slaying the imperious black Shawnee reveals a glimpse of border life far darker than Pompey's skin.

CHAPTER EIGHT

Intrigue on Green River

SPRING 1779

It was spring when George Michael Bedinger left the army of Gen. George Washington to join Col. William Morgan, a veteran of Braddock's Defeat, and his son, Ralph, along with Thomas and Benona Swearingen, John Taylor, John Strode, Samuel Dunes, John Constant, and two slaves. They left Berkeley County, Virginia, passed through Cumberland Gap, and pushed past Hazel Patch to pick up Boone's Trace. By April 6 they were within fifteen miles of Boonesborough.[1]

At Boonesborough that day, a party led by a Captain Starnes had had enough of frontier life and had left for their homes back east. Traveling westerly, Bedinger's band lost the poorly blazed Boone's Trace by midday, wandering for nearly a mile until, through the tangle of cane, they spied the path. As they rode to it, their horses stamped and snorted.

Then they saw: moccasin prints. Wary, they pushed on till dusk and kept their talk low: Had they been seen?

Colonel Morgan chided them, calling them boys: The Indians were gone, he said. The men belled their horses, cut cane for fodder and to spread their blankets on, and gathered wood.

Camping dead center in the trace, feet turned to a high blazing fire and posting no watchmen, the Virginians awoke to a brisk morning and went on their way. They had not gone far when they passed a brake, the dirt pocked with footprints. Indians, it was judged, had spent the night watching them but, mistaking their carelessness for boldness, had feared a trap and did not attack.

188

Hours later the travelers reached Boonesborough. Folks there were much relieved: Captain Starnes's departure had jeopardized the fort's safety. After a time they heard a voice and opened the gates to let in Jacob Starnes, Captain Starnes's son. Shawnees had waylaid them, Jacob sobbed; he was the only survivor.[2]

Bedinger was put in charge of the fort's commissary and signed on as a hunter—a most dangerous task. At dusk four or five hunters would slip out singly and rendezvous miles away, camping without fire. Rising before dawn, they split into groups of two or three and rode away, looking for buffalo sign or deer or elk, avoiding hilltops, ridges, and traces, blowing across tops of their antler powder measures to signal, on summer nights tormented by mosquitoes, on winter nights tormented by cold. They did not shoot until the sun's last rays vanished over the hills.

Buffalo had moved twenty or thirty miles off; it was hard to hunt them and ride back with a load of meat in tow and one's hair in place. Once in a while a hunter might pot a wild hog; the original stock had arrived in 1775 with Richard Henderson, but most of the swine had escaped, thriving on the abundant mast, becoming so fierce that even wolves left them be.

On one hunt, Bedinger, Maj. Thomas and Benona Swearingen, Ralph Morgan, and John Harrison met miles away to camp without fire. They had spied a Shawnee camp; plenty of fresh sign and green tugs and slippery elm bark slivers to boil into gel for wounds told them the camp was new.

At first light, as the men spotted a buff yearling and readied to shoot the calf, Thomas Swearingen sternly rebuked them: "Your scalps will surely be the forfeit of your rashness. You ought to show more self control and fortitude and act like men. Not boys."

"Well Tom," said Benona, "I'll tell you what it is. We'll see who the boys are and who evinces the most fortitude. You shall be the first to say when we shall slay and eat."

Darkness. And again, no fire. The men munched parched corn meal and swatted mosquitoes.

As the sun rose, and on up into the day they came upon a deer. All eyes looked to Tom, who could not hold back. And there, in a quiet hollow, one of them struck flint and steel, sending sparks into a wad of charred punk and tow, and blew the red glow into a flame. Hardly was the deer spitted before they were gorging on the venison; bellies full, they lounged in the grass before hunting in the cane beyond the woods. At dusk a hunter spotted a telltale woolly hump. The men scored again. One of them stuck the buffalo's jugular. As some of the men guarded, others used tomahawks and knives to bone the beef, stuffing it into bags laced up on the spot—two bags could be made from a hide, each holding about one hundred pounds—and tied on packhorses with thick, hairy straps of new-cut tugs.

When they got to the north bank of the Kentucky River, they reined up and hid, listening. Swearingen gave the nod and the men splashed across to Boonesborough, the heavy fort gates swinging to behind them.

Living at the fort then was a man named White, a good hunter, a cool head in a fight, and well thought of. Yet he lacked caution; more than once he had gone off without his gun and had gotten lost, putting at risk the lives of the men who had to go out and find him. John Cradelbaugh vowed to break White of his careless ways.

One day, when White and a friend stole off for a swim in the Kentucky, Cradelbaugh whispered to another, and the two slipped from the fort. Daubing on vermilion and donning blankets, they forded and circled back. As the swimmers neared the far shore, the sumac mysteriously rustled, causing the frolicking twosome to cease splashing, hush their loud talk, and peer into the woods. The bushes parted. Out jumped Cradelbaugh and friend, brandishing guns and knives and sounding forth the dreaded scalp halloo.

White and his companion stared with stupid amazement and panicked, ducking underwater and scrambling for shore. When they surfaced for air and glanced back, Cradelbaugh capered a war dance, cut loose a hideous *hi-yah*!, and leveled his rifle. White screamed, sank, and kicked hard, leaving a swirling wake. The bank was steep where White and his friend splashed ashore, and they floundered trying to scale it. Exhausted, terrified, and naked, White fell backward, rolled down the slope, then clawed his way back up. The two scampered up and over the bank and sprinted away, yelling a warning.

Howling with laughter, Cradelbaugh and his accomplice slipped into the woods. They washed up and hid their blankets. After checking to make sure they looked sufficiently white, they forded the river and walked, deadpan, back to Boonesborough. Everywhere men were grabbing up guns, shot bags, and powderhorns, readying for war. The militia formed a strike force to take the fight to the phantoms lurking on the far bank. A voice yelled to Cradelbaugh:

"See any Indians?"

"No, by Godly!"

But loyal and true, and not one to shirk his duty in keeping Kentucky free of the Indian menace, Cradelbaugh joined in the fray. The men mounted, the gates swung open, and with White (now clothed) in the van, the horsemen pounded off. The men rode and rode, dismounting to stare into the dirt and leaves for sign, but the puzzled Kentuckians could not pick up the trail and reckoned the Indians had fled.

Cradelbaugh kept his masquerade a secret for a long time. White mended his ways and stopped loafing, but later, on a hunt north of the Kentucky, he blundered into an ambush and Indians killed him.

John Cradelbaugh was not Boonesborough's fort's only prankster. Bedinger remembered one greenhorn immigrant who spied a fat skunk ambling along and asked what manner of beast this was. One wag winked. A bear cub, he said.

A bear! He lit out after the little "bruin" at full speed. The skunk stopped, stuck its tail up, and stamped a warning on the ground before him. Heedless, the mighty bear hunter dashed up as the skunk wheeled and shot him an acrid blast that gagged him and sent him reeling. Wood smoke remains the perennial "cure" for hapless victims of a good skunk spraying, so most likely some kind soul kindled a fire, tossed on a few green juniper boughs, and stood the confused, odoriferous bear hunter in the billowing clouds until he was, once again, fit to take his place among polite society.

By 1781 Bedinger had returned to Virginia to fight his second tour of duty in America's Revolution, serving as a teamster at Yorktown. Three years after that, he returned to Kentucky.

SPRING 1784

George Michael Bedinger yearned to go westward to hunt the Green River country. The Green's watershed was mostly unsettled; buffalo, elk, and deer abounded in the barrens, and much of the rich meadowland lay unclaimed. Lewis Fields, a young friend, warned him of the hazards of a solitary jaunt: Should ill befall, who would know his fate? Bedinger was adamant—he was going. Fields was welcome to come along.

"If I had an extra shirt," Fields said, "I'd go, rather than see you go on such a dangerous journey by yourself." Bedinger dug a shirt out of his budget and threw it to him. They set out that day on foot. A week later they passed Henley's Station,[3] bearing southwest. In two weeks' time they hit the Green and followed it to Big Barren's mouth.

That night Bedinger and Fields heard Indian voices, so the hunters hid in a cane thicket and camped without fire. They passed a hard night as mosquitoes feasted, but they did not stir, and by daylight the Indians were gone.

The men struck Big Muddy Creek, Fields leading, picking his way along a path bordering Big Muddy.

Suddenly he screamed, "I'm a dead man!"

Bedinger cocked his rifle and ran ahead. Hearing no shot, he reckoned Fields must have taken an arrow.

"Snake bit!" cried Fields. A cottonmouth three feet long and two ax handles thick lay coiled next to Fields, gaping its white maw and fangs, its thick, V-shaped head cocked at forty-five degrees.

"Don't move!" Bedinger said, fumbling to grab a limb and not step on the mottled dirty-brown pit viper striking at his shins. As he swung, he hit the ground, snapping his club. Yanking his knife, he bent low and stabbed deep, cutting the snake a fatal gash.

Fields moaned. Two fang holes just below his knee pulsed blood. Bedinger tied a rag above the bite; the darkening wound oozed yellow fluid as the venom ate into Fields's veins.[4] His calf and knee began to swell, and as his face turned puffy, his tongue thickened, slurring words that gasped forth in bursts timed with his shallow breathing.

"Don't leave me, Mike."

"Be no trouble on that score."

It was hard, the snake looping over and over on itself in its death throes and turning belly up, but Bedinger was able to bind a quivering hunk of cottonmouth to the hurt leg.[5] He kindled a fire and dipped water in his cup, boiling slippery elm and butternut bark into gel and mixing it with salt and gunpowder to make a poultice. At his touch, Fields swooned, shuddering violently.

Bedinger feared for his friend's life; too, with him down, they were in real danger. It began raining.

Across the water, Bedinger spied a brake. Big Muddy was rising, running fast as he struck out to find a way over. Up ahead he saw ripples over a shoals, so he waded armpit-deep until he felt the bottom rise. He returned to shore.

Bedinger took their rifles, forded, and propped the guns on a log, then came back for Fields. Scooping him up, he cradled him, put him on his shoulders, and waded, water to his neck. He gained the bank, eased the boy into his arms, and walked into the cane to lay him down and wrap him in their blankets.

Night. The critical time. Fields was fighting hard, talking.

Then, shots. Two miles downriver, maybe.

Fields told Bedinger to go see who fired. Perhaps, if it were Indians, skilled in treating snakebite, they would help. Bedinger put his rifle in order, and strapping on his powderhorn and shot bag, walked into the night.

"The croaking of the frogs" guided him along the river, as he groped along in a quagmire of muck, roots, and cattails. He once tripped, rolling end over end for maybe thirty feet to land in a mud hole. He yelled out: If any white men could hear him, they should answer; if any Indians heard him, he came in peace and needed help.

Bedinger returned the camp. Fields had lapsed into a sweaty stupor. Bedinger kept their fire burning and talked to his delirious friend, getting him to sip water.

The hunters remained three weeks in their cove. A week more found Fields hobbling about on a crutch Bedinger whittled for him; where the snake bit, his flesh sloughed off and left a rosy pit deep as a walnut hull. Bedinger fed them on rabbits and squirrels and stalked along Big Muddy to pot fish finning its surface, aiming low.

Here, amid the Big Barren's leg-high grass, green from heavy rains, he came upon a fresh wallow splattered with the loose, pungent, half-digested grassy dung heaps of spring and spied a yearling in a buff drove and shot it. Startled, the buffalo rushed in, horn and hoof, pummeling the bleating yearling, trotting away as he approached. As Bedinger hacked off a hindquarter and hoppused it onto his back, a big yellow wolf ran up, snarling to get at the

The sudden death of a buffalo excites the rest of the drove, causing the buffs to butt and paw at the downed animal. LAND BETWEEN THE LAKES, KENTUCKY. AUTHOR'S COLLECTION.

meat. He had to kick at the animal to keep it off him; finally the wolf turned back to gnaw on the steaming carcass.

Fields was overjoyed when Bedinger slung the meat to the ground; soon they were boiling buffalo in their cups. Bedinger cut four forked saplings five feet tall, pounded them into the ground, and laid poles across the forks. Across the poles he laid small, straight sticks three or four inches apart. After slicing the beef into strips a half inch thick and weighing a pound, he laid them on the rack, kindled a fire underneath and piled it with green hickory, and stretched a blanket over the meat to keep off dew and to keep buzzards away. Making the jerk took two days.

Their jerk ran out the first of June. It was warm now; spring rains were over; the river was down. Fields was better, though he tired easily, but the toil of hunting and tending to Fields and staying hidden was taking its toll on Bedinger. Worse, their ammunition was dwindling.

They started back east. Often Bedinger had to tote his bearskin knapsack, lug Fields arm-in-arm, and carry both rifles. More than once they had to evade Indians.

Spotting a buffalo drove, Bedinger told Fields to pick his target and aim between the horn and ear, where the skull was thinnest. Fields crept from tree to tree until he closed in. He raised up and fired. The buffalo fell.

"Thank God!" said Fields. But as Bedinger ran up to stick him, the buffalo, only stunned, jumped up and charged. Bedinger paused long enough to snap off a shot, then ran hard as the buffalo dashed away to join the herd. Fields fired another round, to no avail. A day later Bedinger shot his last ball at a turkey.

Eighteenth century brass telescope (8" long) with leather case, and French-made compass in wooden cover. MUSEUM OF THE FUR TRADE, CHADRON, NE; PHOTO BY DAVID WRIGHT.

They set their course for Henley's Station. Bedinger spied a warped slip of gnarled buffalo hide stuck in a bush, stripped from a carcass by a hunter or wolf. He singed off the sparse, matted wool and charred the smelly skin to crack into chips. Gulping draughts of water, he choked down bits of burnt hide, but Fields could not eat it. Miles later, Fields came upon a turtle. He cut the animal from its shell and boiled the meat in his tin cup. Bedinger gagged. Fields tried to coax his friend into a taste. Finally, hunger, the aroma of cooked terrapin, and Fields's pleas were too much, and Bedinger took a bite. Surprised, he deemed the turtle fine fare and ate more.

They began to recognize landmarks. Jacob Van Meter's home was only miles off. Two miles past it lay Henley's Station. Bedinger could barely walk. Fields hurried ahead for help.

A kind lady at Van Meter's fed them mush and milk. Bedinger gorged but then ran out and vomited, and he suffered from an aching gut the rest of the day. During his convalescence, he ate when he could and slept like a dead man. Fields did the same, and after a week, both men walked back to the settlements.

FALL 1785

Bedinger readied for his second westward journey, which began on September 20, when he, three surveyors, and Capt. Edward Carrington left the Lower Blue Licks for Green River; two chain carriers, a marker, a hunter, and some slaves accompanied each surveyor. The party numbered twenty-two.

They struck the Green above the confluence of Rough Creek, but rains had swelled the rivulet, making it treacherous to cross. They put up tents,

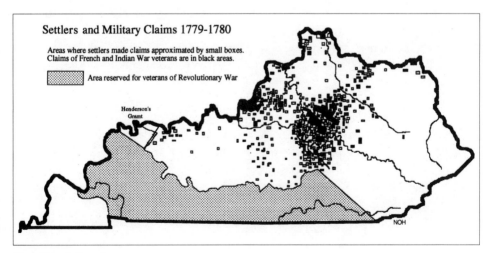

MAP BY NEAL O. HAMMON.

spread blankets and buffalo robes, and took their ease, dining on fish pulled from the creek on linen thread line tied to cane poles. A day or two later, Bedinger scouted a ford and they struck their tents. After a second trip across Rough Creek on horseback, he rigged up a log raft bound with grapevines, put their surveying gear aboard, and poled over. It took three trips back and forth, and the wet and cold (by now it was nearing November) shook him to the bone; soon his joints swelled from rheumatism.

The party pushed on to the Tradewater and along the way saw plenty of beaver sign—dams, mud slides, dens. The hunters set their hand-forged double-longspring traps; a night later they were stretching pelts and feasting on beaver tails, blistering off the leathery hide over a fire to get at the gnarled, greasy flap of gristle and fat. Deer, bears, swans, and geese teemed, and on them all the hunters and surveyors, slaves and crew fared well, putting the rich Green River bottomland to paper via compass and chain.

An evening later the hunters returned in haste: Some Delawares were camped a half mile away.

The men were loath to leave; they had not yet gotten to the lands that they had planned to survey. A quandary: Should they attack first to drive the Indians away? Most voted aye.

Bedinger said no. There were not enough guns, he reasoned. And the warriors might flee for help and return to ambush them. Either way, they could not hunt and survey and fight Indians. Come first light, he said, if someone would go with him, he would go to the Indians and parley.

Before dawn the men rolled out of their blankets and stowed their gear and put their guns in order. Bedinger and Captain Carrington left camp well armed, the rest straggling along in the rear and out of sight. They saw only two warriors and a couple of Delaware women, so they reasoned that it was not a war party. As they waded over, the Delawares ran toward a lean-to for their fusils.

Bedinger hailed them—right hand raised to his right shoulder, palm facing out.

"How de do, brothers!"

"How de do!"

The women fetched up a kettle and stoked the coals to flames and put some bear meat to boiling—a good sign, thought Bedinger. Here White Day was headman. What, White Day asked, was the Big Knife doing this far west?

"Gen'l Clark at the Falls sent us to make peace with our Delaware brothers," he lied.

White Day pondered this one. Clark, the burner of Piqua Town, was a hated foe.

Within minutes, as the charade went on, the entire surveying party arrived, and White Day's woman fed them. Carrington gave White Day his saddle, which his slave had carried up. He longer needed it, he said; his horse had foundered days before; he had left the animal to roam the Tradewater and described to White Day where he thought the horse might be found. White Day gave them four brain-tanned deerskins.

The parley done, the gifts given, the whites shook White Day's hand and left.

A week later Bedinger heard a distant shot. Puzzled, he mounted and galloped off to see who had fired it. A mile or two down the Tradewater, he spied White Day's band and rode to greet them.

"Howdy, brothers!"

"You one damn liar!" White Day said back, glaring through eyes rimmed red from whiskey. White Day had not found Carrington's horse.

Bedinger took a slip of paper from his waistcoat's pocket, scrawled a map of the Tradewater and drew a horse on one fork, and gave it to White Day.

"Maybe you tell truth. Maybe you damn liar," White Day said. "White Day look again. If he not find he take white man's hoss."

Horse-stealing, Bedinger said, would lead to killing. White Day should go look again—it was a gift, he said. If he did not find it, he would pay him for the lost animal.

This would do. Thumping himself on the chest, White Day introduced his men. The face of the first was scarred from a gunpowder burn years before. "This here Powder. And this here Jimmy. And this here Shawnee Captain Buck's son, young Buck." He went on presenting them one by one as Bedinger tied his horse to a sapling.

Suddenly Powder reached forward and grabbed the bridle. Bedinger snatched it back. Powder sauntered to a log and sat down, sullen. He took from his head his battered remnant of a hat—with no crown or brim, it was merely a wool felt band—and pointed at Bedinger's tricorn. Bedinger shook his head.

Powder leaped on him, groping for his hat. Bedinger pushed him back. Powder lunged on. Seconds later he lay sprawled out on the ground, Indians and whites expiring with laughter as Powder retreated to his log, "handling his rifle suspiciously." No one laughed louder than White Day, who took a flask from his budget and poured whiskey into a tin cup and handed it to Bedinger.

Bedinger said he did not drink. White Day soured.

"Drink or I kill!" White Day drew his knife and put the point to Bedinger's chest and made a fist to smack the handle.

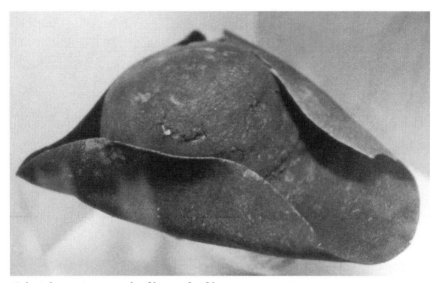

Colonial-era tricorn, made of beaver fur felt. MUSEUM OF THE FUR TRADE, CHADRON, NE; PHOTO BY DAVID WRIGHT.

Bedinger took the cup and passed it to a warrior nearby. White Day lowered his knife, gazing at him, and softened and spoke of the darkest day in Delaware history, the Gnadenhutten massacre.

Bedinger knew of the atrocity. Everyone did. In March 1782 about 150 Scotch-Irish militiamen stormed Rev. David Zeisberger's Moravian mission, Gnadenhutten, and herded the pacifist Delawares into a chapel. Prepare to meet thy God, the avengers announced. Hours later, as the Christians prayed to Jehovah and sang hymns and wept, the Scotch-Irish grabbed a cooper's mallet and took turns breaking the skulls of the thirty-five men, twenty-seven women, and thirty-four children assembled before them.

"My arm fails me, go on with the work. I think I have done pretty well," had declared the first mass murderer, passing the bloodied tool to the man at his shoulder. The first man had taunted the second; no way he could surpass his fourteen, he bet. He was right: The second mass murderer slew one less before giving out. Most of the killers, though, had not been so greedy, wanting only to brain an Indian to get a souvenir. Robert Wallace had not reached ten before he dropped the hammer and ran outside, tears streaming down his face. "You know I couldn't help it!" he had cried out to a sickened friend, one of sixteen who had sat out the spree and who stared in disbelief at Wallace's dank hunting shirt.

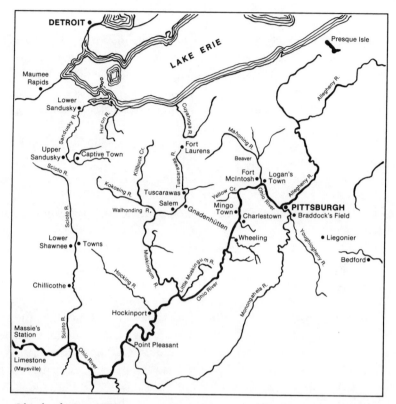

Ohio land, circa 1780. MAP BY JACK TURBEVILLE. AUTHOR'S COLLECTION.

The Long Knives had rifled the corpses for trinkets and cut scalps from battered skulls—the young, the old, the unborn, male and female—and re-crossed the Ohio with eighty horseloads of plunder, voices lifted in song, the missions Salem, New Schoenbrunn, and Gnadenhutten blazing like pitch-pine torches.[6]

Bedinger knew all of this. Everyone did.

"White men kill a good many praying Delaware on the Muskingum. For that White Day kill white men too—this many," White Day said, three times flicking out all his fingers.

As he spoke, two white men in a bark canoe rounded a bend in the Tradewater. Seeing Bedinger, they aimed the bow forward, beached it, and pulled the canoe up on the bank. Bedinger knew one of them, Edward Rice, but not the Irishman with him. As agreed to months before, Rice was bringing supplies to the surveyors; in return, the men were to locate a tract for him. White Day seemed to know Rice and broke the silence:

"Dogs! You afraid, you run away."

The night before, Rice explained to Bedinger, White Day's men had forced them ashore. Rice gave White Day a rum keg, and he and his men got so drunk that their women, fearing violence, hid their weapons. Rice and his men had fled for their lives.

Why, White Day asked again, were so many Big Knives so far from the settlements?

"Some are here to see the country. The rest are heading to French Lick to visit their kin," Bedinger said.

White Day grabbed the ivory end of a surveyor's rule out of Bedinger's pack. "What this?"

"It's only to make lines so I can talk on paper to my friends in the settlements," Bedinger said.

White Day handed it back. Bedinger turned to Rice to ask if he had any flour.

Rice nodded. Twenty-five pounds. White Day said he wanted some. Bedinger and Rice walked to the canoe and hid a one-pound leather wallet of salt in the flour sack's middle. White Day walked to the canoe as the men were tying the bag and grabbed it and hefted it high but felt nothing odd. Bedinger doled out the flour and made his rounds, bidding the Indians adieu.

In December the men made plans to head east to the settlements, but Bedinger, stricken with rheumatism, was unfit to travel. The men shot a bear and gave him the meat. John Stovall, one of the chain carriers, volunteered to stay to help the infirm man.

Neither was dressed for the cold. Both wore buckskin hunting shirts. Bedinger's tattered deerskin breeches he laced from thigh to knee with leather whangs an inch apart and knotted at the ends; from the knees to the ankles, the stitches were of linen thread, less than ten to an inch. He wore a worn camlet[7] jacket, a shirt of green baize, his cocked hat from the Revolution, and moccasins. Stovall's hat was a gray gooseskin worn feather-side-out and tied on with thongs passing under his bearded chin.

For three weeks they hid in the cane under a blanket stretched on poles and heaped wood on the fire to fight off icy gusts boiling off the river. Bedinger befriended another invalid, a parakeet with a broken wing.[8] Two or three times a day, the bird would poke its head out from its tree, dig its bill and its tiny talons into the bark, and zigzag to the ground for scraps. For a day or two the bird shied away, but soon Bedinger had it eating corn and tallow from his hand as he stroked it.

Bedinger, determined to beat the ache swelling his joints, tried an Indian cure: Each morning he stoked the fire and stripped and hobbled to a pond and jumped in. When he could stand it no more he staggered back to his fire to rub himself dry. Water sluicing off his hair froze into icicles, and there were times when he had to break ice to take his plunge, but the dips made him stronger, and he was desperate for home.

Life with Stovall the braggart was getting hard to take. Worse, he stole Bedinger's hatchet, blaming it on Indians. When Stovall's prattle turned to past dark deeds, Bedinger told him that if half of what he said was true, why, he was a rascal indeed—a "gray-haired buccaneer." Wary, Bedinger kept an alert eye.

By Christmas Bedinger could travel. They headed along the Green.

A day or two later they shot a buffalo cow. As Bedinger hacked out the tongue and back meat, Stovall sat on a log behind him, fiddling with his gun lock. Then Stovall's rifle hang-fired, the ball blasting past Bedinger, who lurched backward. Stovall sat, gun across his knees, smoke curling from the muzzle.

He made a feeble excuse: He had plugged his gun's touchhole with tallow and placed a wad of tow with a pinch of powder in the pan to make fire. A spark must have got to the charge, he said.

Bedinger let it go. But a week later, it happened again. At dusk, as the men cut cane to pile on the snow to sleep on and as Bedinger bent over, the air shook, and in a shroud of smoke a hickory ramrod flew past him.

"You sorry dog!" Bedinger said, snatching up his rifle, cocking it, leveling the muzzle to Stovall's head.

Stovall begged him not to shoot, crying out that he had left his ramrod in the barrel, "that he was the damndest fool in the world for his carelessness, and if Bedinger would only spare him, he would walk before him all the way, and would not flash his gun again."[9]

Now, more than ever, Bedinger feared for his life; as he lay on his cane bed, rifle at his side, feet to the fire, he kept a hand on his knife. Stovall, muttering apologies, crawled under the blanket, and they lay back to back. Neither slept much as they shivered and shook.

Morning. Their buffalo meat gone, they pressed on to the Falls.

A wolf dashed out. Stovall's bullet went low, smashing the wolf's front legs, spinning it into a half crawl, sending it squalling under a deadfall. Bedinger cut a sapling to pin the wolf's legs. As the wolf snapped at him, Stovall stabbed it. The men cut and peeled back the pelt to chop out a forequarter, but the sinewy mass was "miserably poor." Stovall boiled up some of the wolf in their kettle and ate it and drank the broth. Bedinger slow-roasted his hunk, but so strong was its smell that he spit out the only piece he ventured to eat.

They walked on, passing drifts along the Green's banks piled leg-deep and ice-covered ponds, breaking through crusts camouflaging pockets of water,

stopping to make fire to dry out, stuffing their moccasins with beech or white
oak leaves, then walking on, hungry, wet, and cold.

Four days later, they saw corn scattered along the trail, and as the ravenous men scooped up the grains, their spirits lifted. Darkness was settling fast
and in a whirl of snow and ice they hastened to camp. A mile later they heard
a whimper, saw a brown head raise, a tail wag. A dog, starving and unable to
walk, was cached in a hollow. Bedinger was moved with pity, so the men
made camp and struck fire; instead of waiting to make ashes to husk the corn,
they boiled it, husks and all, sharing spoonfuls of gruel. Bedinger fed the dog
a little of his own pittance, then the men put their feet to the flames and
pulled their blanket over them as the dog crawled in next to Bedinger. They
broke camp at dawn.

It was a poignant moment, but Bedinger had no choice, so glancing back,
he walked away from the dog as it stared at him.

Stovall led. Bedinger knew the settlements were near. If Stovall was going
to make his move, it would be soon.

At midday a rider spotted them and Bedinger hailed him. Before him
stood two men—gaunt, haggard, unkempt, looking like ill-clad robbers. Bedinger explained they were the last of Captain Carrington's survey crew on the
Green, just trying to get home. How far was it? And why was he out here in
this weather?

"Why, Van Meter's Station is thirteen miles," the rider said. He was out
looking for his dog, which had been mauled by a bear. Had they seen him?

Bedinger described the dog he had befriended. "That's him. Finest bear
dog I ever had," the man said.

The rider gave the two meat enough to last them and rode off in the direction Bedinger pointed. Bedinger, still on guard, could not push the swirl of
emotions from his mind as he neared his journey's end. "It was now early January," he mused, "the 108th day since I had seen a cabin. . . . Within that
long and dreary space of time, how many had been his dangers, how great his
sufferings, and thanks be to God he had escaped them all!"[10]

A day later they reached Van Meter's. For a day or two, the men hardly
did anything but eat and sleep. Bedinger confronted Stovall and told him to
leave, saying that he would pay him for his services the following week. They
met on the appointed day, and Bedinger never saw him after that; years later,
it was rumored he was executed in St. Louis. "Thus perished John Stovall," remembered Bedinger, "brazen, reckless, and bloodthirsty to the last."[11]

Bedinger married Nancy Keene on Christmas Day 1786 in Shepherdstown, Virginia, but she died after giving birth to their first daughter, Sarah.
Saddened by the loss, he returned to Kentucky to settle at Lower Blue Licks.

Simon Kenton and he, with a trusted guide named Morehead, began making plans to trek to the Pacific to search for the Northwest Passage, if it existed, that seemed to elude discovery, and to map out the land and observe its native inhabitants. But rumors of Indian trouble brewing in the Old Northwest prompted President Washington to dispatch Bedinger a commission as a major in the U.S. Army. He accepted, ending hopes for the proposed Kenton and Bedinger expedition, and like most Kentuckians, braced himself for the final waves of red terror that he was confident would surely come.[12]

"The Squirrel Hunter," by David Wright, 1986.

The "Kentucky" Rifle

The subject [of Kentucky rifles] is extraordinarily complex. So complex, in fact, that when I asked Wallace Gusler, former master gunsmith at Colonial Williamsburg, for the name of a history that I could trust, his reply was simple and to the point: "There is none."

—Eliot Wigginton, *Foxfire 5,* 1979

On June 10, 1775, twenty-one year-old George Michael Bedinger mustered with Capt. Hugh Stevenson's sharpshooters—ninety-seven riflemen from Shepherdstown, Virginia (in Jefferson County, West Virginia)—en route to Cambridge, Massachusetts, to serve as snipers for Gen. George Washington. On October 4, 1777, Washington's army—Bedinger in rank with three thousand militia augmenting eight thousand Continentals—eked out a win against Gen. Sir William Howe's nine-thousand-man army at Germantown, six miles northwest of British-occupied Philadelphia. After Valley Forge and another year of skirmishing, in the spring of 1779 Bedinger and ten comrades crossed Cumberland Mountain and forded the Rockcastle, riding westward, rallying to Boonesborough's aid.[1]

With Bedinger went his rifle, a uniquely American firearm thought to have originated in his native Pennsylvania—a gun that became so woven into the lore of the West that it would be labeled the "Kentucky" rifle. Britishers feeling their long-range sting inflicted by the lawless "Shirt-tail Men" knew the cursed "rifle-guns" better as "widow-makers."

The technology needed to rifle a barrel in a spiraling pattern of five to eight grooves to impart "spin" upon a bullet may have existed by 1456, but the earliest rifled barrel with a sure provenance was made in Germany in 1547. The spin was a by-product, incidental to the grooves' intended purpose of serving as soot repositories for the spent powder as it whooshed through the bore and fouled it, hindering reloading. Spiral-grooved barrels were the norm, but a few hunters commissioned rifles bored "straight-cut." "Straight-rifles" offered versatility with a compromise: They were more accurate than smoothbores; they were almost as accurate as spiral-grooved rifles but easier to load; and they handled round-ball, shot, or buck-and-ball loads.[2]

Seventeenth-century rifles (Germanic smiths knew military rifles as *jagerbuchses* and civilian hunting rifles as *pirschbuchses*) tended to be of big caliber, with clubby, stocky butts measuring two inches across, octagonal barrels of twenty-seven to thirty inches (or longer), stocked to the muzzle in English walnut. "Stocky" and "clubby" as descriptions of proportion are not meant to mean clumsy; "jaeger rifles," as they are called, handled well. Their unique lines were founded upon Old World dimensions, well suited to the fine French locks and precision-set triggers fitted to them.

Gunsmiths catered to a well-heeled clientele. Rifles were expensive, sold to hunters and sportsmen at prices far exceeding a peasant's wage. For a member of the "lower classes" to own any gun made his intentions and presence suspect. In 1667 His Majesty Louis XIV forbade commoners on French soil to possess guns with flintlock ignition, outlawing flintlocks even among his infantry (but not among Carignan-Salieres regiments stationed in New France), lest the unlettered masses rise up to depose the Sun King's absolutist domestic tranquility.[3]

In 1712 Norwegian ski troops were armed with rifles; in 1740 Prussia's Frederick II used rifles to arm the first Jaeger corps outside Scandinavia. By 1730 Rhineland smiths were forging barrels of thirty-six inches or more, resulting in arms resembling "transitional" American rifles. During King George's War (the War of Austrian Succession, 1744–48), the English became interested in the rifle's possibilities in warfare. Three decades earlier, among hunters in the New World's backwoods colonies, the rifle—built "lock, stock, and barrel"—had already found a home.

In Pennsylvania and in the Shenandoah Valley, rifles began to take on sleek, shapely proportions. Blacksmiths hammered out long barrels for an improved sighting plane and to better balance them, left barrels fat at the breech, "swamping" (tapering) them at the center and flaring them out at the muzzle, rifling them in slow, twisting spirals that spun a ball one revolution in sixty-six inches; and to spare on powder and ball, reduced bore size from .70 (or more) to calibers averaging from .50 to .54.

In 1761 John Shrite of Reading, Pennsylvania, made the earliest known "Kentucky rifle," which has a barrel length of 43 5/16 inches and is .60 caliber. Though variations existed, a typical pre-Revolutionary rifle, notes Joe Kindig, Jr., in *Thoughts on the Kentucky Rifle in Its Golden Age,* was somewhat shorter and the butt was somewhat heavier than on rifles made twenty or forty years later, but in general, the Kentucky had attained by this time that character that distinguished it from all other firearms. It had an octagonal barrel forty or more inches long, a full graceful stock of plain or slightly curly maple, a brass patch box, other brass mounts, and possibly one or two silver inlays. The patch box was plain with very little engraving and probably no piercings. The relief carving was simple and sparse.[4]

By 1780, avers Kindig, the long rifle reached its esthetic apogee and entered a sort of "Golden Age" lasting until the postwar recession of 1812. Golden Age guns were decorative, some ornate, embellished with silver wire inlay and rococo carving, stocked in fancy curly maple alive with flaming tiger-striped whorls.

Loading this work of art that killed took more time than loading its smoothbore counterpart, but some riflemen were quite adept; good shooters got off two or three rounds a minute. Too, there were tricks to hasten the process where delay might mean either returning to one's cabin or having one's scalp transported across the Ohio in the folds of a gaily beaded sash.

Riflemen toted gunpowder "loose" (instead of in cartridges in leather "belly boxes"), in powderhorns slung over the shoulder. Horners harvested their wares from cattle (along the Mississippi, Indians and Frenchmen utilized buffalo horns) and boiled out the cores, which stunk like burned hair and popped free. Powderhorns might be one- or two-pound capacity, a graceful curl hugging it close to the ribs. Far from home on lonely nights, many a hunter seated near a fire, calloused hand gripping a glass shard or awl or vent pick, painstakingly transformed his horn into a work of folk art, incising on its patinaed surface maps and rivers, hunters and Indians, animals, Bible verses, or mottoes. "IN GOD AND GOD ALONE I TRUST," reads one such scrimshawed horn, whose owner was too humble to boast that he trusted too in his ability to shoot straight. Horn bearers carved their names, followed by a solemn stamp of ownership, as in "CHAS. GOODRICH HIS HORN. FORT TYCONDROGA. ye 16 DEC. 1776."[5]

Keeping one's powder dry was critical, as was keeping locks clicking smoothly, bores rust-free, and guns "in order." Powderhorns—light, sturdy, cheap, available, easy to make, watertight—answered a rifleman's purpose as he yanked out the plug with his teeth and tipped the spout to a hollowed-out antler tine that served as a measure and was tied on a thong to the slender strap of his shot bag. In his near-suicidal one-man raids, Lew Wetzel sprinted through woods with two or three balls pressed between cheek and gum, pouring from the horn down the barrel,

Revolutionary War era powderhorn, 15" in length, with protruding lip drilled with three holes and brass staple near throat for strap. JOHN MONTAGUE COLLECTION; PHOTO BY DAVID WRIGHT.

spitting down a ball, tapping the stock to the ground to seat it and prime, then wheeling to gut-shoot foes from the hip.

(Some folks reckoned that was how Lew did it; no one is sure. But "speed loading" could end fatally: Pouring directly from the horn down the muzzle to a spark smoldering at the breech from a spent round meant a potential grenade at eye's distance. To prevent such calamities, shooters poured powder from the horn into a measure of antler or horn, or cane, brass, or iron.)

The "piece" charged, a hand-cast lead ball .10 to .15 thousandths undersized from the bore's caliber, and swaddled in a patch greased with tallow, was thumbed down the muzzle—some shooters "coned" muzzles for an inch or two to ease loading—and rammed home with a hickory ramrod, the rod pushed back in its ferrules pinned underneath the forestock. The huntsman cradled his rifle, opened the frizzen to prime, snapped the frizzen shut, and raised the horn's narrow end to his mouth to reinsert the spout's plug. Set on half cock, the gun was ready. "Going off half-cocked" was a lethal breach of safety that might end fatally; a "flash in the pan" meant only the priming ignited.

Exaggerated tales of nigh-impossible shots swirl about these guns, but the truth is impressive enough. William Hancock's alleged assassination of Pompey

Leather hunting pouch (also called "shot-bag") and scrimshawed powderhorn, Revolutionary War era, chain lanyard with vent pick and hog-bristle pan whisk, carved antler powder measure below throat of horn. FROM THE KENTUCKY RIFLE HUNTING POUCH, BY MADISON GRANT, PUBLISHED BY JIM JOHNSON, GOLDEN AGE ARMS.

during Boonesborough's 1778 siege was paced off and admired, but Hancock's shot gained fame due to the hue of Pompey's skin. Then there was Jacob Dieverbaugh's spectacular shooting. Dieverbaugh, a hunter for George Morgan, who on a July day in 1768, on a dare and a wager "to try his powder," popped a small rum keg ten shots out of eleven at one hundred yards, then won 100 Spanish dollars in Pennsylvania currency by nailing clean at the same distance a barrel head one hundred times out of one hundred shots. Big Bullet, the Chickamauga who brazenly wore a bag sewn from the hide of a white baby skinned out to its tiny pinkish nails and tanned, was felled by a Tennessean's rifle, just as Simon Kenton downed Big Jim, Shawnee slayer of Boone's firstborn boy, James. Most famous of all was the illiterate Pennsylvanian Sgt. "Sure-shot Tim" Murphy, who at Saratoga on October 7, 1777, settled his rifle's muzzle in a fork and at just over two hundred yards picked off Brig. Gen. Simon Fraser and aide-de-camp Sir Francis Carr Clerke.[6]

Shooting frolics offered valuable prizes: cattle, smoked hams, flour, lead, gunpowder, a guinea or two. But surpassing nighttime candle-snuffing matches, "barking off squirrels," John James Audubon declared, was a most "delightful sport." Audubon, whose eye peered down a rifle flat as keenly as it peered at Florida

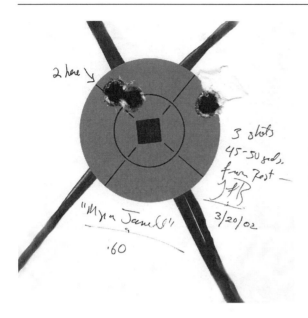

The efficacy of the American long rifle, three shots from a rest at a range of 50 yards as shot by author. AUTHOR'S COLLECTION.

scrub jays freshly rendered in oil on his canvas, claimed he met Daniel "Boon" on the Kentucky's banks one day in 1810 and the two shot their supper without singeing a hair.

> My companion, a stout, hale, and athletic man, dressed in a homespun hunting shirt, bare-legged and moccasined, carried a long and heavy rifle, which, as he was loading it, he said had proved efficient in all his former undertakings, and which he hoped would not fail on this occasion. . . . The gun was wiped, the powder measured, the ball patched with a six-hundred-thread linen, and the charge sent home with a hickory rod. We moved not a step from the place, for the squirrels were so numerous that it was unnecessary to go after them. Boon pointed to one of these animals which had observed us, and was crouched on a branch about fifty paces distant, and bade me mark well the spot where the ball should hit. He raised his piece gradually, until the bead . . . of the barrel was brought to a line with the spot which he intended to hit. The whip-like report resounded through the woods and along the hills in repeated echoes. Judge of my surprise, when I perceived that the ball had hit the piece of bark immediately beneath the squirrel . . . the concussion

"Col. Daniel Boon.," line-and-stipple engraving as rendered by Chester Harding and James O. Lewis, and released by Lewis and Noah Ludlow as a limited-edition in St. Louis two weeks after Boone's death September 26, 1820. Besides being a full-length taken from an oil-portrait rendered "from the life," this unique piece of Americana is the first known depiction of the dress of American riflemen. PATHFINDER PRESS, GALLATIN, TN. AUTHOR'S COLLECTION.

produced by which had killed the animal and sent it whirling through the air. . . . Boon kept up his firing, and before many hours had elapsed, we had procured as many squirrels as we wished.[7]

Audubon's story of "Boon" the squirrel barker is vintage lore dead center in the tradition of Fenimore Cooper's Natty Bumppo and actor James H. Hackett's creation, Nimrod Wildfire, hero of the popular drama, The Lion of the West—The Kentuckian. Whether his tale is true or not is debatable. Audubon's wit and pen were as lively and as imaginative as his camel hair brush dipping from palette to easel. When Boone left for Missouri in 1799, he swore he'd lay his neck on a chopping block rather than set foot in the Bluegrass, whose attorneys had tarnished his good name and whose courts had stripped him of land. According to last-born son, Nathan, and daughter-in-law, Olive, interviewed in 1851 by Lyman Draper, Daniel never wavered from his vow.

Audubon's tale echoes the day's growing storehouse of apocryphal yarns about backwoods Kentuckians—gun-toting, eye-gouging, Bowie-knife-wielding wild men touted to be "half-horse, half-alligator, and a little touched with snapping turtle." Part and parcel of the lore of fighting Kentuckians was their prowess with their "Kentucky" rifles.

How this rifle name came to be is a curious tale.

Daniel Boone died in Missouri on September 26, 1820. That month James O. Lewis—an artist traveling with Sam Drake's "Kentucky Company"—reproduced Chester Harding's full-length Boone portrait rendered from life. Using an upright platen press, Lewis pulled and tinted the images while fellow thespian Noah Ludlow tacked together gilded frames. They would split all profits. Released in St. Louis in a limited edition of 150 prints, Lewis's quaint engravings of "Col. Daniel Boon." sold out—remaindered for $1 apiece.

Their fortune not realized in Boone prints, Lewis left for the Great Lakes and Ludlow resumed acting and tried his hand at singing; for his debut, he rehearsed Samuel Woodward's new ballad, "The Hunters of Kentucky." Readying himself for stage, Ludlow pieced together a ragtag semblance of the garb he recalled Boone wearing in Lewis's engraving, borrowing from a river man a "buckskin hunting-shirt and leggings," with "moccasins . . . a rifle" and an "old slouched hat."

It was a sultry New Orleans night in May 1822 when Drake's troupe opened to a theater "crowded full of river-men" dressed in "linsey-woolsey and blanket coats." After the warm-up act, a comedy, the curtains parted. Dressed, armed, and saluting smartly, Ludlow hit the stage poised and in full regalia. The half-drunken mob of Creoles and flatboat men whooped it up, clapping and stomping so loudly that the floor timbers quaked, roaring approval as the music began, Ludlow peering far out into their midst, palm at his brow, stalking imaginary redcoats stage left and right. The din fading, he returned center stage, shouldered his rifle, and belted out verse one of "The Hunters of Kentucky":

> You gentlemen and ladies fair,
> who grace this famous city,
> Just listen if you've time to spare,
> whilst I rehearse a ditty;
> And for an opportunity,
> conceive yourself quite lucky,
> For 'tis not often here you see
> A hunter from Kentucky.

And then, the dramatic intoning of the refrain—

O Kentucky, the hunters of Kentucky;
O Kentucky, the hunters of Kentucky!

Oh, but this was supreme, ear-tickling fare. Jacksonians through and through, many of the "gentlemen" in his boisterous audience had faced down the Brits with "Old Hickory" on January 8, 1815, at New Orleans. The rowdies could barely hush their caterwauling as Ludlow kicked into verse two:

We are a hardy freeborn race,
Each man to fear a stranger,
Whate'er the game, we join in chase,
Despising toil and danger;
And if a daring foe annoys,
Whate'er his strength and forces,
We'll show him that Kentucky boys
Are "alligator horses."

More cheers, hoots, and hip-hip huzzahs, especially at "Kentucky boys" and "alligator horses." And again, Ludlow's dramatic intoning of the long, slowly drawn-out refrain, sparsely augmented this time with gruff, atonal sing-alongs from the foot-stomping, well-lubricated good old boys . . .

O Kentucky, the hunters of Kentucky;
O Kentucky, the hunters of Kentucky!

Ludlow was ecstatic. "I was saluted with loud applause of hands and feet, and a prolonged howl, such as Indians give when they are especially pleased."
Emboldened now, he sang on lustily:

But Jackson he was wide-awake,
And wasn't scared at trifles,
For well he knew what aim we'd take
With our Kentucky rifles;
So he marched us down to Cypress Swamp,
The ground was low and mucky,
There stood John Bull in martial pomp,
But here was old Kentucky.

At the last line, Ludlow threw his flop hat to the floor and, dropping to one knee, jerked the rifle to his cheek and drew a bead.

This was too much.

Pandemonium broke loose. The crowd arose, clapping, shouting, stomping, yelling, cheering—for a full minute they would not let him go on. Ludlow feared a riot and had to duck a piece of gas pipe hurled his way.

Three verses later, he encored. He sang the entire ballad again. Then encored again.

Three times on opening night, Noah Ludlow sang "The Hunters of Kentucky." And so it went whenever (and wherever) he sang what must that been America's first frontier musical "hit." If he entered a tavern for a late-night toddy, he had to sing "Hunters" or face a duel; if a fan spotted him propped against a post or standing by the road, he was obliged to sing lest he be thought a boor. In short order, he got to where he hated Yankee Woodward's infernal song and printed the lyrics and released them to newspapers from Nashville to New Orleans, from Mobile to Charleston and across the Ohio, so music lovers could learn them for their own satisfaction and leave him alone. This only made matters worse: Now everyone sang "The Hunters of Kentucky" and flocked to theaters demanding to hear Ludlow sing it so they could better learn its clever twists and subtleties and howl along with the Master on the two-line chorus.

"The Hunters of Kentucky" played out, but not its imagery of "Kentucky boys" as "alligator horses" throwing down with "Kentucky rifles" on "John Bull." Andy Jackson adopted the tune for his campaign during his 1828 presidential run, and "Hunters" helped propel him to the White House. Knowing a good marketing ploy when they saw one, enterprising gun builders began to advertise that they built genuine "Kentucky rifles." Sales perked up, and more than sixty years after their invention, this is how American long rifles came to be known.[8]

CHAPTER NINE

Terror in the Bluegrass

WINTER 1783

On December 11, 1783, Spencer Records turned twenty-one, celebrating the first of many birthdays in Kentucky. Like his father, Josiah Records, Spencer stood five foot eight, his skin tanned an olive brown, his face round, and his eyes, like his long hair, black as a raven's wing. Friends knew him as a cheerful, pleasant man possessing great energy and a fast runner. Lean and clothed in a dark linen hunting shirt belted about him, he was often taken for an Indian.

Spencer Records was, in fact, already a skilled woodsman and an experienced Indian fighter, his first brush with frontier warring coming at age fourteen near his family's cabin, less than twenty miles from Fort Pitt. Fearing a raid, Josiah Records had requested Fort Pitt's militia to garrison his mill; the company came and paraded impressively and in good order, but seeing no Indians, it went back to Fort Pitt.

It was during that winter of 1778, in March, that eleven young people, tired of drafty, cramped cabins, left to tap the sugar maples. There were George and William Turner, the two Dever boys, and a lad whose last name was Fulks. With them were five girls—one was fourteen-year-old Betsy Turner, the baby sister of George and William—and a little boy. Spirits high, they camped on Raccoon Creek, two miles below Josiah's mill. Indians heard their skylarking and smelled their wood smoke. At dawn they hit them.

Spencer and his uncle John Finch and others got to the site a day after. Four bodies lay tumbled and pitched in grotesque array about the fire pit—skull-bashed and scalped. Fifty yards away lay another: The lad was fleeing when his assailants delivered a killing blow that left his brains on the leaves.

One of the first realistic depictions of a Kentucky Indian raid ever published, c. 1783.
FROM NARRATIVE OF THE MASSACRE BY THE SAVAGES OF THE WIFE AND CHILDREN OF THOMAS BALDWIN.

One Dever boy lay turned on his right side, his right arm across his chest, pale fingers and thumb eternally reposed in the tear in his chest's left side. The little boy and the girls were gone.

As the men scalloped out a hole, a few balked at the rude burial. Lt. Ephraim Roberts, Spencer's cousin, warned them to hasten lest they reap the same fate. Jamming the bodies in, pushing down stiffening arms and legs, blue and bloodied, they used knives and axes to cut the dirt sides down as fill, tamped it smooth, and piled logs over the grave to keep wolves from digging. "These were the first men that I had seen that had been killed by the Indians," Spencer Records remembered. "A dreadful sight it was to me, the more so, as some of them had been but a short time before, my schoolmates."[1]

But now Records looked westward, as did many Americans.

In the summer of 1783 Uncle John Kiser had sold Josiah Records a tract north of the Kentucky River, and a flurry of activity marked the proposed move as all hands worked to build a flatboat. On November 20 Spencer Records, Uncle John Finch, and his sons John and Josiah pushed the craft into the Monongahela, Kiser going along to show the way. An elm bark canoe and a dugout tied astern bobbed in the broad V wake; as the trip eased by, the men worked to steer the craft in the river's center safe from snipers, veering past rips and eddies and bypassing jetsam, wary of sawyers able to rip out a plank transom in one upending crash, spilling livestock and men into the swirl.

By the twenty-ninth they had landed at the Licking's mouth. On the morrow they put the whiskey and farm tools in the pirogue and canoe and poled up the Licking, forced at times to portage or pull the craft over rills and ripples. After four laborious days, they cached their cargo and returned to the flatboat; by then a steady wash feathering off the banks from a nightlong downpour raised the river enough to float the flatboat to their cache.

With Kiser guarding the boat and livestock, Records and John Finch struck out overland to find the trace crossing the Licking that cut through the cane maze and on to the settlements. At the south fork, Spencer found the buffalo path—now a wagon road blazed the spring of 1780 during Bird's invasion, which left Martin's and Ruddells' Stations ablaze.[2] Three miles past Ruddells' new fort, they saw three families so destitute they had erected an arbor over a sick old woman, having not even a blanket to warm her; that summer, Indians killed some smallpox victims quarantined outside the fort. At Bryan's Station, they feasted on wheat johnnycakes. The Records party wintered at McConnell's Station, a site that became Lexington.

In January Records and three men set out for Stoner's Creek to hunt buffalo, riding twenty miles. They camped, belling their horses to let them crop the sparse graze in the bitter cold.

Morning's leg-deep snowfall kept them from tracking their horses; unable to hunt, they hung their saddles in trees and trudged home. Seeking refuge that night in a brake bent with sleet, they found no wood, only a big hickory stump. Scraping back the snow, they piled the stump heavy with dead cane to get it burning, making a smoky, smoldering fire and passed a hard night, unable to dry their leggings and moccasins, which were crusty with ice when they slogged to Bryan's Station the next day.

In August Spencer Records and Alister McConnell "steered a northwest course . . . struck the south fork of the Licking, then steered a west course and hunted three days." They shot a bull elk, skinned it out, and hung the skin in a tree to retrieve before they returned to McConnell's. Taking a few hunks of the meat, the men rode off to the Licking, and as they broke over the bank's crest, they reined in abruptly: Fresh moccasin prints dotted the mud.

Records and McConnell dogged the trail for miles, until rain drove them to cover, drenching their flintlock's priming. After thumbing out the black ooze dripping from their priming pans and drying them on their hunting shirts, they knew that putting their guns in order "could only be done by picking powder in at the touchhole and shooting them off." Fearing alert ears, they remounted, setting off at a trot for John Kiser's old camp.

Kiser, they saw, had left behind his wagon and supplies—all had been vandalized by Indians. As night was coming on, Records and McConnell belled their mounts and passed the night.

Morning broke, clear.

First things first: Find the horses; prepare to ride; clear the guns. But then, minutes later, the rippling crackle of a dozen gunshots boomed unevenly a half mile off. Records and McConnell circled in the tall grass to spy out Kiser's shelter. Seeing nothing, they crept in and got their blankets, saddles, and rifles, and found their horses.

McConnell leading, the ground soggy and thick with pea vine, their horses left a broad swath as they rode to a ford in the Licking. Four miles into their flight they chanced upon a buffalo drove and dashed among the beasts, whipping them into a trot. Miles later the two reined up where they had dressed the elk two days before. As Records ripped dry bark from the underside of downed trees, gathered dead twigs and sticks, and stripped a juniper of half a handful of its loose, pulpy bark to shred into tinder, McConnell rode back a half mile to spy out their trail, then slipped back to the light of their fire.

Records had cut the elk skin down and pegged the tail end and propped up the neck flap, skin side down. Storm clouds precipitated a bashing rain; puddles swirling under their hide lean-to forced the men to stand.

Finally the rain stopped, and the hunters piled up juniper boughs to lie on till morning. Their trail obliterated, they heaped wood on the fire and stripped, drying their clothes and blankets. Yanking the plugs from their powderhorns, they dashed the black specks into the pans, jabbing vent picks through the touchhole clear to the breech. Thumbing flints to test the edges for sharpness, then snapping frizzens shut, they full-cocked, held aloft, and touched the triggers.

Records and McConnell rode in to McConnell's Station. They had been gone for ten days.

June. "Bellowing time": buffalo rut. Records and three friends rode sixteen miles north of Lexington to Dry Run Creek, where Records shot a bull. He made a jerk rack for the beef, but the tongue he tossed on the coals; a half hour later he picked off bits of the puckered skin, all pocked and bubbled, and slit the steaming tongue lengthwise. The fire smoldering, at midnight Records turned the jerk slabs. Then hefting guns and saddles, all hid in a dark place to eat their parched corn and warm tongue. At daylight they bagged the smoked meat for the ride home.

The last week of November, Records and John Finch shot six buffalo, loading the packhorses with heaps of wild beef. Records salted down his portion, anticipating his father's coming. As Christmas day neared, Josiah

Records's vessel docked at the Limestone wharf. Laban Records, Spencer's younger brother, had come with him.

1785–90

By February 1785 Josiah, Spencer, Laban, and their families were living in Kentucky, though—and typically so—little is said about the female members of the household. Josiah, unimpressed with the tract bought from John Kiser, sold it to buy four hundred acres six miles west of Washington, three miles south of Limestone.

Washington is set on a picturesque, rolling site that Christopher Gist traveled in 1751, and James McBride, whom John Filson wrote about, hunted there after Gist. In 1775 Simon Kenton and Thomas Williams put out a corn crop at the headwaters of Lawrence Creek to establish their claim. In 1784 Kenton erected a fort along a lead trace that became known as Smith's Wagon Road; in 1785 he sold seven hundred acres to two Virginians, William Wood and James Fox, who laid out the township, naming it for America's hero of the Revolution. Daniel Boone was a Washington trustee, and the hamlet boasted more than fifty families by 1786, the year Virginia officially deemed it a city.[3]

Fur buyers, traders, speculators, hunters, surveyors, slaves, families, entrepreneurs, militiamen, mixed-bloods, and an occasional Delaware might all be seen in the bustling town. Near enough to the Ohio for travel and commerce, and within a few minutes' ride of Limestone, Washington offered more protection from the raids emanating from Ohio's Indian towns.

But still, "sometimes" said Spencer, "we had to stand sentry all night . . . for fear the Indians would fall on us." Hunters pursuing dwindling buffalo herds rode miles after dark to hunt.[4] It was hard, dangerous work. "The bone on the back," said Daniel Bryan, a cousin of Daniel Boone's, "was sometimes twenty-one inches high. The brisket of a buffalo, when thrown back . . . would stand up higher than a table. Two men couldn't turn a big bull buffalo, if he had fallen on his side."[5] After gutting the beast, the hunters split it lengthwise to balance on a horse, back foremost, then cracked the spine to drape the carcass over. At the fort, they stripped the meat from the bones; sheared off the reddish brown wool to wash, card, and spin; boiled the stinky cores out of the horns, then heated and shaped and cut the horns into spoons and buttons and myriad other necessities; and tanned the thick, porous hide into spongy shoe leather.[6]

By 1787 Kentuckians had had enough of the Indian menace. In early winter Col. John Todd (one of the few officers who survived the Blue Licks bloodletting in 1782) gathered militiamen from Lexington and struck the wide buffalo trace— "Clark's War Road"—that led to the Ohio.[7]

Colonel Todd's band pushed north, volunteers swelling his ranks. Flanders Callaway, a tall, raw-boned woodsman, rode in front. An experienced fighter, in 1776 he had helped rescue his fiancée Jemima Boone from the Shawnee, and in September 1778 he had fought the Shawnee and their British allies besieging Boonesborough. With bad teeth, illiterate, his lean face pitted from smallpox, Callaway had a countenance, attitude, and demeanor typical of men in Todd's army.

In Washington the militia halted, shouting for volunteers. Spencer Records and a few others joined in. The cavalcade pounded down the wagon road that split the town in half, pushing on.

Todd "crossed the Ohio with his men, one hundred and seventy in all, at Limestone, and proceeded on towards Old Chillicothe, on the north fork of Paint Creek." He led them up and down chert ridges and around the knobs on a trace chiseled out by deer and elk. Nearing Sunfish Mountain, south of Old Chillicothe, they spied four Indians—three men and a boy—and fired on them, killing two and capturing two. Fearing death, the hostages told Todd that more Indians were camped just ahead.

Warrior of the Middle Ground, c. 1780s, showing arm, wrist, and chest tattooing, quilled neck knife sheath, black silk bandana around neck fastened with ring brooch, roached hair. "THE HURON," BY DAVID WRIGHT.

Night came. And as a full moon emerged from marbled cloud tufts to cast a pale light in the dark tangle of woods, cane, and rutted trace, Records and twelve men rode off to reconnoiter. For five miles they stuck to the path. As they neared a stream, they heard dogs barking and tinkling horse bells.

Records reckoned the Shawnee half faces to be four hundred yards off. The whites retreated into the forest, tied horses, whispered plans. But two of their number panicked and fled to warn Todd. Tired, hungry, and edgy, those who remained checked their guns—flipping back frizzens to inspect pans, pecking on flints, pricking vents, greasing linen patches, counting balls, hitching powderhorns and shot bags.

Nearing first light, they heard the faint, rising thuds of hoofbeats. Suddenly Todd's men—forty strong—raced past, forcing Records and his band to mount and fall in. Flanders Callaway was in the van.

The camp dogs heard them. By the time the whites dashed into the camp, the warriors had fled, leaving their parched corn, maple sugar, jerk, meat, blankets, accoutrements, and trade goods for the whites to gloat over so that they could get away.

Three women who got left behind in the rout bolted and ran. Callaway back-shot "an old squaw, which he should not have done," Records said, as he looked upon "her lying on her face with her back naked. She was much pitted with the small pox."[8] One women stood there, trembling. Another, nursing a baby, turned to surrender; as she held out her hands, a teenaged Kentuckian shouted, "Give up, you damn bitch!" and musket-bashed her, knocking her in the dirt, her baby jarred free, provoking gales of laughter from Colonel Todd's gang at the bold audacity of this Long Knife "pup."[9]

Todd's men bound the captives and gathered "horses . . . twinned bags, pewter and etc. which they got from plundering the people as they moved from Virginia to Kentucky"—to auction "at vendue on the spot" to raise money to pay the militia.[10] The army rode to Sunfish Mountain to get the Indians they had left tied there, but both had escaped. The next day Todd's men recrossed the Ohio.

On a spring day in 1787, a certain Smith and Thomas left Washington to look for their horses. The men plunged into the cane and saw their mounts grazing in a clear spot, but Smith spied in the cane's edge four Indians and a white man[11] ten steps from him, guns aimed at his chest. He walked to them, palms up. Thomas was stunned.

They stayed in the cane until dark, before the warriors with their captives and horses headed to Lee's Station two miles away to steal more horses. The Indians tried several times to gain the palisades, but barking dogs drove them back. The warriors hastened to the Ohio and told Smith and Thomas to go home.

Thomas turned to flee. Smith said he would not go without his horse and handed his steel tobacco tin to an Indian to swap for it. The Indian took the tin; he would keep it too, he said. Smith shook his head. Thomas told him to walk away, but Smith kept griping even after getting back his tin. The white man told Smith that if he did not go, he would kill him. They got to Washington as the sun rose.

Fall 1787. Farmers found the scalped bodies of Lot Masters and Hezekiah Wood on Washington's outskirts. Two miles away, near Lee's Station, twelve-year-old Thomas Talmadge sat cooking by a fire one night, when Indians pounced on him and took his scalp. Other than the silver-dollar-size thatch of skin and hair sliced off his crown, he was not hurt. So while the boy moaned and gritted his teeth, a woodsman took an awl and bored a sprinkling of holes into his skull to let the pink cranial fluids ooze out so the gash would scab over. Weeks later the scab blackened and flaked off, leaving a relief map of scar tissue that always felt the sun and cold. Talmadge wore a hat the rest of his days to cover the scar, for no hair ever grew back on his wound.

Near Lee's Station, some hunters from George Stockton's Station stopped at Fox Creek and struck a fire to bed down by. Unseen eyes stared from shadows. As the men stretched their toes to the warmth and drifted to sleep, shots blasting blankets ripped the night. The wraiths charged, attacking the forms lurching from bedrolls, shooting one of Stockman's boys dead; the others tore off into the dark.

As the season warmed, survey teams looked more like militia patrols. Spies scouted ahead; surveyors and their chain carriers and marker men followed single-file; armed cooks guarded the rear. March 1788 brought the yellowish pink blooms of wild day lilies and a hint of green to seas of bluegrass, and it also brought Indians to John Kenton's outpost two miles from Washington. Off to the side of Kenton's Station was the stable. The Indians tomahawked the door and heaved against it, but it was too thick, and its wooden bolt and hinges held firm. A warrior clambered up onto the roof to smash a hole through the shakes and drop to the dirt floor. After he hacked apart the bolt and swung wide the doors, in rushed his comrades, opening stalls and kicking horses into a gallop to drive them to the Ohio.

At daylight one man from the fort ran to Washington to raise a posse. The fifteen vigilantes crossed the Ohio and scoured the shoreline to find the trail, which they followed to White Oak Creek; there their enemy "took an old buffalo road which led up the stream crossing it at every bend, at that time about waist-deep," said Spencer Records. "We had to hold two or three of us together to enable us to cross it."[12] Dismounting to cross the swift, cold waters "eight times that night by moonlight, and twice next morning before sunrise," the whites gained the enemy camp,[13] but their prey scattered. Fearing ambush, the posse gave up the chase.

In the tempest that resumed that spring, two Shawnees stole six horses from Mahan's Station; Spencer and Laban Records and five others, including John Lewis, Joseph Wright, and Dickson Lord, tracked them eight miles to the Ohio, flowing out of its banks from recent downpours. Spencer eyed the muddy ribbon of prints crisscrossing the shore: The high, swift waters, he reasoned, kept the red men from swimming the steeds across.

They reconnoitered. Then, a halloo!

The posse dashed toward the sound and picked up a trail and spied two of the horses. Spencer and Laban and the two others ran ahead of Lord, Wright, and Lewis, as Lord saw lying on the ground an Indian blanket with a fusil pitched across and stooped to grab it. Laban and his man struck the flooded shoreline; Spencer and the other Kentuckian kept twenty yards south of them to watch the bottoms.

Two Indians on a log raft tied with vines floated just offshore: One stood trying to pole it off the bank; the other sat, halters in hand, coaxing the skittish animals—belly-deep and tied nose-to-tail—into the turbid froth. Laban

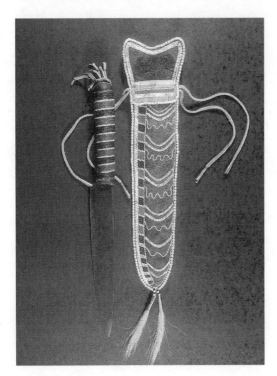

*Scalping knife (blade 7¹/₂")
with fully quilled handle topped
with brass cones. Sheath is
birchbark covered in deerskin
dyed black, edge beaded with
deer-skin hair tufts in brass
cones, quilled with horizontal
and vertical patterns in Ottawa
fashion.* ARTISANS: MICHAEL J. TAYLOR
AND DON MAUDLIN. AUTHOR'S
COLLECTION.

raised his rifle as Spencer dashed to his side. Laban aimed and pulled—then, nothing, save a metallic *clatch!* from the dull flint slamming forward tripping the frizzen. Both Indians dove into the Ohio.

One bobbed to the surface. Spencer fired and missed and was reloading as a second head broke the chop. Again he fired. As the warrior thrashed the reddening shallows in agony, Spencer grabbed Laban's rifle and knapped the flint's edge with the back of his knife blade, cocked, and ended the Shawnee. But his companion ducked under and swam hard, the current pushing him to a stand of poplars out in the river and, finally, out of range.[14]

Spencer waded out, cut a small circle in the skin of the dead man's skull, hitting bone, and grabbed a hank of black hair. A sucking, tearing sound ended with a smack when he kicked his gory prize free, leaving the half-sunken corpse twisting and turning with the ebb and flow of the surge.

The four men walked back, the scalp dangling from Spencer's belt and horses in tow, to where they had seen the other horses and the gun on the blanket. The horses were grazing, but where, pray, were John Lewis, Dickson Lord, and Joe Wright?

Then, a thrashing noise across the heavily leaved limbs of summer caused Spencer to look in a treetop, in time to see the trio shinnying down. Lord declared that he "thought they should stay there and if an Indian should escape . . . they would kill him."

Ha! Lord's lame play brought laughter, but not from Spencer, who chided them for cowardice, which might have cost them their lives. One of the horses saved was Lord's; Spencer threatened to sell it and divide the cash. It "was a long time before they heard the last about hiding in the tree-top," and Lewis, Lord, and Wright gained local fame as news of their deed spread.

On May 27, 1789, Judge Robert Rankin of Washington, Kentucky, "ordered that Spencer Records, John Kenton, Simon Kenton, I. L. Turner, Joshua Baker, Peter Lee and Lawrence Williams be recommended to his Excellency the governor as proper persons to be commissioned as Captains of the Militia of this County."[15] From then on until raids in the Bluegrass ceased, Capt. Spencer Records would have a strong hand in helping keep Mason County safe. Still, horses were stolen, and that spring Indians killed and scalped Amos Woods in view of Clark's Station.

In the summer of 1789 a Virginian named Coleman moved to Washington to secure a claim on the Licking and hired Simon Kenton and ten men to go with him to see his land. As Kenton led, the men rode out of Washington, southward. Five miles from town, they fell into a trace and took it past Camp Creek. At a ford the trace ran down to the rivulet on a steep, fifty-yard slant, crossed it, and rose as the trail stretched on; where the creek and the trace met, the left bank rose to a six-foot bluff. Hidden behind the knoll was a grassy meadow dotted with hardwoods, and there, at midday, Kenton halted to eat and rest the horses. He posted a mounted sentry at the splice of the creek and trace; the rest rode over the bluff.

Tobias Wood and Spencer Records were hunting on foot that day and struck the trace where the horsemen had ridden by and saw their tracks. The two reckoned Indians had raided a few outlying cabins and stolen some horses.

Wood and Records ran close to the path for about a mile and heard a horse snort just as they reached Camp Creek. Whispering, they spotted Kenton's sentry at the same time that Kenton's sentry saw them and took them for Indians and fled up the trace and dropped over the knoll. As he disappeared from view, the two woodsmen treed. "We both had black hair and were bareheaded. Both of us had on dark colored hunting shirts," remembered Spencer Records.[16]

They heard horses and men fleeing past the knoll. Then a booming voice, Kenton's.

"Stand your ground. Not a man run!"

Records hallooed, emerging from the trees. Coleman, impressed with their daring, tried to hire both on the spot for the sum of "fifty cents a day in cash." But Records and Wood said no, and after bidding Kenton good-bye, they retrieved their hats and began their hunt anew.[17]

On December 1 Spencer and Laban Records and John Hughey set off to hunt for Isaac Sellers, Laban's father-in-law, who had not returned from hunting. They read the sign easily enough: Sellers had taken his slave boy and dog and two horses and made his way along Locust Creek and camped. At his half-faced shelter they found his corpse, scalped and stripped, and Spencer and Laban walked to the old man's body and rolled it over. His nose had been cut off, his tongue severed, his throat slashed. The men lugged the body to a fallen tree and hacked out a hole with belt axes and a makeshift shovel split from an ash. Wrapping Sellers in a blanket, they laid him in the earth and, after heaping logs on his grave, stole back to Washington.[18]

In March 1790 Spencer and Laban were hunting near the same area when they rode to the head of a run to stay the night and walked the horses away two hundred yards to stake them. Only because it was bitter cold did they make a fire, but before getting into their blankets, they reprimed and took off their moccasins to put in their blankets to thaw and dry. Shot bags and powderhorns strapped on, rifles half cocked and primed at their sides, dogs at their heads, Spencer and Laban put their bare feet to the embers.

Spencer dreamed that he and his brother were hunting and camping on this very spot, just as they were. He dreamed that they had put out the horses from the camp at the head of the run, just as they had done. And as he dreamed on, he dreamed his dog raised its head and looked down the run and growled.

Spencer awoke. A premonition? He went back to sleep. Oddly, he awoke from the same dream.

As he lay awake, his dog raised its head, looked down the run, and growled. Spencer turned to Laban. "Indians creeping in," he said.

As Laban lay still, Spencer raised to put on his moccasins, tying the leather whangs across his heels. As he lay back down Laban sat up and did the same and they crept off to their horses.

1790

Washington's population was more than five hundred and boasted 119 houses and twenty-one slaves.[19] That February John May—for whom Maysville was named—and his clerk, Charles Johnston, traveled to Virginia to settle their legal affairs. For the return trip, May bought a flatboat at Kelly's Station at the Little Kanawha and was joined by Jacob Skyles, seeking passage to ship goods and horses to Lexington. Stopping at Point Pleasant, May gained more passengers: a man named Flinn and two sisters named Fleming, who were going west to find husbands.

On March 20, as dawn lifted, May's boat rounded a bend just past the Scioto's mouth. Flinn stood on deck in his night dress, peering down at an ominous black pall boiling up from the Ohio shore and hovering on the water, steaming river fog and smoke as one. Flinn yanked on the rudder to steer to the Kentucky shore and roused May, Skyles, and Johnston.

Two grimy-faced men—"Devine and Thomas," the terrified whites called aloud, identifying themselves by their own names—stood under the smoke, waving, pleading for help: Shawnees had captured them at Kennedy's Bottom, Devine hollered, and they had escaped; even now they feared their captors were near. The two ran along the water's edge as the boat slipped by.

Flinn and the Fleming girls begged May to stop, though Skyles and Johnston reckoned it was a trap. May ordered the boat be put close to the north shore. Flinn leaned on the till. Devine and Thomas shouted praises to glory.

As the hull scraped sand Flinn jumped ashore. Gunfire rattled the willows. In the smoky din Indians seized Flinn. Johnston and Skyles fired, but as May waved his white nightcap to show surrender, a lead ball punched into his head. Seconds later, Johnston crumbled as one Fleming girl fell—her jaw blasted away. A bullet jolted Skyles's right shoulder, boring across his back and into his left shoulder. Horses on board lay dead or dying. A painted horde swarmed over the boat's high gunwales, as three more flatboats hove into view.[20]

The Indians pressed their hostages into duty to intercept the oncoming flotilla, warriors hunkered below gunwales. As Thomas Marshall's craft veered sharply toward the other two, the red men loosed a volley. Marshall's crew gave up two of their boats to escape in the third, leaving behind $2,000 in goods and twenty-eight horses.[21] After Marshall moored at Limestone, Capt. Spencer Records raised a third of a company supplied with six days' provisions and at dusk rendezvoused with another hundred fighters to cross the Ohio.

The next morning the militiamen were led around by a priggish officer who paraded them single-file along the Ohio's banks. Laban Records, on point, advised striking to the hills, but the officer refused until Laban showed him tracks. "Quit the river and take to the hills," commanded the officer. The men on the shoreline obliged, cutting northeast toward Old Chillicothe. At a ford Laban saw fresh sign bearing northeast. "For God's sake," the commander ordered, "make to the river." At the Scioto's mouth, they found Marshall's flatboats. Cloth, clothes, horses, weaponry, and supplies were gone; two copper stills were beaten useless; ruined cakes of chocolate and packets of pins lay scattered about.

On April 8 a desolate broadhorn spinning past Limestone was intercepted and docked; near a blood-splashed gunwale, John Boyd found a fragment of a letter:

> Around the sapling to which I am chained . . . a part of my merchandise is scattered, and a small bundle of pencils presenting themselves to my view gave me the hint of writing to you. . . . In the hope and expectation that you will receive it, and that an expedition will be carried forward against these daring pirates, I shall offer my advice which from my knowledge of their situation. . . . They have a train of spies on each bank of the river, which extends as far down as Limestone; so that it is impossible to steal a march on them, by following the meanders of the Ohio. . . . From the North-East they apprehend no danger. . . . Cross a few leagues above the mouth of Scioto River, then form in two divisions, one to file off to the right and conceal themselves on the trace which leads to their station camp, the other to follow the course of the river, and make the charge.[22]

Ten days later Gen. Charles Scott's 1,000 Regulars and 230 Kentuckians met at Limestone and crossed the river, their noise and gab scattering native spies before them. After a fifteen-mile chase, the army shot four Indians and took their scalps to show off back at Limestone.

Spencer Records married Elizabeth Elrod on April 15, 1790, and settled six miles west of Washington.[23] He built a two-story split log cabin "to have room to load and shoot, with port-holes above and below. The door was made of strong puncheons, pinned with a two inch pin, and barred with a strong bar, so that it could not possibly be forced open."[24]

That August, Laban Records and John Hughey were hired as spies to patrol the Ohio at £5 6s. per day. Both had been handpicked by Simon Kenton and were in his employ. Laban took one scalp that summer and avenged the death of Isaac Sellers, stabbing the Indian through the head with his fifteen-inch knife; it was, he said, just like "thrusting through a pumpkin." He tacked the scalp to his cabin's garret, in spite of his mother's protests.[25]

Along the Washington road, Jonathan Livingston was driving his wagon of goods, whiskey, and hides to Limestone when Indians stepped into the path, took him captive, cut free his horse, and stole as much booty as they could carry. Rolled up in his greatcoat was a whiskey jug and soon the warriors became drunk as they rode the woods and ridges back to the Ohio. But the terrain, coupled with their drunkenness, slowed them considerably, and after many hours of starting and stopping to find their way, the Indians, with Livingston, swam their mounts across the broad river.

Word of the mischief ignited Washington. Spencer and Laban Records and John Hughey led a posse that rode out at dawn, heading for a flatboat they knew to be moored some eight miles away. Upon boarding, they double-manned the oars and brought the craft near the far shore, all the while watching for tracks to emerge at the shore's edge. Spotting the muddy prints, they beached and hit the trail for four miles. At a hastily erected lean-to the path split three ways; the whites took the center trail. Two miles later the trail split again; Spencer took the right fork and camped. At daylight they took up the chase anew.

Then, just ahead, halloos! The whites followed two more miles.

Emerging from a brush heap into a clearing, scouts spotted the four Indians seventy yards away, one riding a packhorse laden with deerskins. Hughey fired first, knocking the warrior off his mount, forcing him to drop a new rifle and stagger into some timber. Laban's rifle hang-fired, but he held steady and hit his mark high in the back, turning him off to one side; yet somehow the man stayed on his feet and kept running. His face painted and wearing a calico hunting shirt with a greatcoat hoppused high on his back, the man struggled to keep pace.

"Shoot him again!"

"No! Don't shoot! Take him prisoner!"

Upon hearing, the man turned and ran to Spencer, Laban, and Hughey, yelling "Oh, my wagon! My wagon!"

It was Livingston. His greatcoat showed sixteen holes, cut by shards of the smashed whiskey bottle ripping through its folds. The packhorse with its burden and his rifle, the one dropped by the wounded Indian, were returned to him, but Livingston gave both to his rescuers to thank them for their trouble.

Looming on Kentucky's horizon was statehood, but Capt. Spencer Records's adventures continued.[26] So too did the Indian wars.

"William Augustus Bowles, Director General of the Creek Nation."
PAINTED FROM LIFE IN LONDON, MARCH 1791, BY THOMAS HARDY.

"Aping the Manner of Savages"

"The jury Mr. Webster demands," said the stranger, sipping at his boiling glass. "You must pardon the rough appearance of one or two; they will have come a long way."

And with that the door blew open and twelve men entered one by one.

If Jabez Stone had been sick with terror before, he was blind with terror now. For there was Walter Butler, the Loyalist, who spread fire and horror through Mohawk Valley in the times of the Revolution; and there was Simon Girty, the renegade, who saw white men burned at the stake and whooped with the Indians to see them burn. His eyes were green like a catamount's, and the stains on his hunting shirt did not come from the blood of deer.

—Steven Vincent Benet, *The Devil and Daniel Webster,* 1937

To Jonathan Livingston, whom Spencer Records rescued from the Shawnees even though Livingston ran from him (thinking Records was an "enemy Indian" in pursuit of the Indians who had captured him), Records "looked Indian"—sun-darkened skin, eyes like onyx, compact frame fleshed out lean and tight from a diet of wild meat and parched corn and kept taut by woods running and hunting, spying, and skirmishing. His shoulder-length shock of black hair, plaited back in a thick braid, greased and bound with a whang, resembled an ebony scalp lock; such a look was enhanced when on the trail Records stripped down to leggings and clout and doffed his black fur felt beaver to don a linen or silk head rag or club his hair back in a thick queue.

To be "taken for an Indian" in Spencer's day near Limestone on the Ohio, dead across from the "Indian shore," was no compliment and might end tragically: Peter Harper, "a half-Indian," was killed in a case of mistaken identity, as was Joseph Rogers, a nephew of George Rogers Clark. Captured near the Lower Blue Licks on December 28, 1776, young Rogers ran to greet his uncle's army as his rescuers marched on Piqua in 1782, but being "dressed fine in Indian dress," he was fired upon and died as his uncle George crouched by his side and wept. Near Cassidy's Station, in Fleming County, famed scout Michael Cassidy shot dead a comrade attired "in Indian dress."[1]

Records, Harper, and Rogers "looked Indian." None of them were "white Indians." But there were those who did—for reasons of preference, profession, or coercion—"ape the manner of savages."

In early February 1778, on the Upper Blue Licks, Daniel Boone—inexplicably, so it seemed to many—surrendered his twenty-six salt boilers to Black Fish's Shawnee war party 120 strong. Over the next five years, most of the hostages were freed or escaped. A few died in captivity. At least three of the captives—Micajah Callaway, Jack Dunn, and Joseph Jackson—"turned Indian."

Micajah Callaway lived five years in the Middle Ground as a Shawnee. Ezekiel Lewis was with Col. Archibald Lochry's flotilla when famed Mohawk leader Joseph Brant and Wyandot warriors ambushed them on the Ohio on August 24, 1781, killing thirty-seven Americans and capturing seventy. Lewis reported seeing Callaway with Brant: "'Cage Callaway was the worst savage amongst them!"[2] George Rogers Clark secured Callaway's release in Louisville in July 1783; due to his linguistic skill and knowledge of Indians and the Ohio land, he became one of General Clark's scouts and mediators.

Called "a renegade destitute of principles," Jack Dunn escaped from the Shawnees in 1778 or 1779. In 1780 he deserted Col. Ben Logan's Kentucky regiment and tried to betray them to the Mackujay sept he had once lived with. Fearing trickery from this turncoat, the Shawnees called off the raid and took Dunn back to their village on the Scioto, staked him, and set him aflame.[3]

Joseph Jackson, a salt-boiler-turned-Shawnee, returned to Kentucky in 1800 to "make a good citizen," he told Lyman Draper, who met him in 1844, noting that in appearance and mannerisms, Jackson was "Indian in every respect." In the end, though, poor Jackson, unhappily married, melancholy, and unable to reconcile his past, hanged himself.[4] Jackson was a haunted man: In 1782 he had fought the Americans at Blue Licks; in 1790 he fought Col. Josiah Harmar's army; in 1791 he fought Gen. Arthur St. Clair; in 1794 he fought Gen. Anthony Wayne at Fallen Timbers. Perhaps what is most remarkable is that Joseph Jackson could have lived in Kentucky after his Shawnee life without fearing a noose from his neighbors.

Great Lake warriors captured Steven Ruddell in 1780 during Ruddell's Station's capitulation to the Brits and Indians. Ruddell grew to manhood among

Shawnees, married, and spoke fluent Algonquin and pidgin English. Of Ruddell and his family, observed by Daniel Trabue during a truce as Ruddell and his "squagh" rode up and reined their horses:

> They all alighted and came in the fort and all had the appearrence of Indians. They were all painted and very Dirty and shabby. . . . They had some silver trenkits hanging about thir necks and brests, and some broaches in their brechcloaths, and beeds in their leggans and Moxckersons, I suppose they thought themselvs fine; yet they weare all Dirty looking creaturs. They all Drank Whiskey and ate very hearty.[5]

The prisoners exchanged, Ruddell's parents—stunned at the sight of this wild man, once lost but now found, who was their boy—persuaded him to trim his hair and wash up and don breeches and weskit, stockings and shoes. Ruddell obeyed but did not take to the new look: Two hours later he "was dressed again in his Indian garb." Ruddell stayed with his kinsmen, who adored this one born out of due

John Norton, from life, c. 1810. Mixed-blood Iroquois/Anglo, and adopted by the Cherokee. Note red ruffled shirt, blue matchcoat, spike tomahawk, turban, and ostrich plumes. Norton was well educated, keenly intelligent, and in 1816 wrote his very lucid memoirs.

season; in time, he felt the Holy Ghost stir within, heeded the Macedonian Call, and took to the pulpit as a Baptist preacher. "Steven had a good deal that reminded you of the Indian in his manner," said one parishioner who heard Brother Ruddell proclaim the Gospel but was taken aback by the blue-black whorls tattooed upon his pastor's face—"he wasn't a pretty speaker."[6]

Shawnees seized Johnny Tanner (age nine) near the Big Miami in 1789 and took him northward and sold the boy to the Ojibway, who took him in as one of their own and renamed him The Falcon. In 1800 Tanner married an Ojibway and began his family. Seventeen years later he returned to Kentucky to reenter a lost world Shawnee captors had snatched from him. But Tanner's aloof ways, dress, manner of living, halting English, Ojibway wife, and visits from his kin cast him under a cloud among neighbors. A year later The Falcon was roaming the Great Lake's verdant rim of tamarack and spruce and living life as an Ojibway but spending time around his own race to learn their ways. Torn between two worlds, and accused of a murder he did not commit—accused because he was thought to be a "half-breed"—the enigmatic Tanner vanished in 1846.[7]

Some whites managed to see past color. The enlightened comments of Nicholas Cresswell, the young Brit who lived among the Delawares in the late 1770s, differed sharply from those of his peers. "I have . . . a great regard for Indians. If we take an impartial view of an Indian's general conduct with all the disadvantages they labor under, at the same time divest ourselves of prejudice, I believe every honest man's sentiments would be in favor of them."[8]

Settlers may have been suspicious of John Tanner, but they despised one name above all others. In his last years in Canada, settled in forced exile west of the Detroit River at the British outpost Fort Malden, Simon Girty had become a living legend—America's first frontier villain.

Americans—and especially those in Ohio land—hated Girty with a burning malevolence too dark for words. In the heat of a good fight, though, some of the more articulate Kentuckians did manage to find a few choice ones: "A no-good son of a bitch" is what Aaron Reynolds called him to his broad, round face (but from afar and safely from behind Bryan's Station's palisades) in August 1782. Moravian minister John Heckewelder felt the sting of his presence and declared Girty was "as brutal, depraved, and wicked a wretch as ever lived." Hunters named worthless curs for him to give them greater pleasure when they loosed them in cornfields to gut-shoot them for sport. At night mothers would wag a finger in the faces of restless children to admonish—"You be good or Simon Girty will get you."

Born in 1741 near Harrisburg, Pennsylvania, Simon Girty, named for his Irish father who was shot in a duel before his ten-year-old son's eyes, grew up hard even when judged by the harsh standards of the frontier. An Indian raid in 1756 changed his life: Forced to watch stepfather John Turner die at the stake, Simon

Though this is a fictitious sketch of Simon Girty, of unknown date and provenance, this image—depicting trade silver, wampum, chevron-patterned sash, peace medallions, leggings with ring brooches on flaps, quilled strips on coat, and feather-cap (gastoweh)—is a remarkably accurate depiction of the hybrid blend of attire worn by 18th century "white Indians."

and his three brothers were separated to make them into "white Indians." For nine years Simon lived in New York among the Senecas but was freed during the French and Indian War.

Labeled a "drunken and unfit person" during the Revolution, prone to fisticuffs when in his cups, and a defender of Indian rights, at Fort Pitt Girty was denied a captain's commission and became an outcast; an "Indian lover" is what they called him, and his Indian ways and associations did nothing to assuage such talk. More than once his life was threatened, and he struck back with the ultimate unholy bargain: Simon Girty—patriot, spy, and interpreter fluent in a variety of Algonquin and Iroquoian tongues—defected to the British Indian Department the night of March 28, 1778, to join with George III's tawny minions against liberty and against his own flesh and blood.

Americans were shocked: Few men could incite Indians like Girty could. Worse, as viewed through their eyes, Girty had "turned Indian," sinking past mere depravity to natural man's most craven state, that of an unredeemed "white savage." Haughty and unrepentant to the end, Simon seemingly reveled in his sins, siring mixed-blood issue and lending a strong hand in the darkest of deeds that resulted in the deaths of scores of Kentucky's sons.

His was an impressive roster of British and Indian military coups against Americans. In 1779 Girty's Indians besieged Fort Laurens in southern Ohio. Months later, his forces fell upon an Ohio River flotilla bound for Kentucky, killing forty-two. In 1780 Simon, along with brothers James and George, and with hundreds of Great Lake Indians and British partisans, journeyed to the Bluegrass with Capt. Henry Bird and seized Ruddells' and Martin's Stations—Simon helped negotiate terms of surrender. In 1781 his Wyandots ravaged Squire Boone's Painted Stone Station, leaving, it was rumored, sixty dead; Girty wounded Squire—"I really made Boone's white shirt fly," he laughed, recounting the raid—and very nearly killed Daniel's younger brother. In Ohio in June 1782, a coalition of British-allied native forces defeated Col. William Crawford's attacking Virginians, and Girty watched as Delawares slow-roasted Crawford. Eyewitness accounts differ as to whether Girty lifted a hand to help the tormented man. That August, during what Kentuckians called the Year of Blood, Girty and his allies besieged Bryan's Station, killing two, wounding two, destroying 300 hogs, 150 cattle, and all the sheep; two days later the contingent ambushed 180 Americans at Blue Licks, killing more than 70: one-thirteenth of Kentucky's militia. In 1791 his Wyandots so distinguished themselves in St. Clair's defeat that Girty was given the captured American cannons.

Little wonder Gen. Anthony Wayne offered $1,000 for Girty's scalp, a bounty that was never collected.

Simon Girty threatened white captive O. M. Spencer during young Spencer's eight-month captivity at Blue Jacket's Town in 1792. Spencer deemed Girty "the very picture of a villain" and said he wore "the Indian costume, but without any ornament; and his silk handkerchief, while it supplied the place of a hat, hid an unsightly wound in his forehead."[9]

By the time of his death in 1818, Girty's reputation and tales of his much-embellished exploits evolved into myth and legend, making him the personification of evil incarnate: America's archetypal renegade. And though he had saved the lives of more than twenty captives, befriended Daniel Boone during his Shawnee captivity in 1778, was blood brother to Simon Kenton and rescued him from the stake, by the end of his life American novelists would deem renegade Girty the vilest miscreant cur of the Allegheny west. In the end, Simon Girty, like other "marginal men" of his day and kind, lived in two vastly different worlds, in many ways a stranger to both.[10]

CHAPTER TEN

Reckonings & Resolutions

LATE 1780s

When Daniel Boone was not hunting or surveying—and most of the time, he was surveying, drawing plats, registering claims, hustling up business for more of the same—he was helping Rebecca at their new inn at Limestone on the banks of the Ohio: "a grate Landing place," destined to become a major riverine port.[1] For Boone and others of that unique vanishing breed that once plied its livelihood peering down the hammered flat of a hand-forged octagon rifle barrel to sight a silver sliver between an iron rear sight, Kentucky was fast closing in, and they were making do as they could.

Daniel Boone's woes were the woes of all the original hunters of Kentucky. The once fabled island in the wilderness had been claimed many times over, resulted in two generations of courtroom wrangling, lawsuits, and litigation.

Where there were once seas of bluegrass and cane, there were now farms belted by split-rail fences. Then came Boone's legal headaches: Attorneys challenged many of the old woodsman's surveys, forcing him to retain a lawyer to lead him through mazes of litigation, and more than once after his court depositions, blackguarding claimants threatened his life far more than did any Shawanoe raiders. Boone learned that he had unknowingly erected Boone Station on a land grant officially claimed by another, which led to a long, drawn-out legal affair appearing on the court docket as Boofman vs. Hickman; in the end, Boone was forced to move.[2]

But not only were Boone's dwindling acres "shingled over"; the very face of the land and its once teeming herds was changing. Elk were gone or going

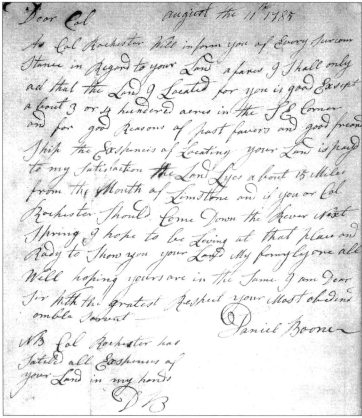

Letter of Daniel Boone's, dated August 11, 1785, written to Col. Thomas Hart in Hagerstown, Maryland, confirming he has surveyed a plot of land for Hart near Limestone (Maysville), Kentucky: "I shall only ad that the Land I Located for you is good except about 3 or 4 hundered acres in the SE Corner . . . the Land Lyes about 15 miles from the Mouth of Limestone and if you or Col. Rochester should come down the river next Spring I hope to be leving at that place and rady to show you your land." FRANK T. SIEBERT COLLECTION.

fast. Buffalo droves numbered less than twenty head, if that, and were rarely seen except west of the Green and along the Mississippi's western shores. Deer herds had been radically thinned. Beaver and otter were trapped out. Bounty hunters with packs of baying Plott hounds bred in North Carolina shot panthers out of trees and trapped and shot black bears and black wolves as garden pests.

Disappearing as quickly as the game were the canebrakes and the darkly canopied forests of oaks, hickories, maples, sycamores, and poplars that once soared skyward. Rapacious market hunting followed by land clearing by

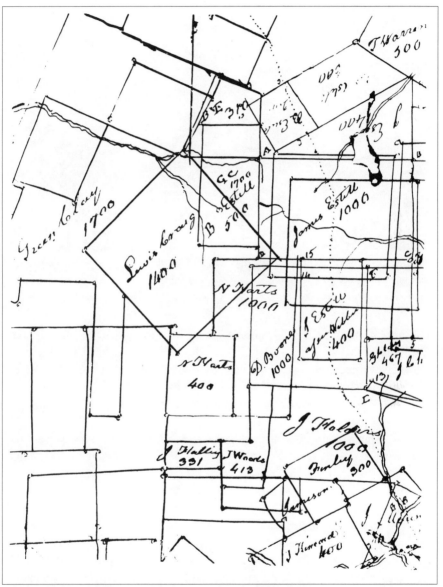

"Shingled" (or overlapping) land claims, featuring names of famous Kentuckians, including Daniel Boone, Nathaniel Hart, James Estill, and Lewis Craig.

Woodcut, c. 1845, that probably was rendered earlier than date of publication and accurately depicts a frontier "house-raising." Such affairs not only built log cabins, but strong bonds of community. "THE RAISING," FROM THE WESTERN MISCELLANY, JULY, 1848.

igniting fires that raged uncontrollably, ravaging the countryside and torching lush habitat into cinders, had transformed hardwood stands and vast, shimmering savanna into scorched earth thick with columns of tall dead trees black from where they had been girdled and torched. And everywhere, it seemed, were squatter-filled pigsty log cabins propped up in the midst of crooked, weed-choked corn rows.

Most citizens of the United States—and certainly Kentuckians were no different—thought little of sacred pacts between Indians and foreign absolutist kings. Most Americans perceived Indians as a kind of unpredictable, violent human vermin having no claim to lands left, in their eyes, "undeveloped."

Yet, in spite of the inevitability of it all (or perhaps, because of the inevitability of it all), spates of volley fire echoed across the Ohio's often bloodied waters. Shawnees captured John Kinsaulla, Robert Clark, and some slaves and put a woman and her four sons under the tomahawk; in Bourbon County warriors killed and scalped two boys and beat their heads in. Settlers vanished. Indians were shot for sport. Algonquins meted out stern retribution, only to be met by Kentuckian eye-for-an-eye justice.

Mid-September 1786, Col. Benjamin Logan ferried his force of eight hundred men across the Ohio River in flatboats launched from Limestone's wharfs, gained the Indian shore, regrouped his army, and tore into the Middle Ground's vitals in a desperate effort to halt the red pestilence. Col. Daniel Boone commanded one militia company. Cutting a half moon of fire and lead from the Scioto to the Great Miami, on October 6 the Big Knives split their ranks to hit the Shawnee towns.

But most of the warriors had fled northwest to the Wabash, leaving their Shawanoe towns and villages to old men and captives, women and children. Mackacheck, New Piqua, Will's Town, McKee's Town, Blue Jacket's Town, Moluntha's Town, and Wapakoneta smoldered by week's end. Twenty Shawnees died, thrice that were captured. Indians killed three Kentuckians and wounded two as billowing smoke from over two hundred burning wigwams, cabins, and all manner of lodges clouded the settling dusk. The army destroyed more than fifteen thousand bushels of corn, slaughtered as much livestock as they could, and loaded plunder valued at £1,000 on long strings of captured horses to take home, ensuring starving times again for the Ohio Indians.

It was in this fight that Simon Kenton shot Big Jim. "Mind that fellow, I know him. He killed my boy James," Boone shouted to Simon as the woodsman fired and drew steel and plunged after Big Jim the Cherokee as he crouched in a brake shooting twice and reloading, Kenton finishing off with a knife this infamous one who had tortured to death Boone's son in 1773. For Boone, the sight of the leering, wildly painted man with the high cheekbones sucking a last defiant breath brought haunting remembrances of Powell's Valley and the first casualties of Lord Dunmore's War. Rangers scalped Big Jim's corpse as Boone stood by, silent.

The fighting was fierce, pitiless, brutal. One young warrior the Americans captured they scalped alive and set free. A handful of George Rogers Clark's enraged Kentuckians chased a band of Indians into a cabin, buttressed its doors shut from the outside, and set the cabin aflame, cursing and shooting those leaping through the inferno's flames attempting to save themselves.

During the rout's final salvos, hot-headed Maj. Hugh McGary again did what he did so well, distinguishing himself almost as finely as he had distinguished himself at the battle of Blue Licks. After Moluntha, the venerable Shawnee chieftain, gave himself up and sat conferring with Logan's officers under the flapping shade of his own American flag, negotiating terms for prisoner exchanges, McGary charged up brandishing a woodsman's ax, swore "by God" he would give the old man "Blue Licks play," and split Moluntha's skull, leaving him writhing in blood and brains. As McGary moved in to slice Moluntha's scalp off his near-bald pate, Logan's soldiers wrestled the enraged Kentuckian to the ground.

Colonel Logan, furious his orders to spare all prisoners had been so blatantly disobeyed, immediately relieved Major McGary of his command.

Unrepentant to the end, McGary swore "by God, he would chop him down or any other man who should attempt to hinder him from killing at any time." McGary's actions inspired Thomas Kennedy to turn mad dog, his battered, high-swinging Scottish basket-hilt slashing at the cowering Indian women, nearly decapitating the first one he swung on, cutting the fingers off two or three of the others as they raised their hands to fend his broadsword off. Lt. Col. James Trotter tongue-lashed McGary and the "Squaw Hacker," as the Kentuckians called Kennedy after that, but took no real action.[3]

Col. Benjamin Logan's war expedition was to be Daniel Boone's last Indian fight. After it, Boone, sickened by it all, turned more to himself and to his family and looked to the future.

Of a truth, Ohio Indians, too, were sickened by it all.

More than a century and a half of migrations, wanderings, and warring were enough to convince the Shawanoes that the century's closing would bring sweeping changes, but no certain peace. With their British allies defeated (and especially so after the War of 1812), the Shawanoes faced a precariously uncertain future.

Old habits and Indian customs were dying hard; but truly, inexorably, irrevocably, the old ways were dying, and with their steady diminution came the decaying of the lives and culture of a people whose ancient homeland had been invaded by a strange, powerful enemy that appeared as a plague of locusts, perennially devouring all sustenance. In 1787 the U.S. Congress passed the Northwest Ordinance, federalizing Indian lands east of the Mississippi River, west of the Blue Ridge, and north of the Ohio.

A triune path now lay before Ohio land's Algonquins: to fight; or to make peace; or to emigrate westward. For the next score of years, the five septs of the Shawanoes—never in their history a united people—would, at various times, attempt to take all three paths.

Col. Benjamin Logan's torching of clusters of wigwams and council longhouses along the Great Miami's banks blunted the sharp tines of the near constant raids emanating south of the Great Lakes. By 1787 whites and reds had agreed to terse terms of a prisoner swap to be held at Limestone, across from Daniel Boone's tavern (where the Shawanoes often ferried across to visit their beloved white brother, Sheltowee, and buy whiskey and supplies), but across on the Indian shore.

Nearing noon August 20, about seventy warriors showed themselves on the Ohio's far bank. Faces were bronzed and flecked with vermilion and smeared with bear grease and soot; blue lines thinly painted from temples to eyes masked some of the warriors who stood there clad in stroud match-coats and leggings of blue and red wool and looking just as they were: fierce men of the Shawnee; proud; defiant; haughty; wary. Quilled hair locks heavy from brooches pinned in braided ebony strands radiated celestial flashes from newly shaven heads bobbing in quiet conversation. Arms, ears, and raiment shimmered with sterling. Strands of blue, black, and white glass beads adorned necks.

The Chillicothe's Big Men—Captain Johnny, Black Snake, and The Wolf—looked like aboriginal kings coming from a far country. Captain Johnny was to speak for the red men.

A bateaux of whites rowed over to parley and greet the prisoners. Col. Benjamin Logan was to speak for the white men.

Daniel Boone, Levi Todd, Robert Patterson, James Trotter, Isaac Ruddell, Simon Kenton, John Crow, and others stood with Logan. Kentuckians looked beyond the warrior delegation to peer at the hostages, seeking recognition of loved ones lost yet never forgotten. Sunburned faces marked by dirt, paint, and tattoos peered back at Kentuckians.

Central to the negotiations was Micajah Callaway, the late Col. Richard Callaway's nephew. Captured February 1778 on the Lower Blue Licks with Daniel Boone's salt-boilers, 'Cage was adopted (unlike his irascible brother James, whom Black Fish sold at Detroit and Lt. Gov. Henry Hamilton shipped to Canada). For five years he roamed the Middle Ground as a white savage. In 1783 he was freed during a hostage exchange and became one of George Rogers Clark's most trusted spies. Now Callaway stood with the whites, looking into the dark eyes of those he once called kin, fluidly putting Shawnee talk into English and vice versa.

For twenty days the parley lasted. From their tavern stores, Daniel and Rebecca Boone furnished the Indians 21 gallons of whiskey, 230 pounds of "Flower," 100 pounds of hog bacon, and 100 pounds of jerked beef. Boone paid go-between Micajah Callaway £6 for his services. In a show of goodwill, the young warrior Blue Jacket,[4] exhibiting the novel sort of leadership that would bring him renown among Shawanoes and incite fear among whites, invited Boone's son Daniel Morgan on a deer hunt. Both rode away as Indians and whites feasted and danced and sang. Daniel Morgan and Blue Jacket returned days later.

The prisoners were exchanged. The parley ended. So too ended most displays of goodwill between the races.[5]

A year earlier, Canadian-born *métis* trader Louis Lorimier, perceiving the indelible script on the wall after Col. Benjamin Logan's assault upon his outpost at Piqua Town, had fled the headwaters of the Big Miami for Spanish

Grave of Louis and Charlotte Lorimier, Cape Girardeau, Missouri, Lorimier Cemetery.
PHOTO BY ROGER RESSEL. AUTHOR'S COLLECTION.

Illinois, and from there entered the rich, low-lying alluvium of Ste. Genevieve, Missouri. Lorimier moved southward, nearer to expatriate bands of Shawnees and Delawares settled near Cape Girardeau, where, in time, he and his Shawnee wife died and were buried.[6]

By the time of Lorimier's Illinois-to-Missouri exodus, more than two thousand of his wife's Algonquin kinsmen were living in Upper Louisiana along the Saline, Apple, Cinque Hommes, and Flora Creeks, and were there with the approval of Manuel Gayoso de Lemos, governor general of Spanish Louisiana, who hoped that the Shawnee and Delaware towns would create a buffer between the hostile Little and Big Osages to the West and the influx of white settlers from the East. Many feared that the Osage Nation, suspicious of the horde of White Eye invaders—Spanish, French, British, and now Americans—were bent on taking up the war club. As were the Sauk and Fox.

EARLY 1790s

Though the era of Indian wars was not over east of the Mississippi, the epic battles occurring south of the Ohio between Kentuckians and the Shawnees and their allies were reduced to sporadic guerrilla warfare and to surprise waylays along the twists, and turns, and oxbows, and in the shallows along the Beautiful River's north shore.

One of the last Indian-fueled Kentucky flatboat tragedies to occur was perhaps the most ironic of them all.

In March 1791 Capt. William Hubble poled his flatboat from the Great Kanawha en route to Kentucky. His passengers were Daniel Light; William Plascut and his family; John Stoner, a Dutchman; two young men named Ray and Tucker; and a Mr. Kilpatrick with his two daughters. Below the mouth of the Scioto on March 23, Hubble came upon a flotilla of six more flatboats; the boatmen were drunken, boisterous, dancing to fiddler's jigs, passing whiskey jugs amidst toasts and huzzahs. Hubble pulled away from the revelry echoing up and down the river. Jacob Greathouse's flatboat pulled away to follow Hubble. Greathouse and his crew and their women were deep in their cups. Their flatboat lagged behind.

Daylight came slowly. Thick fog curled from the river. Blankets tacked up in the stern of Captain Hubble's flatboat whipped with the wind. The whites heard a scurry on the Indian shore as three canoes nosed from the fog. The whites counted thirty warriors, stiletto deerhair roaches visible in the dawn. Hubble's men flung chairs and tables overboard to clear the plank deck and make ready.

"Don't fire till the flash of your guns singes their eyebrows!" cried Hubble, as a crash of gunfire raked them starboard, leaving Tucker with a hip wound and Light badly gut-shot. As Hubble took aim, a musket ball smashed into his gun lock. He seized a firebrand and jammed it into the pan, the blast of priming searing his right hand. He charged, firing a brace of pistols, and felt the sting of a hot lead ball plow into his right arm. The raiders backed away. For a moment.

Upriver, as Captain Hubble's flatboat pulled ahead, Jacob Greathouse's flatboat eased from the rising mist. More shots. The Indians swarmed in anew, overpowering Greathouse and crew, tying up the women. As a few warriors poled the commandeered flatboat to the north bank, the rest of the whooping cadre paddled hard for Hubble's flatboat, propping the women in the bow as human shields. Hubble's men fired away. Again they repelled the Indians as their flatboat drifted dangerously near the Ohio's north shore.

A waiting ambush party rushed down the banks and fired, wounding several and killing Kilpatrick, but, providentially it seemed, the current caught Hubble's flatboat and sent it careening downriver. It was about midnight, on this March 24, that William Brooks, one of Boone's old salt boilers and himself an ex-Shawnee captive, heard their cries, roused the men, and helped guide Hubble and his crew in.[7] Only two men and Kilpatrick's two girls had escaped injury.

Hitched to the cleats at Limestone's wharf, Hubble's riddled, bloodstained flatboat created quite a stir by morning. Folks stared, counting more than one hundred bullet holes punched through a tattered blanket tacked to the craft's stern. Kentuckians shifted the gray, bloodied corpses from litters to ox-drawn carts, exhibiting the bodies about town as word got out that more flatboats were en route and it was feared the Indians had seized Jacob Greathouse's crew.[8]

On April 5 Alexander D. Orr led about three hundred men out of Limestone to find any stragglers and learn the fate of the Greathouse party. Gen. Simon Kenton and Capt. Spencer Records numbered among the militia. As the army neared the Greathouse wreckage, a haggard teenage boy wandered to them. His last name, he said, was Black. His father had been with Greathouse. Young Black led them past three Indian corpses dark with flies and cached under logs.

The Kentuckians threw off the logs to mutilate the bodies. "Though they smelled badly," said Kenton, "Joe Lemon went and scalped them."

A rod or two later they came upon Greathouse's flatboat. "There lies my poor old father." The boy pointed to the bloated corpse on the deck lying amid the dead horses. A pack of hogs loosed from their pens had rooted around the bodies, gorging, as the Kentuckians shooed them away to shovel the offal into the river. A woman's body and that of a big man were on shore, their naked corpses at the foot of a sapling and their tethered viscera entwined. A gash just above their crotches showed where the ends of their intestines had been severed and yanked out by the hank and tied to the tree; after cinching up their bowels, the Indians had whipped the pair around and around the sapling, slowly winding out their entrails in their circuitous death march.

The Indians it seemed had not forgotten that day on Yellow Creek in 1774 and had, the woodsmen agreed, reserved an especially macabre killing for Jacob Greathouse, one of the accused murderers of Chief Logan's seed.

The militiamen buried their dead in the sand, heaped logs upon the shallow graves, and with haste, ferried across to the Kentucky shore; some of the woodsmen floated Greathouse's flatboat down to Limestone, where throngs of the town's citizens lined the wharf to stare at the derelict, ill-fated vessel.[9]

North of the Ohio on the eve of the nineteenth century, thrice Americans took the fight to the Indians living in the Old Northwest, in what were destined to be some of the bloodiest Indian battles in American history.

In the fall of 1790, the urbane Philadelphia Quaker Brig. Gen. Josiah Harmar, commander of the U.S. Army in the far western theater, ferried more than 1,100 militiamen and 320 Regulars across the Ohio to take President George Washington's Indian war to the Middle Ground Algonquins. "Exhibit to the Wabash Indian our power to punish them for their positive depredations, for their conniving at the depredations of others, and for their refusing to treat with the United States when invited to," President Washington ordered his field general.[10] Harmar the drunkard had exuded full confidence of success to his commander-in-chief, especially after bracing himself with his daily cognac. But Little Turtle's eager contingent of Miami, Wea, Shawnee, Delaware, Sauk, Potawatomi, and Ottawa forces routed Harmar's troops, killing about seventy, and as bad, seizing hundreds of weapons and four hundred heavily burdened packhorses.

On November 4, 1791, Harmar's successor, Brig. Gen. Arthur St. Clair, unknowingly led his American forces (more than 1,000 strong) straight into Little Turtle's well-orchestrated ambush. After Little Turtle sprang his trap and St. Clair retreated, 632 American soldiers lay dead or dying, and another 200 camp followers were killed. Little Turtle—who lost 66 warriors—had dealt the United States its greatest defeat ever in its unrelenting wars upon American Indians. That military men of the day compared St. Clair's Defeat to Braddock's Defeat must have had special resonance to Gen. Edward Braddock's most celebrated survivor, who had become America's greatest hero of its Revolution and Father of his country.

But at the battle of Fallen Timbers in 1794, famed Revolutionary War veteran Brig. Gen. "Mad" Anthony Wayne soundly defeated Little Turtle's warriors, and the following year Ohio Valley Algonquins signed the Treaty of Greenville.[11]

New issues divided Kentuckians. Where once it was harvesting deerskins, slaughtering buffalo, contesting survey titles, and haggling over shingled land claims, heated debates now arose over government, slavery, toll roads, taxes—and, in the wake of Bourbon County's "Great Awakening" at Cane Ridge, even over biblical interpretations concerning man's salvation, spiritual gifts, and the "work" of the church.

The old Long Knife George Michael Bedinger had served as major for Brig. Gen. Arthur St. Clair, commanding during St. Clair's doomed Ohio expedition the Winchester Battalion of Sharpshooters. Afterward, Bedinger served two terms in the Kentucky legislature and two terms in the U.S. House of Representatives. In 1829 he made his last bid for Congress but was unsuccessful, perhaps because some of his ideas seemed radical. Privately operated toll roads, he averred, should be abolished in favor of public roads maintained at public expense. He believed that the electoral college went against democratic ideals and pushed to amend the Constitution to end the system. "I feel favorable to such an amendment as would give to the people themselves the entire election of the President and Vice-President of the United States."

Slavery was dividing Kentucky—as it was all of America—into pro-Union and secessionist camps. Bedinger's moral dilemma was typical of any Kentucky landowner grappling with this issue, but his feelings and sensitivity to the Africans' sad plight made him rather unique among his peers. He owned slaves yet opposed their importation and freed his slaves when they reached age thirty. "Slavery is an unhappy thing," he wrote. "If I once own them, responsibility seems to fasten on me." Banning slavery would not help the economic and social plight of Africans, he believed, so he contributed to the American Colonization Society to "raise enough money to send to Liberia freed American Negroes who wished to go."[12]

There were happier times, though. Many years before, in 1775, Bedinger had joined the ranks of Capt. Hugh Stevenson's riflemen of Shepherdstown, Virginia. To show their thanks to the men pledging their loyalty to America, they butchered a cow and held a great barbecue. Townspeople, wives, and sweethearts came to bid them well and composed a song—"That Seat of Science, Athens"—to mark the event. It was proposed, amid many toasts and huzzahs, that fifty years from the day, on June 10, 1825, at the same place, those patriots still living would reunite. Fifty years later, as decreed, the survivors met.

Out of Stevenson's company of ninety-seven, only five yet lived, and three of those could not attend. George Bedinger, who now walked with two canes due to rheumatism, rode from Blue Licks back to Shepherdstown. The only other person to show up was his brother Henry. Townspeople fixed a feast, the militia paraded and fired volleys, dignitaries made speeches, and the two men were treated like royalty.

Even after cholera swept Kentucky in 1833, leaving two of his children dead, Bedinger never lost his zest for life nor his faith. "I have not of late attended to much of my earthly business. I often read Dutch and English scriptures and compare the two. Have a cheerful mind of my own." Survived by his wife and five children, George Michael Bedinger died in 1843 at eighty-seven.[13]

With the civilizing of "progress," crime came to Kentucky.

At the century's turn, the most infamous mass murderers in frontier history, Wiley and Micajah Harpe, went on a killing spree in Adair County and hacked to death little John Trabue, second child of Daniel and Mary Trabue, and threw his mutilated remains down a sinkhole.[14] Kentuckians finally caught up with this new breed of desperadoes, who hid out with their gang of pirating cutthroats in Cave-in-Rock, Illinois, overlooking the Ohio, to plunder oncoming vessels and terrorize passengers. "Big Harpe" (Micajah) was hanged until dead, decapitated, and his head piked for a road marker; the tiny Kentucky community near Hopkinsville became officially known as "Harpes Head," and for years Big Harpe's rotting skull became a rather famous curiosity. To the south, a bounty hunter shot Wiley "Little Harpe" on the Natchez Trace, cut his head off and rolled it up in a mud-ball to preserve it, and took it to the courthouse to claim the high sheriff's blood money.

Yet Daniel Trabue, one of the old pioneers, even while relating little John's death, betrayed no acrimony, no cry for vengeance, trusting in his faith in God to sustain him. Trabue, who in 1778 recorded the court-martial trial of Daniel Boone, in 1801 witnessed Kentucky's spiritual revival at Cane Ridge and the doctrinal clashes between Baptists and Immersionists (called "Campbellites" and "Stone-ites" for Thomas and Alexander Campbell and Barton W. Stone, leaders of the "Immersionist movement").[15] Mary Trabue passed away on September 25, 1828; Daniel on September 10, 1840.

Some of the hunters of Kentucky, like Michael Cassidy and William Clinkenbeard, lived out their days in the Bluegrass, which they had helped subdue. Others did not. Capt. Spencer Records resigned as captain in the Mason County militia and in 1801 moved to Ohio, as did Simon Kenton. Records died in the fall of 1849, six miles north of Columbus.

When old Kenton returned to Kentucky briefly from Ohio to visit, he hitched a wagon ride a few miles south of Limestone to take a sack of corn to a Washington gristmill. As David Hunter's team topped a rise, Hunter reined in momentarily. Kenton, musing and drawing on his pipe stem, gazed at the land before him, all clapboarded cabins and barns and greening pastures and cattle and horses where once there were buffalo rattling in canebrakes.

"What a change. What a change," Kenton exclaimed, shaking his head in amazement.

As the leather snapped and the wagon eased on, passing a certain spring—memorably dubbed "the Shitting Spring" by Kenton and Daniel Boone years before for the many dung piles a Shawanoe hunting party had deposited upon its banks—flowing on land claimed by Hunter's father, Hunter's venerable passenger grinned and spun a few yarns about his adventures with Boone, but in the end, Kenton realized that the fabled island in the wilderness he once knew, explored, hunted, trapped out, and helped wrest from the Shawanoes was no more.[16]

Like the redoubtable Simon Kenton, nearly all of the old pioneers gave up the hunt as they aged, as rheumatism swelled their joints, and as the game vanished. All but one.

In 1789 Daniel and Rebecca Boone and their youngest children left Kentucky for a six-year sojourn in western Virginia. Boone returned to the Bluegrass in 1795, erecting his last Kentucky cabin on Brushy Fork, in Nicholas

County. In 1799 sixty-four-year-old Boone moved again—this time walking to Spanish Missouri, soon to be made French territory, which in 1803 Napoleon ceded to President Thomas Jefferson in the Louisiana Purchase.

So, America again caught up with Colonel Boone, destined to be a living legend. And so again did America's courts and legal system strip the most famous hunter of Kentucky, now living in Missouri, of his land—about one thousand acres in all.

But, his legal problems aside, Boone was delighted with what he saw of America's true Far West. Frontier Missouri was like Kentucky of old. Game was aplenty. So too were the Indians—the Osages, Iowas, Sauks, and Fox. To Boone, the tall, handsome Osages were not the fierce adversaries his adopted Shawanoe kinsmen were, though he had several run-ins with them and was twice robbed of his pelts, stripped of his capote during a heavy snow, and beaten with ramrods. Back home in St. Charles County, along the Missouri River bottoms, a sprawling progeny clamored around the beloved Grandfather Boone, who lived out his days hunting and trapping with his sons, two or three coureurs de bois, and Daniel Morgan's slave, a young black man named Derry Coburn, whose quiet company Boone enjoyed because, as he put it, the two of them thought so much alike.[17]

And his Shawnee family that had emigrated with Louis Lorimier, some of the very ones who had captured him at the Lower Blue Licks in 1778 and had fought against him at the siege of Boonesborough, now visited Sheltowee at least once or twice a year, bringing ponies as gifts. Boone and his sons appeared at their towns in turn. One of their number, Charles "Indian" Phillips, Boone hired to accompany him on his far western jaunts to dress his peltry, to cook for him, and to properly bury him should he die on the trail. The old hunter's grandchildren remembered Phillips as being "tall and spare," and that he "wore Indian leggings and moccasins" and "walked and acted like an Indian"—"all were afraid of him." Maybe. But for old Sheltowee, feeling his age and rheumatism, and through with the worries Kentucky had brought him, Phillips the Shawnee was the perfect comrade.[18]

Boone's last hunts took him as far west as Fort Riley, Kansas, the Platte River, and possibly beyond. Rebecca died in 1813. Daniel lasted until dawn, September 26, 1820, days shy of his eighty-sixth birthday.

When he left the Bluegrass in 1799, Daniel Boone had vowed never to return—"he was soured on civilization," he told Peter Houston. Boone's last-born son, Nathan, declared that to his last breath, his famous father never wavered from his vow.[19]

But in 1792 the land Boone shunned after his departure became the fifteenth state added to the Union. A year later some Cherokees and Shawnees swooped down upon Morgan's Station (in Montgomery County), killing two and seizing at least twenty hostages; in their retreat northward, the Indians tomahawked twelve of the captives. The attack on Morgan's Station was a gory, horrific affair, but it was Kentucky's last Indian raid.[20]

Aside from filling militia levies to take the warring elsewhere—to the Old Northwest against Tecumseh's alliance; to New Orleans to fight with Andrew Jackson at John Bull's final stand; to the Old Southwest against Osceola's Seminoles—by the new century's dawn, the United States had clearly won its first West.

Americans poured down the Ohio River and came by the thousands via Daniel Boone's buffalo trace, which Kentucky's first governor, Col. Isaac Shelby, had widened twenty years after Boone blazed it, as announced in the *Kentucky Gazette,* October 15, 1796: "The Wilderness Road from Cumberland Gap to the settlements in Kentucky is now completed. Wagons loaded with a ton weight may now pass with ease, with four good horses." By 1800 Kentucky's population was 220,955, including 40,343 slaves.[21]

Kentucky's frontier era had ended. The hunters of Kentucky were no more.

EPILOGUE

The First Shall Be Last

1847

Presbyterian circuit rider John Dabney Shane guided his horse-drawn buggy southeast over the low, hilly Bluegrass farmland and toward the border separating Clark from Montgomery County. He was about six miles from Mount Sterling, approaching where Stone Quarry Road forked off to Kiddsville. He was looking for Maj. Jesse Daniels's house.

Reverend Shane was in his midthirties. He was a stern-looking man capable of a fixed stare and having a firm jawline and a bold, prominent chin. He wore his headful of wavy dark hair parted on the right, pomaded the front to a glossy sweep across to his opposite temple, and broad-brushed the rest hard left. He dressed in fashion befitting a parson—white shirt, collar starched and pointy ends stabbing upward touching flesh, cravat knotted tight, dark vest, dark suit with wide lapels and cuffs halfway down his wide, fleshy hands. Standing, he appeared slender but thick-hipped, narrow-shouldered, and medium tall. Sitting, his knees rose almost as high as his waist. In the parlance of the day, John Shane was split-high: His height was mostly in his legs.

A graduate of Union Theological Seminary, after receiving his ordination from the West Lexington Presbytery in 1845, Reverend Shane had declined a located pastorship to better render "to God, the things that are God's" by serving as a "domestic missionary." Sermons he dutifully prepared and preached at the eight or nine churches on his route. In erudition he was not lacking: He could read the Old Testament in Hebrew and the New

Testament in Greek; he understood schools of biblical criticism and exegesis; and he was entirely conversant with the day's issues.

Unmarried to his last day on earth in 1864, friends knew John Shane as a kind, disciplined fellow who, despite his serious demeanor and passion for "bibliomania," was excellent company.

A devoted bibliophile, Reverend Shane had amassed almost 350 catalogs of various sorts, technical books, dictionaries, and nearly one thousand books on theology, history, science, geography, and the like (including thirty books alone on the secret fraternity the Freemasons). Besides his burgeoning library, he had hundreds of magazines, journals, and papers, and took care in assembling his many scrapbooks, pasting into the swelling volumes hundreds of clippings, essays, and interviews. He stored all of it back in his Cincinnati home (the city where he was born in 1812), in rooms "shelved all around from floor to ceiling, divided and subdivided by partitions."

Shane's antiquarian bent blossomed in his role as pastor; in his tours to comfort the ailing and visit the fatherless and widows, Shane also visited Revolutionary War veterans, pioneer folk, and aging survivors of Indian wars, writing down their reminiscences and collecting what miscellany he could from attics, from hair and leather traveling trunks, from antique portmanteaus stashed in mansion cocklofts.

Reverend Shane, naturally inquisitive as he was, was gleaning a trove of lore about Clark County, Kentucky.

A leg of the fabled Warriors' Path once cut through here, he had learned. White-haired men in homespun yarning about buffalo spoke so vividly it almost seemed as if the rheumy-eyed hunters had shot out the wild cows only weeks before. Near here was a thirty-five-hundred-acre plain drained by Upper Howard and Lulbegrud Creeks, where once stood the one-acre palisaded Shawnee town Eskippakithiki. Kentuckians called the fertile veldt Indian Old Fields for the scores of fallow corn hills blanketing it.

Indian Old Fields yielded some of Clark County's best harvests. White hickory, cherry, black locust, and black walnut saplings dotted its dense brakes and swaying savanna that grew higher than a horse's back. Between the young timber, none of it bigger around than a man's thigh, William Risk, Elisha Bishop, and Thomas Gough had plowed up cinders from ancient fire pits and unearthed squaw axes, gun barrels, pottery chards, British mortising hatchets, bits of iron hoes and kettles, and tarnished sterling brooches.

A farmer Mrs. Gough knew who had once tilled a fine patch of buffalo clover snagged an old trade kettle bail, stalling his ox team to a halt until the bail finally tore loose from the dirt. The man reckoned it was a tree root until he reached the row's end and yanked the rusty iron bail off the plowshare and examined it. That ended the day's plowing. He hunted mighty hard for the bailless kettle, Mrs. Gough recalled to the Reverend, sure it was heavy with gold. All he found was a stone pipe.

The big sugar maples skirting Indian Old Fields, Risk had discovered, disclosing his curious find to Shane, had been tapped several score years before; in augering them anew, Risk was forced to bore through bark six inches thick, closing off the old taps.

All of this greatly interested Reverend Shane. He had even heard rumors of Indians actually visiting Clark County this century. So it was, then, when Shane braked his buggy beside Maj. Jesse Daniels's cabin, he had arrived as an oral historian on a mission, this time rendering "to Caesar the things that are Caesar's," as he philosophically put it.

Yes, Indians had visited his land twice that he knew of, said Major Daniels. They had camped on his land for a day or two, a tall old man and his two grandsons. Daniels was very much surprised to learn from the man's

Kishkalwa, a Shawanoe chieftain, warred against the Ojibway and Miami, fought the Long Knives at Point Pleasant in 1774, and at age eighty in Missouri, esteemed himself in battle against the Osage. In 1825, he led an Indian delegation to the White House and sat for artist Charles Bird King.

"chat," he said, that the old Shawanoe "seemed acquainted with the ground he was on."

Daniels, though, was thoroughly baffled by their peculiar behavior, their incessant walking over and over his farmland to look at apparently nothing, visiting springs and licks—they "seemed to know them all," he said—and again and again, pointing at nothing that Daniels could see, talking and shaking heads, their emotions giving way to "great demonstrations of joy," and then, finally, walking away, the strangely acting trio heading, Maj. Jesse Daniels figured, toward Red River.

Indians fascinated Reverend Shane. He was grateful to Daniels for allowing him the privilege of painstakingly recording his reminiscences. Daniels continued.

After that first visit, he said to Reverend Shane, he did not see any more Indians until, several years later, a second Shawanoe party visited. He was sure that it was after the War of 1812, after the Shawanoes were no longer allied with the British.

This second entourage was much like the first—an old man with two grandsons, Daniels said. The second old Indian claimed to be some sort of a "king"—neighbors who came to stare at them reckoned he might have been Catahecassa, Black Hoof. But some thought that the famous Black Hoof had been born in Florida during the old English wars; this "king" claimed Indian Old Fields as his birthplace. Whether this was Black Hoof, signer of the Greenville Treaty in 1795 and Fort Wayne's Treaty in 1803, and the Black Hoof who had defied to his face the great Tecumseh by placating Americans instead of fighting them, Daniels was not sure, he said.

During this second visit, he said, another curious personage appeared: Pastor Steven Ruddell.

Rev. John Shane knew the Lakes Indians had seized young Ruddell in 1780 after burning his father's fort. When his parents "redeemed" him a decade later, Steven spoke broken English, wore leggings and a clout and earbobs, and had an Indian wife and a brood of mixed-blood children. After he reconverted to white ways and turned minister, he had given up Indian life but had retained fluency in his second tongue.

Apparently, Pastor Ruddell had come to visit the Shawanoes and interpret for the "king," Daniels thought, saying so to Shane.

With Ruddell at hand, Daniels said, the Shawanoe king gave a speech, pausing as the Baptist pastor with the strangely tattooed face put his Algonquin talk into English, the king relating his people's history and their enduring love for this spot of land. He had brought his two grandsons to see this place, the king declared through Ruddell, so that they might, many winters from now, recall it to their grandchildren.

Major Daniels continued, Reverend Shane's dip pen edging left-to-right on the broad paper lined with his cramped chirography.

Explained the king to the listening whites and to his grandchildren: Shawanoes lived on this land the Creator gave to them until one year before the Braddock fight at Fort Duquesne, Ruddell, interpreting, said. Then: "Some tribes from the south proving too hard for them," the Shawanoes migrated closer to the Red and then into Ohio land.

Daniels thought the king was referring to the Catawbas of South Carolina, but he might have been referring to the Cherokees of North Carolina. He was not sure.

After the king's speech, the three Indians left. That was the last Daniels saw of them.

Shane kept taking notes, writing concisely and compactly, abbreviating for speed—"towd" for "toward"; "2d" for "second"; "abt" for "about." As Daniels ended his curious tale, Shane carefully read his words back to him for clarification, correcting and amending as needed to make his document accurate.

Before he left the good company of Maj. Jesse Daniels, Reverend Shane paused to scribble onto foolscap leaf Daniels's parting observation about the old gray-haired Shawanoe visiting with his two grandsons: "No person comprehended the object of their visit, and they departed again, leaving the whole subject involved in the deepest mystery (as they came)."[1]

And thus, so it was. The poignancy of the obvious seemed to be lost upon Maj. Jesse Daniels and even upon the very astute Rev. John Dabney Shane. Tiny bands of Shawnees, their nation being forced into Kansas, Oklahoma, and Texas, and even into Canada, were returning one last time to the bluegrass island in the wilderness, bringing their grandchildren with them to see what was left of their sacred homeland, of Speleawee-theepee, of Red River, of Eskippakithiki, of *Kanta-Ke!*

Kanta-Ke:
A Selected Chronology

A.D. 1000–1200: Early Fort Ancient Era; founding of mound-building sites in Inner Bluegrass of Jessamine, Bourbon, and Greenup Counties, among others.

1200–1400: Middle Fort Ancient Era; larger native farming villages and hunter-farmer communities, each housing from one hundred to three hundred, proliferate in Mason, Boone, Bourbon, and other Counties.

1400–1750: Late Fort Ancient Era: As village size and native hunter-farmer population increase in northeastern Kentucky, number of villages decline as protohistoric era merges with contact era.

1543: Rumors of Luis de Moscoso, successor to Hernando de Soto, reach Kentucky's western edge via the Mississippi; first epidemics appear.

1550: Fort Ancient site of Hardin Village established on Ohio River floodplain in northeastern Greenup County and occupied until about 1675.

1570: Birth of the Iroquois Confederation: Cayuga, Mohawk, Oneida, Onondaga, and Seneca—the "Five Nations."

1607: Jamestown, Virginia, established. England's charter of ownership mentions "Kentucky," thought to be an island in a far-off sea.

1608: August. Capt. John Smith treats with the Susquehannas.

1634–39: The Five Nations war against the Hurons, already ravaged by smallpox epidemics; by 1636 the "fevers" spread among Delaware in Maryland.

1641: Epidemics reach the Cayugas, Onondagas, and others.

1649: Five thousand Huron die of disease and starvation; by 1669 epidemics spread west of St. Lawrence.

1651: The Five Nations exterminate the Neutrals of Huronia.

1654: Col. Abraham Wood of Virginia explores branches of the Ohio and Mississippi and first hears of Kentucky.

1655: Dutch conquer Swedes.

1656: Iroquois conquer Eries.

1660–76: The Five Nations war against Susquehannas and Shawnees, driving all but a remnant of Shawnees from their Ohio Valley homeland and into Pennsylvania, western Kentucky, and the Southeast.

1663: Father Hierosme Lalemant's "relation" to France produces Europe's first published account of Kentucky; his is a fulsome depiction of an earthly paradise he never saw.

1665–85: Era of largest Shawnee dispersals.

1669: Spanish adventurers float the Ohio to its forks in search of silver mines and portage to Onondaga Lake, New York; Iroquois kill all twenty-three.

1673: Father Jacques Marquette and Louis Joliet arrive at the mouth of the Ohio and mention "Chaoanons" (Shawnees) living to the east in about forty villages.

1674: Gabriel Arthur escapes Shawnees on the Scioto to return to Fort Henry, Virginia.

1675: Iroquois defeat Susquehannas.

1676–79: Epidemics spread to Great Lakes tribes; Iroquois temporarily halt warring to bury dead; by 1690 the Iroquois suffer new waves of epidemics.

1683: William Penn signs Great Treaty with Delawares.

1684: The Five Nations become protectorates of British empire, ceding vast trans-Appalachia territory, which includes Kentucky.

1689: King William's War (War of the League of Augsburg) begins; ends in 1697 with the Treaty of Ryswick.

1692: Huguenot partisan from Fort St. Louis, Martin Chartier, leads sixty Shawnee families to Cecil County, Maryland.

1694: Capt. Arent Schuyler of New York reports more than seven hundred "Shanwan Indians" living in the lower Ohio Valley, "loaden wth. beavor and peltries."

1697: Shawnees settle Pequea Creek, Pennsylvania.

1700: De l'Isle's map of Louisiana designates the Shawanoe (Cumberland) River as the "Rivière des anciens Chaouanons," for Shawnee villages established there.

1701: William Penn signs treaty with Shawnees and Susquehannas.

1702: Queen Anne's War (War of the Spanish Succession) begins; ends in 1713 with the Treaty of Utrecht.

1704: Chief Oretyagh, a Conestoga, protests rum trade. (1) 1704–17. Epidemics ravage Illinois tribes.

1718: Eskippakithiki established in Clark County; a 1736 French census numbers population at two hundred families.

1720s: Shawnees and Delawares living along the Potomac and elsewhere begin migrating back to the Ohio Valley.

1722: Tuscaroras join Iroquois Confederation, making the Five Nations the "Six Nations."

1729: Chaussegros de Lery, French engineer, conducts expedition down the Ohio, surveying and mapping the river.

1730: Lower Shawneetown (Hardin Village or Bentley site, Greenup County) established at confluence of Ohio and Scioto; by 1751 Lower Shawneetown's resident population—not counting visiting Iroquois, Wyandots, Cherokees, Delawares, Miamis, Piankashaws, or others—reaches between twelve hundred and fifteen hundred.

1731–33: Montreal, the Great Lakes, and west to the Maumee besieged by new epidemics spread to the Middle Ground and southeastern tribes.

1734: Iroquois emissaries meet with Ohio and Allegheny Shawnees, imploring them to return to the Susquehanna. (1) Daniel Boone born near Reading, Pennsylvania, November 2 (Gregorian calendar, or "New Style").

1735: French-Canadians en route to Illinois voyage up "the Fine River, or Ohio," discover at Big Bone Lick (Boone County) "skeletons of seven elephants"; such exotic reports inspire more explorations.

1737: Pennsylvania's fraudulent "Walking Purchase." Thomas and John Penn seize in eighteen hours a twelve-hundred-square-mile tract in Lehigh Valley on upper Delaware River.

1738: Pennsylvania Shawnee protest rum trafficking and "Walking Purchase."

1739: Baron de Longueil leads more than 440 French and Indians down Ohio to war against Chickasaws dwelling at its mouth; at Big Bone Lick he collects ice age–era fossils and bones for Louis XV; many French explorers, hunters, and soldiers will follow in his wake.

1742: Cherokees attack John Peter Salling, taking Salling's party down the Ohio and Mississippi in buffalo boats.

1744: Publication of N. Bellin's map, "Carte of La Louisiane," reflecting M. Lery's 1729 surveys. (1) June–July. Lancaster Treaty: Governors of Virginia, Maryland, and Pennsylvania purchase from Iroquois land to the Ohio's headwaters, interpreting the deed, wrongly, to include Ohio Valley. (2) King George's War (War of the Austrian Succession) begins; ends in 1748 with the Treaty of Aix-la-Chapelle. (3) Irish emigrant George Croghan licensed as a Pennsylvania Indian trader.

1745: Peter Chartier's Shawnees of western Pennsylvania visit Lower Shawnee-town; within several years, tribal Big Men, like Big Hominy, are living there.

1748: Gov. Robert Dinwiddie, with Arthur Dobbs, Thomas Lee, George Mason, and others, form the Ohio Land Company.

1749: Expedition down Allegheny and Ohio by Pierre Joseph de Celeron, who buries lead plates at mouths of all major tributaries, proclaiming the Ohio Valley French territory; arrives at Lower Shawneetown August 22; departs August 26.

1750: April 13. Dr. Thomas Walker leads first English expedition through Cumberland Gap; returns to Albemarle County, Virginia, July 13. (1) October 31. Christopher Gist departs Maryland and penetrates Ohio, reaching Lower Shawneetown on January 29 and returning to Yadkin Valley May 19, 1751.

1752: February. George Croghan's trader John Findlay resides at Eskippakithiki; Lakes Indians rob Findlay, torch outpost, kill three of his men and capture six. (1) Lewis Evans's first map of Kentucky published. (2) June 13. The Six Nations, Shawnees, Delawares, and Wyandots meet at Logstown to reaffirm 1744 Treaty of Lancaster; Twightwees (Miamis) of Ohio and Lower Shawnee Town Shawnees are absent. (3) August 4. Andrew Montour, along with Capt. William Trent, meet Iroquois and Algonquins at Lower Shawneetown to seal Logstown treaty, giving gifts to Shawnees and Twight-wees to strengthen England's claims over Ohio Valley.

1754: James McBride and his hunters float the Ohio to the Kentucky's mouth; he returns to the colonies to proclaim his "discovery of the best tract of land in North-America and probably in the world." (1) April 16. French erect Fort Duquesne at Forks of Ohio. (2) July 4. George Washington surrenders Fort Necessity to French, igniting the French and Indian War (Seven Years' War), which ends in 1763. (3) Death of Queen Alliquippa.

1755: July 9. Maj. Gen. Edward Braddock's force of fifteen hundred ambushed near Fort Duquesne. (1) Murders committed by Shawnees and Delawares upon Pennsylvanians.

1756: After losses from French and Indian raids the year before, "Suffering Traders" petition British Crown for reimbursement of £86,912. (1) December. Pennsylvania offers bounty for scalps of Delaware men, women, or children.

1763: Pontiac's Rebellion; Pontiac forms confederation of western tribes. (1) June 22. Rumors that Capt. Simon Ecuyer, commandant of Fort Pitt, during a parley presents smallpox-infected blankets and a handkerchief to Delaware chiefs. (2) England's Proclamation Line following French and Indian War prohibits colonists from settling trans-Appalachia.

1765: Daniel and Squire Boone hunt eastern Kentucky but fail to penetrate Bluegrass. Boones explore north Florida. (1) May–June. George Croghan tours Ohio River.

1766: June 18. Capt. Harry Gordon, chief engineer in the Western Department in North America, departs Fort Pitt via the Ohio for the Illinois country. (1) Capt. James Smith and other Long Hunters explore Cumberland basin.

1767: Woodsman James Harrod visits Kentucky.

1768: October. Treaty of Hard Labor. (1) November. Fort Stanwix Treaty.

1769: Hancock Taylor and three companions depart Virginia, float the Ohio to the Falls, thence to New Orleans, possibly skirt Texas, and return home by sea. (1) Daniel Boone's first Kentucky long hunt, May 1769–May 1771. (2) June. James Knox's Long Hunter brigade enters Cumberland Gap to hunt the Cumberland into central Kentucky and western Tennessee; Knox and company will return for future hunts.

1771: Spring. During John Donelson's Kentucky surveying expedition, he "mistakes" the Kentucky for the Levisa Fork of the Big Sandy, doubling Virginia's size of its claims with the Cherokee. (1) Simon Kenton, John Strader, and George Yeager descend the Ohio to hunt Kentucky's canelands.

1772: Lord Dunmore carves Fincastle County (Kentucky) from Botetourt County (Virginia).

1773: Spring-Summer. Capt. Thomas Bullitt's Kentucky expedition; Bullitt reaches Falls on July 8. (1) Late September. Daniel Boone's first attempt to settle Kentucky; Indians attack detached party on October 9, killing five, including James Boone.

1774: John Floyd's expedition into Kentucky. (1) April 30. Murder of family of John Logan, chief of the Mingoes, igniting Lord Dunmore's War. (2) June–August. Daniel Boone and Michael Stoner warn Fincastle County surveyors, covering eight hundred miles in sixty-two days. (3) October 10. Battle of Point Pleasant; Shawnees "officially" cede claims to Kentucky.

1775: March. Sycamore Shoals Treaty between North Carolinians of the Transylvania Company and Cherokees (Virginia's royal governor Lord Dunmore protests purchase); Daniel Boone's axmen blaze Wilderness Road. (1) April 19. American Revolutionary War erupts at Lexington and Concord, Massachusetts. (2) May 8. Boonesborough formally established. (3) June. Leestown begun. (4) June 17. Battle of Bunker Hill. (5) Summer. Logan's Station (St. Asaph's) established. (6) Summer. Attacks on Harrod's Town. (7) October. McClellan's Station (Georgetown) established. (8) October 11. Gen. Benedict Arnold reaches Quebec. (9) December 1. Land office for Henderson's "Proprietors of the Colony of Transylvania" enters deeds for 560,000 acres.

1776: January 1. U.S. Continental Army formed. (1) March 17. British leave Boston. (2) April. Leestown attacked; Boonesborough attacked. (3) May. General Arnold retreats from Quebec. (4) Virginia consolidates westernmost claims into "Kentucky County." (5) June 8. First cabins built at Lexington. (6) July 4. America declares her independence. (7) July 14. Shawnees capture Jemima Boone and Fanny and Betsy Callaway. (8) August 26. Washington beaten at battle of Long Island. (9) September 15. Washington beaten at battle of New York. (10) October. Lt. Gov. Henry Hamilton, "Hair Buyer" of Detroit, offers bounties for American scalps; sends Indians against Americans. (11) December 23. George Rogers Clark arrives in Kentucky with five hundred pounds of gunpowder. (12) December 29. McClellan's fort attacked; fort abandoned two days later.

1777: "Year of the Three Sevens." (1) January 1. Washington defeated at Brandywine. (2) March 7. Attack on Harrod's Town. (3) April 24. Boonesborough attacked; Daniel Boone wounded; Simon Kenton saves Boone's life. (4) May 20–June 2. Logan's Station besieged; Boonesborough's militia chases Indians to Ohio. (5) July 4–6. First siege of Boonesborough. (6) August 1. Capt. John Holder arrives at Boonesborough with forty-eight men. (7) October 17. British surrender at Saratoga. (8) November. Principal Shawnee chief Cornstalk and three unarmed Shawnees slain while under American custody at Point Pleasant.

1778: February 7. Shawnees capture Daniel Boone's team of about thirty salt boilers. (1) March. Simon Girty, Matthew Elliott, Alexander McKee, and other Tories desert Fort Pitt and defect to Loyalists. (2) May. Salt boiler Andrew Johnson escapes. (3) June 15. Daniel Boone escapes. (4) July. Salt boiler William Hancock escapes. (5) Late August. Boone makes a scouting and horse-stealing foray to Paint Lick Creek. (6) September 7–16. Second siege of Boonesborough. (7) September 13. Kenton captured. (8) October. Daniel Boone's court-martial trial; Boone promoted to major of the militia; he returns to North Carolina.

1779: February 25. George Rogers Clark recaptures Vincennes. (1) April. Capt. Robert Patterson begins building Fort Lexington. (2) April. Col. Evan Shelby musters two thousand men to war against Chickamauga Cherokees. (3) May. John Bowman campaigns against Chillicothe; Blackfish killed. (4) September. Daniel Boone returns, leading emigrants from North Carolina. (5) December. Daniel Boone establishes Boone's Station.

1780: "Year of the Hard Winter." (1) March 19. Col. Richard Callaway and Pemberton Rawlings killed near Boonesborough. (2) April 19. Fort Jefferson (erected at the confluence of the Ohio and Mississippi) begun. (3) June 24. Martin's and Ruddell's (Hinkston's) Stations surrender to British captain Henry Bird. (4) July. Fort Jefferson attacked. (5) August.

Fort Jefferson attacked. (6) July-August. George Rogers Clark musters four-fifths of Kentucky's militia to attack Piqua town and Chillicothe town. (7) October 7. Battle of King's Mountain. (8) November. Kentucky counties of Jefferson, Lincoln, and Fayette formed.

1781: January 17. Battle of Cowpens. (1) February 27. Attack on Montgomery's cabin. (2) March 1. Strode's Station attacked. (3) March. Floyd's Defeat. (4) May 9. McAfee's Station attacked. (5) May. Squire Boone's Station attacked. (6) June 4. Daniel Boone captured by British rangers in Charlottesville, Virginia. (7) June 8. Fort Jefferson abandoned. (8) August 24. Lochry's Defeat. (9) September 14. Long Run massacre. (10) September 17. Lord Cornwallis seeks terms with Washington, ending Revolution in eastern theater.

1782: "Year of Blood." (1) March 1. Strode's Station attacked. (2) March 20. Estill's Station attacked. (3) March 22. Estill's Defeat. (4) June 11. Death of Col. William Crawford. (5) July 6. George Rogers Clark's row galley launched. (6) August 14. Holder's Defeat. (7) August 16–17. Siege of Bryan's Station. (8) August 19. Battle of Blue Licks. (9) September. Kincheloe's Station burned. (10) November 1–17. George Rogers Clark retaliates against Shawnees.

1783–89: April 10, 1783. Killing of John Floyd. (1) September 3, 1783. American Revolution ends; Treaty of Paris signed. (2) Fall 1783. Benjamin Logan fights Indians on Big Sandy. (3) Fall 1784. John Filson's *The Discovery, Settlement, and Present State of Kentucke* published. (4) January 31, 1786. George Rogers Clark and Shawnee sign treaty. (5) February-September 1786. Daniel Boone negotiates prisoner exchange at Limestone (Maysville). (6) October 6, 1786. George Rogers Clark's and Benjamin Logan's campaign against Ohio Indians. (7) 1787. John Bradford's *Kentucky Gazette* begins publication. (8) March 1787. Chickamaugas attack along Wilderness Road. (9) July 17, 1789. Chenowith massacre. (10) 1789. America elects George Washington as president.

1790: September–October. Gen. Josiah harmer's disastrous campaign into Ohio land.

1791: November 4. Little Turtle's pan-Indian confederation defeats Gen. Arthur St. Clair's army, killing 632 militia and an estimated 200 campfollowers.

1792: Kentucky becomes America's fifteenth state.

1793: April 1–2. Shawnees and Cherokees raid Morgan's Station, the last Kentucky Indian raid.

1794: August 20. Battle of Fallen Timbers, conducted by Gen. "Mad" Anthony Wayne, ends Shawnee threats to Kentucky settlements.

APPENDIX B

"Suffering Traders'" Inventories, c. 1748–56

Author's note: Costs for trade goods are listed in English denominations in right-hand columns in the following order: pounds, shillings, pence. Spellings, figures, and math have not been altered from original documents.

[INVENTORY LIST: ST, 37–38]

"Goods sent to Twightwee Town with Andrew McBryer," c. 1752.

16 Ps. of Stroud	@ £10	£160	0	0
5 Ps. of Duffell	@ £10	50	0	0
7 Ps. of Halfthicks	@ £5	35	0	0
3 hundred powder	@ £10	30	0	0
600 Lead	@ £2	12	0	0
36 Holland Ruffled Shirts	@ 25/each	45	0	0
154 Plain Linnen Shirts	@ 10/	77	0	0
3 Pieces of Embost Flannel	@ £4 ..10	13	10	0
3 Pieces of Callimancoe	@ £3 ..10	10	10	0
32 Thousand of Wampum	@ 60/	96	0	0
28 Vermillion	@ 18/	25	4	0
27 Groce Gartering	@ 40/	54	0	0
20 Ps. of Ribbon	@ 15/	15	0	0
10 Pins Heads		10	0	0
8 Groce of Rings	@ 30/	12	0	0
12 Brass Wire	@ 5p	3	0	0
4 Pieces of Handkerchiefs	@ 60/	12	0	0
22 Dozen of Knives	@ 12/	13	4	0
18 Dozen of Brass Pen-knives	@ 20/	18	0	0
4 Groce Awl Blades	@ 30/	6	0	0
28 coats	@ 20/	28	0	0

Transporting these Goods from Philadelphia to the Twightwee Town
about 500 miles on Horseback & paying the Servants Wages . . . . .217 . . .10 . . .0

£942 . . .18 . . .0

[INVENTORY LIST: ST, 39–40]

"Goods sent up the River Kentucky [in 1753] . . . under care of David Hendricks
to trade with the Cherokees, who was hunting there, which came from Carolina, he
was surprised by a Party of Chipawas . . . and French-men who took him and five
more of our People Prisoners, only one and an Indian who was in Company
making their Escape."

42 Robed Strouds	@ 30/	.£63 . . . .0 . . .0
12 Plain Strouds	@ 20/	.12 . . . .0 . . .0
22 Calimancoe Bed Gowns	@ 12/	.13 . . . .4 . . .0
40 Plain Shirts	@ 10/	.20 . . . .0 . . .0
24 Ruffled Shirts	@ 25/	.30 . . . .0 . . .0
2 Ps. of Calimancoe	@ 70/	.7 . . . .0 . . .0
2 Ps. of Handkerchiefs	@ 60/	.6 . . . .0 . . .0
12 Vermillion	@ 18/	.10 . . .16 . . .0
30 Made Coats	@ 20/	.30 . . . .0 . . .0
15,000 Wampum	@ 60p	.45 . . . .0 . . .0
15 Dozen Knives	@ 12/	.9 . . . .0 . . .0
14 Dozen Silver Broches	@ 12/	.8 . . . .8 . . .0
12 Silver Arm Bands	@ 20/	.12 . . . .0 . . .0
12 Womens Silver Hair Plates	@ 20/	.12 . . . .0 . . .0
1 Riding Saddle		.3 . . . .0 . . .0
2 Pack Saddles		.2 . . . .0 . . .0

Transporting these Goods from Philadelphia on Horseback to the River Kentucky
where they were taken, about 600 miles and paying the Servants Wages
. . . . .84 . . .10 . . .0

£367 . . .18 . . .0

[INVENTORY LIST: ST, 43]

"Goods and Skins taken from our Men as they were coming down the Big Miamis
& ca. by a Party of Indian Warriors."

3 Guns	.90 Bucks @ 7/6	.£33 . . .15 . . .0
2 Axes	4 "	.1 . . .10 . . .0
3 Tomahawks	3 "	.1 . . . .2 . . .6

3 Kettles . . . . .20 " .7 . . .10 . . .0
12 Blankets . . . . .26 " .9 . . .15 . . .0
1 Coat . . . . 4 " .1 . . .10 . . .0
1 Cannoe . . . . .60 " . . . . .22 . . .10 . . .0
10 Shirts . . . . .20 " .7 . . .10 . . .0
3 Strouds . . . . 9 " .3 . . . .7 . . .6
some small Goods . . . . 1 Doe . . . . .0 . . . .3 . . .9
25 Buck Skins . . . . .25 " .9 . . . .7 . . .6

                                                            98 . . . .1 . . .3

[INVENTORY LIST: ST, 44–45]

"Account of the losses of George Croghan and William Trent, June 14, 1756, . . .
taken by French and Indians."

18 Ps. of Stroud . . . .@ £10 p. Ps . . . .£180 . . . .0 . . .0
7 Ps. of Duffell . . . .@ £10 . . . . .70 . . . .0 . . .0
10 Ps. of Half Thicks . . . . .50 . . . .0 . . .0
160 Plain Shirts . . . .@ 10/ . . . . .80 . . . .0 . . .0
48 Ruffled Shirts . . . .@ 25/ . . . . .60 . . . .0 . . .0
18 Thousand of Wampum . . . .@ 60/ . . . . .54 . . . .0 . . .0
300 Powder . . . .@ £10 . . . . .30 . . . .0 . . .0
10 Ct. Lead . . . .@ 40/p. Ct . . . . .20 . . . .0 . . .0
1000 Flints . . . . .1 . . . .0 . . .0
36 Groce Gartering . . . .@ 40/p. Gro: . . . . .72 . . . .0 . . .0
24 Ps. Ribbon . . . .@ 15/ . . . . .18 . . . .0 . . .0
30 Dozen Knives . . . .@ 12/ . . . . .18 . . . .0 . . .0
6 Pieces of Calimancoe . . . .@ 70/p. Ps . . . . .21 . . . .0 . . .0
4 Pieces of Embost Serge . . . . .18 . . . .0 . . .0
8 Pieces of Hankerchiefs . . . .@ 50/ . . . . .20 . . . .0 . . .0
60 coats . . . .@ 20/ . . . . .60 . . . .0 . . .0
50 Dozen Silver Broches . . . .@ 12/ . . . . .30 . . . .0 . . .0
20 Silver Arm Bands . . . .@ 25/ . . . . .25 . . . .0 . . .0
20 Womens Hair Plates . . . .@ 20/ . . . . .20 . . . .0 . . .0
12 Horses with Saddles and Bells . . .@ £10p. Ps . . . . .120 . . . .0 . . .0
Carriage of the above Goods from Philadelphia there . . . . .287 . . .10 . . .0

                                                            £1255 . . . .0 . . .0

[INVENTORY LIST: ST, 73]

"Account of Robert Callender, George Croghan and Michael Teaffe with Mitchell and Company, May 1756"

12 yds blue Damask	@ 4/	£2	.8 ...0
5 yds 3/4 Check	@ 5/6	1	.7 ...6
1 Handker		.6	...6
6 yds Shallon	@ 3/	.18	...0
1 Whipp		.12	...0
4 Scanes of Sewing Silk		.4	...0
2 yds Buckram	@ 2/6	.5	...0
1 yd. Linen		.3	...0
2 Bottles Snuff		.11	...0
2 pair Silk Stockings	@ 20/	.2	.0 ...0
2 Quire writing paper		.3	...0
14 1/2 yds: worsted damask	@ 4/6	.3	.3 ...0
5 yds Muslin	@ 13/	.3	.5 ...0
[?] Needles		.1	...6
1 Scarlet Short Cloak		1	.15 ...0
3 Wipps		1	.3 ...6
20 Keggs	@ 2/6	.2	.10 ...0
		£20	.16 ...0

[INVENTORY LIST: ST, 74]

"Account of William Trent with Abraham Mitchell, 1749/50 Capt. William Trent."

	To a Pewter Standish	£0	.15 ...0
21st	To dressing a hatt	£0	.2 ...6
March 7th	To 4 brass Blunder busses	.5	.8 ...0

1752

May 29th	To 2 beaver hatts at ...45/	£4	.10 ...0
	To 1 Castor hatt 25/	£1	.5 ...0

1750

6 Mo: 9th	To 1 Handsaw and vice	£1	.0 ...6
	To 1 Rasp	.1	...1

1751

To 1 pair Shears ....4 ...6
To 1 Frying pann ....9 ...4
To 1¹/2 yds: Cambrick .....@ 10/ ....12 ...0
To 1¹/2 yds: Callicoe .... 4/6 ....6 ...9
To 6 yds .... " .... 5/6 ....1 ...13 ...0
To 10 yds Linnin .... 3/6 ....1 ...15 ...0
To 2¹/2 yds Durov .... 3/ ....7 ...6
To 1 silk Handker ....9 ...6
To 4¹/2 yds Shalloon .... 3/4 ....14 ...7
To 4¹/2 yds Tamy .... 2/8 ....12 ...0
To 2 yds Striped Holland ... 5/ ....10 ...0
To 3 yds Linin .... 2/9 ....8 ...3
To 2 Laces ....1 ...0
To 1 yd womans Stockings ....8 ...0
To 1 Hatt ....18 ...0
To 1 Handker ....7 ...6
To 1 pr Stockings ....8 ...0
To 10 lb Sugar ....6 ...8

£11 ...14 ...5

[INVENTORY LIST: ST, 76]

"Account of George Croghan with Abraham Mitchell and Company" c. 1756.

April 8th	To 2 Silk Caps ....£1 .....5 0	
	4 yards of Onbrigo ..@ 2/ 8 0	
	10 yards ....2 ....13 ...6¹/2	
	1 Oz Indigo 8	
	6 lb. of Sugar ......@ 8/ 4 0	4 ...12 ..9¹/2
10	To a Hatt £1	
	3¹/2 Yards Check	
	Linnen ....@ 3/3 ....11 ...4¹/2	1 ...11 ..4¹/2
12	To 20 lb of Sugar ...@ 8d ..£13 4	
	2¹/2 lb. Nails ....@ 10 d ...2 1	15 5
15	To a Silk Handkffs £9 6	
	To a pair of Stocking 7 6	17 ....

May 6	To 6 Yards Buckram . . . . .2/6 . . . . .15 . . . .
	To ¼ lb. Indigo . . . . .2 . . .6
	To Sundries . . . . .7 . . . .
July 9	To 2 Sheets of Pins . . . . .2 . . .8
Aug. 5	To 2 Bottles Snuff . .£11 . . . .
	2½ oz of Indigo . . . .@ 10d . . .2 1
	1 oz Cinnamond 2 6
	1 Paper Pins 1 4

16 . . .11

9	To Cash lent 12
	To 6 Quire Paper . . . . .9 . . . .
21	To 10 lb. Sugar . . . . .@ 8d . . . . .6 . . .8
24	To 5 Yard of Muslin . 6/ . . . . .1 . . .10 . . . .

£24 . . . .6 .3½

[INVENTORY LIST: ST, 83–85]

"Account of losses of John Fraser . . . taken by French and Indians at Battle of Great Meadows. July 3d, 1754."

27 Peices Stroud . . . .@ . .£9 ..10 . . .0	236 . . .10 . . .0
18 " Duffills . . . .@ . . .9 ..10 . . .0	171 . . . .0 . . .0
13 " Halfthicks . . . .@ . . .4 ..10 . . .0	57 . . .10 . . .0
46 " Garlis made into shirts . . . .@ . . .4 . . .0 . . .0	184 . . . .0 . . .0
6½ " Callicoes . . . .@ . . .5 . . .0 . . .0	32 . . .10 . . .0
5 Ct. Gunpowder . . . .@ . . .9 ..10 . . .0	47 . . .10 . . .0
9 " Bar Lead . . . .@ . . .2 . . .0 . . .0	18 . . . .0 . . .0
5 Peices silk handkerchiefs . . . .@ . . .4 . . .0 . . .0	20 . . . .0 . . .0
6 " Callimancoes . . . .@ . . .3 . . .0 . . .0	18 . . . .0 . . .0
24 Groce Gartering & Bed Lace . . . . .@ . . .1 ..10 . . .0	36 . . . .0 . . .0
17 Peices Broad Ribbons . . . .@ . . .1 . . .0 . . .0	17 . . . .0 . . .0
23 " Narrow Ribbons . . . .@ . . .0 ..10 . . .0	11 . . .10 . . .0
13000 Black Wampum . . . .@ . . .3 . . .0 . . .0	390 . . . .0 . . .0
8000 White " . . . .@ . . .2 . . .0 . . .0	160 . . . .0 . . .0
4 Groce silver Broaches . . . .@ . . .7 . . .4 . . .0	28 . . .16 . . .0
3 Dozen silver hair plates . . . .@ . . .1 . . .0 . . .0	36 . . . .0 . . .0
6 Dozen silver Wrist bands . . . .@ . . .4 . . .4 . . .0	25 . . . .4 . . .0
3 Dozen silver Arm bands . . . .@ . . .1 . . .0 . . .0	36 . . . .0 . . .0
10 Suits Wearing Apparel . . . .@ . .15 . . .0 . . .0	150 . . . .0 . . .0

A Compleat sett of Armorers tool . . . .@ . .50 . . .0 . . .0	50 . . . .0 . . .0
Sundry household furniture . . . .@ . .50 . . .0 . . .0	50 . . . .0 . . .0
1 horse Load Beaver & other Furs . . .@ . .64 . . .0 . . .0	64 . . . .0 . . .0
2 horse Load Deer & Bear skins . . . . .@ . .34 . . .0 . . .0	34 . . . 0 . . .0
Carried up	£1873 . . .10 . . .0
Brass Kettles . . . .@ . . .8 . . .0 . . .0	24 . . . .0 . . .0
34 lb Vermillion . . . .@ . . .0 . .15 . . .0	25 . . .10 . . .0
7 Peices 7/8 Garlis Whole . . . .@ . . .3 . . .5 . . .0	22 . . .15 . . .0
34 Dozen Large Knives . . . .@ . . .0 . .10 . . .0	17 . . . .0 . . .0
22 " Pen Knives . . . .@ . . .0 . . .6 . . .0	6 . . .12 . . .0
7 Rifled Guns . . . .@ . . .6 . . .0 . . .0	42 . . . .0 . . .0
4 Smooth Guns . . . .@ . . .4 . . .0 . . .0	20 . . . .0 . . .0
2 Cases Neat Pistoles & furniture . . . .@ . . .7 . .10 . . .0	7 . . .10 . . .0
4 Dozen Pipe Tomyhawks . . . .@ . . .0 . .12 . . .0	28 . . .16 . . .0
5 Dozen hunting Tomyhawks . . . . . .@ . . .2 . . .0 . . .0	10 . . . .0 . . .0
7 Peices silver Ribbon . . . .@ . . .1 . .10 . . .0	10 . . .10 . . .0
4 Dozen Indian Weeding Boughs . . . .@ . . .2 . . .0 . . .0	8 . . . .0 . . .0
100 Strings forked Wampum . . . .@ . . .0 . . .3 . . .0	15 . . . .0 . . .0
35 Carring sadles . . . .@ . .30 . . .0 . . .0	30 . . . .0 . . .0
4 hunting " . . . .@ . .12 . . .0 . . .0	12 . . . .0 . . .0
6 Dozen Plain Gun Locks . . . .@ . . .3 . .12 . . .0	21 . . .12 . . .0
6 Dozen [gun lock] Bridles . . . .@ . . .0 . .15 . . .0	18 . . . .0 . . .0
A Large Quantity Small Goods	35 . . . .0 . . .0
Cash in Pennsylvania Currency	75 . . . .0 . . .0
15 ct. Flower . . . .@ . . .0 . .15 . . .0	16 . . . .5 . . .0
44 Bushels Indian Corn . . . .@ . . .0 . . .3 . . .0	6 . . .12 . . .0
5 Carrying horses . . . .@ . .10 . . .0 . . .0	50 . . . .0 . . .0
Paid for the Carriage & Expences sd. Goods from	
Philadelphia to the Ohio . . . .@	80 . . . .0 . . .0
1755 Goods Lost at the Battle of the Monghela vizt. Cloaths	
& other Baggage Amounting to	40 . . . .0 . . .0
Cash in Spanish Dollars	35 . . . .0 . . .0
Carried up	£2530 . . .12 . . .0
5 Milk Cows & Calves . . . .@ . . .5 . . .0 . . .0	25 . . . .0 . . .0
2 Riding Horses . . . .@ . .15 . . .0 . . .0	30 . . . .0 . . .0
	£2585 . . .12 . . .0

[INVENTORY LIST: ST, 123–29]

"Goods Taken from James Young and John Frazier in Partnership Trading with the Indians on . . . Lake Erie, Nov. 24th, 1750. Taken by a French officer and 30 men."

To 2¹/₂ pieces of Stroud at £10 P piece	£25	....	
To 3 pieces of Duffells at £10 P piece	30	....	
To 4 " of ⁷/₈ Garlix at £3 P piece	12	....	
To 4 Duzn. Large Cutto knifs at 17s P Duzn	3	8	....
To 2 " of Brass Penn Knifs at 10s P Duzn	1	....	
To 3 Gross of Gartring at £2 P Gross	6	....	
To 4 " of Bed Lace at £2 P "	8	....	
To 6 pieces of Broad Pd. away Ribband at 12s p piece	3	...12	....
To 4 pieces Small Tenpenny at 10s P Gross	2	....	
To 1 " Tandum Hollan	6	...15	....
To 3 Duzn. black hafted knife at 8s P Duzn	1	4	....
To 3 lb of Vermillian at 18s P lb	2	...14	....
To 50 lb Gun Powder at £10 P hundred	5	....	
To 300 lb of Lead at £2 P hundred	6	....	
To 3000 of Black wampum at £3 p Thousd	9	....	
To 4000 of White " at £1 10s "	6	....	
To 1 Duzn. of Best Worsted Stockings	4	4	....
To 1 Piece of Callimanco at	3	....	
To 4 Brass Kettles wt. 15 lb at ³/₆s P lb	2	...12	...6
To 4 Duzn. Shoe buckles at 2d P Duzn	0	8	....
To 4 lb. of White Beads at ³/₆ p lb	0	...13	...6
To 6 Hatchets at	0	4	...6
To ¹/₂ Gross Morris Bells at 17s P gross	0	8	...6
To ¹/₂ piece of Silk handkerchiefs at £3 p piece	1	...10	...0
To making 40 shirts at 1s P shirt	2	....	
To making one piece of Tandum at 5s P shirt	1	...15	....
To Thread and Ruffling for the whole	1	....	
To 1 Piece of Purple half thicks at	5	...10	....
To 1 " of White " "	4	...10	....
To Horse Load of Skins and Furrs	40	....	
To the Carriage of the goods from Philada to Harris's Ferry ..	2	....	
To the Carriage of the goods in the place Where we were			
Robbed and other Expenses	20	....	
	£217	9	....

JULY 20, 1753

To Goods Taken from Wm. Willson at

Wayningo by the French . . . .   9 . . . .

£226 . . . .9 . . .0

JULY 3RD 1754

"Goods Taken from James Young & John Frazier . . . by French & Indians at Great Meadows at Geo. Washington's Defeat."

To 8 pieces of Stroud at £9 10s p piece . . . .   £76 . . . .

To 25 butt Strouds and Robed with Gartering Ribbaning

& Bed Lace of diferent sorts at £2 5s . . . .   56 . . . .5 . . . .

To paid the Taylor 10s p. stroud . . . .   12 . . .10 . . . .

To 8 pieces of Duffells at £9 10s p. piece . . . .   76 . . . .

To 4   " ⁷/₈ Garlix   at £3 10s p piece . . . .   15 . . .12 . . . .

To 9   " ³/₄ "   at £3 15s p.   " . . . .   33 . . .15 . . . .

To 2   " Tandum Hallan at £6 10s p. " . . . .   13 . . . .

To 1 Do. Lawn . . . .   1 . . .13 . . . .

To making the Garlix at 12s p piece . . . .   5 . . . .8 . . . .

To making the Ruffled Shirts at 1/6 p shirt . . . .   2 . . . .8 . . . .

To making the Tandum Linen at 5s p shirt . . . .   3 . . .10 . . . .

To 2 lb of Thread at 11s p lb . . . .   1 . . . .2 . . . .

To 1 patch of Cambrick . . . .   1 . . .10 . . . .

To 2 Pieces Purple halfthicks at £5 10s p piece . . . .   11 . . . .

To 3   "   White halfthicks at £4 10s . . . .   13 . . .10 . . . .

To 5 casks of Gun powder at £9 10 hundd . . . .   22 . . . .

To 1 bask of Lead at £2 p hundred . . . .   10 . . . .

To 8 Gross of Gartring and Bed lace at £1 10s p groce . . . . . .   12 . . . .

To 10 pieces of broad Ribbon at 12s p piece . . . .   6 . . . .

To 8   "   of small   "   at 10s p piece . . . .   4 . . . .

To 2   "   of silk handcherchiefs at £3 p piece . . . .   6 . . . .

To 8 lb of Vermillion at 16s p lb . . . .   6 . . . .8 . . . .

To 8 Doz. black hafted knifs at 10s p Doz . . . .   4 . . . .

To 4 Doz. Penn knifs at 9 P Doz . . . .   1 . . .16 . . . .

To 2 Doz. Brass knifs at 12s p Doz . . . .   1 . . . .4 . . . .

To 4 Doz. large Cutto knifs at 16s p Doz . . . .   3 . . .4 . . . .

To 6 lb White Beads at ³/₆ p lb . . . .   1 . . . .1 . . . .

To 8 lb Brass wire at ⁴/₆ p lb . . . .   1 . . .16 . . . .

To 1 Double Gross of Morris Bells at 17s p gross	1 . . .14 ....
To 60 lb of Brass Kettles at 3s 6d p lb	10 . . .10 ....
To 2 pieces of Stampt Linen made into shirts	8 . . .10 . . .8
To 2 " of Callimanco at £3 17s p piece	7 . . .14 ....
To 160 lb of Tobaco at £1 p hundred	1 . . .12 ....
To 1 Bagg of Flints	1 ....
To a quantity of back debts which was taken	98 . . .10 . . .4
To 200 lb of deer skins at 2s p lb	20 ....
To 1000 of Black Wampum at £3 p thousand	30 ....
To 8000 of White " at £1 10s p thousand	12 ....
To 35 strings of Forket Wampum at 2s 3d p string	3 . . .18 . . .9
	£598 . . .16 . . .9

To 6 doz. Silver Broches at 13s p doz	3 . . .18 ....
To 9 large Silver Crosses at 4/6 p piece	2 . . . .0 . . .6
To 6 Baarcletts at 10s p piece	3 ....
To 4 Hair plates at £1 p piece	4 ....
To 4 Arm bands at £1 2s p piece	4 . . . .8 ....
To the carriage of the Goods from Phil. to Harris's Ferry	10 ....
To the Carriage of them to the Ohio and back to the great Meadows with provisions and wages with other Expences attending the same	100 ....
	£726 . . . .3 . . .3

"Goods & Cash Taken from James Young . . . on East side of Lake Earie, Nov. 24th 1750."

To 3 Horses at £10 Each	£30 ....
To 1 Neat Gun	2 . . . .5 ....
To 2 Carring Saddles	2 ....
To 1 Ridding Saddle	1 . . .15 ....
	£36..

Taken at Great Meadows—

To 1 Great Coat	£3 ....
To 6 Cotton Shirts at £1 each	6 ....
To 1 Jacket of Superfine Cloath	3 ....
To 1 Beaver hatt	1 ....
To 1 set of shoe buckles and buckles	2 . . . .5 ....

To a purse of Gold	16	...18	....
To 4 Carring Saddles	4		....
To a pair of shoes and pumps	0	...15	....
	£72	...18	....

To total of the losses at Lake Erie	£217	9	....
To total at Col. Washington's defeat	726	3	...3
To James Young's losses exclusive of partnership	72	...18	...0
Total of the whole	£1016	...10	...3
Taken from William Wilson	9		....
	£1025	...10	...3

"Losses of Robert Callender & Michael Teaffe, May 1, 1756, . . . taken by French & Indians . . . at the Time the French drove the English off Ohio River & the Waters thereof."

7 pieces of Stroud @ £9 10s p piece	66	...10	...0
7 pieces of Duffils @ [same price]	66	...10	...0
300 lb. wt. of Powder @ £9 10s p 100	28	...10	...0
600 lb. wt. of Lead @ £2 0s p 100	12	0	...0
10 pieces of Linnen @ £3 p piece	30	0	...0
20 lb. wt. of Paint @ 18/ p pound	18	0	...0
20 gross of Gartering at £1 15s p gross	35	0	...0
	£256	...10	...0

"Goods in the care of Thomas Burney at the above mentioned Time he was attack'd by Indians & French & several of White People kill'd & Burney made his Escape but was since Kill'd at the Defeat of General Braddock."

Brot: over	£316	...10	...0
3000 of Wampum of the Value of			
30 Bucks @ 7/6	11	5	...0
100 Raccoon Skins of the Value of			
25 Bucks @ 7/6	8	...17	...6
6 Parchment Skins of the Value of			
6 Bucks @ 7/6	2	5	...0
2 Bed Gowns of the Value of			
10 Bucks @ 7/6	3	...15	...0
1 Quart of Powder (1 Buck)	0	7	...6

Lead (3 Bucks)	1	...2	...6
6 ruffled shirts (15 Bucks)	5	...12	...6
1000 Wampum (10 Bucks)	3	...15	...0
	£353	...10	...0

"Goods with Joseph Campbell who was employ'd by Teaffe & Callender . . . for which Teaffe & Callender never received Satisfaction . . . of Campbell because he being killed by an Indian & his Books not found."

20 strouds @ 2 Bucks & a Doe p stroud .....50 Bucks	18	...15	...0
10 Match Coats ....25 Bucks	9	7	...6
12 Quarts of powder ....12 Bucks	4	...10	...0
Lead ....10 Bucks	3	...15	...0
[?] gross of garter ....12 Bucks	4	...10	...0
Ribboning ....7 Bucks	2	...12	...6
Wampum ....20 Bucks	7	...10	...0
Knives ....11 Bucks	4	2	...6
a Rifle Gun ....20 Bucks	7	...10	...0
7 Kettles ....35 Bucks	13	2	...6
6 lb. wt. of paint ....36 Bucks	14	0	...0
15 Blankets ....37 Bucks/a doe.	14	11	...3

"Also an Acct: of Horses lost on the Ohio [when] the English were drove from thence by French & Indians."

23 Horses & Mares @ ....9 ..0 ..0 each	207	0	...0
	£296	...93	...6

[The last three Fort Pitt inventories were excerpted from ST, pages 167–73.]

List 1

"A list of a large assortment of Indians goods suitable at this time at Pittsburg. November 24th, 1761."

4 bales blue stroud with dark blue narrow straight List

1 bale scarlet red stroud with dark List

4 ps. black stroud

20 bales French matchcoats of different sizes

15 bales English matchcoats

3 bales of the best blanketing

3 bales of yard wide Napet[?] purple of white halfthicks

1 bale plain white halfthicks

10 ps. stripped Holland

30 ps. callico of the brightest flourishing colors

15 ps. stamped linnen

30 ps. Irish $^7/_8$ linnen

30 ps. garlix

10 ps. check linnen

5 doz. silk handkerchiefs: Dublin Manufactory of the largest sort & several colors, but few of them dark colors

4 doz. silk handkerchiefs of the common kind

80 gross bedlace of the best & cleanest colors, viz: green, blue, red, scarlet

20 gross bedlace: crimson and yellow

20 gross scarlet gartering

100 ps. plain ribbon of several deep colors, viz: mostly green, dark and light blue, yellow & some pink color

50 ps. flowered ribbon

$^1/_2$ doz. childrens shoes & hose 1 doz.

12 doz. cuttoe knives of several sizes

1 doz. common pistal cap knives

12 doz. brass handled pen knives

1000 gun flints

5 lb. vermillion

6 doz. horn combs of several sorts

12 gross small white beads

50 Qr. cask FF gunpowder

30 C bar-lead; each bar to weigh 1 lb.

12 nests—brass kettles with small iron ears, small bales & small hoop about the mouth

12 nests—tin kettles with small iron ears, small bales & small hoop about the mouth

2 doz. snuff boxes of a small size

1 doz. spring steel tobacco boxes

1 doz. painted fram'd looking glasses

2 doz. pocket looking glasses

6 lb. colored threads

6 doz. brass [jews'] harps

4 gross brass rings plain & different sort of stones

6 nest trunks

10 lb. scarlet or clear red colored cruel or worsted yarn

5 lb. green colored cruel or worsted yarn

5 lb. yellow colored cruel or worsted yarn

1 gross large Morris bells

Of this country manufactory of the under-named articles as much as you think
 proper

 black wampum (the best that can be got)

 white wampum (very little)

 a considerable quantity of silver [items] well-assorted,

viz: arm-bands of several sizes, wrist-bands, hair-plates, brooches, ear-bobs,
 hair-bobs

rifle-guns: only a few

List 2
NOVEMBER 24, 1761

"A list of all kinds of goods proper for presents to the Indians in the northern department of America"

Strouds: deep blue, lively red, black

English match-coats

French match-coats

blanketing

white half-thicks napt.

purple half-thicks

$3/4$ garlix

$7/8$ garlix

Irish linen about 1/ P yard

coarse cambricks & thread to make them up

calicoes

callimancoes: lively colors

bed-lace: red, yellow, green, blue (lively colors)

star gartering

scarlet gartering

figured gartering

ribbon: red, yellow, green, blue (lively colors)

Imbost serges different colors

worsted caps

womens worsted stocking: red, yellow, green

gunpowder

bar-led

flints

vermillion

cuttoe knives (large & small)

pen knives

brass wire (different sizes)

jews harps

fine tongs

brass & tin kettles

Morris bells

pipe & hunting tomahawks

gun hammers

light guns, about 1 guinea each

spun worsted: red, yellow, green, blue

white beads, different sizes

looking glasses

colored thread

sorted needles

Made up clothing, such as laced coats, laced jackets, and embroidery, which may be purchased at second-hand, well-cleaned

gold- and silver-laced hats

silver ware, which it to be made by William Evans, [a] jeweler near St. John's turnpike who has the patterns for them

silver gorgets & hair-plates

silver arm-bands & nose rings

silver wrist chains

silver crosses (large & small)

silver ear-bobs

silver rings

silver brooches round

silver brooches made like a heart

silver bells of the size of Morris bells (smaller sort)

A number of medals to be made larger than a crown piece with silver chains to them, to hand about the Indian chiefs neck with the King on one side & his coat of Arms on the other.

List 3

"A list of an assortment of goods to suit the white people about the fort"

1 ps. superfine scarlet bed cloth

1 ps. @ 18/ or 20 P yard

1 ps. superfine blue bed cloth

2 ps. rattenale or shalloon

1 ps. red shalloon

1 ps. blue shalloon

1 ps. white shalloon, the best & finest kind

1 ps. white tammy or durant

1 ps. scarlet durant

10 or 12 double gross of the best silver wash'd buttons with ivory of bone bottoms that will cost about 40/ or 45 P double gross

3 double gross hard metal jacket buttons

4 single gross common yellow metal jacket buttons

1 lb. of the best scarlet scaff twist

1 lb. of the best blue scaff twist

4 lb. coarse white thread

10 or 12 lb. blue and red thread

2 lb. black thread

1 lb. yellow or buff colored thread

2 lb. sewing silk of several colors but mostly blue and scarlet

1000 needles of several sizes

2 packets [of] pins

6 knit patterns for breeches, scarlet

3 buff colored breeches

20 yards scarlet hair shagg

20 yards scarlet worsted shagg

1 doz. cotton caps

1 doz knee bindings: scarlet, blue & buff

1 ps. black mode

For queuing hair: 8 ps. black satin ribbon; 8 pieces black padusauy ribbon

1 ps. black callimanco

1 ps. green callimanco

1 ps. blue callimanco

1 ps. narrow camblet

1 ps. dark colored hair binding

1 ps. striped poplin

1 ps. silver colored poplin

4 patterns manchesters poplin

4 ps. chintz

1 ps. cotton fine

2 ps. cambrick sorted

4 ps. lawn sorted

1 doz. gazes [gauze?] handkerchiefs

1 ps. flowered lawn

1 doz. newest fashion hat, black

2 doz. bonnets

2 doz. womens fine stocking

1 doz womens cotten stockings middling coarse

2 doz. large cotten stockings, men

$^1/_2$ doz. white thread no. 8

2 doz. white thread no. 12

2 doz white thread no. 10

2 doz. white thread no. 22

1 doz. best large men thread stockings, white

1 doz. germinton mixed thread stockings

For the soldiers if you intend to supply the officers with their necessaries: shirts well-made ruffled at the breasts; yarn stockings, germinton or fulled stockings, shoes.

ABBREVIATIONS

CAH: Charles A. Hanna, *The Wilderness Trail*

DB: Daniel Boone

DM: Draper Manuscripts, State Historical Society of Wisconsin, Madison

DT: Daniel Trabue

FCHQ: *Filson Club Historical Quarterly*

GMB: George Michael Bedinger

IWW: Neal O. Hammon, "Into Western Waters, 1773–1775"

JDS: John Dabney Shane

JLH: Josephine L. Harper, *Guide to the Draper Manuscripts*

JMF: John Mack Faragher, *Daniel Boone: The Life and Legend of an American Pioneer*

JN: James Nourse

JSJ: J. Stoddard Johnson, ed., *First Explorations of Kentucky*

KY: John E. Kleber, ed., *The Kentucky Encyclopedia*

LH: Ted Franklin Belue, *The Long Hunt: Death of the Buffalo East of the Mississippi*

LCD: Lyman Copeland Draper

LIFE: Lyman C. Draper, *The Life of Daniel Boone,* edited by Ted Franklin Belue

NC: Nicholas Cresswell

NOH: Neal O. Hammon

NOM: Nancy O'Malley, *"Stockading Up": A Study of Pioneer Stations in the Inner Bluegrass Region of Kentucky*

PH: Peter Houston, *A Sketch in the Life and Character of Daniel Boone*, edited by Ted Franklin Belue

REV: Richard L. Blanco, ed., *The American Revolution, 1775–1783: An Encyclopedia*

RKHS: *Register of the Kentucky Historical Society*

SR: Spencer Records

ST: Kenneth P. Bailey, ed., *The Ohio Company Papers, 1753–1817: Being Primarily Papers of the "Suffering Traders" of Pennsylvania*

TFB: Ted Franklin Belue

WIK: Daniel Trabue, *Westward into Kentucky: The Memoirs of Daniel Trabue*, edited by Chester Raymond Young

NOTES

PROLOGUE. THE CONTESTED LAND, 1200–1744

1. For Ohio River, see R. E. Banta, *The Ohio*, 2nd ed. (Lexington: University Press of Kentucky, 1998); also, *KY*, "Ohio River," 691–92.
2. In the days of George Rogers Clark, this slip of land was called Corn Island.
3. For bison in eastern America, see TFB, *LH*; in trans-Mississippian, see Andrew C. Isenberg, *The Destruction of the Bison: An Environmental History, 1750–1920* (New York: Cambridge University Press, 2000); also, Shepard Krech III, *The Ecological Indian: Myth and History* (New York: W. W. Norton & Company, 1999).
4. TFB, "18th Century Tattooing," in William H. Scurlock, ed., *The Book of Buckskinning VIII* (Texarkana, TX: Scurlock Publishing, 1999), 34–69.
5. Adapted from William E. Sharp, "Fort Ancient Farmers," in *Kentucky Archaeology*, edited by Barry Lewis (Lexington: University Press of Kentucky, 1996), 161–82.
6. Constructing precontact activity in Kentucky is theoretical. For this, see James Bennett Griffin, *The Fort Ancient Aspect: Its Cultural and Chronological Position in Mississippi Valley Archaeology* (Ann Arbor: University of Michigan Press, 1943); also A. Gwynn Henderson, ed., *Fort Ancient: Cultural Dynamics in the Middle Ohio Valley* (Madison, WI: Prehistory Press, 1992); A. Gwynn Henderson, Cynthia E. Jobe, and Christopher A. Turnbow, *Indian Occupation and Use in Northern and Eastern Kentucky during the Contact Period (1540–1795): An Initial Investigation* (Frankfort: Kentucky Heritage Council, 1986).
7. A. Gwynn Henderson, "Dispelling the Myth: Seventeenth- and Eighteenth-Century Indian Life in Kentucky," *RKHS* 90 (1992): 1–25; running counter to Henderson's notions are those by LCD, *LIFE*, 522–23, n. 4.
8. Montagnais warrior, 1634, and Robert Juet, 1609, quoted in Carolyn Gilman, *Where Two Worlds Meet: The Great Lakes Indian Fur Trade* (St. Paul: Minnesota Historical Society, 1982), 5.
9. Joseph François Lafitau, c. 1650, quoted in Daniel K. Richter, *Ordeal of the Long-House: The Peoples of the Iroquois League in an Era of European Colonization* (Chapel Hill: University of North Carolina Press, 1992), 79–80.
10. For European wares, see Gilman, *Two Worlds;* see also Dr. Ruth B. Phillips, *Patterns of Power: The Jasper Grant Collection and Great Lakes Indian Art of the Early Nineteenth Century* (Kleinburg, Ontario: McMichael Canadian Collection, 1984); Ted J. Brasser, *Bo'jou Neejee!: Profiles of Canadian Indian Art* (Ottawa, Ontario: National Museum of Man, 1976); also, Wilber R. Jacobs, *Wilderness Politics and Indian Gifts: The North Colonial Frontier, 1748–1763* (Lincoln: University of Nebraska Press, 1966).

11. Cadwallader Colden, quoted in Peter C. Mancall, *Deadly Medicine: Indians and Alcohol in Early America* (Ithaca, NY: Cornell University Press, 1995), 70.

12. Accounts of torture and cannibalism during the Beaver Wars are legion, and the deleterious results of trade upon tribal stability are well documented. As certain contemporary political elements may either doubt the validity of my depictions or wish to challenge them, I refer them to references cited in footnote 13.

13. Data for Beaver Wars from Francis Jennings, *The Ambiguous Iroquois Empire: The Covenant Chain Confederation of Indian Tribes with English Colonies from Its Beginnings to the Lancaster Treaty of 1744* (New York: W. W. Norton, 1984); Richter, *Long-House;* and William C. Sturtevant, gen. ed., *Handbook of North American Indians,* vol. 15, *Northeast,* Bruce Trigger, vol. ed. (Washington, DC: Smithsonian Institution, 1978); for maps and migration patterns, see Helen Hornbeck Tanner, ed., *Atlas of Great Lakes Indian History* (Tulsa: University of Oklahoma Press, Newberry Library, 1987); graphic firsthand accounts found in compendium edited by Reuben Gold Thwaites, *Jesuit Relations and Allied Documents,* 73 vols. (New York: Pagent, 1959); for the region's social and cultural complexity, see Richard White, *The Middle Ground: Indians, Empires, and Republics in the Great Lakes Region, 1650–1815* (New York: Cambridge University Press, 1991).

14. Tanner, *Atlas,* 169–74.

15. NOH, *Early Kentucky Land Records, 1773–1780,* Filson Club Publications, 2nd ser., no. 5 (Louisville, KY: Butler Book Publishing, 1992), xi.

16. Richter, *Long-House,* 190–91.

17. In February 1704 a band of *Compagnies franches de la Marine* and Abenaki descended on Deerfield, Massachusetts, killing fifty-six English. John Demos, *The Unredeemed Captive: A Family Story from Early America* (New York: Vintage Books, 1994), 15–25.

18. William Augustus, duke of Cumberland, who after his slaughter of Scottish highlanders at Culloden, April 16, 1746, was known by his own subjects as "Butcher Cumberland."

19. Quoted in Randolph C. Downes, *Council Fires on the Upper Ohio,* 2nd ed. (Pittsburgh: University of Pittsburgh Press, 1977), 19; for migrations, see CAH, 1: 119–60; Chartier's Town was near Tarentum, in Allegheny County.

20. Tribal divisions from Jerry E. Clark, *The Shawnee* (Lexington: University Press of Kentucky, 1977), 5–27, 28–29; and James H. Howard, *Shawnee!: Ceremonialism of a Native American Tribe and Its Cultural Background* (Athens: Ohio University Press, 1981), 5–11, 24–30; also, John Sugden's *Blue Jacket: Warrior of the Shawnees* (Lincoln: University of Nebraska Press, 2000), 7–11, 17ff.

21. Quoted in James H. Merrill, *Into the American Woods* (New York: W. W. Norton & Company, 1999), 268.

22. For Andrew Montour, see CAH, 1: 223–46.

23. Quoted in Merrill, *American Woods,* 55.

CHAPTER 1. FORBIDDING GATEWAY

1. See David M. Burns, *Gateway: Dr. Thomas Walker and the Opening of Kentucky* (Middlesboro, KY: Bell County Historical Society, 2000); DM, 1D: 181–229, "Border Forays and Adventures"; JSJ; *LIFE,* 47–61, 536–42; Alexander Canady McLeod, "A Man for All Seasons: Dr. Thomas Walker of Castle Hill," *FCHQ* 71 (1997): 169-201; Keith Ryan Nyland, "Doctor Thomas Walker (1715–1794): Explorer, Physician, Statesman, Surveyor and Planter of Virginia and Kentucky" (Ph.D. diss., Ohio State University, University Microfilms, 1971); Charles Royster's *The Fabulous History of the Dismal Swamp Company: A Story of George Washington's Times* (New York: Alfred A. Knopf, 1999).

2. In southwestern Virginia, near Abingdon.

3. For Winston, see *LIFE,* 537.

4. Quote in Royster, *Dismal Swamp,* 8.

5. For Patton, see Kenneth P. Bailey, *The Ohio Company of Virginia and the Westward Movement, 1748–1792,* 2nd ed. (Lewisburg, PA: Wennawoods Publishing, 2000), 22–29, 150–52.

6. Burns, *Gateway,* 24.

7. NOH, *Land Records,* xi.

8. "Influences in Religion," November 3, 2001, 1:45 P.M., http://www.users.voicenet.com/~wordinfo/deutsch/religion.htm; "The Brethren," November 3, 2001, 1:52 P.M., http://religiousmovements.lib.virginia.edu/nrms/brethren.html.

9. Near Knoxville.

10. Walker's cabin, built near Barbourville, was occupied until 1835.

11. Having grained and brain-tanned deerskins using eighteenth-century techniques, my rendering here is speculative, based upon my experiences and research and knowing what tools and resources Walker had with him.

12. JSJ, 75.

13. Robert L. Kincaid, *The Wilderness Road* (New York: Bobbs-Merrill Company, 1947), 52; quote regarding Walker's proposed far western foray from Royster, *Dismal Swamp*, 45.

FIRST INTERLUDE. WARS & RUMORS OF WARS

1. Near present-day Jacksonville, Florida.

2. For Spanish occupation, see David J. Weber, *The Spanish Frontier in North America* (New Haven, CT: Yale University Press, 1992), 60–64.

3. Rene Chartrand, *The French Soldier in Colonial America,* Historical Arms Series, no. 18 (Bloomfield, Ontario: Museum Restoration Service, 1984), 7.

4. The eastern diamondback rattlesnake *(Crotalus adamenteus adamenteus),* the world record for which is eight feet, six inches, is not only the longest rattlesnake on earth, but also has the largest girth. Like most rattlers, the snake's venom is predominately hemotoxic and can be delivered deep into the muscle and in massive doses.

5. The coral snake *(Micrurus fulvius fulvius)* possesses neurotoxic venom. Like all of Florida's flora and fauna, rattlers and corals suffer from diminishing habitat. In the case of the former, the destructive "sport" of "Rattlesnake Round-Ups," which wantonly destroy annually thousands of these magnificent reptiles, also ruin habitat by gassing tortoise holes that share the reptile's habitat, and deprive what's left of nature's ecosystems of the eastern diamondback's role in rodent control.

6. See Grace Nute, *The Voyageurs* (St. Paul: Minnesota Historical Society, 1955).

7. Data regarding French arms and warfare from Chartrand; for wars, see Howard H. Peckman, *The Colonial Wars, 1689–1702* (Chicago: University of Chicago Press, 1964), 8–12, 21–24, 54–57, 77–78.

8. The fer-de-lance *(Bothrops andianus asper)* and its subspecies live throughout South and Central America and the Caribbean, reach lengths of eight feet, and possess a virulent hemotoxic venom.

9. For New Netherland, the English, and imperial conflicts, see Ted Morgan, *Wilderness at Dawn: The Settling of the North American Continent* (New York: Simon and Schuster, 1993), 152–164, 193 ff; and Arthur Quinn, *A New World: An Epic of Colonial America from the Founding of Jamestown to the Fall of Quebec* (New York: Berkeley Books, 1994), 188–227.

CHAPTER 2. ODYSSEUS OF THE MIDDLE GROUND

1. Quoted in SJS, 101–2.

2. SJS, 90.

3. Quoted in Allan Powell, *Christopher Gist: Frontier Scout* (Hagerstown, MD: Privately published, 1992), 66.

4. For Gist, see Bailey, *Ohio Company,* Wennawoods; William M. Darlington, *Christopher Gist's Journals* (Pittsburgh: J. R. Weldin & Company, 1893); JSJ, pages 85–100 are biographical, 101–66 consist of Gist's journal (from which quotes herein from journal are taken), 167–85 are an appendix; many references in CAH.

5. Nine years thence, the site was named "Ligonier" for Gen. Lord John Ligonier, commander of the British Army.

6. Having built sweat lodges and undergone "sweats" myself, I have presented my reconstruction of the event.

7. For Shannopin and Alliquippa, see CAH, 1: 228, 229, 251, 270–72, 289; Merrill, *American Woods,* 68–69, 237.

8. Reuben Gold Thwaites, ed., *Early Western Travels, 1748–1765,* 2nd ed. (Lewisburg, PA: Wennawoods Publishing, 1998), 31–32.

9. Quoted in Michael H. McConnell, *A Country Between: The Upper Ohio Valley and Its Peoples, 1724–1774* (Lincoln: University of Nebraska Press, 1992), 88, 90–91; CAH, 1: 356–58.

10. Quoted in CAH, 2: 320.

11. SJS, 118.

12. CAH, 2: 268–71; Albert T. Volwiler, *George Croghan and the Westward Movement, 1741–1782* (Cleveland: Arthur H. Clark Company, 1926), 35.

13. See Demos, *Unredeemed Captive,* 15–25.

14. John Heckewelder, *History, Manners, and Customs of the Indian Nations Who Once Inhabited Pennsylvania and the Neighboring States,* 2nd ed. (Bowie, MD: Heritage Press, 1990), 206.

15. Henderson, *Indian Occupation,* 21–62, Celeron's visit, 33–35; A. Gwynn Henderson, "The Lower Shawnee Town on Ohio: Sustaining Native Autonomy in an Indian 'Republic,'" in Craig Thompson Friend, ed., *The Buzzel about Kentuck: Settling the Promised Land* (Lexington: University Press of Kentucky, 1999), 25–55; journal of Father Jean Bonnecamps in Thwaites, *Jesuit Relations,* 69: 175–83.

16. Terry G. Jordan, *The American Backwoods Frontier: An Ethnic Ecological Interpretation* (Baltimore: Johns Hopkins Press, 1989), 219–20; CAH 1: 255.

17. For Old Brit, see Tanner, *Atlas,* 44–46; McConnell, *Country Between,* 72, 76, 86; White, *Middle Ground,* 213, 220–23, 230, 232–35.

18. The Carolina parakeet, a green-and-yellow parrot larger than the domestic parakeet, flourished throughout the Southeast. A few last survivors were seen in the 1920s near Ormand Beach, Florida, according to a letter December 11, 1969, from Clifford A. Willis, administrative assistant, Division of Marine Resources, Florida Department of Natural Resources, to Frank O. Belue.

19. Conclusion adapted from Francis Jennings, *Empire of Fortune: Crowns, Colonies and Tribes in the Seven Years War in America* (New York: W. W. Norton, 1990), 19.

SECOND INTERLUDE. CRUCIBLE OF FIRE

1. Fred Anderson, *Crucible of War: The Seven Years' War and the Fate of Empire in British North America, 1754–1766* (New York: Alfred A. Knopf, 2000), 77–123; Jennings, *Fortune,* 139–61; for firsthand accounts of the Braddock debacle, see Winthrop Sargent, *The History of an Expedition against Fort Du Quesne in 1755 Under Major-General Edward Braddock,* 2nd ed. (Lewisburg, PA: Wennawoods Publishing, 1997); Quinn, *A New World,* 426–70.

2. Stewell Elias Slick, *William Trent and the West,* 2nd ed. (Lewisburg, PA: Wennawoods Publishing, 2001).

3. Quoted in Anderson, *Crucible of War,* 96.

4. Ibid., 100.

5. Much information on Dr. Thomas Walker, including this curious episode, is found in Charles Roster's *Dismal Swamp,* 229–30; *LIFE,* 538.

CHAPTER 3. DEER SLAYERS & FINCASTLE SURVEYORS

1. For Wawundochwalend, see Heckewelder, *Indian Nations,* 206.

2. Henderson, *Indian Occupation,* 25ff.

3. See Tanner, *Atlas,* 44–46; McConnell, *A Country Between,* 72, 76, 86; White, *Middle Ground,* 213, 220–23, 230, 232–35.

4. For James Smith, see John J. Barsotti, ed., *Scoouwa: James Smith's Indian Captivity Narrative* (Columbus: Ohio Historical Society, 1992); James Smith, *An Account of the Remarkable Occurrences in the Life and Travels of Col. James Smith,* 2nd ed. (Cincinnati: Robert Clarke, 1870); Harriette Simpson Arnow, *Seedtime on the Cumberland* (New York: Macmillan, 1960), 134–38.

5. Regarding Long Hunters, a researcher wading through primary and secondary sources will be confronted by an array of conflicting dates and stories, especially so concerning the forays of Col. James Knox. For Will Emery, see Robert M. Addington, *History of Scott County, Virginia* (Baltimore: Regional Publishing, 1977), 35 (compare with Robert Hancock to LCD, c. 1853, DM 24C: 17{2});

Brent Altsheler, "The Long Hunters and James Knox Their Leader," *FCHQ* 5 (1923): 166–85; James R. Bently, ed., "Letters of Thomas Perkins to Gen. Joseph Palmer, Lincoln County, Kentucky, 1785," *FCHQ* 49 (1975): 145; John B. Dysart to LCD, March 27, 1849, DM 5C: 60(2)–61(2); Gen. William Hall, *Early History of the South-West*, 2nd ed. (Nashville: Parthenon Press, 1968), 33–36; *LH*, 85–96; *LIFE*, 254–80 (for alternate interpretation to Draper, see Arnow, *Seedtime*, 158–69).

6. Quoted in IWW, 20.

7. NOH, *Land Records*, xiii.

8. Quoted in IWW, 13–14.

9. Quoted in Downes, *Council Fires*, 160.

10. Downes, *Council Fires*, 156.

11. IWW, 24, 25

12. IWW, 53.

13. Downes, *Council Fires*, 154–55.

14. IWW, 61.

15. For Lord Dunmore's War (1774) see Reuben Gold Thwaites and Louise Phelps Kellogg, eds., *Documentary History of Dunmore's War*, (Madison: State Historical Society of Wisconsin, 1905).

16. Arthur Campbell to John Murray, May 5, 1774, DM 3QQ: 111.

17. James Robertson to William Preston, August 11, 1774, DM 3QQ: 73–73(1).

18. Arthur Campbell to William Preston, October 1, 1774, DM 3QQ: 109.

19. Thwaites, *Dunmore's War*, 39.

20. NOH, *Land Records*, xiii.

21. IWW, 81.

22. NOH, *Land Records*, 284.

23. For Lord Dunmore's War, see *LIFE*, 299–322; for "Logan's Lament," *LIFE*, 327–28, note o.; in 1786 John Logan's Iroquois nephew, seeking praise from the council, who had pronounced Logan "too great a man to live," killed him.

THIRD INTERLUDE. THE LONG HUNTERS

1. Quoted in *LH*, 109.

2. NC, 103.

3. *Virginia Gazette*, June 22, 1739; quoted on p. 120 in James P. McClure, "The Ohio Valley's Deerskin Trade: Topics for Consideration," *Old Northwest* 15 (1993): 115–33.

4. Kathryn E. Holland Braund, *Deerskins and Duffels: Creek Indian Trade with Anglo-America, 1685–1815* (Lincoln: University of Nebraska Press, 1993).

5. For Indians and nature, see Krech, *Ecological Indian*, and Calvin Martin, *Keepers of the Game: Indian-Animal Relationships and the Fur Trade* (Berkeley: University of California Press, 1978); Stephen Aron, "The Significance of the Kentucky Frontier," *RKHS* 91 (1993): 308.

6. For Long Hunters, see Arnow, *Seedtime*, Macmillan; LCD, *LIFE*, 254–80; see also *LH*, 85–96.

7. Quoted in *LH*, 166–67.

CHAPTER 4. INTO WESTERN WATERS

1. On March 6, 1769, James Nourse sailed for Virginia, bought a plantation near the Potomac, and in April 1775 left for Kentucky. "Journey to Kentucky in 1775: Diary of James Nourse," *Journal of American History* 29.2 (1925): 121–38, 29.3: 251–60, 29.4: 351–64; NOH, *RKHS* 69 (1971): 198–203; Nicholas Cresswell, *The Journal of Nicholas Cresswell, 1774–1777*, 2nd ed. (New York: Dial Press, 1928), 62ff.

2. Settlers wore chestnut bark and leggings as "snake boots." Laurence M. Klauber, *Rattlesnakes: Their Habits, Life Histories, and Influence on Mankind*, 2nd ed. (Berkeley: University of California Press, 1972), 982–84.

3. George Washington built Fort Necessity at Great Meadows following an ambuscade near Fort Duquesne. On July 4, 1754, Washington surrendered Necessity to Coulon de Villiers. Dale Van Every, *Forth to the Wilderness: The First American Frontier, 1754–1774*, 2nd ed. (New York: Quill, 1987), 66, 67 n., 69, 73–75.

4. On July 27, 1774, Hancock Taylor, James Strother, and Abraham Haponstall were ambushed on the Kentucky.

5. NC, May 1, 1775, *Journal*, 69.

6. John Campbell and John Connolly bought Charles Warranstaff's tract at the Falls. Campbell and Connolly, accused of being Tories, forfeited their tract.

7. CAH, 1: 199, 202, 203, 206, 244; 2: 80. Montour's Island is near Pittsburgh's airport. McKee's Island is known as Brunot Island.

8. Between Beaver and Rochester, Pennsylvania.

9. Near Moundsville, West Virginia.

10. George Rogers Clark to Matthew Carey, n.d., DM 53J: 81.

11. Near St. Mary's, West Virginia.

12. Twenty miles above Parkersburg. Two islands of Big Tree Island remain: Middle Brother and Lower Brother Island.

13. *Sanguinaria canadensis.*

14. Fort Gower was on the Hocking, at Hockingsport, Ohio.

15. Twitty and his slave Sam were shot March 25 during a raid on Boone's axmen. Felix Walker was wounded. Reuben Gold Thwaites and Louise Phelps Kellogg, eds., *Revolution on the Upper Ohio*, (Madison: State Historical Society of Wisconsin, 1905), 6–17.

16. Near Huntington. The Guyandotte lies twenty miles above Big Sandy and sixty miles above the Scioto. CAH 2: 123, 161.

17. JN, May 10, 1775, "Diary," 29.2: 127–28.

18. Ibid., 127.

19. NC, May 13, 1775, *Journal*, 73–74.

20. "Middle Ground" defined here as the lands bordered by the Ohio and Mississippi Rivers and the Great Lakes.

21. Manchester Island, Ohio, is a turtle sanctuary.

22. Bracken Creek, near Augusta, Kentucky, marker 426.

23. NC, May 18, 1775, *Journal*, 75–76.

24. James McAfee identifies Jacob Drennon as Jack Drennon. NOH, James McAfee's journal, July 9, 1773, in IWW, 32.

25. See "Drennon's Spring," *KY*, 271.

26. Harrod's Landing, NC, May 24, 1775, *Journal*, 78.

27. NC, June 11, 1775, *Journal*, 84–85.

28. NC, May 26, 1775, *Journal*, 79, near the northwest corner of Franklin County.

29. JN, May 29, 1775, "Diary," 29.3: 251.

30. "The great buffalo crossing was at Leestown, now part of northern Frankfort, at marker 64.5. The trace went up the bluff . . . to where present U.S. 60 intersects with U.S. 460." Quoted in NOH, "Historic Lawsuits of the Eighteenth Century: Locating the Stamping Ground," *RKHS* 69 (1971): 214.

31. Nourse's journal may be the first recorded glimpse of the central Bluegrass. JN, May 30, 1775, "Diary," 29.3: 252.

32. *Tradescantia virginia.*

33. NOH notes: "Nourse, Taylor, et al. . . . should have camped at what was soon to be Leestown, waited for Willis Lee. Later they could have hiked over to Boonesborough or Woodstock and hired either [John] Floyd or [James] Douglas to survey for them. These would have been valid as both were legal surveyors." NOH to TFB, June 1, 1994; NOH, *Land Records*, 46.

34. Harrod's Landing is on the Kentucky, marker 97.5.

35. JN, June 4, 1775, "Diary," 29.3: 256.

36. NC, June 4, 1775, *Journal*, 81.

37. A discrepancy. After JN described Harrod's to NC, he recorded: "Mr. Nourse informs me there is about thirty cabins in it, built of logs and covered with clapboards, but not a nail in the whole town." See NC, June 6, 1775, *Journal*, 82; JN, June 5, 1775, "Diary," 29.3: 256.

38. The killings were the same attacks Nourse learned about on May 8.

39. John Gabriel Jones represented Kentucky in the legislature. Indians killed him in December 1776.

40. See William Stewart Lester, *The Transylvania Company* (Spencer, IN: Samuel R. Guard, 1935), 86–87.

41. Boone's first fort was a palisaded blockhouse near where Boonesborough State Park's restrooms are located today. Henderson tried to induce his men to build a fort but had little luck, as most were claiming land. The fort remained unfinished until just before the Shawnees attacked in 1778.

42. Harrod's Town settlers first harvested wheat in 1777. *LIFE*, 424.

43. Five miles past Harrod's Town, between Danville and Harrodsburg, and a mile west of U.S. Highway 127 was Boiling Springs. Knob Lick was on the northeastern side of Junction City.

44. JN, June 25, 1775, "Diary," 29.4: 352; his survey was south of Cynthiana.

45. Reuben and Edmund Taylor left to meet Hancock and Willis Lee (they were related) and establish Leestown. Indians killed Willis in April 1776. In the 1800s Frankfort absorbed Leestown. "Leestown," *KY,* 542.

46. JN, June 28–29, 1775, "Diary," 29.4: 361; Big Hill (three miles southeast from Berea), paralleling Roundstone Creek.

47. NC, June 11, 1775, *Journal,* 84.

48. At Lower Blue Licks, it took 840 gallons of water to make a bushel of salt. *LIFE,* 459–60.

49. NC, June 14, 1775, *Journal,* 86.

50. This canoe most likely had carried Haptonstall, Taylor, and Strother when they were attacked in July 1774.

51. NC, June 15–16, 1775, *Journal,* 87.

52. During the ice age, Big Bone Lick was a bog that trapped mammoths, mastodons, tapirs, sloths, and buffalo; twenty-two species have been identified. In 1739 Charles Lemoyne de Longueil shipped fossils to Louis XV; a few wound up with Ben Franklin, who concluded elephants once roamed America. Thomas Jefferson commissioned William Clark to investigate but sent the bones to the world's museums. "Big Bone Lick," *KY,* 76; Samuel W. Thomas, "George Rogers Clark: Natural Scientist and Historian," *FCHQ* 41 (1967): 202–26.

53. Tales of white buffalo east of the Mississippi are very rare.

54. NC, June 19, 1775, *Journal,* 89.

55. Near Portsmith.

56. Indians and Anglo hunters shot game with abandon, leading to the extermination of buffalo and elk in the East.

57. NC, August 19, 1775, *Journal,* 102–3; NC, September 1, 1775, *Journal,* 109.

58. James Nourse died in Annapolis in 1784. Three of his sons settled in Kentucky. Nicholas Cresswell died in 1804, willing his Indian mementos to his children.

FOURTH INTERLUDE. WARFARE & TACTICS

1. *LIFE,* 498–99.

2. Richard Lea to LCD, c. 1862, DM 9E: 124.

3. John Cuppy to LCD, May, 1860, DM 9S: 36–37.

4. Ibid.

5. Ibid., 21.

6. Ibid., 26.

CHAPTER 5. THE PATHFINDER

1. William Fleming Papers, Special Collections, Leyburn Library, Washington and Lee University, Lexington, Virginia; this undated letter, c. November 1777, found in ms. PP4.

2. Ear-slitting as a fashion died out by the early 1800s. See Heckewelder, *Indian Nations,* 207.

3. Nicholas de Finiels, who met Louis Lorimier in 1797 at Cape Girardeau, Missouri, believed he was of *métis* extraction. Nicholas de Finiels, *An Account of Upper Louisiana,* edited by Carl J. Ekberg and William E. Foley (Columbia: University of Missouri Press, 1989), 34–35; see Alice Ford, *Audubon, by Himself* (Garden City, NY: Natural History Press), 49.

4. For Pompey, compare DM 24C: 81(1) with DM 8S: 143; regarding "Black Dick," see E. J. Roark to LCD, c. 1885, DM 16C: 81(2); for Pompey's death, see Seventh Interlude.

5. TFB, "Terror in the Canelands: The Fate of Daniel Boone's Saltboilers," *FCHQ* 68 (1994): 3–34; Stephen Aron, *How the West Was Lost: The Transformation of Kentucky from Daniel Boone to Henry Clay* (Baltimore: Johns Hopkins University Press, 1996), 41–47.

6. *WIK*, 57.

7. Robert Hancock to LCD, February 25, 1853, DM 24C: 17(2–3); see also Joseph Jackson to LCD, April 1844, DM 11C: 62(13).

8. Quoted in Joseph Jackson to LCD, April 1844, DM 11C: 62(13).

9. *WIK*, 57.

10. Quoted in *LIFE*, 497.

11. TFB, "Did Daniel Boone Shoot Pompey, the Black Shawnee, at the 1778 Siege of Boonesborough?" *FCHQ* 67 (1993): 5–22.

12. *WIK*, 63–64.

13. TFB, "Terror," 3–34.

14. John Filson, *The Discovery, Settlement, and Present State of Kentucke,* originally published in 1784 (New York: Corinth Books, 1962), 73.

15. Prior to January 1, 1778, preempted claims could be had at $40 per hundred acres.

16. Swivel guns were large-bore muskets (or rifles) set on a mechanism. Carl P. Russell, *Firearms, Traps, and Tools of the Mountain Men* (Albuquerque: University of New Mexico Press, 1981), 77–84; George C. Neuman, Frank J. Kravic, and George C. Woodbridge, *Collector's Illustrated Encyclopedia of the American Revolution,* 2nd ed. (Texarkana, TX: Rebel Publishing, 1989), 272.

17. As late as 1817, Boone was attempting to retrieve his swivels. See Samuel Gibson to John D. Shane, c. 1843–49, DM 12CC: 124.

18. PH, DM 20C: 84 (15–16).

19. Ibid., (17).

20. GMB to LCD, c. 1843, 1A: 21, 22, 24, 27.

21. NOM, 171–78.

22. Boone believed the landlord drugged him and robbed him, or that an accomplice absconded with the cash. He sold his land to pay off the debt, but, recalled Nathan Boone, "it was a great loss." NB to LCD, DM 6S: 145–46; see JMF, 208–9; Boone may have owned about thirty thousand acres in Kentucky; for Boone's Station dispute, see NOM, *Stockading Up,* 175–78; also JMF, 242–45.

23. William Byrd, *The Writings of Colonel William Byrd of Westover in Virginia, Esquire,* 2nd ed., edited by John Spencer Bassett (New York: Burt Franklin, 1970), 225.

24. For tanning, see PH, DM 20C: 84 (24–26).

25. See "Perticulars of E Boons Death," E. B. Scholl to LCD, January 5, 1856, DM 23C: 104; also in NOM, 174.

26. Maj. John Redd to LCD, November 30, 1849, DM 10NN: 101; for buttons, see Daniel Bryan to JDS, c. 1843, DM 22C: 14(14).

27. James Boone, n.d., family record, DM 1C: 59.

28. Quoted in Filson, *Kentucke,* 80; Nathan Boone said that in 1783 his father moved five miles west of Boone's Station to Marble Creek and was there until 1785, then moved to Limestone. Conversely, Daniel Bryan noted that "after he left Marble Creek he moved up on Sandy [River] or K[anawha], because he was so troubled by preemptions and etc." Compare NB to LCD, 1851, DM 6S: 159, with Daniel Bryan to JDS, c. 1843, DM 22C: 14(14).

FIFTH INTERLUDE: FROM BOONE TO BUMPPO TO POE

1. From Basil Davenport's Foreword, James Fenimore Cooper, *The Deerslayer* (New York: Dodd, Mead and Company, 1952).

2. Quoted in Mark Twain, "Fenimore Cooper's Literary Offenses," in Charles Neider, ed., *The Comic Mark Twain Reader: The Most Humorous Selections from His Stories, Sketches, Novels, Travel Books and Speeches* (New York: Doubleday and Company, 1977), 470.

3. *Deerslayer,* 153.

4. Mark Twain's best-known and most caustic Cooper burlesque is cited in note 2.

5. Gary Edgerton, "'A Breed Apart': Hollywood, Racial Stereotyping, and the Promise of Revisionism in The Last of the Mohicans," *Journal of American Culture* 17.2 (1994): 1–17; for a portfolio of

black-and-white pictures of United Artists' 1936 version, see *Literary Prints: The Last of the Mohicans* (Logan, IA: Perfection Form Company, 1936).

6. Dan Gagliasso, "Flintlocks in Film," *Dixie Gun Works Blackpowder Annual* (1993): 46–49, 99.

7. For seven weeks during the long, hot summer of 1991, I served in the French and Indian War as a Hollywood extra in Michael Mann's *The Last of the Mohicans,* portraying a French marine on one day, a redcoat the next, and sometimes both on the same day.

CHAPTER 6. HUGUENOT LONG KNIFE

1. *WIK,* 164, fn. 5; DT's memoirs originally found in DM 57J, the George Rogers Clark Papers. In 1981 University Press of Kentucky published an annotated version as *WIK.* In May 1879 the *Richmond Standard* published six pages of the memoir. Also, Marco Sioli, "Huguenot Traditions in the Mountains of Kentucky: Daniel Trabue's Memories," *Journal of American History* 84 (1998): 1313–33.

2. See Carolyn D. Wallins, *Elisha Wallin: The Longhunter* (Johnson City, TN: Overmountain Press, 1990).

3. Bennet Belue's inciting Cherokees and Chickasaws against Americans are topics of two letters between Indian agent Gen. Joseph Martin and Patrick Henry. See John Donelson, journal entry, March 4, 1780, DM 11ZZ: 14; Joseph Martin to Patrick Henry, July 2, 1789, DM 1XX: 30–31; Joseph Martin to Patrick Henry, January 18, 1791, DM 1XX: 31.

4. *WIK,* 44, 46.

5. Logan's Station (St. Asaph's) was west of present-day Stanford in Lincoln County. See Anita J. Stanford, "Bryan's Station," *KY,* 133–34.

6. *WIK,* 48.

7. For Joel Sappington, see Joshua McQueen, c. 1842, DM 13CC: 122; for Nathan Boone, c. 1851, DM 6S: 208; for Simon Kenton, see Fielding Belt to LCD, n.d., DM 21S: 208–9.

8. See Charles Gano Talbert, *Benjamin Logan: Kentucky Frontiersman* (Lexington: University Press of Kentucky, 1976).

9. Quoted in Kenneth C. Carstens, "George Rogers Clark," *KY* 195.

10. *WIK,* 166, fn. 44.

11. Ibid., fn. 46.

12. Ibid., 54.

13. It was not until June 1779 that Kenton and two of Daniel Boone's salt boilers, Jesse Copher and Nathaniel Bullock, escaped from Detroit and made their way down the Wabash to Kentucky.

14. For land bills, see *WIK,* 68, 173, fn. 68–69.

15. August William Derleth, *Vincennes: Portal to the West* (Englewood Cliffs, NJ: Prentice-Hall, 1968), 72.

16. *WIK,* 75.

17. A. Campbell, c. 1780, DM 13CC: 82–87; Filson, *Kentucke,* 73.

18. SR, c. 1842, DM 23CC: 33–35; William Clinkenbeard to John D. Shane, c. 1843, in Lucien Beckner, trans., "Reverend John D. Shane's Interview with Pioneer William Clinkenbeard," *FCHQ* 2 (1928): 104–6, 112. For Clinkenbeard, see DM 11CC: 54–66. William Fleming, March 20, 1780, Newton D. Mereness, ed., *Travels in the American Colonies,* (New York: Macmillan, 1916), 636; see also James and Samuel McAfee, c. 1842, DM 14CC: 115.

19. Rachel Denton to LCD, January 5, 1856, DM 23C: 104(2); Edna Kenton, *Simon Kenton: His Life and Period, 1755–1836* (Reprint. Salem, NH: Ayer, 1993), 148.

20. *WIK,* 72.

21. In 1785 Trabue and his family moved to Fayette County, later relocating to Adair County. Mary passed away on September 25, 1828, Daniel on September 10, 1840.

SIXTH INTERLUDE. BUFFALO FOR THE KILLING

1. Quoted in TFB, *LH,* 17. All data on eastern buffalo herein adapted from *LH.*

2. Hugh Bell to LCD, c. 1841, DM 30S: 263.

3. John Hanks to LCD, c. 1843, DM 12CC: 144.

4. Thwaites, *Jesuit Relations,* 65: 73–75.

5. *WIK,* 74.

6. For restrictions on buffalo killing at Boonesborough c. 1775, see *LIFE,* 367.

CHAPTER 7. TO EARN ONE'S FREEDOM

1. Quoted in Lewis Collins, *History of Kentucky* (Covington, KY: Collins and Company, 1882), 13; Bessie Taul Conkright, "Estill's Defeat; or, The Battle of Little Mountain," *RKHS* 22 (1924): 313; see GMB to LCD, DM 1A: 69; for Monk Estill, see TFB, "Monk Estill," *KY,* 298; for James Estill, see *The Biographical Encyclopedia of Kentucky of the Dead and Living Men of the Nineteenth Century* (Cincinnati: J. M. Armstrong, 1878), 51–52; see TFB, "Blacks on the Western Frontier," *REV,* 1: 128–29; William Loren Katz, *Black Indians: Hidden Heritage* (New York: Macmillan, 1986), i; Marion B. Lucas, "African Americans on the Kentucky Frontier," *RKHS* 95 (1997): 121–34.

2. Z. F. Smith, *The History of Kentucky* (Louisville, KY: Prentiss Press, 1895), 191–92.

3. Joseph Collins, March 26, 1778, quoted in Lester, *Transylvania Company,* 195.

4. For formulas, see Eliot Wiggington, ed., *Foxfire 5* (Garden City, NY: Anchor, 1979), 246–48, 252–60; for Boone's gunpowder formula, c. 1788, see DM 27C: 35.

5. GMB to LCD, c. 1843, DM 1A: 19.

6. For John Evans Finlay, see DM 12ZZ: 77; also, Mark Odle, "Tools and Techniques of Bark Tanning," in William H. Scurlock, ed., *The Book of Buckskinning VII* (Texarkana, TX: Scurlock Publishing, 1995) 222–48.

7. Jerry Estill moved to Shelby County and became one of Kentucky's first black Baptist preachers, a detail often wrongfully attributed to Monk Estill. One root of this error is in my essay "Monk Estill," *KY,* 298. When the editor returned the page proof, a portion of my entry had been rewritten to read that Monk Estill "became a Baptist preacher and lived in Shelbyville." On May 9, 1991, I responded: "I find no evidence Monk Estill became a Baptist preacher. . . . Please revise." The editor did not revise. In 1997 the error reappeared on p. 43 of Lowell H. Harrison and James C. Klotter's *A New History of Kentucky* (Lexington: University Press of Kentucky, 1997). The editorial error is now "official" history.

8. For Strode's Station, see NOM, *Stockading Up,* 161–66; regarding Strode, see Clinkenbeard to JDS, c. 1843. See Clinkenbeard's memoirs in DM 11CC: 54–66.

9. See Collins, *Kentucky,* 2: 527.

10. For "go-betweens," see Merrill, *American Woods;* and Larry B. Nelson, *A Man of Distinction among Them: Alexander McKee and British-Indian Affairs along the Ohio Country Frontier, 1754–1799* (Kent, OH: Kent State University Press, 1999).

11. Simon Girty, c. 1781, quoted in Consul Wilshire Butterfield, *History of the Girtys,* 2nd ed. (Columbus: Long's College Book Company, 1950), 190–91, 372–73.

12. After the battle, many people remarked about Jenny Gass's portentous dream. See Roxann Gess Smith, "Notes and Biography for David Gass," February 21, 2000, http://www.transport.com/-gess-whoto/index21.html.

13. Near Irvine.

14. Little Mountain was a pre-Columbian mound 25 feet high and 125 feet across that "developers" leveled in 1846 for the intersection of Locust and Queen Streets in Mount Sterling, Kentucky.

15. According to historian Harry G. Enoch, "The battlefield is on Hinkston Creek, a little north of Mt. Sterling, near where I-64 crosses the creek. The interstate, in fact, partly covers the field." See Enoch, *In Search of Morgan's Station and The Last Indian Raid in Kentucky* (Bowie, MD: Heritage Books, 1997), 8–9, 17–18.

16. Col. John Todd, commander at the battle of Blue Licks, attempted a similar three-pronged maneuver.

17. William Miller, unable to hear Estill's commands, feared his men would be cut off. Yet all but two of Estill's men condemned his retreat. William Champ, who did not, said Miller told him that in the cane, "he could not see the Indians and felt foolish exposing himself." Yelverton Peyton told LCD that "Miller was as brave as any man." All, however, blamed Miller's retreat for the loss. Twenty years later David Cook swore he would kill him, given the chance. Miller, who lived to be ninety-five, said little to justify his actions.

18. Men who fought at Little Mountain include James Berry (wounded), Adam Caperton (killed), William Champ, David Cook (wounded), John Colefoot (killed), Benjamin Dunaway, Capt. James Estill (killed), Monk Estill, Forbes (first name unknown; killed), David Gass, Peter Hackett, William Irvine (wounded), Johnson (first name unknown; wounded), David Lynch, Jonathan McMillan (killed), M. McNeely (killed), William Miller, Yelverton Peyton, Joseph Proctor, Reuben Proctor,

John South, Jr. (killed), Samuel South, and one other man (name unknown; killed). Accounts differ on who was killed, who was wounded (and how many, either four or six), and who was present. This list is not complete, nor does it agree perfectly with other compilations.

No one is sure how many Indians died, nor of the fate of the French-Canadians. During his Ohio Valley campaign, George Rogers Clark rescued two prisoners, Margaret Polly and a Mrs. Gatliff, who had heard the Wyandot version of the battle and believed their losses numbered twenty casualties.

Joseph Proctor became a Methodist circuit rider; three times he joined George Rogers Clark and Benjamin Logan to take the fight to the Ohio Indians. William Irvine, scarred and forever carrying a ball and two buckshot, served as a delegate from Madison County to the Virginia Conventions of 1788 and 1789 and was a presidential elector in 1805, 1813, and 1817. Samuel South was active in Madison County politics from 1800 to 1813, was appointed general, and led a regiment in the War of 1812.

19. References for events leading up to and during the battle of Little Mountain (alternately, "Estill's Defeat"), including dialogue, paraphrases, and events, are from works cited previously and TFB, "Death in the Bluegrass: The Battle of Little Mountain," *Dixie Gun Works Blackpowder Annual,* 1995: 66–69; primary sources are from depositions, survivors' recollections, and eyewitness accounts collected by LCD, c. 1843–45, DM 13C: 38–59. I am grateful to genealogist William Dunniway, whose forebear Benjamin Dunaway survived Estill's Defeat, and whose correspondence of February 10, 1997, helped fill in the names of Estill's militia.

20. Quoted in TFB, *REV* 1: 135.
21. Ibid.
22. Filson, *Kentucke,* 77–78.
23. John Floyd to Gov. Thomas Jefferson, April 16, 1781. Floyd's letters, transcriptions by NOH; Monk Estill married three times, begat thirty children, and died in Madison County in 1835.

SEVENTH INTERLUDE. KILLING POMPEY

1. John Mason Peck, *Life of Daniel Boone, the Pioneer of Kentucky,* vol. 13, in Jared Sparks, ed., *The Library of American Biography,* 2nd ser. (Boston: Charles C. Little, 1847), 87.
2. NOH, ed., *My Father, Daniel Boone: The Draper Interviews with Nathan Boone* (Lexington: University Press of Kentucky, 1999), 68, 69, 70; see TFB, "Black Shawnee," 5–22; also see TFB, "Who Shot the Black Shawnee," *Muzzleloader,* January/February 1992: 46–48.
3. *LIFE,* 516.
4. E. J. Roark to LCD, September 10, 1885, 16C: 81(2).
5. Joseph Jackson to LCD, May 17, 1884, DM 11C: 62(16).
6. Ephraim McClean to LCD, DM 16C: 7(3–4).
7. John Gass to JDS, c. 1843–49, DM 11CC: 4.
8. John Bakeless, *Daniel Boone: Master of the Wilderness,* 3rd ed. (Lincoln: University Press of Nebraska, 1989), 218.
9. Elijah Bryan to LCD, December 16, 1884, DM 4C: 33(5).

CHAPTER 8. INTRIGUE ON GREEN RIVER

1. Anecdotes and dialogue relating to GMB from interviews with LCD, c. 1843, interviews with Benjamin Drake, c. 1839, and GMB's letters in DM 1A: 14–53; William Dodd Brown, ed. "A Visit to Boonesborough in 1779: The Recollections of Pioneer George M. Bedinger," *RKHS* 86 (1988): 315–29; biographical data excerpted from Josephine L. Harper, *Guide to the Draper Manuscripts* (Madison: State Historical Society of Wisconsin, 1983), 1; Biographical Directory of the United States Congress, February 21, 2000, http://bioguide.congress.gov/scripts/biodisplay.pl?index=B000301.
2. Kentuckians remembered the Starnes episode as "a most dismal massacre."
3. Located in an area then known as Severn Valley (named for explorer John Severn), near Elizabethtown, county seat of Hardin County.
4. Having lost part of my left thumb to two copperhead bites—the first June 30, 1988; the second February 15, 1989—I know a bit about how Fields must have felt, though his bite was much worse. The hemotoxic venom from a western cottonmouth moccasin *(Agkistrodon piscivorus leucostoma)* causes massive tissue damage and necrosis. Too, because cottonmouths are aquatic and eat fish and frogs, their saliva teems with bacteria that often lead to infection.

5. This bit of folklore was standard treatment for snakebite. Binding the serpent to the wound was believed to "draw" the poison. A dead chicken, a split bean, or a toad, with appropriate incantations and mysterious potions, was thought to work equally well.

6. This outrage shocked Indians and whites alike, but no one brought the killers—whom some saw as frontier heroes—to trial. Regarding the massacre of the Moravian Delawares and the subsequent retaliation, see TFB, "Crawford's Sandusky Expedition (May-June 1782)," *REV,* 1: 416–20; see also Earl P. Olmstead, "Moravian Indian Missions on the Muskingum River," *REV,* 2: 1099–1103; and C. Hale Sipe, *The Indian Wars of Pennsylvania,* 2nd ed. (Lewisburg, PA: Wennawoods Publishing, 1995), 647–53, 659–64.

7. A blend of red wool and silk.

8. Probably a Carolina parakeet *(Conurus carolinensis),* extinct in Kentucky since the late 1800s.

9. GMB to LCD, DM 1A: 50.

10. Ibid., 52.

11. Bedinger never specified Stovall's crime, saying only that "pursuing his career in infamy, [Stovall] was finally detected, convicted and executed several years later in St. Louis." See GMB to LCD, DM 1A: 53ff; see Clifford C. Gregg and Charles G. Talbert, "George Michael Bedinger, 1756–1843," *RKHS* 65 (1967): 41–46.

12. In 1791 he served as major for Gen. Arthur St. Clair, commanding the Winchester Battalion of Sharpshooters during St. Clair's Ohio expedition. He also served two terms in the Kentucky legislature and two terms in the U.S. House of Representatives. On February 11, 1793, he eloped with sixteen-year-old Henrietta Clay, who bore him nine children, and in 1829 he made his last unsuccessful bid for Congress. Survived by his wife and five children, Bedinger died in 1843 at eighty-seven.

EIGHTH INTERLUDE. THE "KENTUCKY" RIFLE

1. LCD, c. 1843, interview with Benjamin Drake, c. 1839, and letters, notes, and land claims in DM 1A: 14–53; Brown, "Pioneer George M. Bedinger," 315–29.

2. De Witt Bailey, "Rifle," *REV,* 2: 1405–7; De Witt Bailey, "Riflemen," *REV,* 2: 1407–9; Henry Kauffman, *The Pennsylvania-Kentucky Rifle* (New York: Bonanza Books, 1960); Joe Kindig, Jr., *Thoughts on the Kentucky Rifle in Its Golden Age* (New York: Bonanza Books, 1964); Robert Lagemann and Albert Manucy, *The Long Rifle* (New York: Eastern Acorn Press, 1980); also Wiggington, *Foxfire 5,* 208–21.

3. Chartrand, *French Soldier,* 7–8.

4. Kindig, *Kentucky Rifle,* 30.

5. Don Wright, "Design and Construction of Powder Horns," in William H. Scurlock, ed., *The Book of Buckskinning II* (Texarkana, TX: Rebel Publishing Company, 1983), 111–48.

6. For Hancock, see TFB, "Black Shawnee," 5–22; for Dieverbaugh, see Mark A. Baker, "What It Takes to Tarry in the Country," *Muzzleloader* (July-August 2001): 12–18; for Big Bullet, see John Tucker to LCD, c. 1841, DM 30S: 288; for Big Jim, see Nathan and Olive Boone to LCD, c. 1851, DM 6S: 160–61; for Murphy, see Brian E. Hubner, "Timothy Murphy," *REV* 2: 1130–32.

7. Quoted in Bakeless, *Daniel Boone,* 398–99.

8. For Noah Ludlow, the Harding-Lewis engraving of "Col. Daniel Boon.," and Samuel Woodward's "The Hunters of Kentucky," see Clifford Amyx, "The Authentic Image of Daniel Boone," *Missouri Historical Review* 82 (1988): 153–64; Roy T. King, "Portraits of Daniel Boone," *Missouri Historical Review* 33 (1939): 171–83; Leah Lipton, *A Truthful Likeness: Chester Harding and His Portraits* (Washington, DC: National Portrait Gallery, Smithsonian Institution, 1985); Noah M. Ludlow, *Dramatic Life as I Found It,* 2nd ed. (St. Louis: Benjamin Blom, 1966), 191–238, 241, 250–51; John Francis McDermott, "How Goes the Harding Fever?" *Missouri Historical Society Bulletin* 8 (1951): 53–59; Charles Van Ravenswaay, "A Rare Midwestern Print," *Antiques* 43 (1943): 77, 93; St. Louis, Missouri, *Gazette,* "Advertisements in the Pioneer Press," *Missouri Historical Review* 26 (1932): 395; lyrics in Wiggington, *Foxfire,* 211–12.

CHAPTER 9. TERROR IN THE BLUEGRASS

1. Unless otherwise stated, episodes, dialogue, and quotes pertaining to SR were taken from his memoir, "A Brief Narrative Giving an Account of the Time and Place of the Birth of Captain Spencer

Records, His Moving and Settlements: With Incidents That Occurred Relative to the Wars with the Indians with a Brief Account of his Father, Josiah Records: Written by Himself, the Said Spencer Records," composed October 1842 and found in DM 23CC: 1–108; ancillary material found in LCD's interview with John N. Records (son of SR), circa 1863, in DM 19S: 108–17; see also LCD's interview with George Edwards, c. 1863, in DM 19S: 71–95; SR, DM 23CC: 10.

2. In Harrison County.
3. See "Washington," *KY,* 934.
4. SR, DM 23CC: 39–40.
5. Daniel Bryan to LCD, n.d., DM 22CC: 14(9).
6. SR, DM 23CC: 36–38.
7. U.S. Route 68 overlaps the trace once named for George Rogers Clark.
8. SR, DM 23CC: 44.
9. This episode with dialogue is from John N. Records to LCD, c. 1863, DM 19S: 110.
10. Auctioning off loot, or "selling at vendue," helped pay the militia; "twilled bags," as erroneously inscribed in the original text, appears here corrected as "twinned," a finger-weaving technique.
11. The white man confessed that he was born in Lancaster County, Pennsylvania, and was kidnapped and raised as an Indian.
12. SR, DM 23CC: 50.
13. Ibid., 55–56.
14. Near Newmarket, Ohio.
15. Quoted in G. Glenn Clift, *History of Maysville and Mason County* (Lexington, KY: Transylvania Printing Company, 1936), 1: 84; see also 56, 59, 68, 71, 85, 111, 123, 385.
16. SR, DM 23CC: 59.
17. Simon Kenton said of that day in 1789, "I thought I had men I could depend on, the way they boasted." It was a fact, Spencer replied, that "the more men brag and boast when there is no danger, the less may be expected of them when there is danger."
18. John Records to LCD, c. 1863, DM 19S: 113; alternate rendering in George Edwards to LCD, c. 1863, DM 19S: 94; John Hughey to LCD, December 6, DM 10BB: 26(1–2); Ophra Peyton to LCD, December 3, 1866, DM 10BB: 27 and William Hughey to LCD, December 24, 1866, DM 10BB: 28(4).
19. See Clift, *Maysville,* 100–101.
20. Devine and Thomas said that they had been seized before the episode and were forced to be decoys. Flinn and the Fleming girl were given up in a prisoner exchange. Jacob Skyles's fate is unknown.
21. Clift, *Maysville,* 97–99.
22. Quoted in Ibid., 95–96.
23. SR, DM 23CC: 70.
24. George Edwards to LCD, c. 1863, DM 19S: 93.
25. Laban's revenge in citations in note 18.
26. Spencer and Elizabeth had "thirteen living children, and one still-born, eighty-seven grandchildren . . . [and] seven great-grandchildren." He resigned as captain of Mason County's militia in 1795, moved to Ross County, Ohio, and died in 1849.

NINTH INTERLUDE. "APING THE MANNER OF SAVAGES"

1. Clinkenbeard, *FCHQ* 2: 110, 120, 125.
2. Ezekiel Collins to LCD, c. 1843, DM 30J: 80.
3. *LIFE,* 469, 482.
4. J. Breckenridge to JDS, c. 1843–49, DM 11CC: 35; Joseph Jackson to LCD, c. 1840, DM 11C: 62ff.
5. *WIK,* 140–41.
6. Judge Adam Beatty to JDS, c. 1843–49, DM 16CC: 307.
7. John Tanner, *The Falcon: A Narrative of the Captivity and Adventures of John Tanner during Thirty Years' Residence among the Indians in the Interior of North America,* edited by Louise Erdrich (New York: Penguin Books, 1994).
8. NC, *Journal,* 117.

9. O. M. Spencer, *The Indian Captivity of O. M. Spencer,* edited by Milo Milton Quaife (New York: Citadel Press, 1968), 47–48.

10. A perusal of these works provides a good start in trying to unravel the myth and lore that swirls about Simon Girty: James Axtell, "The White Indians of Colonial America," *The European and the Indian: Essays in the Ethnohistory of Colonial North America* (New York: Oxford University Press, 1981): 168–206; Butterfield, *Girtys;* Colin C. Calloway, "Neither White nor Red: White Renegades on the American Indian Frontier," *Western Historical Quarterly* 17, no. 1 (1986): 43–66; also by Calloway, "Simon Girty: Interpreter and Intermediary," in James A. Clifton, ed., *Being and Becoming Indian: Biographical Studies of North American Frontiers* (Prospect Heights, IL: Waveland Press, 1989): 38–58; Philip Hoffman, "Simon Girty," *REV, I:* 660–64.

CHAPTER 10. RECKONINGS & RESOLUTIONS

1. Quoted in JMF, 235.
2. For the Boone's Station dispute, see NOM, *Stockading Up,* 175–78; JMF, 242–45.
3. For Logan's campaign and Boone's role, see JMF, 252–54.
4. For many years there has existed a controversy over whether the renowned Shawnee warrior named Waweyapiersenwaw (or Blue Jacket) was an adopted white man named Marmaduke Van Sweringen or a full-blooded Shawnee. According to recent scholarship by John Sugden, he was Shawnee. See Sugden, *Blue Jacket,* Lincoln.
5. For prisoner exchange and negotiations, see JMF, 255–60.
6. See de Finiels, *Upper Louisiana,* 32–41.
7. Quoted in Clift, *Maysville,* 95–96.
8. SR, DM 23CC: 70; see George Edwards to LCD, c. 1863, DM 19S: 93.
9. For more on the Hubble disaster, see Clift, *Maysville,* 105–6; also, Jemima Hawkins to LCD, c. 1863, DM 19S: 46–47.
10. For George Washington's Indian policies, see Wiley Sword, *President Washington's Indian War: The Struggle for the Old Northwest,* 2nd ed. (Norman: University of Oklahoma Press, 1995), 35, 56, 75, 81–84, 86–87.
11. See Sword, *Indian War,* 145, 205–6. Sword presents a complete, well-written scholarly analysis of this entire era.
12. GMB to LCD, DM 1A: 50.
13. This and subsequent in-text quotes regarding later years are from Gregg and Talbert, *RKHS,* 65 (1967): 41–46.
14. For the Harpes, see Jonathan Daniel, *The Devil's Backbone: The Story of the Natchez Trace* (New York: McGraw-Hill, 1962), 114–24; Louanna Furbee and W. D. Snively, Jr., *Satan's Ferryman: A True Tale of the Old Frontier* (New York: Frederick Unger, 1968), 46–56.
15. Baptists viewed immersion as nonessential to salvation, as "an outward showing of an inward grace." "Immersionists" deemed immersion essential to salvation—"for the remission of sins"—citing from Bible passages like Mark 16:16 and Acts 2:38. See J. M. Pendleton, *Baptist Church Manual* (Nashville: Broadman Press, 1966), 87, 96–97.
16. For anecdote, see LCD to Charles A. Marshall, November 21, 1884, DM 10BB: 48–48(25).
17. For DB's life west of the Mississippi, see JMF, 264–319; also, for firsthand recollections of Nathan and Olive Boone, see NOH, *My Father.*
18. DM 30C: 41, 66. Delinda Craig to LCD, c. 1868.
19. Quoted in Houston, *Sketch,* 33.
20. For an interesting account of this sad affair, see Enoch, *Morgan's Station,* Heritage Press.
21. Quoted in NOH, *RKHS* 68 (1970): 124.

EPILOGUE: THE FIRST SHALL BE LAST

1. In constructing my epilogue, including quotes, descriptions, and context, I drew from the following resources: Henderson, Jobe, and Turnbow, *Indian Occupation,* 77–93; James D. Horan, *The McKenny-Hall Portrait Gallery of American Indians* (New York: Bramhall House, 1986), 158–59; Elizabeth A. Perkins, *Border Life: Experience and Memory in the Revolutionary Ohio Valley* (Chapel Hill: University of North Carolina Press, 1998), 15–24.

BIBLIOGRAPHY

I find it almost impossible to conceive how anyone—whether writer, historian, dedicated aficionado, or the most casual history "buff"—can attempt to write valid Kentucky frontier history without delving heavily into the vast archival repository known as the Draper Manuscript Collection; the original handwritten 491 volumes are housed in the State Historical Society of Wisconsin, in Madison, and are available on microfilm. Certainly in my many periodical and magazine essays, and in my four books to date, I have mined Lyman C. Draper's expansive, near-bottomless work; indeed, my third book, *The Life of Daniel Boone* (published by Stackpole Books in 1998), is an edited transcription of Draper's voluminous—but sadly, unfinished—manuscript of the same title.

So it is the work of Lyman C. Draper (and that of Rev. John Dabney Shane, another "oral history" pioneer in Kentucky whose bulging tomes the foresighted Draper purchased after Shane's death) that any genuine student of the era should peruse and peruse with zeal. I continue to do so.

Reuben Gold Thwaites, who succeeded Draper as Wisconsin's State Historical Society secretary, certainly contributed (besides a well-written Daniel Boone biography based upon his predecessor's work) his strong hand in harnessing some of Draper's most critical Kentuckiana. Very useful to my narrative sketches herein were Thwaites's well-edited compendiums concerning Lord Dunmore's War and the American Revolution in the western theater.

Books on famous frontier Kentuckians like Daniel Boone, Simon Kenton, George Rogers Clark, and other men of that distinct class are legion; indeed, books on Boone and other forms of "Boone-iana" (including flintlocks of dubious provenance and artificially aged powderhorns and the like that fetch high prices from unsuspecting buyers) have become a sort of thriving cottage industry. It is more difficult, however, to locate the equally competent though "lesser lights," which is this book's focus. A dedicated researcher must scour the end notes of books (and journal essays) dealing with the legendary and famous and not-so-famous in hopes of finding tantalizing clues regarding the whereabouts and lives of their not-so-well-known peers. To be sure, writings dealing with such a wide and varied group—the heroes, rogues, slaves, and common men—run the gamut in terms of quality. Many are well researched and well written. Others are only moderately useful. Some are romantic gush and dreadfully written.

Not surprisingly, many of the best and most incisive writings about frontier Kentucky continue to be authored by modern-day Kentuckians. Much of it, too, is housed in two of the commonwealth's most distinguished historical repositories, the Filson Historical Society (in Louisville), and the Kentucky Historical Society (in Frankfort). Both historical societies are responsible for generations of ongoing scholarship found in their journals (published quarterly), *Filson Club Historical Quarterly* and *The Register of the Kentucky Historical Society*. Any researcher of the era would do well to visit both historical mother lodes and plumb the depths of their many archival resources, including their publications.

Kentuckians contributing to retrieving and preserving the commonwealth's past are numerous, and some of the most influential contemporary works are those written by Nancy O'Malley, A. Gwynn Henderson, and Elizabeth Perkins. Their books (and articles) were especially valuable to my research in making sense of Kentucky's early historic (and precontact) era. Additionally, writings from all three contain generous quantities of eighteenth-century excerpts about frontiersmen, forts, Indians and Indian relations, treaties, skills, everyday life, slaves, race relations, religion, and much more—most taken from the Draper Manuscripts, thus making their work especially useful to researchers unable to access the complete collection of Lyman C. Draper's work.

Too, Neal O. Hammon's interest in frontier Kentucky remains unstinting and his pen undeterred; it is gratifying to see that his many writings—published journal essays dealing with such esoterica as buffalo traces, land grants, and lawsuits over survey claims, and three books—are finally receiving some of the aplomb they have been long due. In addition, Hammon was kind enough to send me his copies of his transcriptions of the Daniel Boone, William Fleming, and John Floyd Papers. His unpublished book manuscript, "Into Western Waters, 1773–1775," also was extraordinarily useful, and I do hope that someday it is put into print for all time. Perusers of my end notes will frequently see "NOH" listed, and I cannot commend NOH's work heartily enough.

Besides these fine folks mentioned above and all the works listed below, as Kentuckians did in the past, many Kentuckians continue to unearth and share their family histories in articles, journal essays, genealogical newsletters, and self-published books. Though some of it is uncritical and self-congratulatory, much of it is not and sheds much light and insight into the life and times and culture long past.

PRIMARY SOURCES: MANUSCRIPTS

Daniel Boone Papers. Compiled by Neal O. Hammon, n.p., Filson Club, Louisville, KY.

John Floyd Papers. Compiled by Neal O. Hammon, n.p., Filson Club, Louisville, KY.

Lyman C. Draper Manuscript Collection. Microfilm ed. Madison: State Historical Society of WI, 1980.

    Series A. George M. Bedinger Papers.

    Series C. Daniel Boone Papers.

    Series D. Border Forays.

    Series E. Samuel Brady and Lewis Wetzel Papers.

    Series J. George Rogers Clark Papers.

    Series S. Draper's Notes.

    Series BB. Simon Kenton Papers.

    Series CC. Kentucky Papers.

    Series NN. Pittsburgh and Northwest Virginia Papers.

    Series QQ. William Preston Papers.

    Series XX. Tennessee Papers.

    Series ZZ. Virginia Papers.

William Fleming Papers. Special Collections, Leyburn Library, Washington and Lee University, Lexington, VA.

William Fleming Papers. Compiled from the Draper Manuscript Collection, by Neal O. Hammon, n.p., personal copies.

PRIMARY SOURCES: ARTICLES
Beckner, Lucien, trans. "Reverend John D. Shane's Interview with Pioneer William Clinkenbeard." *FCHQ* 2 (1928).

Bently, James R., ed. "Letters of Thomas Perkins to Gen. Joseph Palmer, Lincoln County, Kentucky, 1785." *FCHQ* 49 (1975): 145.

Brown, William Dodd, ed. "A Visit to Boonesborough in 1779: The Recollections of Pioneer George M. Bedinger." *RKHS* 86 (1988): 315–29.

"Journey to Kentucky in 1775: Diary of James Nourse." *Journal of American History* 29.2 (1925): 121–38; 29.3: 251–60; 29.4: 351–64.

PRIMARY SOURCES: BOOKS
Bailey, Kenneth P., ed. *The Ohio Company Papers, 1753–1817: Being Primarily Papers of the "Suffering Traders" of Pennsylvania.* Arcata, CA: n.p., 1947.

Barsotti, John J., ed. *Scoouwa: James Smith's Indian Captivity Narrative.* Columbus: Ohio Historical Society, 1992.

Byrd, William. *The Writings of Colonel William Byrd of Westover in Virginia, Esquire.* 2nd ed. Edited by John Spencer Bassett. New York: Burt Franklin, 1970.

Cresswell, Nicholas. *The Journal of Nicholas Cresswell, 1774–1777.* 2nd ed. New York: Dial Press, 1928.

de Finiels, Nicholas. *An Account of Upper Louisiana.* Edited by Carl J. Ekberg and William E. Foley. Columbia: University of Missouri Press, 1989.

Filson, John. *The Discovery, Settlement, and Present State of Kentucke.* Originally published 1784. Many editions available. New York: Corinth Books, 1962.

Hall, Gen. William. *Early History of the South-West.* 2nd ed. Nashville: Parthenon Press, 1968.

Heckewelder, John. *History, Manners, and Customs of the Indian Nations Who Once Inhabited Pennsylvania and the Neighboring States.* 2nd ed. Bowie, MD: Heritage Press, 1990.

Houston, Peter. *A Sketch in the Life and Character of Daniel Boone.* Edited with an introduction by Ted Franklin Belue. Mechanicsburg, PA: Stackpole Books, 1997.

Johnson, J. Stoddard, ed. *First Explorations of Kentucky.* Louisville, KY: John P. Morgan and Company, 1898.

Ludlow, Noah M. *Dramatic Life as I Found It.* 2nd ed. St. Louis: Benjamin Blom, 1966.

Mereness, Newton D, ed. *Travels in the American Colonies.* New York: Macmillan, 1916.

Smith, James. *An Account of the Remarkable Occurrences in the Life and Travels of Col. James Smith.* 2nd ed. Cincinnati: Robert Clarke, 1870.

Spencer, O. M. *The Indian Captivity of O. M. Spencer.* Edited by Milo Milton Quaife. New York: Citadel Press, 1968.

Tanner, John. *The Falcon: A Narrative of the Captivity and Adventures of John Tanner during Thirty Years' Residence among the Indians in the Interior of North America.* Edited by Louise Erdrich. New York: Penguin Books, 1994.

Thwaites, Reuben Gold, ed. *Early Western Travels, 1748–1765.* 2nd ed. Lewisburg, PA: Wennawoods Publishing, 1998.

———. *Jesuit Relations and Allied Documents.* 73 vols. New York: Pagent, 1959.

Thwaites, Reuben Gold, and Louise Phelps Kellogg, eds. *Documentary History of Dunmore's War.* Madison: State Historical Society of Wisconsin, 1905.

———. *Revolution on the Upper Ohio.* Madison: State Historical Society of Wisconsin, 1905.

Trabue, Daniel. *Westward into Kentucky: The Memoirs of Daniel Trabue.* Edited by Chester Raymond Young. Lexington: University Press of Kentucky, 1981.

SECONDARY SOURCES: ARTICLES AND WEBSITES

Altsheler, Brent. "The Long Hunters and James Knox Their Leader." *FCHQ* 5 (1923): 166–85.

Amyx, Clifford. "The Authentic Image of Daniel Boone." *Missouri Historical Review* 82 (1988): 153–64.

Aron, Stephen. "The Significance of the Kentucky Frontier." *RKHS* 91 (1993): 298–323.

Baker, Mark A. "What It Takes to Tarry in the Country." *Muzzleloader* (July–August 2001): 12–18.

Belue, Ted Franklin. "Death in the Bluegrass: The Battle of Little Mountain." *Dixie Gun Works Blackpowder Annual* (1995): 66–69.

———. "Did Daniel Boone Shoot Pompey, the Black Shawnee, at the 1778 Siege of Boonesborough?" *FCHQ* 67 (1993): 5–22.

———. "Terror in the Canelands: The Fate of Daniel Boone's Saltboilers." *FCHQ* 68 (1994): 3–34.

———. "Who Shot the Black Shawnee?" *Muzzleloader* (January–February 1992): 46–48.

Biographical Directory of the United States Congress, February 21, 2000, http://bioguide.congress.gov/scripts/biodisplay.pl?index=BOOO301.

"The Brethren." November 3, 2001. 1:52 P.M. http://religiousmovements.lib.virginia.edu/-nrms/brethren.html.

Calloway, Colin C. "Neither White nor Red: White Renegades on the American Indian Frontier." *Western Historical Quarterly* 17, no. 1 (1986): 43–66.

Conkright, Bessie Taul. "Estill's Defeat; or, The Battle of Little Mountain." *RKHS* 22 (1924): 311–22.

Edgerton, Gary. "'A Breed Apart': Hollywood, Racial Stereotyping, and the Promise of Revisionism in The Last of the Mohicans." *Journal of American Culture* 17, no. 2: (1994): 1–20.

Gagliasso, Dan. "Flintlocks in Film." *Dixie Gun Works Blackpowder Annual* (1993): 46–49, 99.

Gregg, Clifford C., and Charles G. Talbert. "George Michael Bedinger, 1756–1843." *RKHS* 65 (1967): 41–46.

Hammon, Neal O. "Early Roads into Kentucky." *RKHS* 68 (1970): 100–24.

———. "Historic Lawsuits of the Eighteenth Century: Locating the Stamping Ground." *RKHS* 69 (1971): 214.

Henderson, A. Gwynn. "Dispelling the Myth: Seventeenth- and Eighteenth-Century Indian Life in Kentucky." *RKHS* 90 (1992): 1-25.

"Influences in Religion." November 3, 2001, 1:45 P.M. http://www.users.voicenet.com/-wordinfo/deutsch/religion.html.

King, Roy T. "Portraits of Daniel Boone." *Missouri Historical Review* 33 (1939): 171–83.

Literary Prints: The Last of the Mohicans. Logan, IA: Perfection Form Company, 1936.

Lucas, Marion B. "African Americans on the Kentucky Frontier." *RKHS* 95 (1997): 121–34.

McClure, James P. "The Ohio Valley's Deerskin Trade: Topics for Consideration." *Old Northwest* 15 (1993): 115–33.

McDermott, John Francis. "How Goes the Harding Fever?" *Missouri Historical Society Bulletin* 8 (1951): 53–59.

McLeod, Alexander Canady. "A Man for All Seasons: Dr. Thomas Walker of Castle Hill." *FCHQ* 71 (1997): 169–201.

Sioli, Marco. "Huguenot Traditions in the Mountains of Kentucky: Daniel Trabue's Memories." *Journal of American History* 84 (1998): 1313–33.

Smith, Roxann Gess. "Notes and Biography for David Gass." February 21, 2000, http://gesswhoto.com/olden-daze/index21.html

St. Louis, Missouri, *Gazette*. "Advertisements in the Pioneer Press." *Missouri Historical Review* 26 (1932): 395.

Thomas, Samuel W. "George Rogers Clark: Natural Scientist and Historian." *FCHQ* 41 (1967): 202–26.

Van Ravenswaay, Charles. "A Rare Midwestern Print." *Antiques* 43 (1943): 77, 93.

SECONDARY SOURCES: BOOKS

Addington, Robert M. *History of Scott County, Virginia*. Baltimore: Regional Publishing, 1977.

Anderson, Fred. *Crucible of War: The Seven Years' War and the Fate of Empire in British North America, 1754–1766*. New York: Alfred A. Knopf, 2000.

Arnow, Harriette Simpson. *Seedtime on the Cumberland*. New York: Macmillan, 1960.

Aron, Stephen. *How the West Was Lost: The Transformation of Kentucky from Daniel Boone to Henry Clay*. Baltimore: Johns Hopkins University Press, 1996.

Axtell, James. *The European and the Indian: Essays in the Ethnohistory of Colonial North America*. New York: Oxford University Press, 1981.

Bailey, Kenneth P. *The Ohio Company of Virginia and the Westward Movement, 1748–1792*. 2nd ed. Lewisburg, PA: Wennawoods Publishing, 2000.

Bakeless, John. *Daniel Boone: Master of the Wilderness*. 3rd ed. Lincoln: University Press of Nebraska, 1989.

Banta, R. E. *The Ohio*. 2nd ed. Lexington: University Press of Kentucky, 1998.

Belue, Ted Franklin. *The Long Hunt: Death of the Buffalo East of the Mississippi*. Mechanicsburg, PA: Stackpole Books, 1996.

The Biographical Encyclopedia of Kentucky of the Dead and Living Men of the Nineteenth Century. Cincinnati: J. M. Armstrong, 1878.

Blanco, Richard L. *The American Revolution, 1775–1783: An Encyclopedia*. 2 vols. New York: Garland Publishing, 1993.

Brasser, Ted J. *Bo'jou Neejee!: Profiles of Canadian Indian Art*. Ottawa, Ontario: National Museum of Man, 1976.

Braund, Kathryn E. Holland. *Deerskins and Duffels: Creek Indian Trade with Anglo-America, 1685–1815*. Lincoln: University of Nebraska Press, 1993.

Burns, David M. *Gateway: Dr. Thomas Walker and the Opening of Kentucky*. Middlesboro, KY: Bell County Historical Society, 2000.

Butterfield, Consul Wilshire. *History of the Girtys*. 2nd ed. Columbus: Long's College Book Company, 1950.

Cassidy, Samuel M. *Michael Cassidy: Frontiersman*. Lexington, KY: Self-published, Shenco Printers, 1979.

Chartrand, Rene. *The French Soldier in Colonial America*, Historical Arms Series, no. 18. Bloomfield, Ontario: Museum Restoration Service, 1984.

Clark, Jerry E. *The Shawnee*. Lexington: University Press of Kentucky, 1977.

Clift, G. Glenn. *History of Maysville and Mason County*. Lexington, KY: Transylvania Printing Company, 1936.

Clifton, James A., ed. *Being and Becoming Indian: Biographical Studies of North American Frontiers*. Prospect Heights, IL: Waveland Press, 1989.

Collins, Lewis. *History of Kentucky*. Covington, KY: Collins and Company, 1882.

Cooper, James Fenimore. *The Deerslayer*. Foreword by Basil Davenport. New York: Dodd, Mead and Company, 1952.

Daniel, Jonathan. *The Devil's Backbone: The Story of the Natchez Trace*. New York: McGraw-Hill, 1962.

Darlington, William M. *Christopher Gist's Journals*. Pittsburgh: J. R. Weldin & Company, 1893.

Demos, John. *The Unredeemed Captive: A Family Story from Early America*. New York: Vintage Books, 1994.

Derleth, August William. *Vincennes: Portal to the West*. Englewood Cliffs, NJ: Prentice-Hall, 1968.

Downes, Randolph C. *Council Fires on the Upper Ohio*. 2nd ed. Pittsburgh: University of Pittsburgh Press, 1977.

Draper, Lyman C. *The Life of Daniel Boone*. Edited with an introduction by Ted Franklin Belue. Mechanicsburg, PA: Stackpole Books, 1998.

Enoch, Harry G. *In Search of Morgan's Station and The Last Indian Raid in Kentucky*. Bowie, MD: Heritage Books, 1997.

Faragher, John Mack. *Daniel Boone: The Life and Legend of an American Pioneer*. New York: Henry Holt and Company, 1992.

Ford, Alice. *Audubon, by Himself*. Garden City, NY: Natural History Press, 1963.

Friend, Craig Thompson, ed. *The Buzzel about Kentuck: Settling the Promised Land*. Lexington: University Press of Kentucky, 1999.

Furbee, Louanna, and W. D. Snively, Jr. *Satan's Ferryman: A True Tale of the Old Frontier*. New York: Frederick Unger, 1968.

Gilman, Carolyn. *Where Two Worlds Meet: The Great Lakes Indian Fur Trade*. St. Paul: Minnesota Historical Society, 1982.

Griffin, James Bennett. *The Fort Ancient Aspect: Its Cultural and Chronological Position in Mississippi Valley Archaeology*. Ann Arbor: University of Michigan Press, 1943.

Hammon, Neal O. *Early Kentucky Land Records, 1773–1780*. Filson Club Publications, 2nd ser., no. 5. Louisville, KY: Butler Book Publishing, 1992.

———. "Into Western Waters, 1773–1775." n.p., n.d.

———. *My Father, Daniel Boone: The Draper Interviews with Nathan Boone*. Lexington: University Press of Kentucky, 1999.

Hanna, Charles A. *The Wilderness Trail*. 2 vols. New York: Knickerbocker Press, 1911.

Harper, Josephine L. *Guide to the Draper Manuscripts*. Madison: State Historical Society of Wisconsin, 1983.

Harrison, Lowell H., and James C. Klotter. *A New History of Kentucky*. Lexington: University Press of Kentucky, 1997.

Henderson, A. Gwynn, ed. *Fort Ancient: Cultural Dynamics in the Middle Ohio Valley*. Madison, WI: Prehistory Press, 1992.

Henderson, A. Gwynn, Cynthia E. Jobe, and Christopher A. Turnbow, *Indian Occupation and Use in Northern and Eastern Kentucky during the Contact Period (1540–1795): An Initial Investigation*. Frankfort: Kentucky Heritage Council, 1986.

Horan, James D. *The McKenny-Hall Portrait Gallery of American Indians*. New York: Bramhall House, 1986.

Howard, James H. *Shawnee!: Ceremonialism of a Native American Tribe and Its Cultural Background*. Athens: Ohio University Press, 1981.

Isenberg, Andrew C. *The Destruction of the Bison: An Environmental History, 1750–1920*. New York: Cambridge University Press, 2000.

Jacobs, Wilber R. *Wilderness Politics and Indian Gifts: The North Colonial Frontier, 1748–1763*. Lincoln: University of Nebraska Press, 1966.

Jennings, Francis. *The Ambiguous Iroquois Empire: The Covenant Chain Confederation of Indian Tribes with English Colonies from Its Beginnings to the Lancaster Treaty of 1744*. New York: W. W. Norton, 1984.

————. *Empire of Fortune: Crowns, Colonies and Tribes in the Seven Years War in America.* New York: W. W. Norton, 1990.

Jordan, Terry G. *The American Backwoods Frontier: An Ethnic Ecological Interpretation.* Baltimore: Johns Hopkins Press, 1989.

Katz, William Loren. *Black Indians: Hidden Heritage.* New York: Macmillan, 1986.

Kauffman, Henry. *The Pennsylvania-Kentucky Rifle.* New York: Bonanza Books, 1960.

Kenton, Edna. *Simon Kenton: His Life and Period, 1755–1836.* Reprint. Salem, NH: Ayer, 1993.

Kincaid, Robert L. *The Wilderness Road.* New York: Bobbs-Merrill Company, 1947.

Kindig, Joe, Jr. *Thoughts on the Kentucky Rifle in Its Golden Age.* New York: Bonanza Books, 1964.

Klauber, Laurence M. *Rattlesnakes: Their Habits, Life Histories, and Influence on Mankind.* 2nd ed. Berkeley: University of California Press, 1972.

Kleber, John E., ed. *The Kentucky Encyclopedia.* Lexington: University Press of Kentucky, 1992.

Krech, Shepard, III. *The Ecological Indian: Myth and History.* New York: W. W. Norton & Company, 1999.

Lagemann, Robert, and Albert Manucy. *The Long Rifle.* New York: Eastern Acorn Press, 1980.

Lester, William Stewart. *The Transylvania Colony.* Spencer, IN: Samuel R. Guard, 1935.

Lipton, Leah. *A Truthful Likeness: Chester Harding and His Portraits.* Washington, DC: National Portrait Gallery, Smithsonian Institution, 1985.

Mancall, Peter C. *Deadly Medicine: Indians and Alcohol in Early America.* Ithaca, NY: Cornell University Press, 1995.

Martin, Calvin. *Keepers of the Game: Indian-Animal Relationships and the Fur Trade.* Berkeley: University of California Press, 1978.

McConnell, Michael H. *A Country Between: The Upper Ohio Valley and Its Peoples, 1724–1774.* Lincoln: University of Nebraska Press, 1992.

Merrill, James H. *Into the American Woods.* New York: W. W. Norton & Company, 1999.

Morgan, Ted. *Wilderness at Dawn: The Settling of the North American Continent.* New York: Simon and Schuster, 1993.

Neider, Charles, ed. *The Comic Mark Twain Reader: The Most Humorous Selections from His Stories, Sketches, Novels, Travel Books and Speeches.* New York: Doubleday and Company, 1977.

Nelson, Larry B. *A Man of Distinction among Them: Alexander McKee and British-Indian Affairs along the Ohio Country Frontier, 1754–1799.* Kent, OH: Kent State University Press, 1999.

Neuman, George C., Frank J. Kravic, and George C. Woodbridge. *Collector's Illustrated Encyclopedia of the American Revolution.* 2nd ed. Texarkana, TX: Rebel Publishing, 1989.

Nute, Grace. *The Voyageurs.* St. Paul: Minnesota Historical Society, 1955.

Nyland, Keith Ryan. "Doctor Thomas Walker (1715–1794): Explorer, Physician, Statesman, Surveyor and Planter of Virginia and Kentucky." Ph.D. diss., Ohio State University, University Microfilms, 1971.

O'Malley, Nancy. *"Stockading Up": A Study of Pioneer Stations in the Inner Bluegrass Region of Kentucky.* Archaeological Report 127. Frankfort: Kentucky Heritage Council, 1987.

Peck, John Mason. *Life of Daniel Boone, the Pioneer of Kentucky.* Jared Sparks, ed. *The Library of American Biography,* Vol. 13 in 2nd ser. Boston: Charles C. Little, 1847.

Peckman, Howard H. *The Colonial Wars, 1689–1702.* Chicago: University of Chicago Press, 1964.

Pendleton, J. M. *Baptist Church Manual.* Nashville: Broadman Press, 1966.

Perkins, Elizabeth A. *Border Life: Experience and Memory in the Revolutionary Ohio Valley.* Chapel Hill: University of North Carolina Press, 1998.

Phillips, Dr. Ruth B. *Patterns of Power: The Jasper Grant Collection and Great Lakes Indian Art of the Early Nineteenth Century.* Kleinburg, Ontario: McMichael Canadian Collection, 1984.

Powell, Allan. *Christopher Gist: Frontier Scout.* Hagerstown, MD: Privately published, 1992.

Quinn, Arthur. *A New World: An Epic of Colonial America from the Founding of Jamestown to the Fall of Quebec.* New York: Berkeley Books, 1994.

Richter, Daniel K. *Ordeal of the Long-House: The Peoples of the Iroquois League in an Era of European Colonization.* Chapel Hill: University of North Carolina Press, 1992.

Roster, Charles. *The Fabulous History of the Dismal Swamp Company: A Story of George Washington's Times.* New York: Alfred A. Knopf, 1999.

Russell, Carl P. *Firearms, Traps, and Tools of the Mountain Men.* Albuquerque: University of New Mexico Press, 1981.

Sargent, Winthrop. *The History of an Expedition against Fort Du Quesne in 1755 under Major-General Edward Braddock.* 2nd ed. Lewisburg, PA: Wennawoods Publishing, 1997.

Scurlock, William H, ed. *The Book of Buckskinning II.* Texarkana, TX: Rebel Publishing Company, 1983.

———. *The Book of Buckskinning VII.* Texarkana, TX: Scurlock Publishing, 1995.

———. *The Book of Buckskinning VIII.* Texarkana, TX: Scurlock Publishing, 1999.

Sharp, William E. "Fort Ancient Farmers." *In Kentucky Archaeology,* edited by Barry Lewis. Lexington: University Press of Kentucky, 1996.

Sipe, C. Hale. *The Indian Wars of Pennsylvania.* 2nd ed. Lewisburg, PA: Wennawoods Publishing, 1995.

Slick, Stewell Elias. *William Trent and the West.* 2nd ed. Lewisburg, PA: Wennawoods Publishing, 2001.

Smith, Z. F. *The History of Kentucky.* Louisville: Prentiss Press, 1895.

Sturtevant, William C., gen. ed. *Handbook of North American Indians.* Vol. 15, *Northeast.* Bruce Trigger, vol. ed. Washington, DC: Smithsonian Institution, 1978.

Sugden, John. *Blue Jacket: Warrior of the Shawnees.* Lincoln: University of Nebraska Press, 2000.

Sword, Wiley. *President Washington's Indian War: The Struggle for the Old Northwest.* 2nd ed. Norman: University of Oklahoma Press, 1995.

Talbert, Charles Gano. *Benjamin Logan: Kentucky Frontiersman.* Lexington: University Press of Kentucky, 1976.

Tanner, Helen Hornbeck, ed. *Atlas of Great Lakes Indian History.* Tulsa: University of Oklahoma Press, Newberry Library, 1987.

Van Every, Dale. *Forth to the Wilderness: The First American Frontier, 1754–1774.* 2nd ed. New York: Quill, 1987.

Volwiler, Albert T. *George Croghan and the Westward Movement, 1741–1782.* Cleveland: Arthur H. Clark Company, 1926.

Wallins, Carolyn D. *Elisha Wallin: The Longhunter.* Johnson City, TN: Overmountain Press, 1990.

Weber, David J. *The Spanish Frontier in North America.* New Haven, CT: Yale University Press, 1992.

White, Richard. *The Middle Ground: Indians, Empires, and Republics in the Great Lakes Region, 1650–1815.* New York: Cambridge University Press, 1991.

Wiggington, Eliot, ed. *Foxfire 5.* Garden City, NY: Anchor, 1979.

INDEX

Numerals in **bold** typeface indicate an illustration.

THE GREAT SETTLEM

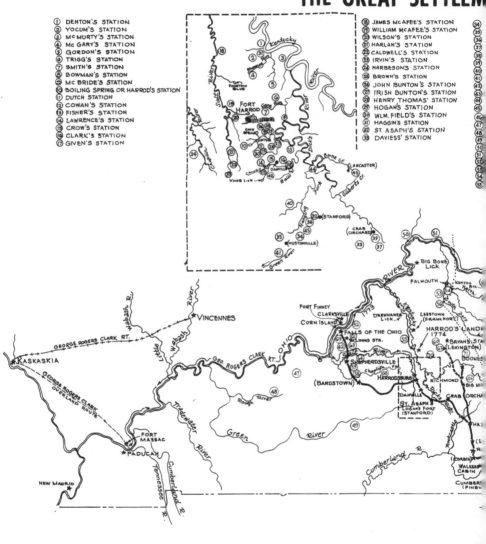

1. DENTON'S STATION
2. YOCUM'S STATION
3. McMURTY'S STATION
4. McGARY'S STATION
5. GORDON'S STATION
6. TRIGG'S STATION
7. SMITH'S STATION
8. BOWMAN'S STATION
9. McBRIDE'S STATION
10. BOILING SPRING OR HARROD'S STATION
11. DUTCH STATION
12. COWAN'S STATION
13. FISHER'S STATION
14. LAWRENCE'S STATION
15. CROW'S STATION
16. CLARK'S STATION
17. GIVEN'S STATION

18. JAMES McAFEE'S STATION
19. WILLIAM McAFEE'S STATION
20. WILSON'S STATION
21. HARLAN'S STATION
22. CALDWELL'S STATION
23. IRVIN'S STATION
24. HARBESON'S STATION
25. BROWN'S STATION
26. JOHN BUNTON'S STATION
27. IRISH BUNTON'S STATION
28. HENRY THOMAS' STATION
29. HOGAN'S STATION
30. WLM. FIELD'S STATION
31. HAGGIN'S STATION
32. ST. ASAPH'S STATION
33. DAVIESS' STATION